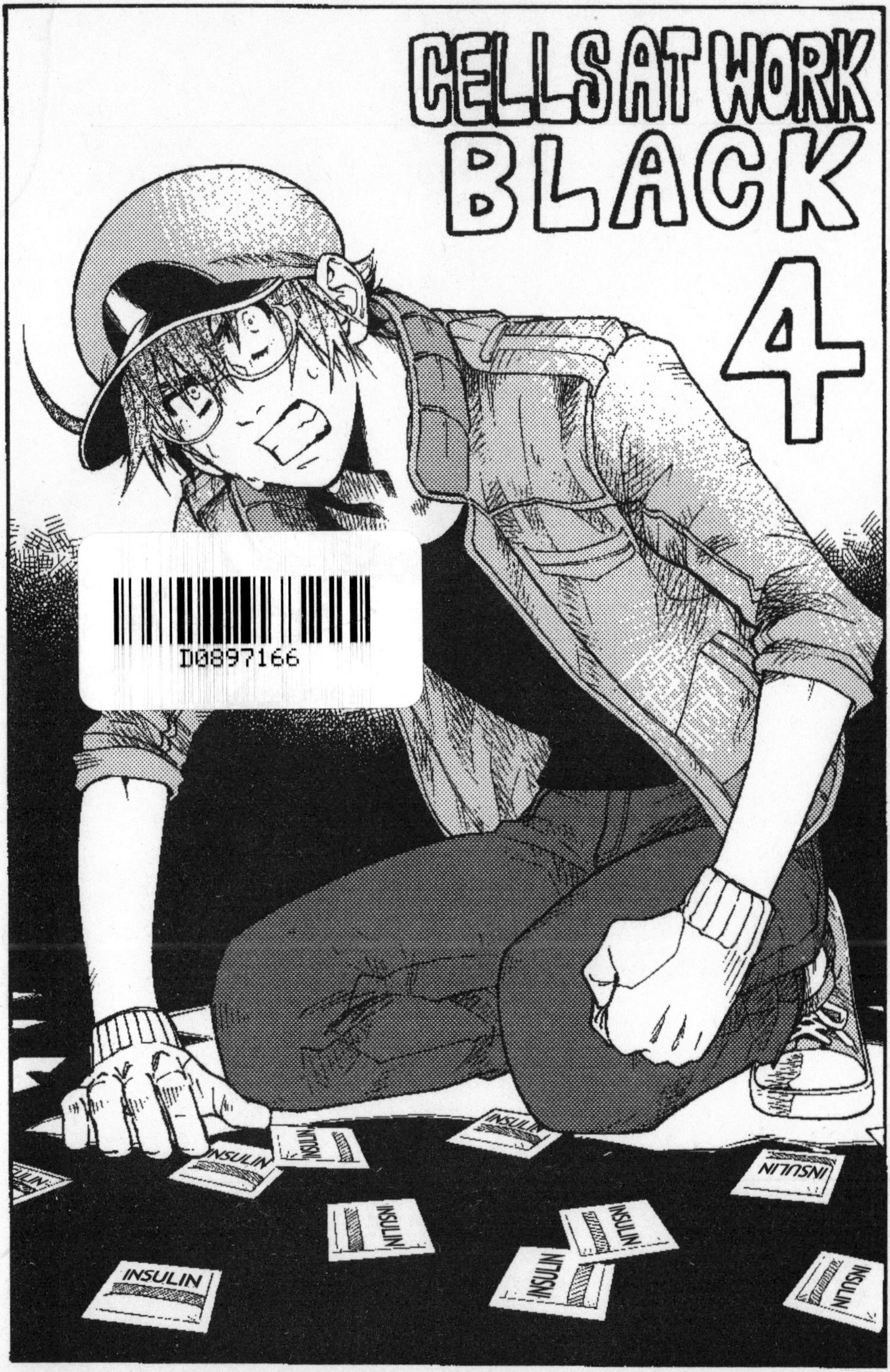
CELLS AT WORK
BLACK
4
INSULIN
INSULIN
INSULIN
INSULIN
INSULIN
INSULIN
INSULIN
INSULIN
INSULIN
INSULIN

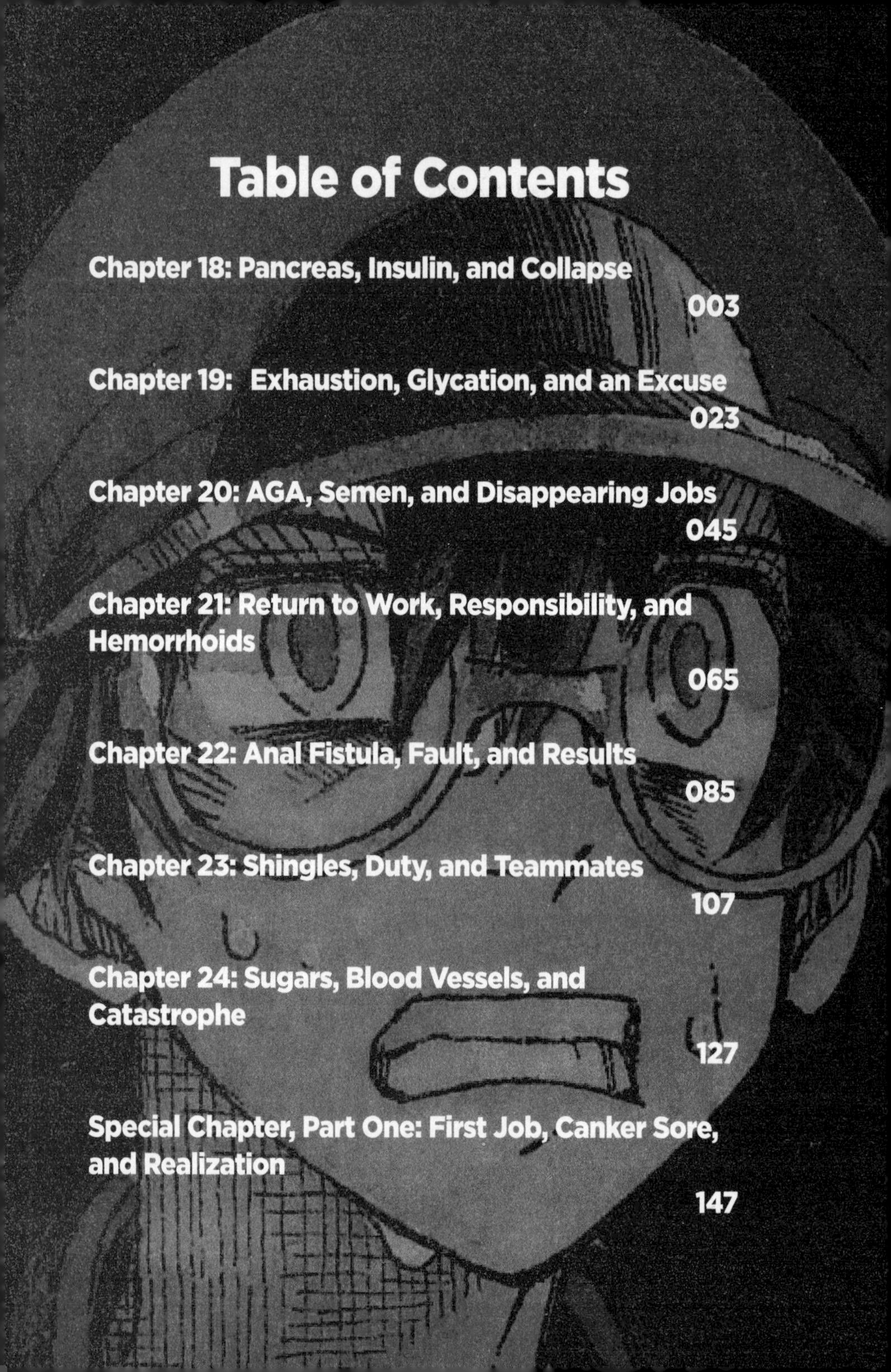

Table of Contents

18. PANCREAS, INSULIN, AND COLLAPSE

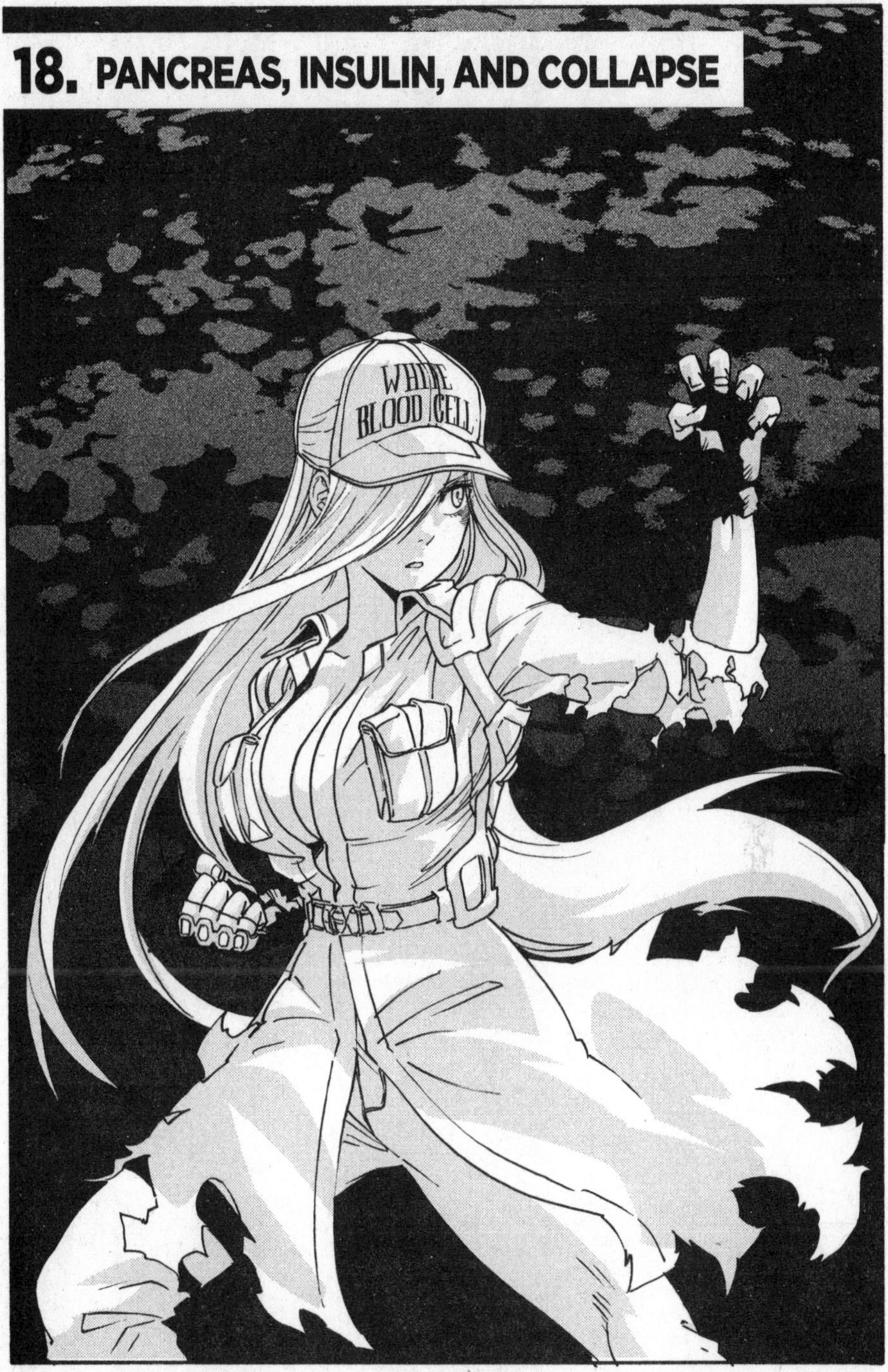
WHITE
BLOOD CELL

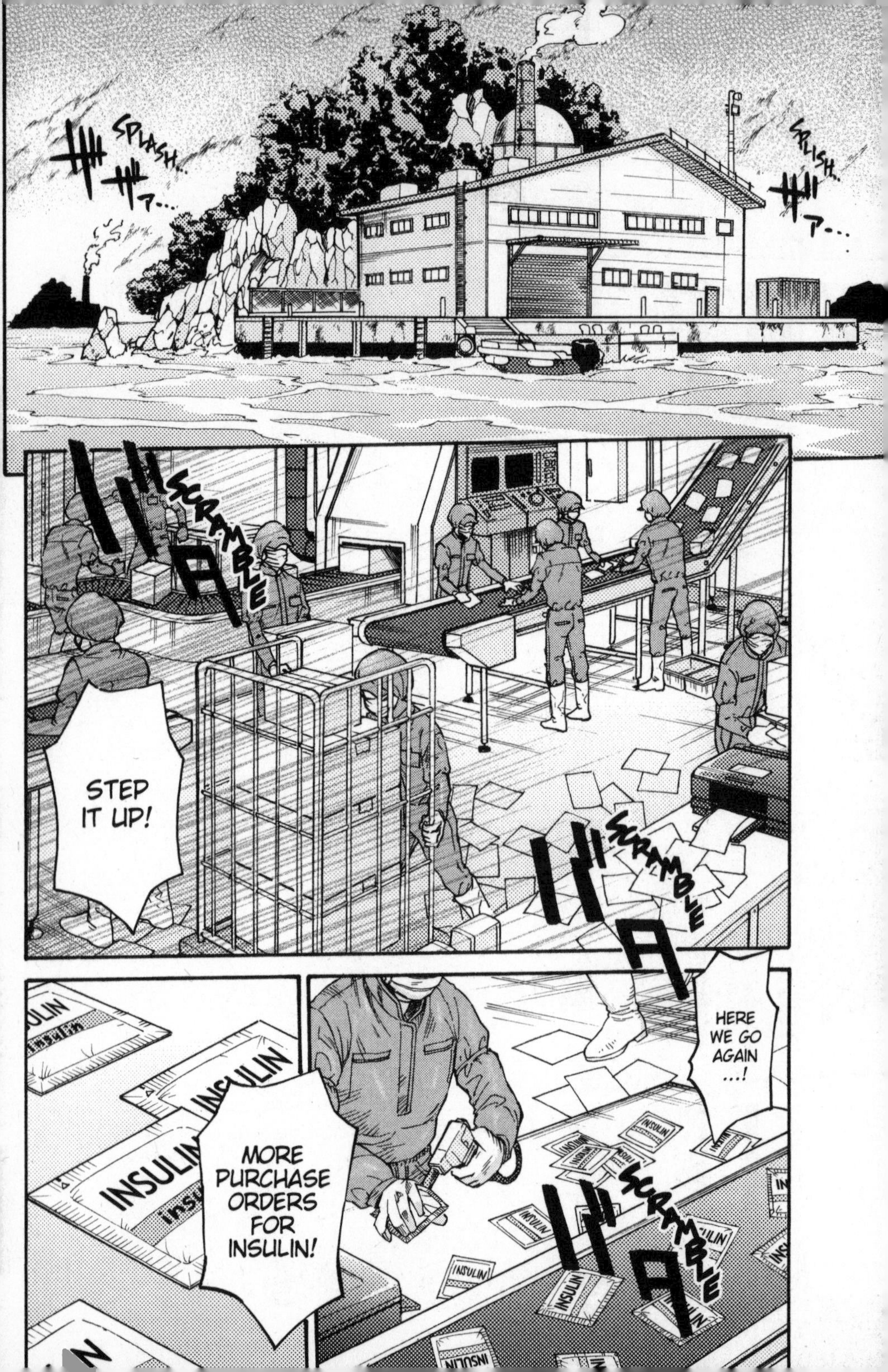
SPLISH...
ザァ...
SPLASH...
ザァ...
SCRAMBLE
STEP IT UP!
SCRAMBLE
HERE WE GO AGAIN ...!
SCRAMBLE
MORE PURCHASE ORDERS FOR INSULIN!
INSULIN

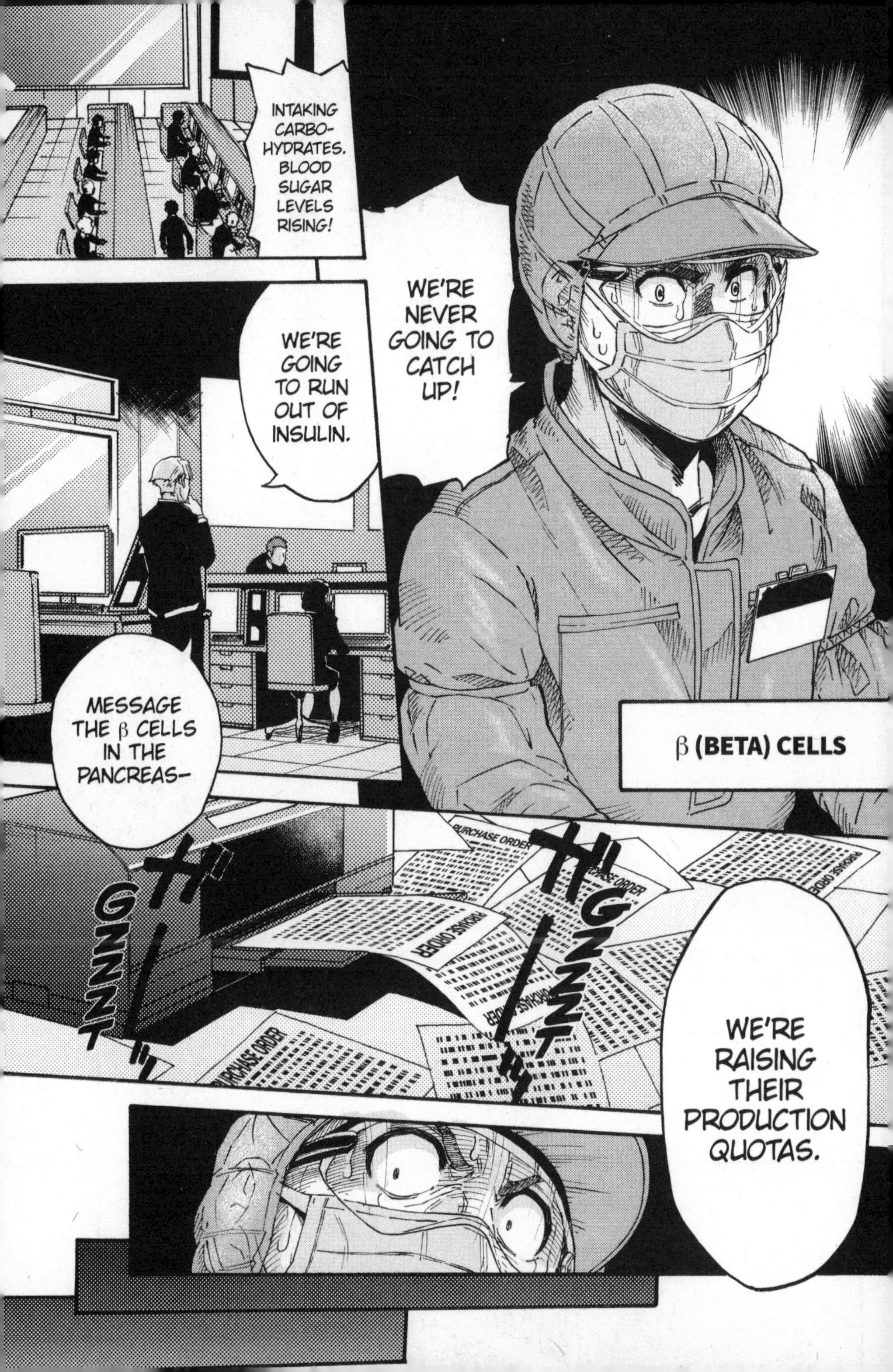
WE'RE NEVER GOING TO CATCH UP!
β (BETA) CELLS
INTAKING CARBO-HYDRATES. BLOOD SUGAR LEVELS RISING!
WE'RE GOING TO RUN OUT OF INSULIN.
MESSAGE THE β CELLS IN THE PANCREAS–
GZZZT
PURCHASE ORDER
GZZZT
WE'RE RAISING THEIR PRODUCTION QUOTAS.

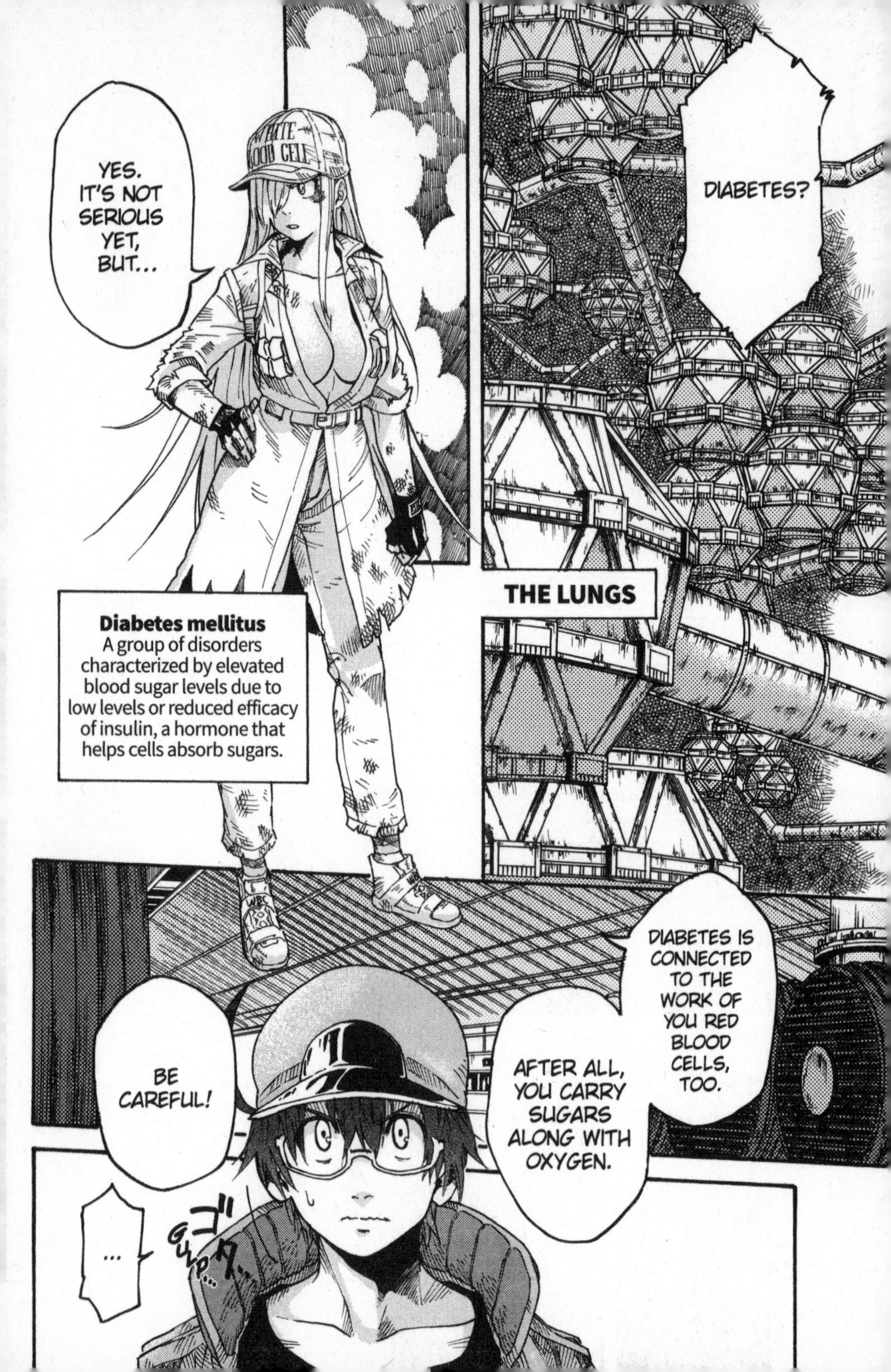
DIABETES?
THE LUNGS
YES. IT'S NOT SERIOUS YET, BUT...
Diabetes mellitus
A group of disorders characterized by elevated blood sugar levels due to low levels or reduced efficacy of insulin, a hormone that helps cells absorb sugars.
DIABETES IS CONNECTED TO THE WORK OF YOU RED BLOOD CELLS, TOO.
AFTER ALL, YOU CARRY SUGARS ALONG WITH OXYGEN.
BE CAREFUL!
...
GULP...

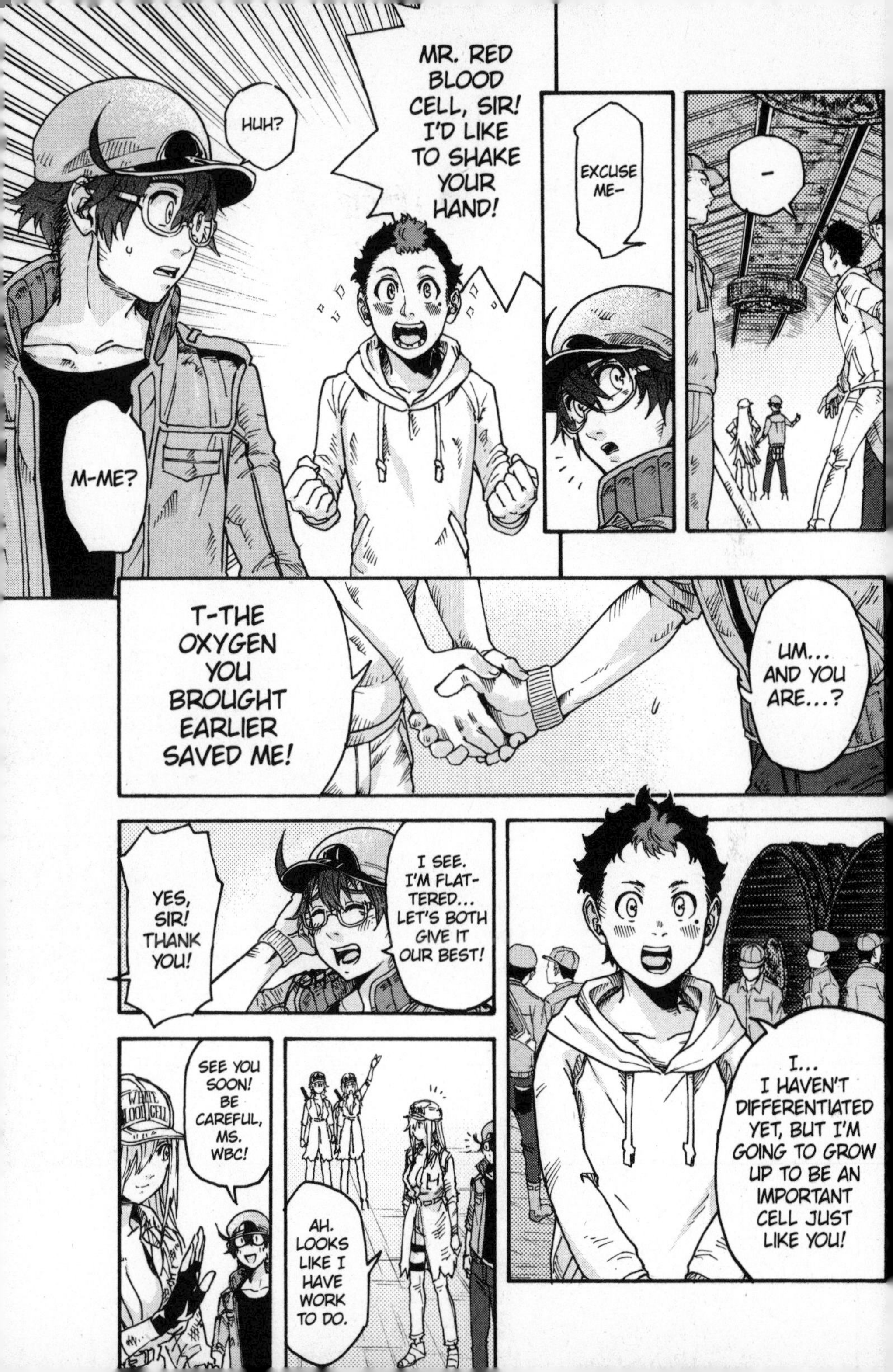
-
EXCUSE ME-
MR. RED BLOOD CELL, SIR! I'D LIKE TO SHAKE YOUR HAND!
HUH?
M-ME?
UM... AND YOU ARE...?
T-THE OXYGEN YOU BROUGHT EARLIER SAVED ME!
I... I HAVEN'T DIFFERENTIATED YET, BUT I'M GOING TO GROW UP TO BE AN IMPORTANT CELL JUST LIKE YOU!
I SEE. I'M FLATTERED... LET'S BOTH GIVE IT OUR BEST!
YES, SIR! THANK YOU!
AH. LOOKS LIKE I HAVE WORK TO DO.
WHITE BLOOD CELL
SEE YOU SOON! BE CAREFUL, MS. WBC!

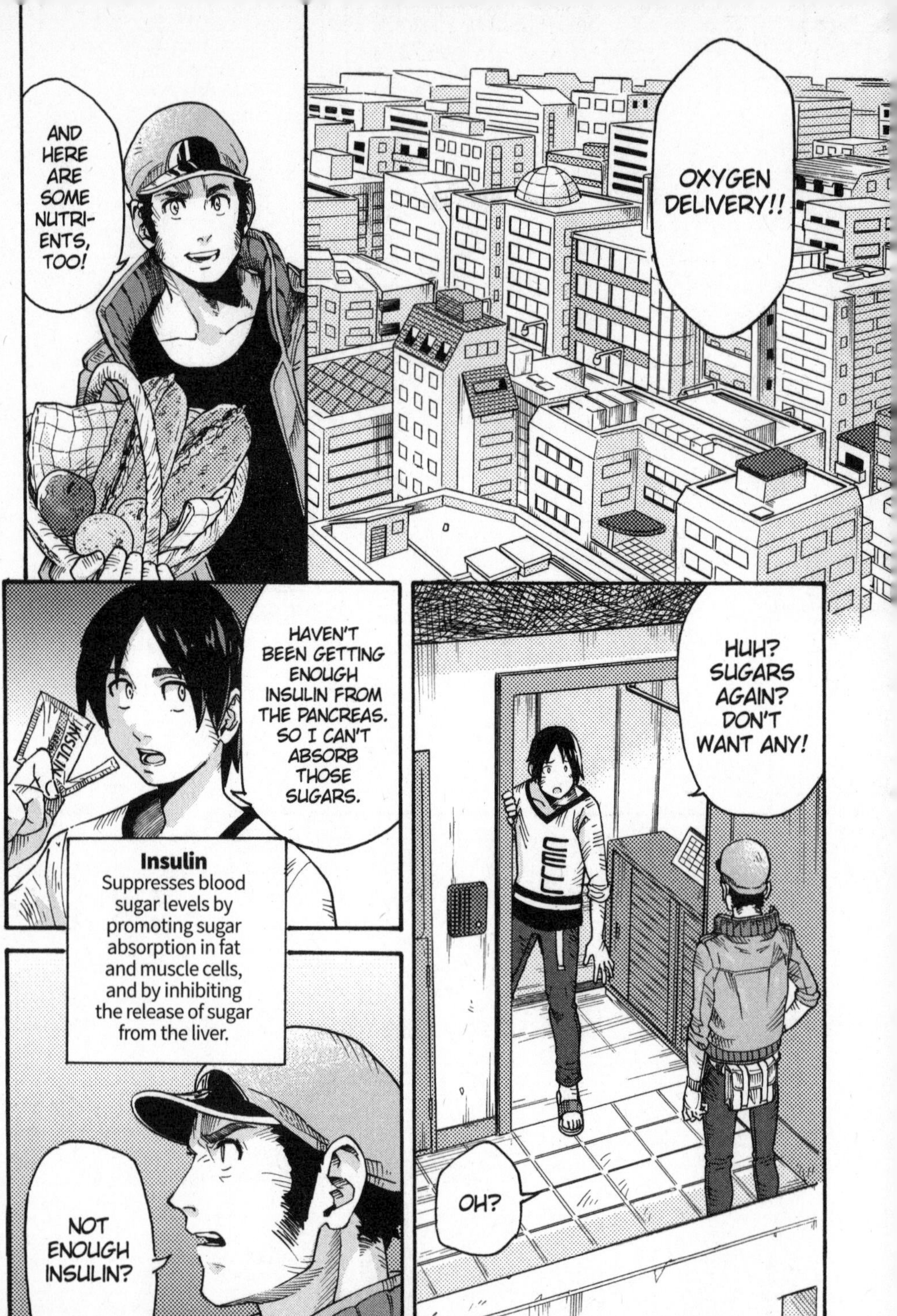
OXYGEN DELIVERY!!
AND HERE ARE SOME NUTRI-ENTS, TOO!
HUH? SUGARS AGAIN? DON'T WANT ANY!
OH?
HAVEN'T BEEN GETTING ENOUGH INSULIN FROM THE PANCREAS. SO I CAN'T ABSORB THOSE SUGARS.
Insulin
Suppresses blood sugar levels by promoting sugar absorption in fat and muscle cells, and by inhibiting the release of sugar from the liver.
NOT ENOUGH INSULIN?

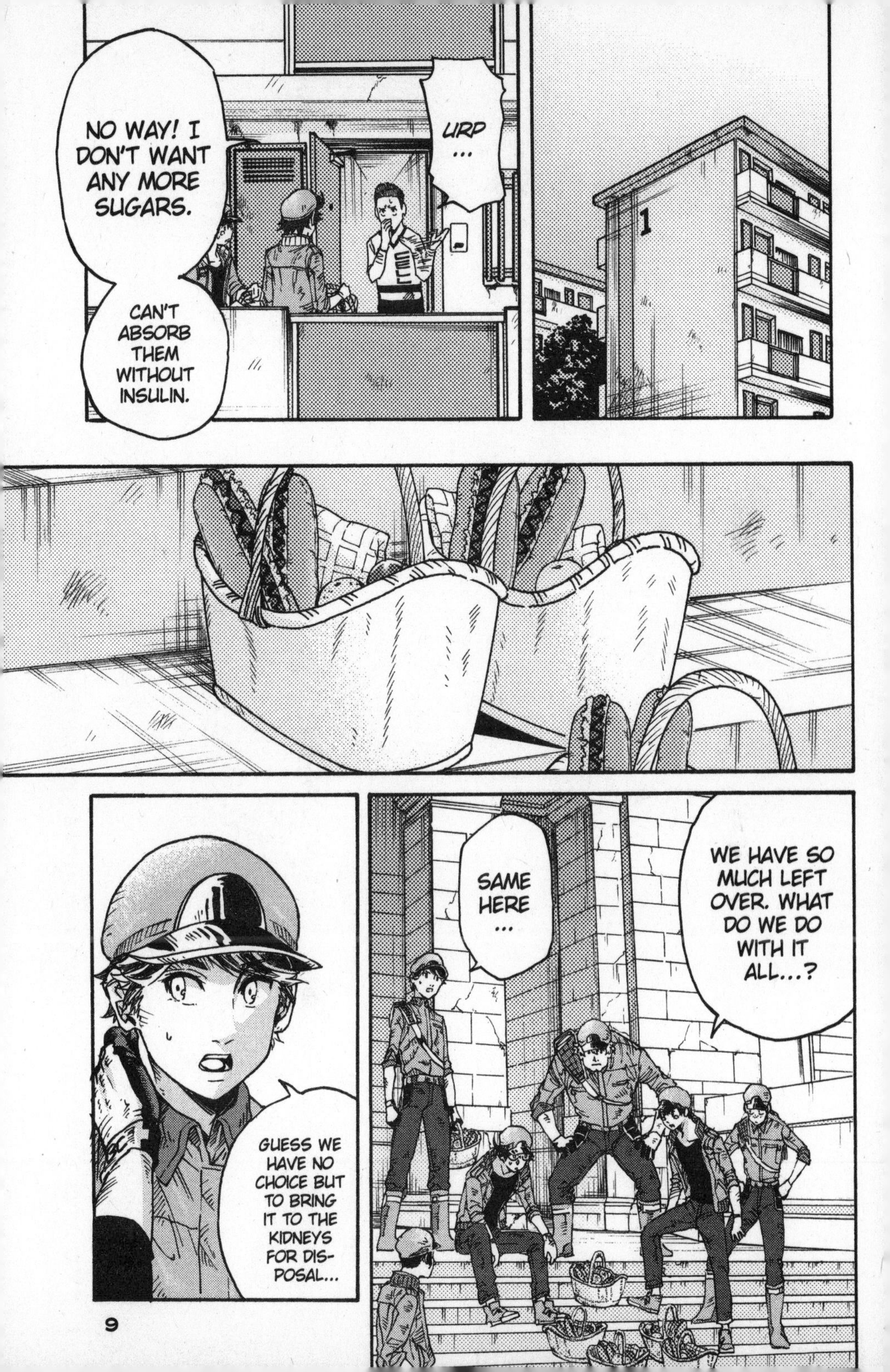
URP ...
NO WAY! I DON'T WANT ANY MORE SUGARS.
CAN'T ABSORB THEM WITHOUT INSULIN.
WE HAVE SO MUCH LEFT OVER. WHAT DO WE DO WITH IT ALL...?
SAME HERE ...
GUESS WE HAVE NO CHOICE BUT TO BRING IT TO THE KIDNEYS FOR DIS-POSAL...

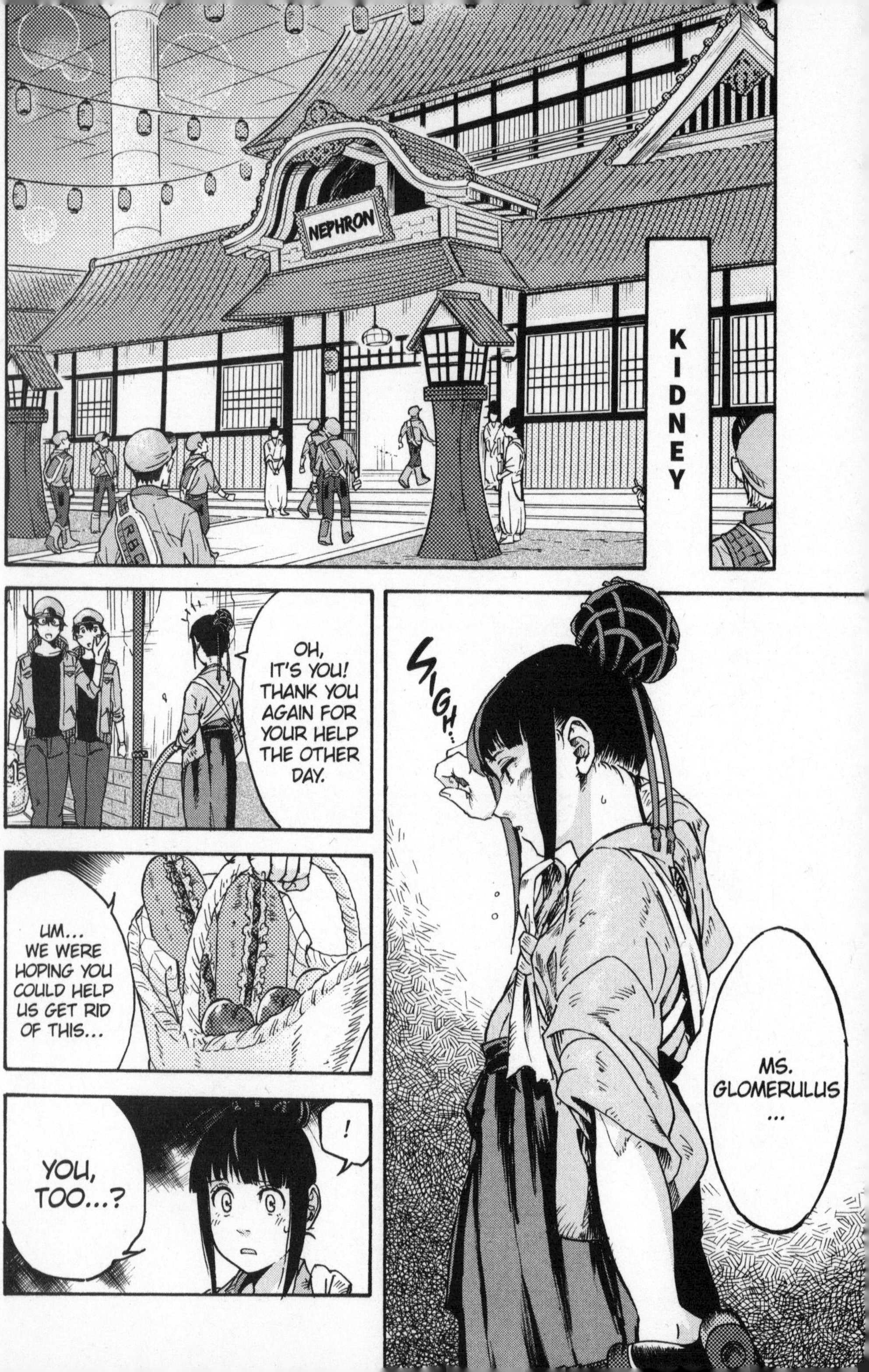
NEPHRON
KIDNEY
SIGH...
MS. GLOMERULUS...
OH, IT'S YOU! THANK YOU AGAIN FOR YOUR HELP THE OTHER DAY.
UM... WE WERE HOPING YOU COULD HELP US GET RID OF THIS...
!
YOU, TOO...?

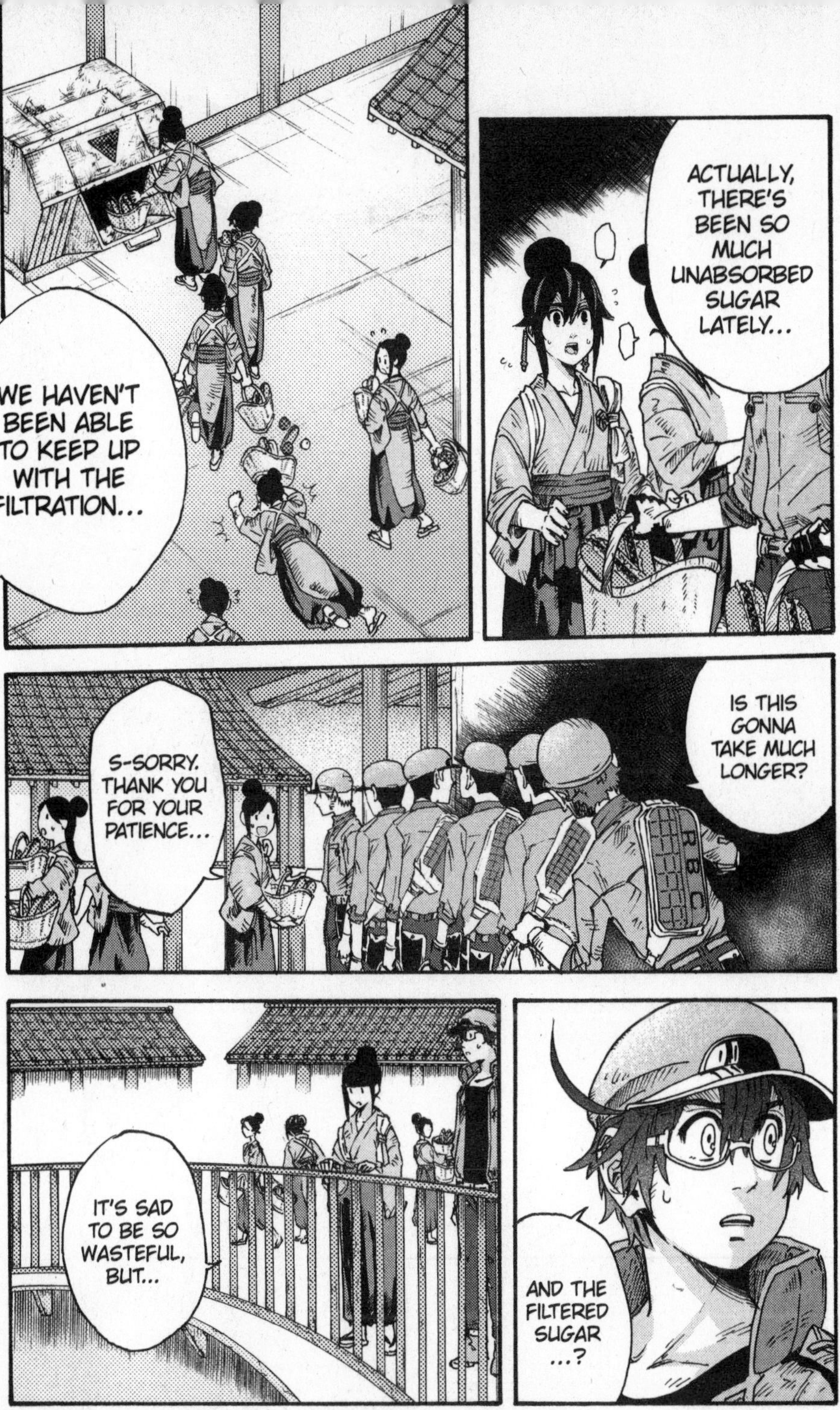
ACTUALLY, THERE'S BEEN SO MUCH UNABSORBED SUGAR LATELY...
WE HAVEN'T BEEN ABLE TO KEEP UP WITH THE FILTRATION...
IS THIS GONNA TAKE MUCH LONGER?
S-SORRY. THANK YOU FOR YOUR PATIENCE...
AND THE FILTERED SUGAR ...?
IT'S SAD TO BE SO WASTEFUL, BUT...

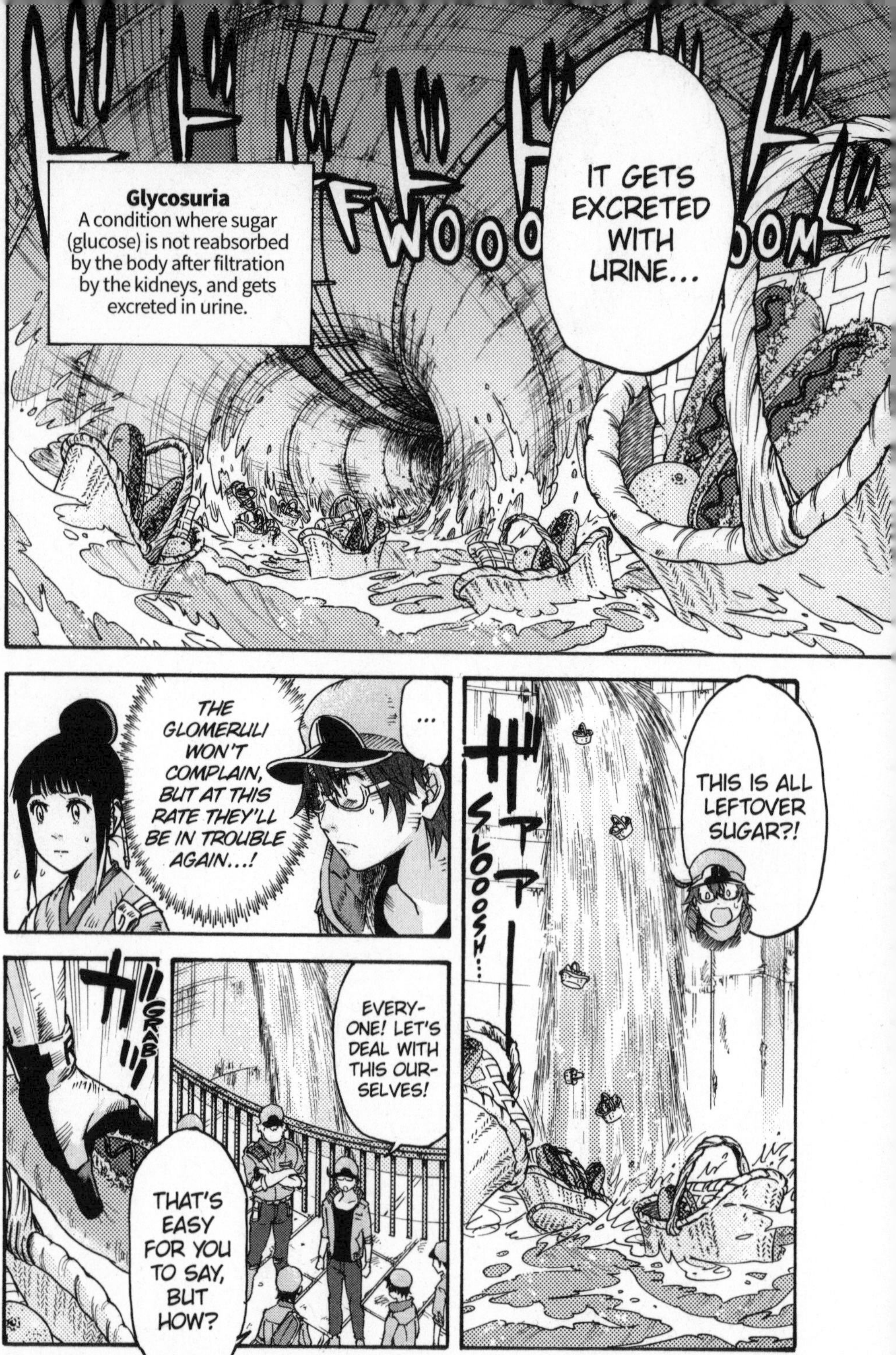
IT GETS EXCRETED WITH URINE...
FWOOO OOM
Glycosuria
A condition where sugar (glucose) is not reabsorbed by the body after filtration by the kidneys, and gets excreted in urine.
THIS IS ALL LEFTOVER SUGAR?!
SLOOOOSH...
...
THE GLOMERULI WON'T COMPLAIN, BUT AT THIS RATE THEY'LL BE IN TROUBLE AGAIN...!
EVERY-ONE! LET'S DEAL WITH THIS OUR-SELVES!
THAT'S EASY FOR YOU TO SAY, BUT HOW?
GRAB

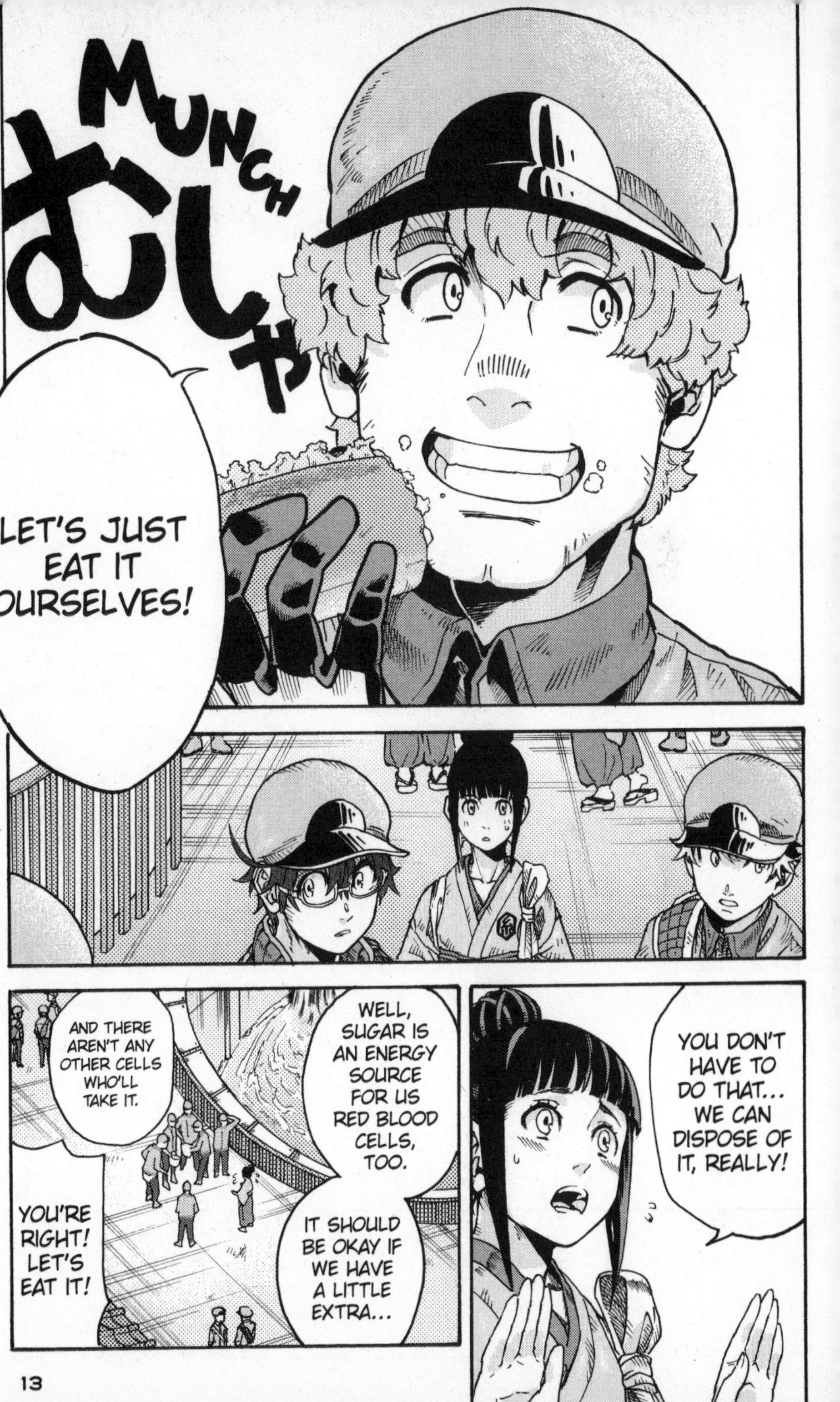

MUNCH
むしゃ
LET'S JUST EAT IT OURSELVES!
YOU DON'T HAVE TO DO THAT... WE CAN DISPOSE OF IT, REALLY!
WELL, SUGAR IS AN ENERGY SOURCE FOR US RED BLOOD CELLS, TOO.
AND THERE AREN'T ANY OTHER CELLS WHO'LL TAKE IT.
IT SHOULD BE OKAY IF WE HAVE A LITTLE EXTRA...
YOU'RE RIGHT! LET'S EAT IT!

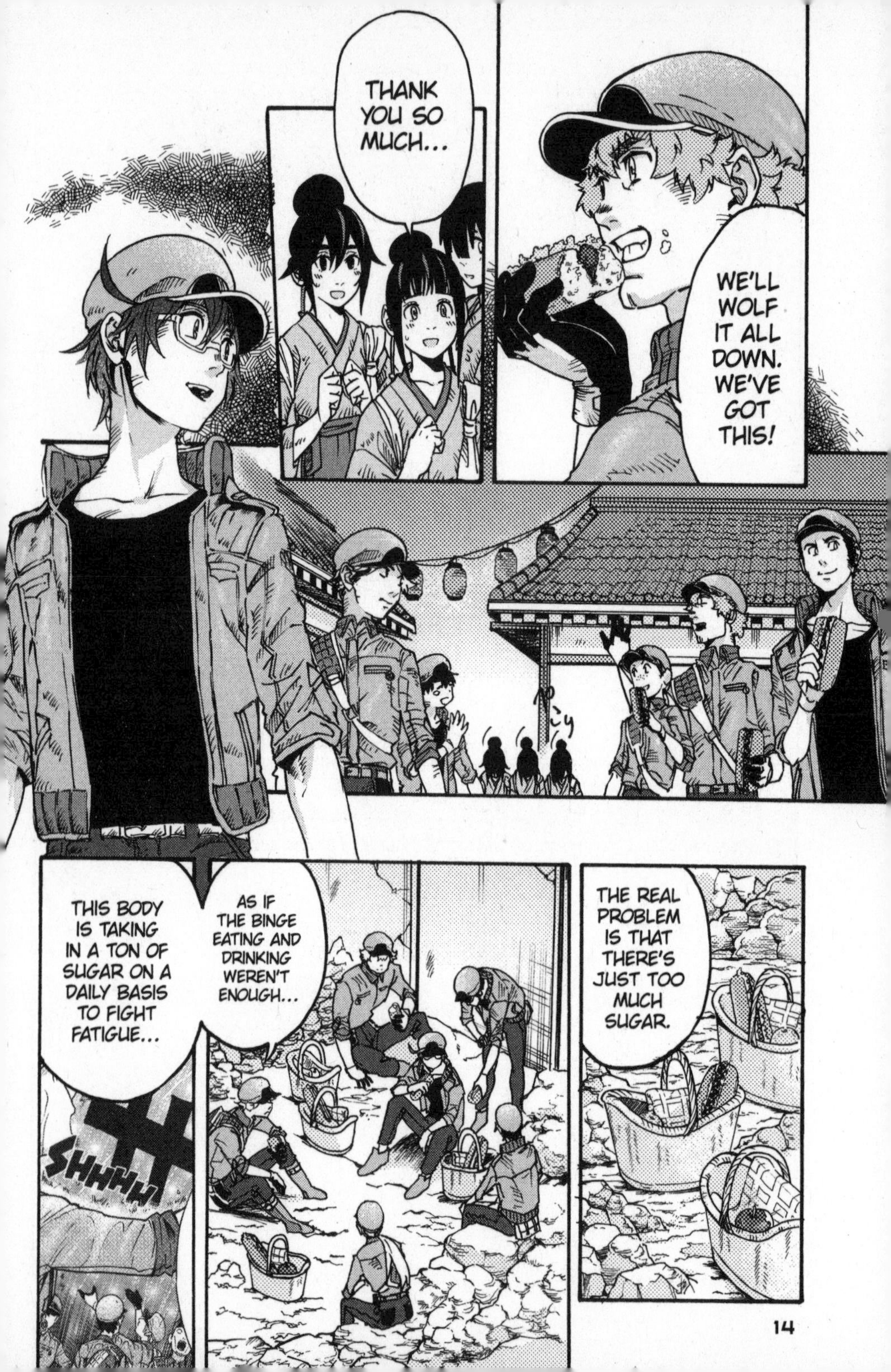
WE'LL WOLF IT ALL DOWN. WE'VE GOT THIS!
THANK YOU SO MUCH...
THE REAL PROBLEM IS THAT THERE'S JUST TOO MUCH SUGAR.
AS IF THE BINGE EATING AND DRINKING WEREN'T ENOUGH...
THIS BODY IS TAKING IN A TON OF SUGAR ON A DAILY BASIS TO FIGHT FATIGUE...
SHHHH

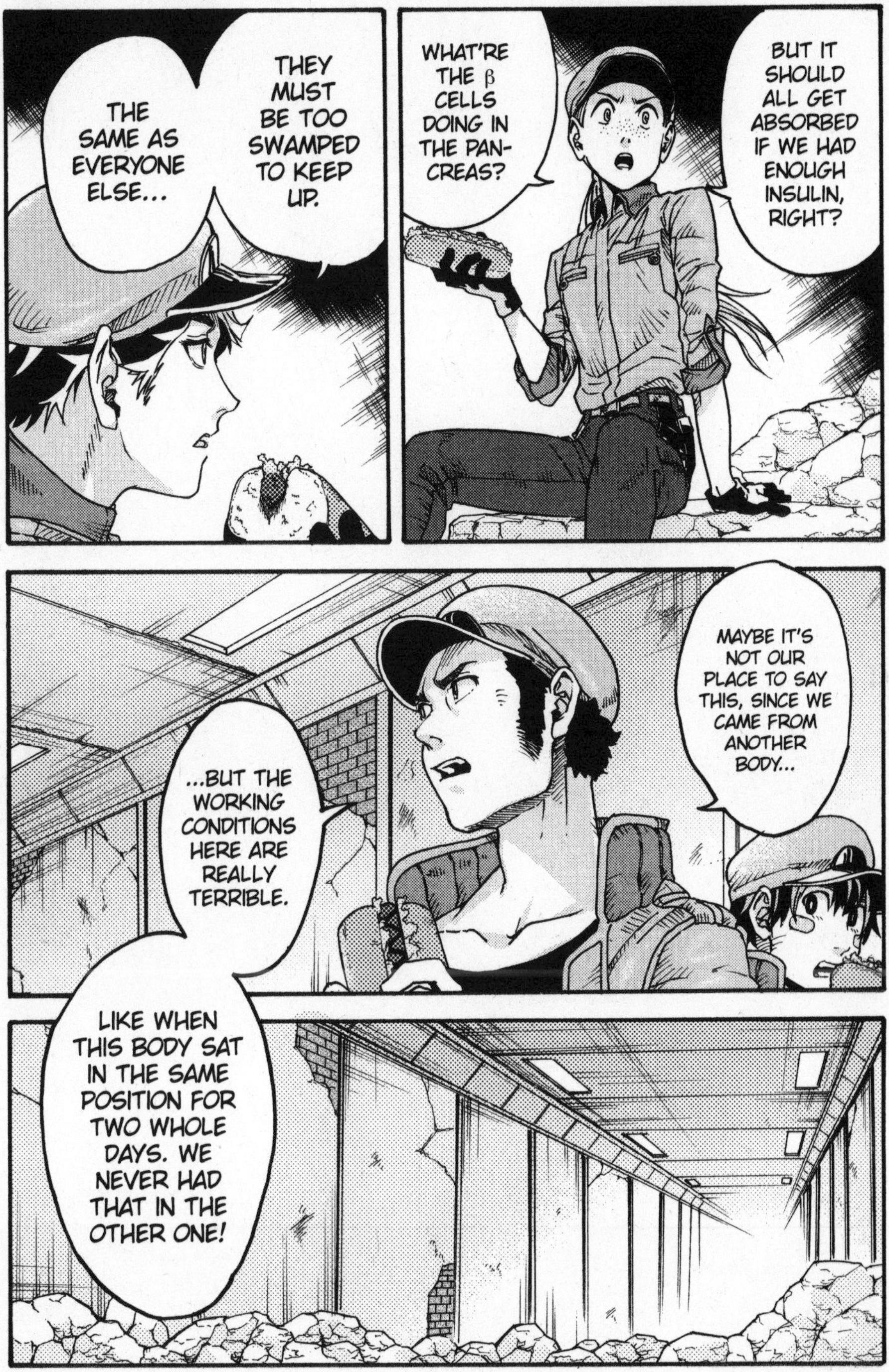
BUT IT SHOULD ALL GET ABSORBED IF WE HAD ENOUGH INSULIN, RIGHT?
WHAT'RE THE β CELLS DOING IN THE PAN-CREAS?
THEY MUST BE TOO SWAMPED TO KEEP UP.
THE SAME AS EVERYONE ELSE...
MAYBE IT'S NOT OUR PLACE TO SAY THIS, SINCE WE CAME FROM ANOTHER BODY...
...BUT THE WORKING CONDITIONS HERE ARE REALLY TERRIBLE.
LIKE WHEN THIS BODY SAT IN THE SAME POSITION FOR TWO WHOLE DAYS. WE NEVER HAD THAT IN THE OTHER ONE!

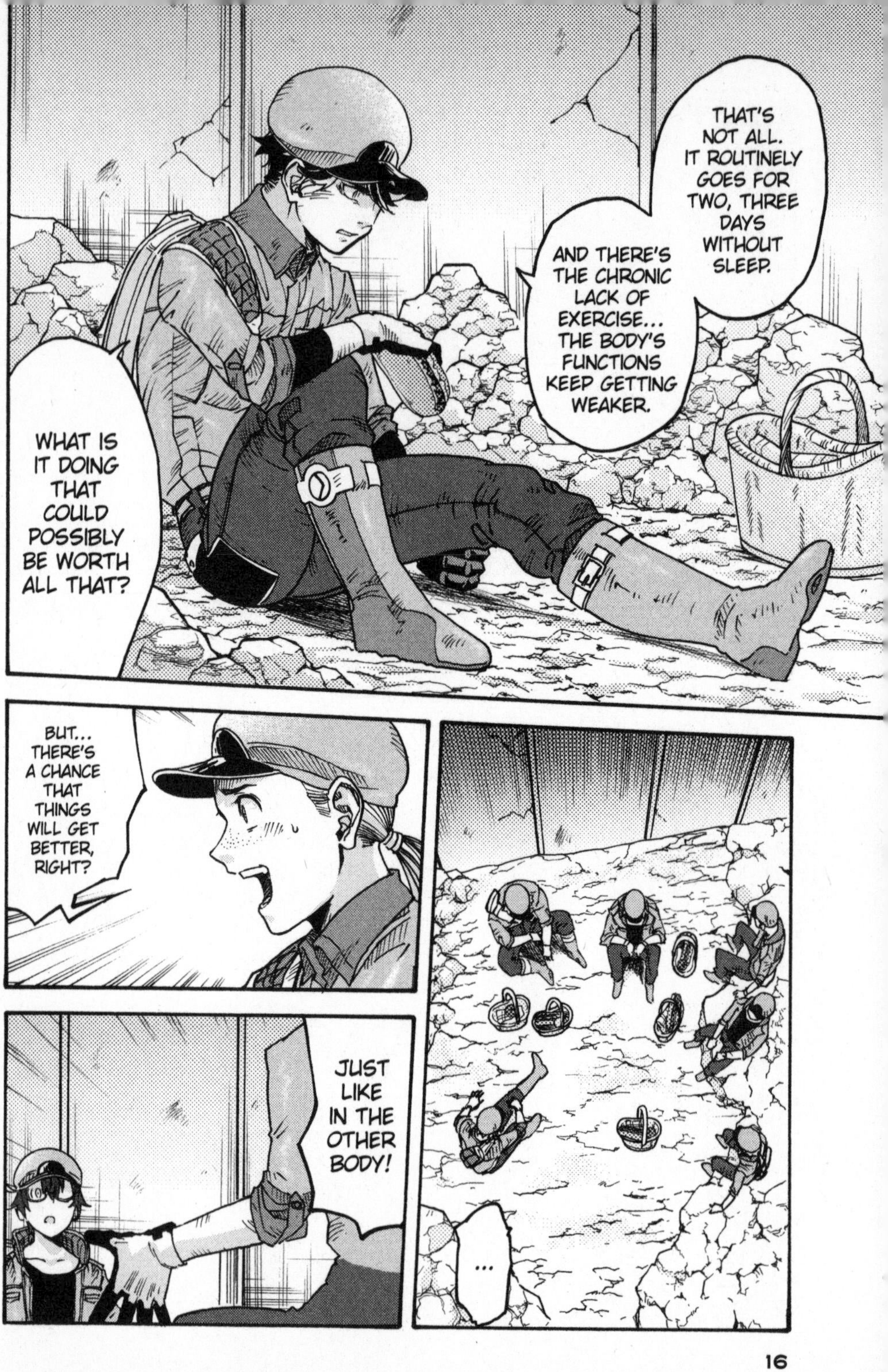
THAT'S NOT ALL. IT ROUTINELY GOES FOR TWO, THREE DAYS WITHOUT SLEEP.
AND THERE'S THE CHRONIC LACK OF EXERCISE... THE BODY'S FUNCTIONS KEEP GETTING WEAKER.
WHAT IS IT DOING THAT COULD POSSIBLY BE WORTH ALL THAT?
...
BUT... THERE'S A CHANCE THAT THINGS WILL GET BETTER, RIGHT?
JUST LIKE IN THE OTHER BODY!

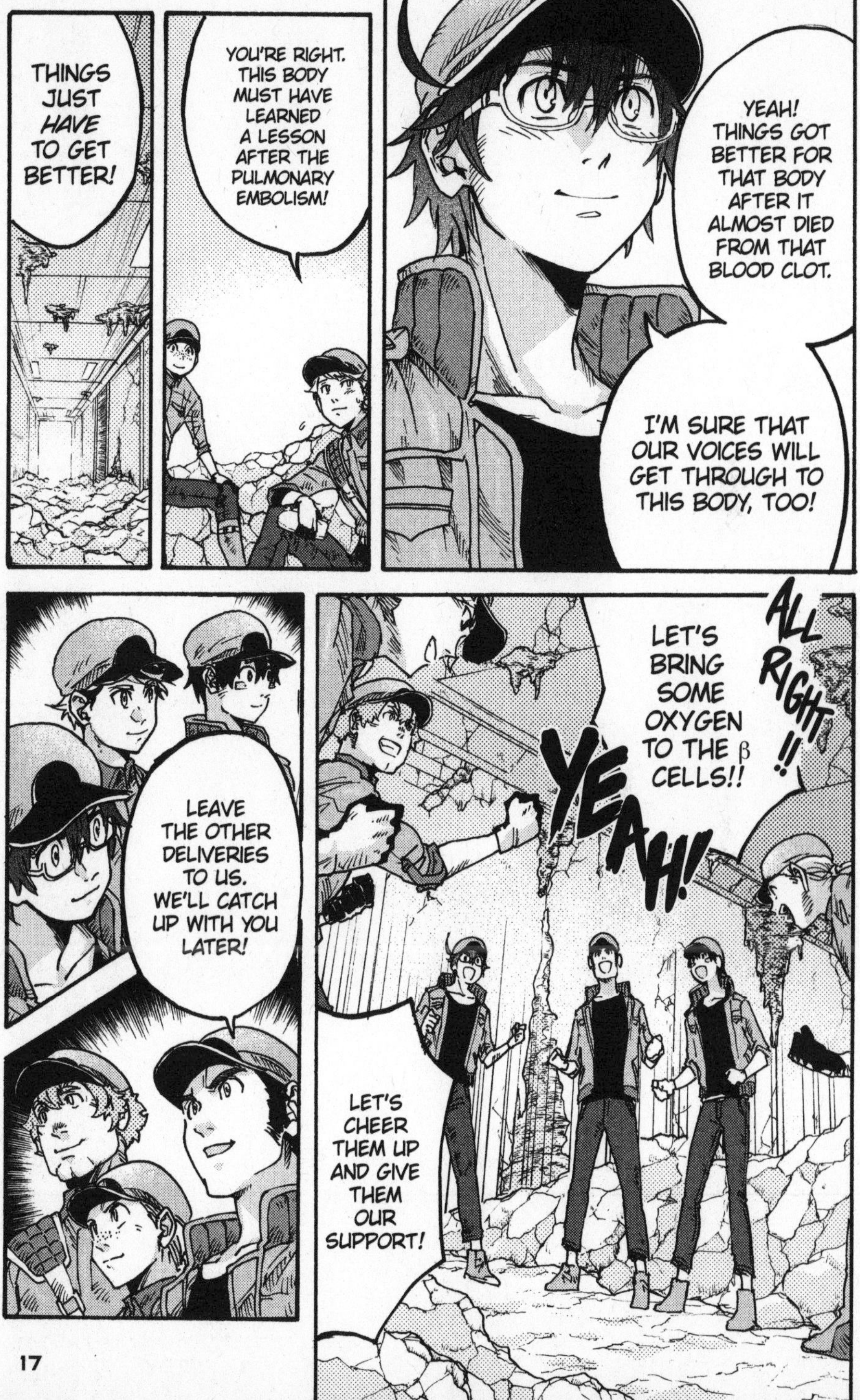
YEAH! THINGS GOT BETTER FOR THAT BODY AFTER IT ALMOST DIED FROM THAT BLOOD CLOT.
I'M SURE THAT OUR VOICES WILL GET THROUGH TO THIS BODY, TOO!
YOU'RE RIGHT. THIS BODY MUST HAVE LEARNED A LESSON AFTER THE PULMONARY EMBOLISM!
THINGS JUST *HAVE* TO GET BETTER!
ALL RIGHT!!
LET'S BRING SOME OXYGEN TO THE β CELLS!!
YEAH!
LET'S CHEER THEM UP AND GIVE THEM OUR SUPPORT!
LEAVE THE OTHER DELIVERIES TO US. WE'LL CATCH UP WITH YOU LATER!

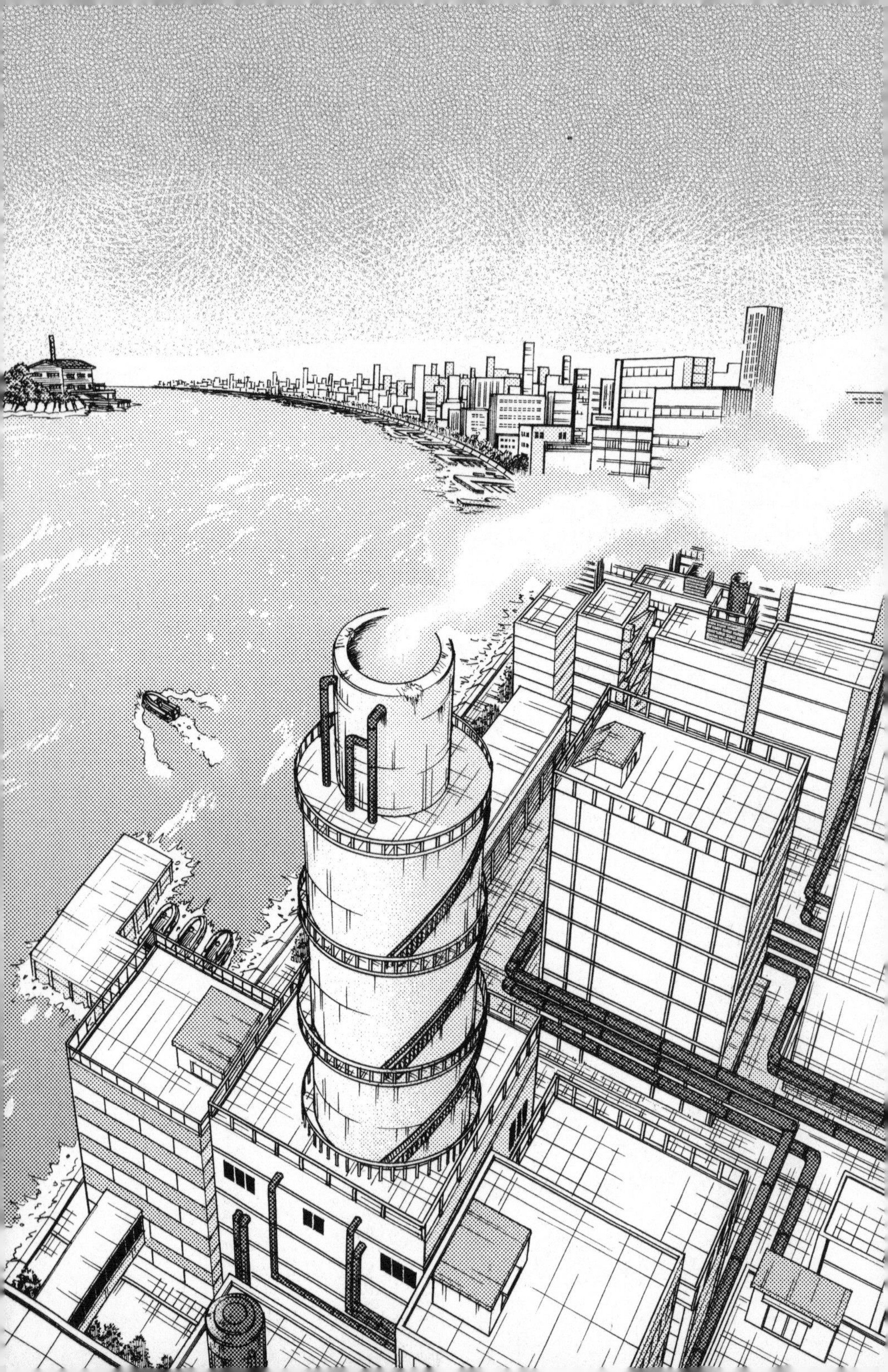

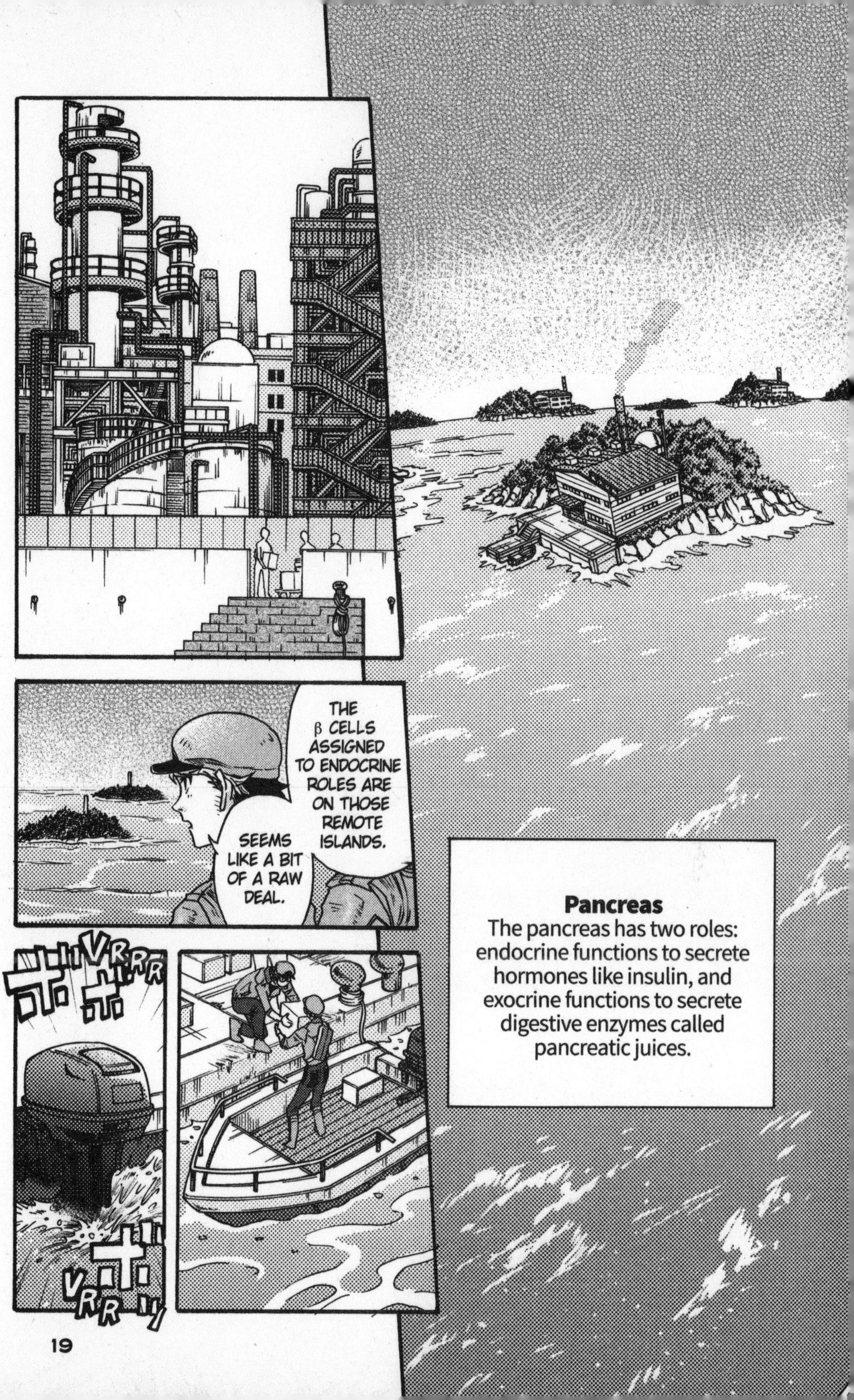
Pancreas
The pancreas has two roles: endocrine functions to secrete hormones like insulin, and exocrine functions to secrete digestive enzymes called pancreatic juices.
THE β CELLS ASSIGNED TO ENDOCRINE ROLES ARE ON THOSE REMOTE ISLANDS.
SEEMS LIKE A BIT OF A RAW DEAL.
VRRRR
VRR

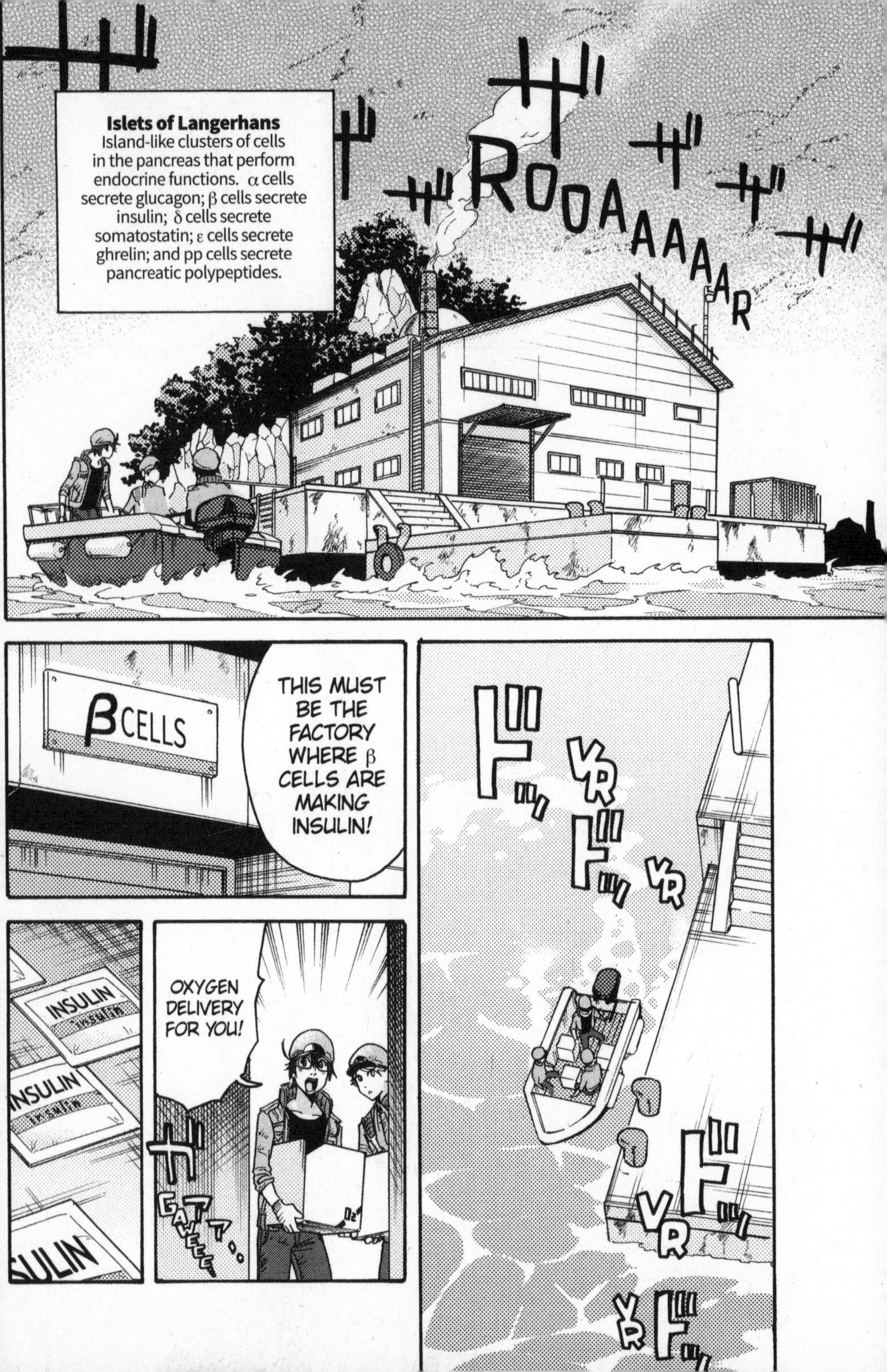
Islets of Langerhans
Island-like clusters of cells in the pancreas that perform endocrine functions. α cells secrete glucagon; β cells secrete insulin; δ cells secrete somatostatin; ε cells secrete ghrelin; and pp cells secrete pancreatic polypeptides.
ROOAAAAAR
VR
VR
VR
VR
βCELLS
THIS MUST BE THE FACTORY WHERE β CELLS ARE MAKING INSULIN!
OXYGEN DELIVERY FOR YOU!
GAWEEET
INSULIN
INSULIN
INSULIN

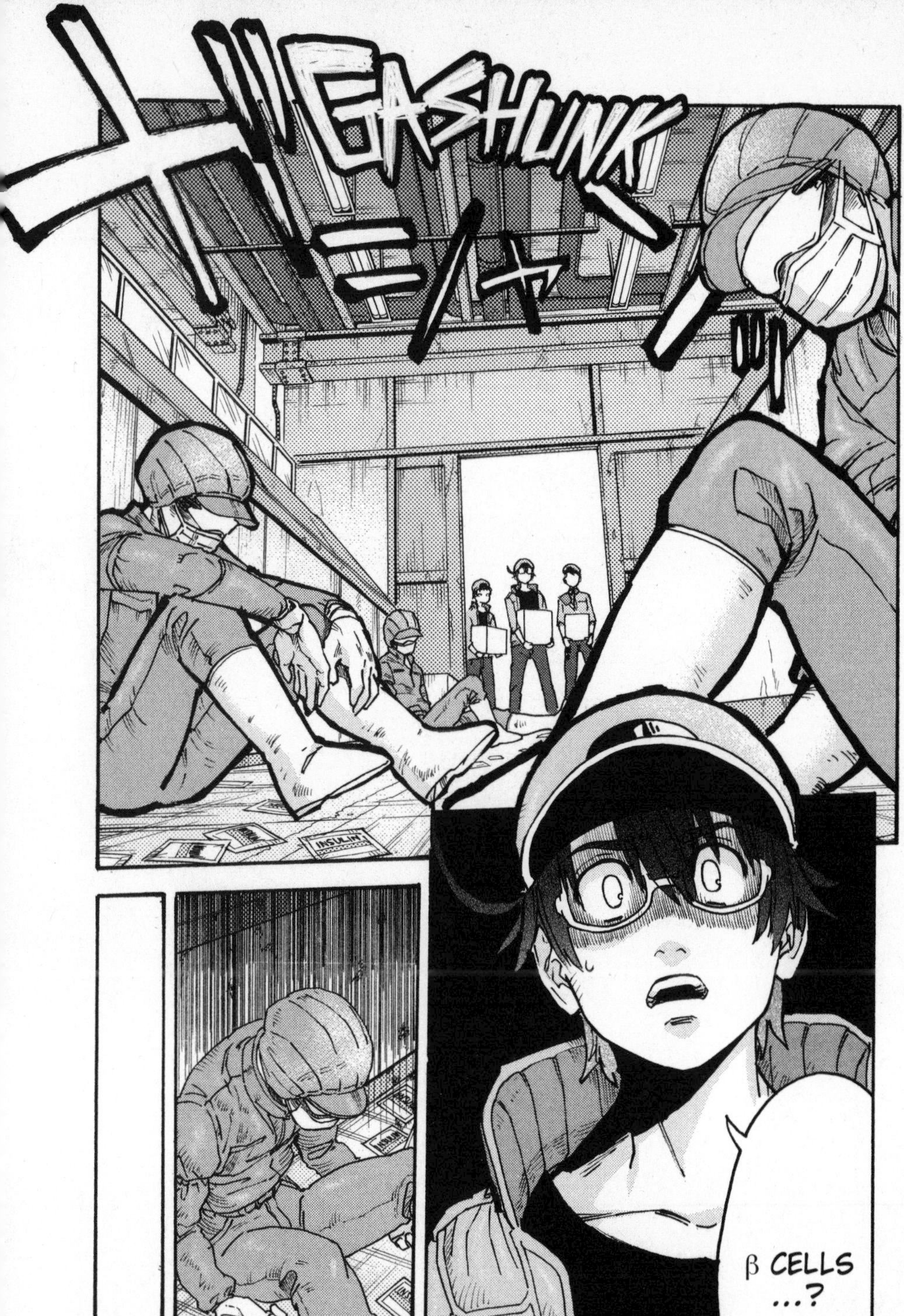
GASHUNK
INSULIN
β CELLS
...?

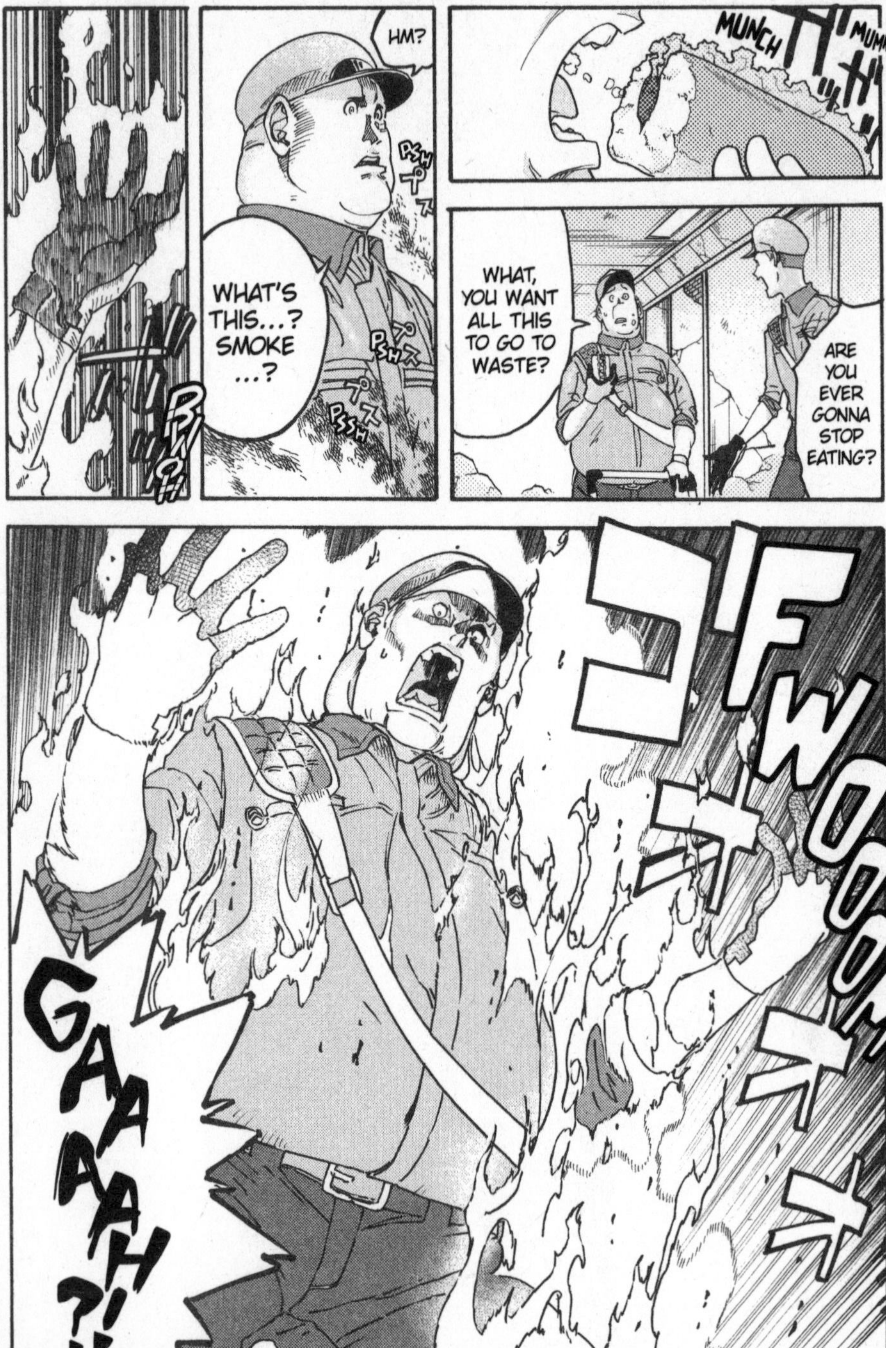
MUNCH
MUMNCH
ARE YOU EVER GONNA STOP EATING?
WHAT, YOU WANT ALL THIS TO GO TO WASTE?
HM?
PSH
WHAT'S THIS...? SMOKE ...?
PSH
PSSH
FWOOOOM
GAAAAH?!!

CHAPTER 18 - END

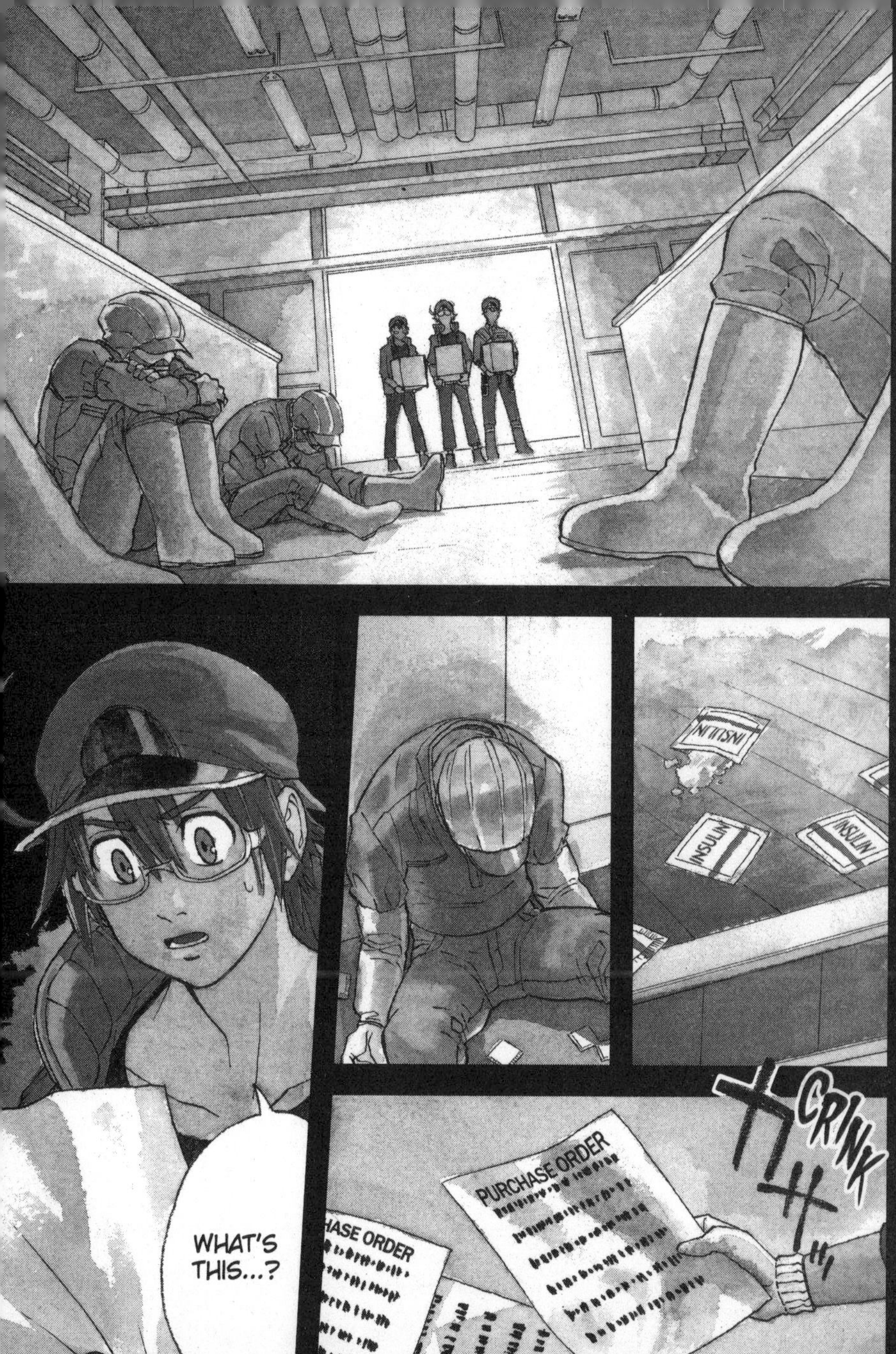
INSULIN
INSULIN
INSULIN
CRINK
PURCHASE ORDER
HASE ORDER
WHAT'S THIS...?

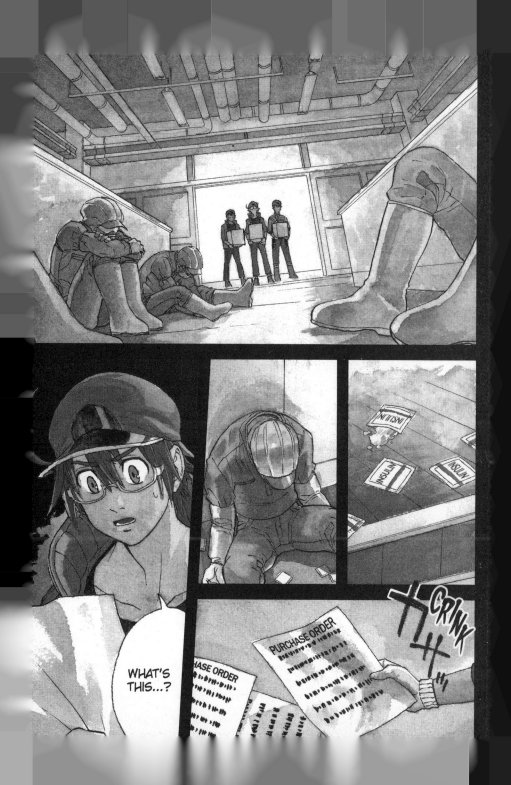

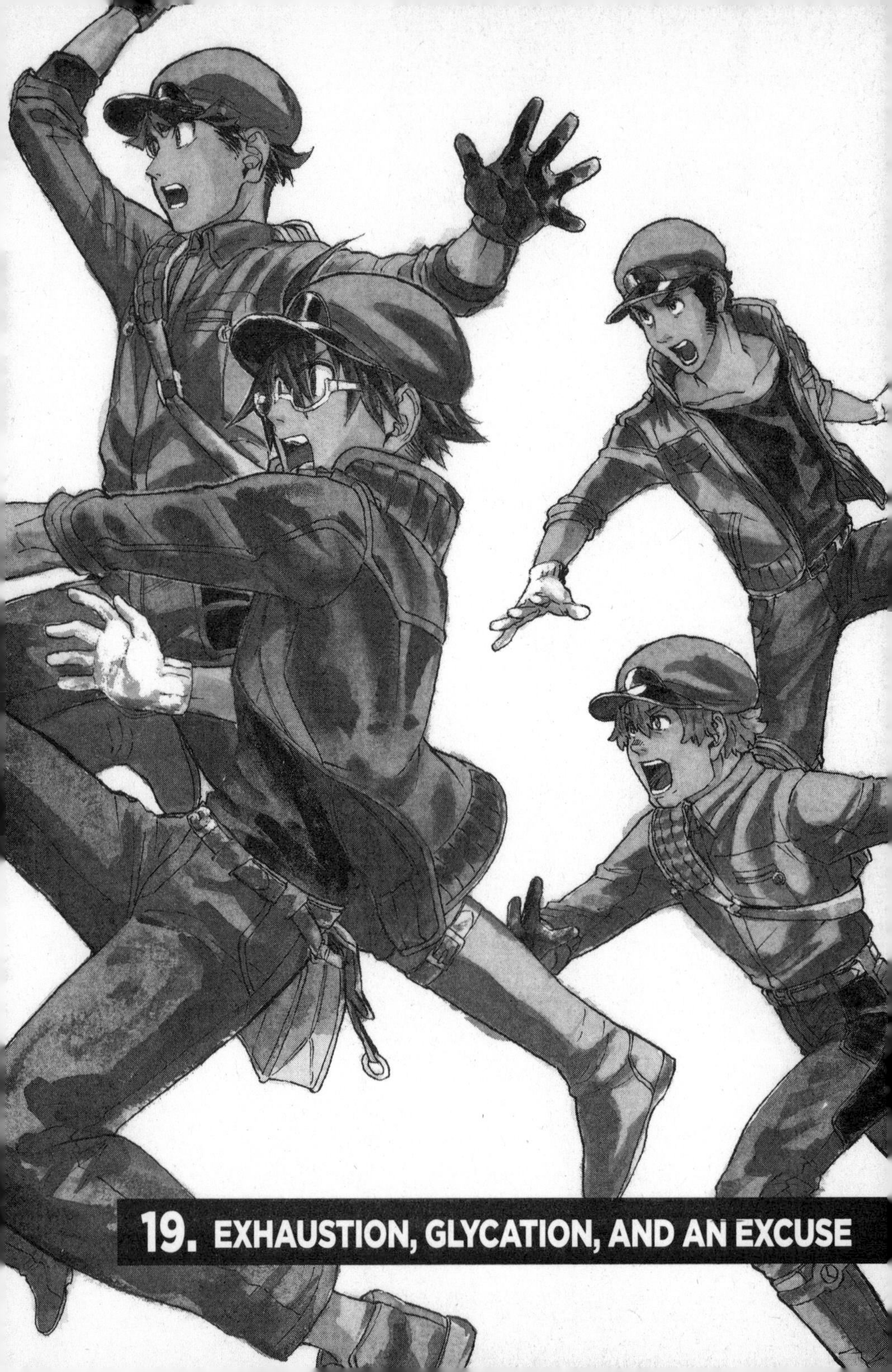

19. EXHAUSTION, GLYCATION, AND AN EXCUSE

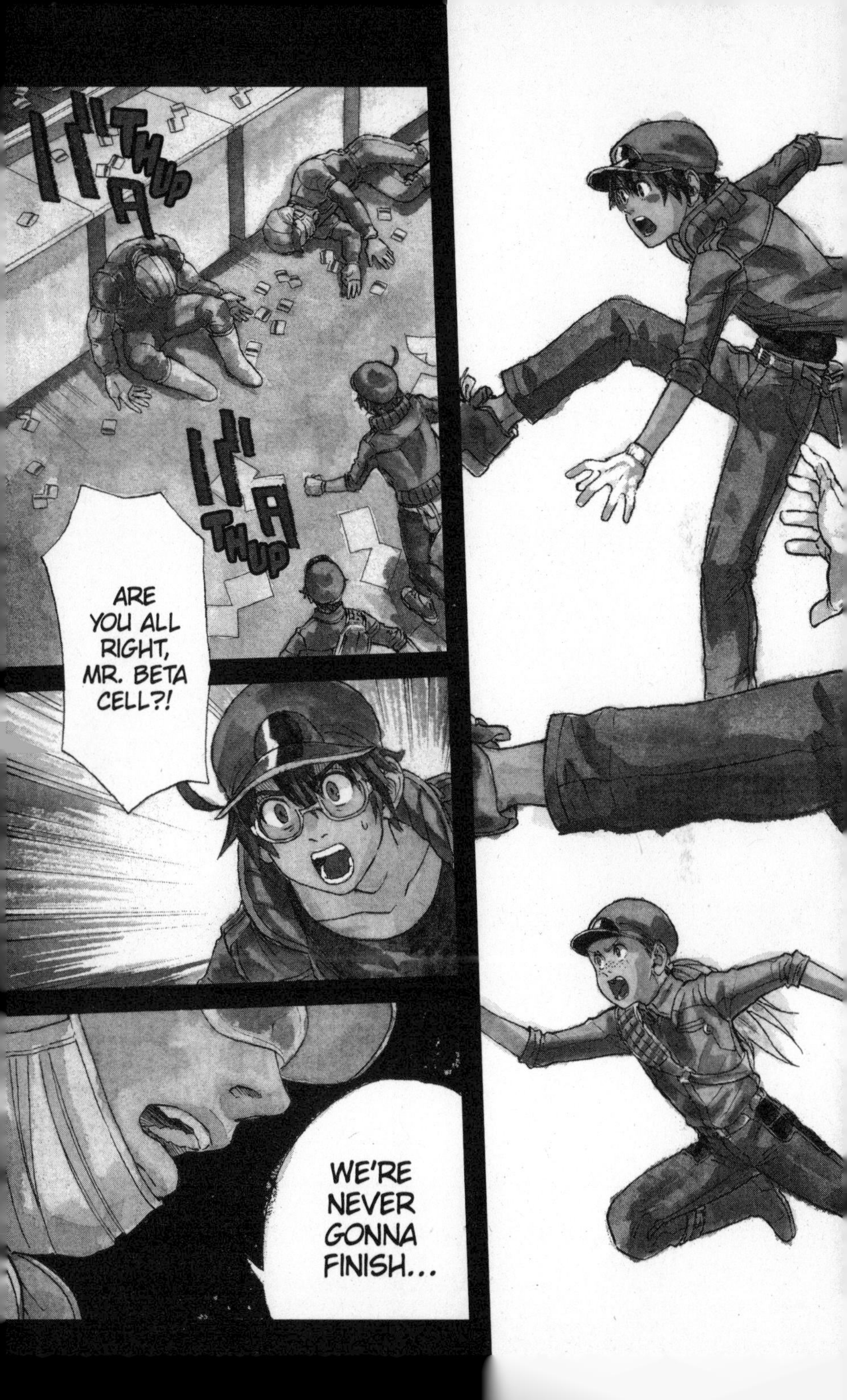
THUP
THUP
ARE YOU ALL RIGHT, MR. BETA CELL?!
WE'RE NEVER GONNA FINISH...

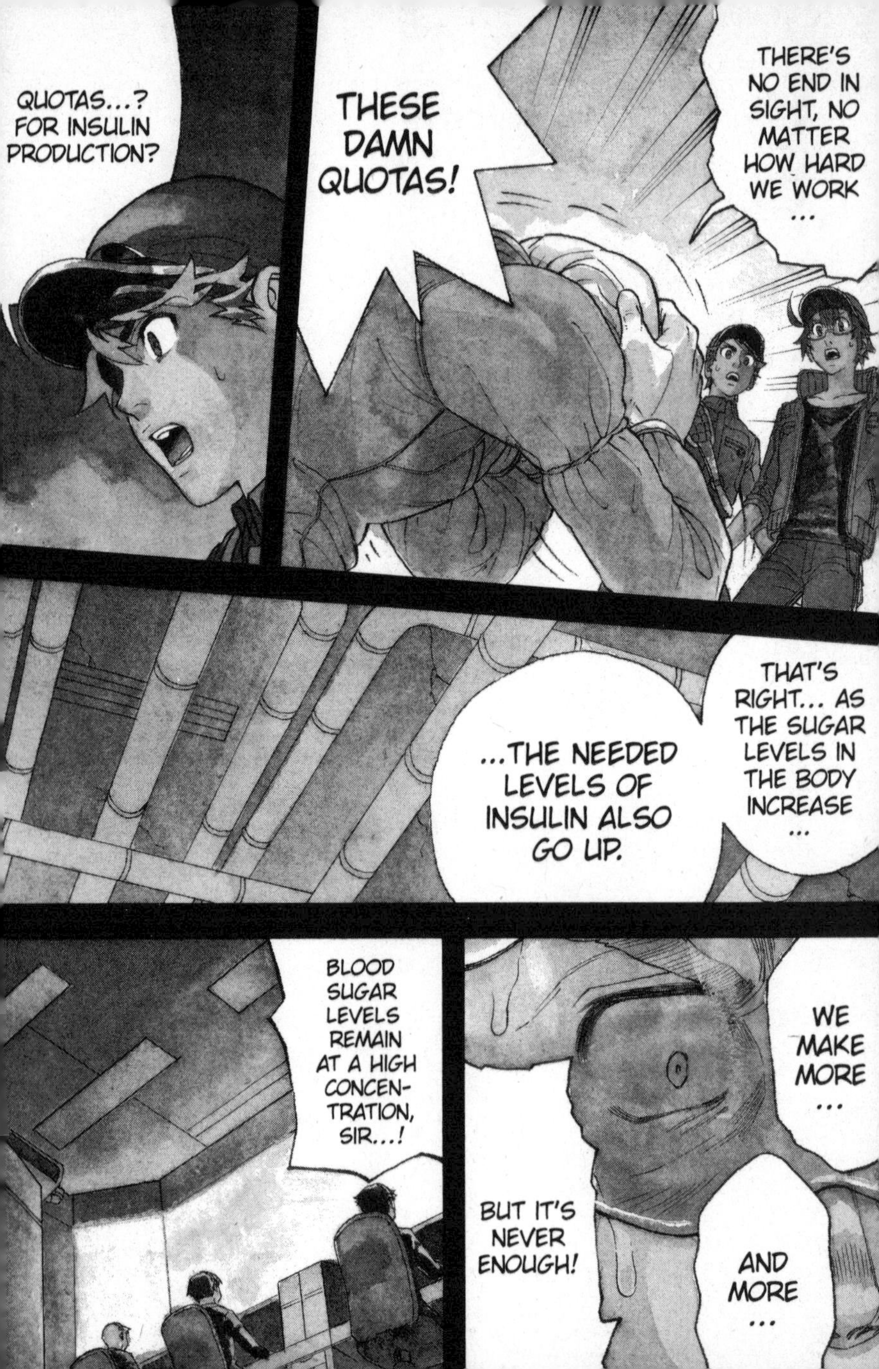
THERE'S NO END IN SIGHT, NO MATTER HOW HARD WE WORK …
THESE DAMN QUOTAS!
QUOTAS…? FOR INSULIN PRODUCTION?
THAT'S RIGHT… AS THE SUGAR LEVELS IN THE BODY INCREASE …
…THE NEEDED LEVELS OF INSULIN ALSO GO UP.
WE MAKE MORE …
AND MORE …
BUT IT'S NEVER ENOUGH!
BLOOD SUGAR LEVELS REMAIN AT A HIGH CONCENTRATION, SIR…!

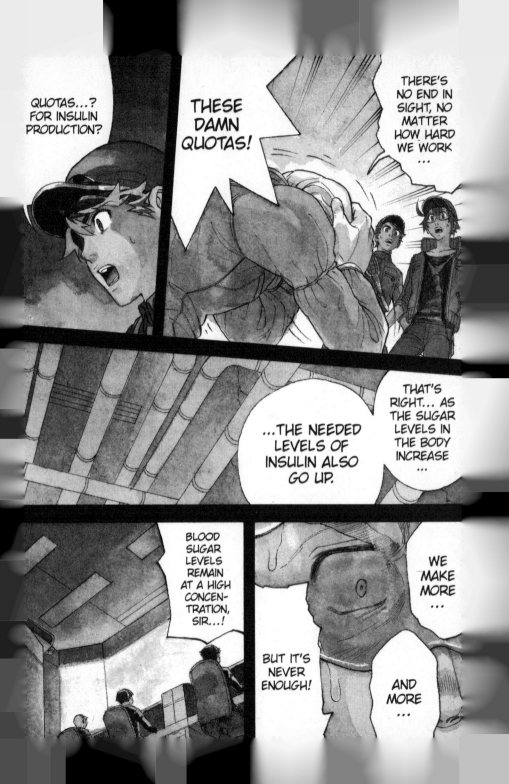

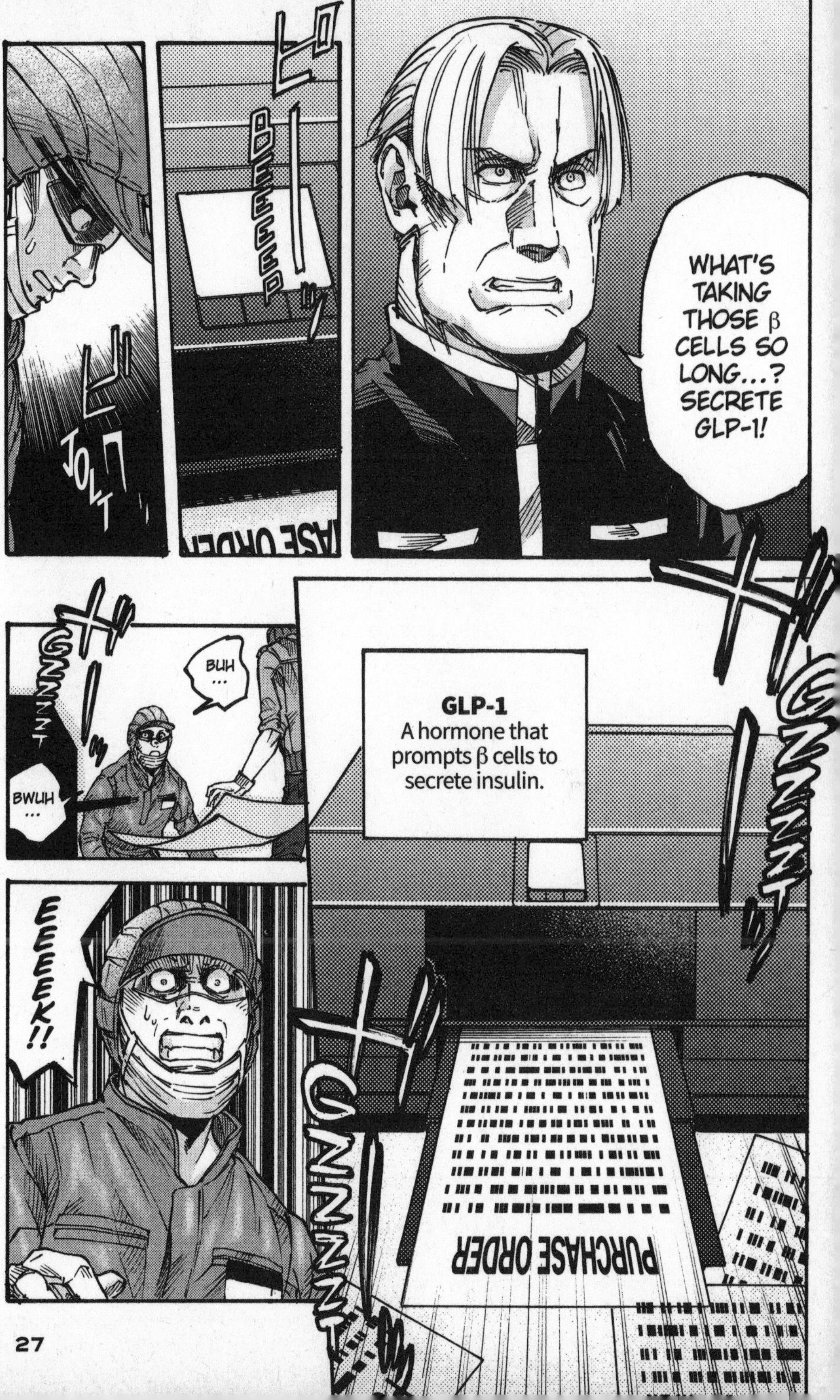

WHAT'S TAKING THOSE β CELLS SO LONG...? SECRETE GLP-1!
BEEEEP
PURCHASE ORDER
JOLT
GNNNNT
GLP-1
A hormone that prompts β cells to secrete insulin.
GNNNNT
PURCHASE ORDER
GNNNNT
BUH ...
BWUH ...
EEEEEK!!

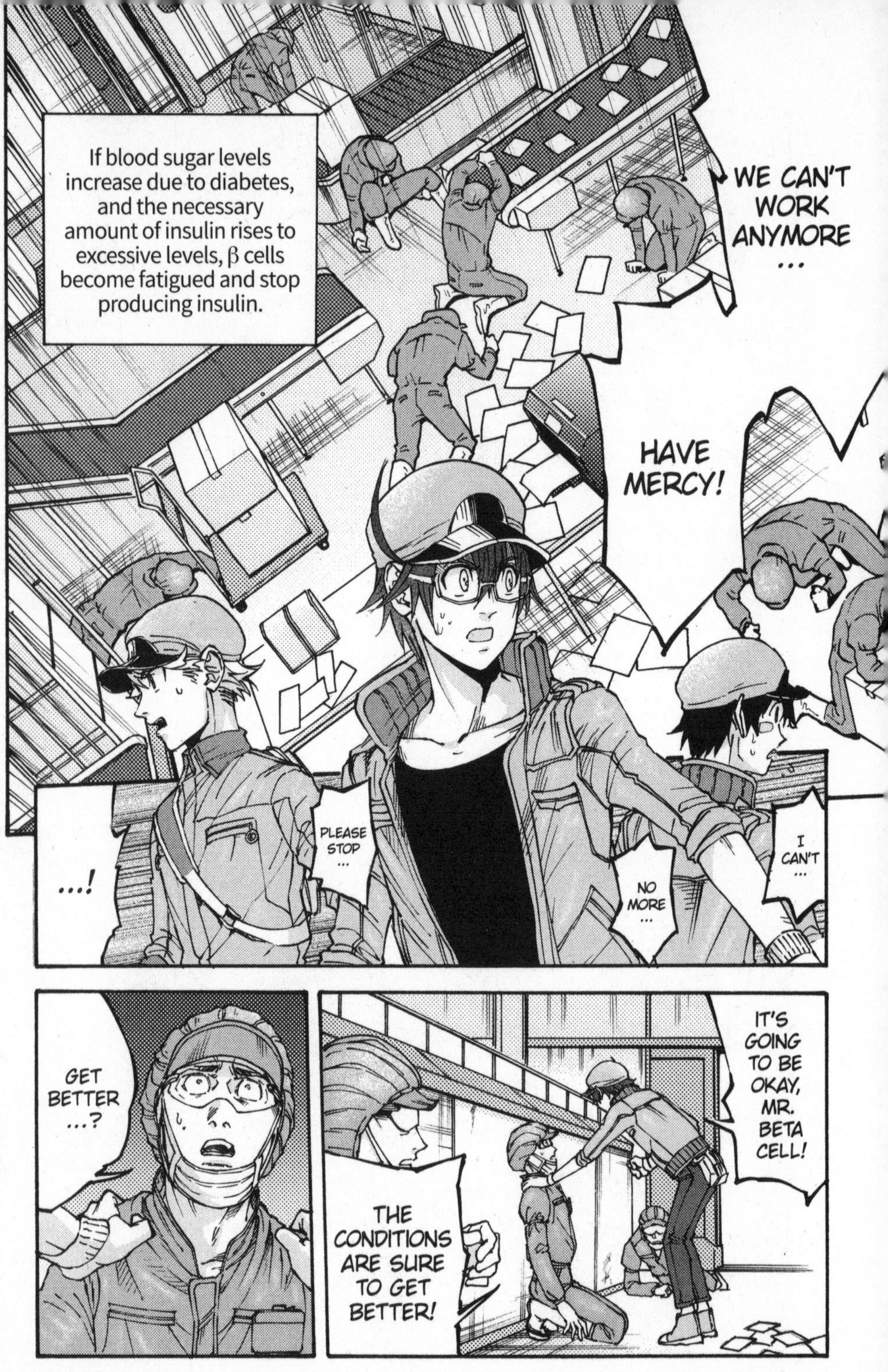
WE CAN'T WORK ANYMORE ...
If blood sugar levels increase due to diabetes, and the necessary amount of insulin rises to excessive levels, β cells become fatigued and stop producing insulin.
HAVE MERCY!
I CAN'T ...
NO MORE ...
PLEASE STOP ...
...!
IT'S GOING TO BE OKAY, MR. BETA CELL!
THE CONDITIONS ARE SURE TO GET BETTER!
GET BETTER ...?

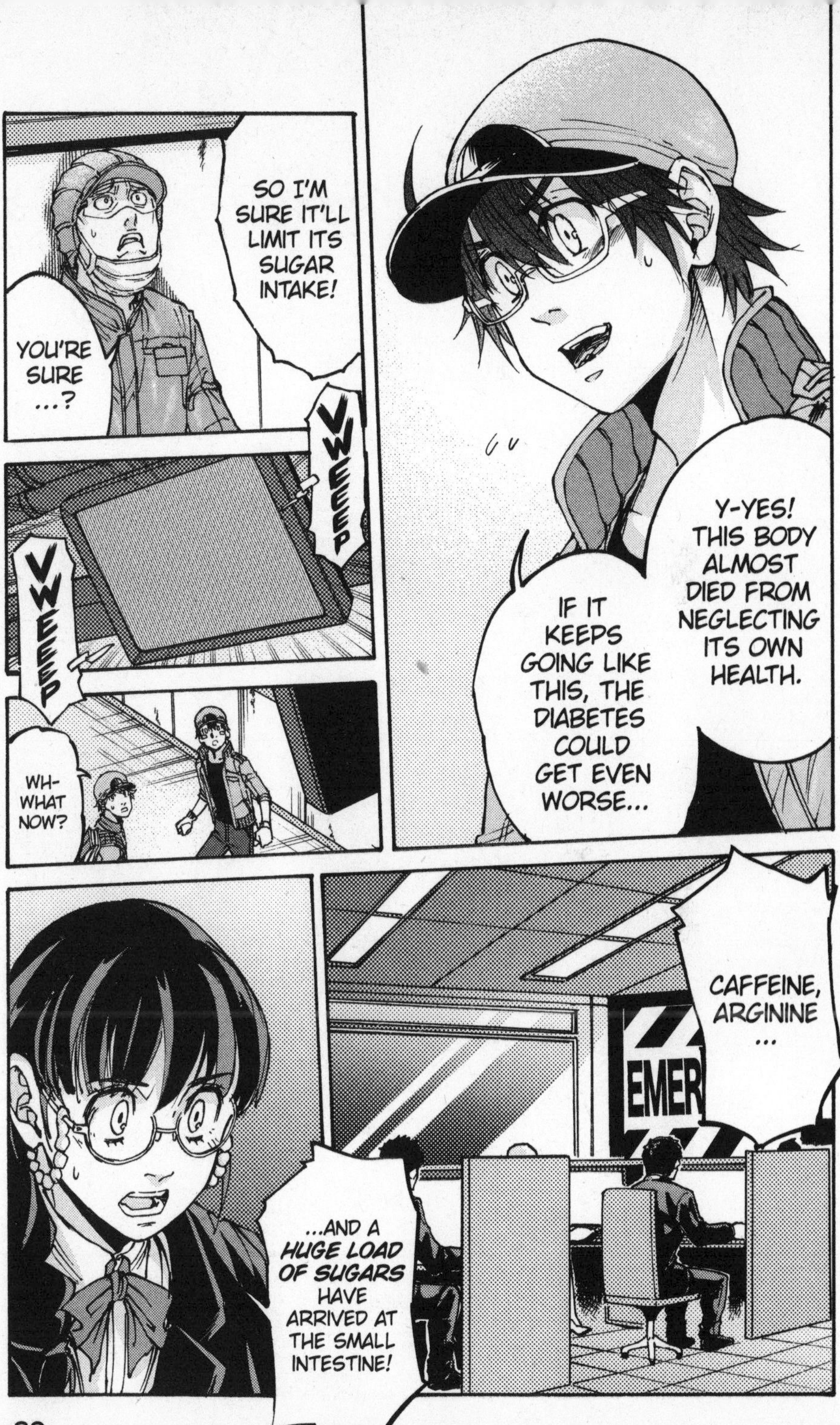
Y-YES! THIS BODY ALMOST DIED FROM NEGLECTING ITS OWN HEALTH.
IF IT KEEPS GOING LIKE THIS, THE DIABETES COULD GET EVEN WORSE...
SO I'M SURE IT'LL LIMIT ITS SUGAR INTAKE!
YOU'RE SURE ...?
VWEEEP
VWEEEP
WH-WHAT NOW?
CAFFEINE, ARGININE ...
EMER
...AND A *HUGE LOAD OF SUGARS* HAVE ARRIVED AT THE SMALL INTESTINE!

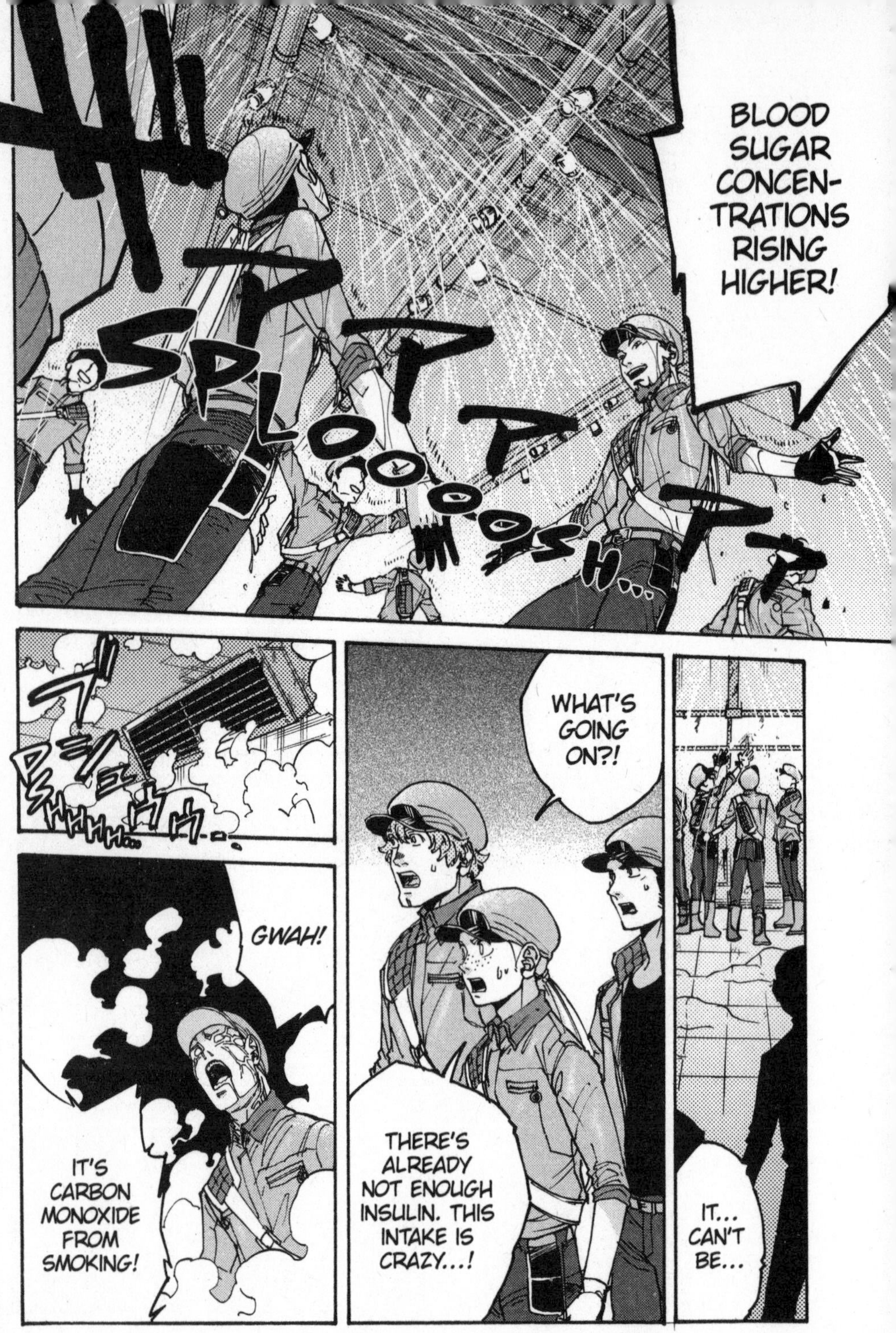

BLOOD SUGAR CONCEN-TRATIONS RISING HIGHER!
SPLOOOOOSH...
IT... CAN'T BE...
WHAT'S GOING ON?!
THERE'S ALREADY NOT ENOUGH INSULIN. THIS INTAKE IS CRAZY...!
GWAH!
IT'S CARBON MONOXIDE FROM SMOKING!

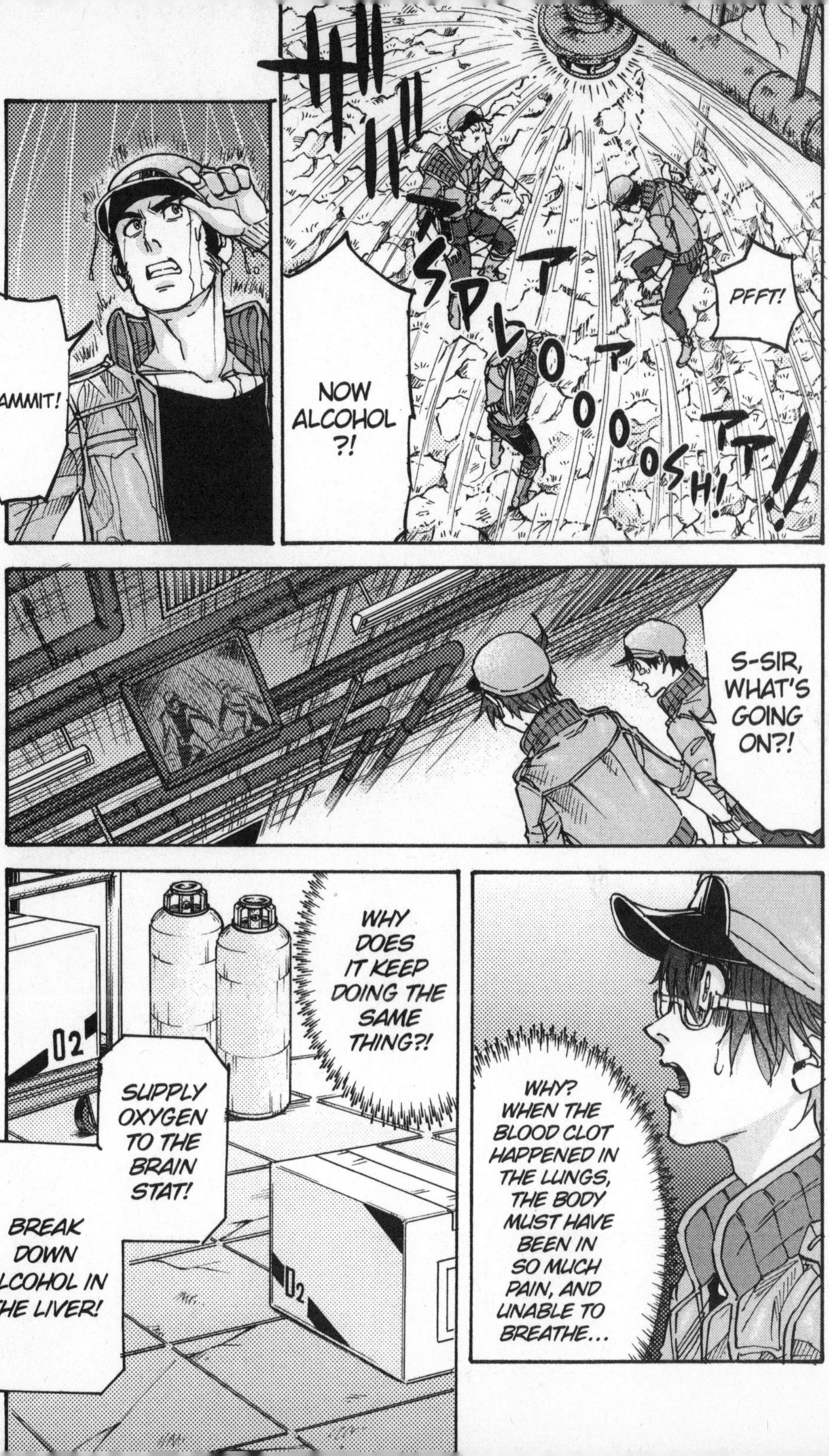
SPLOOOOSH!!
PFFT!
NOW ALCOHOL?!
DAMMIT!
S-SIR, WHAT'S GOING ON?!
WHY? WHEN THE BLOOD CLOT HAPPENED IN THE LUNGS, THE BODY MUST HAVE BEEN IN SO MUCH PAIN, AND UNABLE TO BREATHE...
WHY DOES IT KEEP DOING THE SAME THING?!
O2
SUPPLY OXYGEN TO THE BRAIN STAT!
BREAK DOWN ALCOHOL IN THE LIVER!
O2

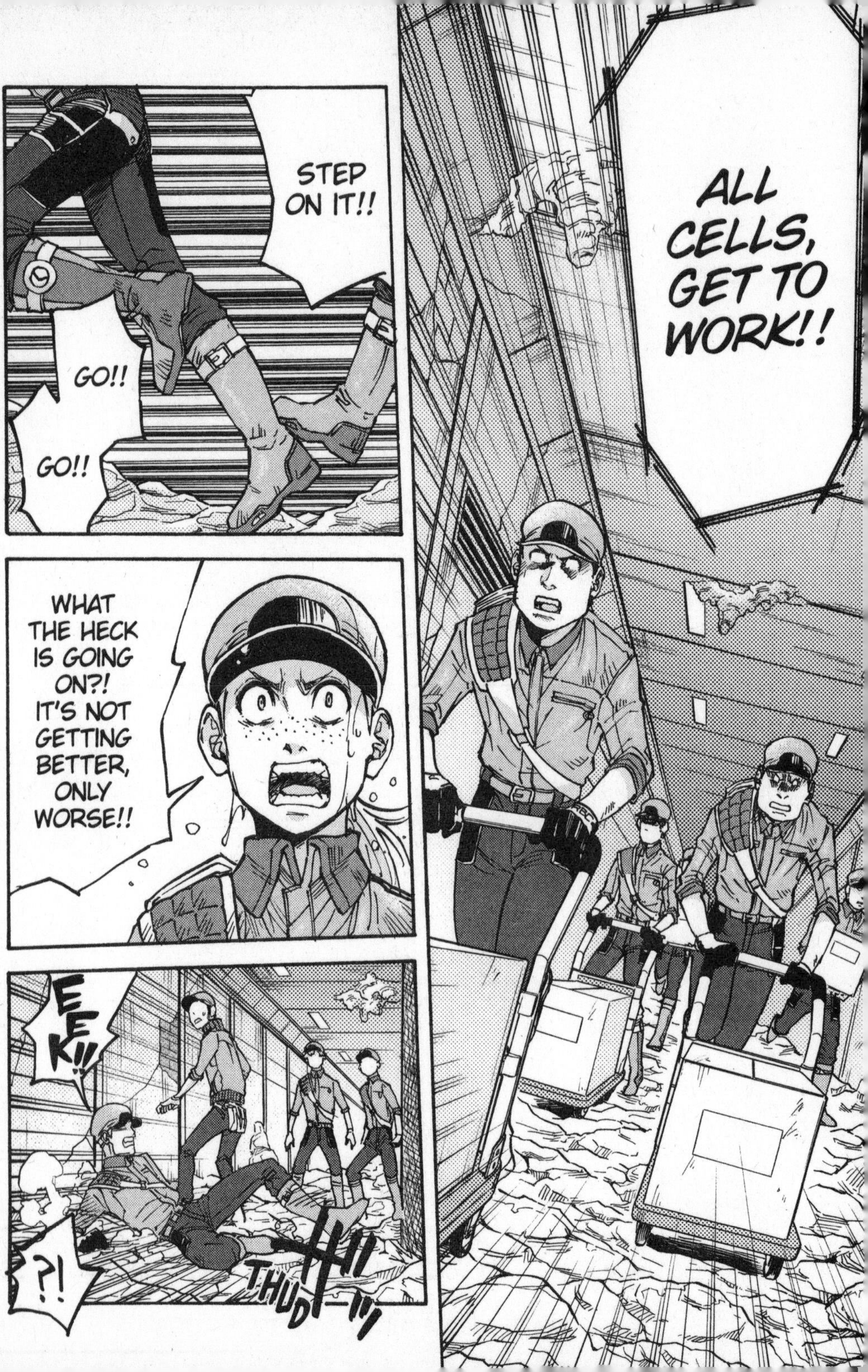
ALL CELLS, GET TO WORK!!
STEP ON IT!!
GO!!
GO!!
WHAT THE HECK IS GOING ON?! IT'S NOT GETTING BETTER, ONLY WORSE!!
EEEK!!!
?!
THUD

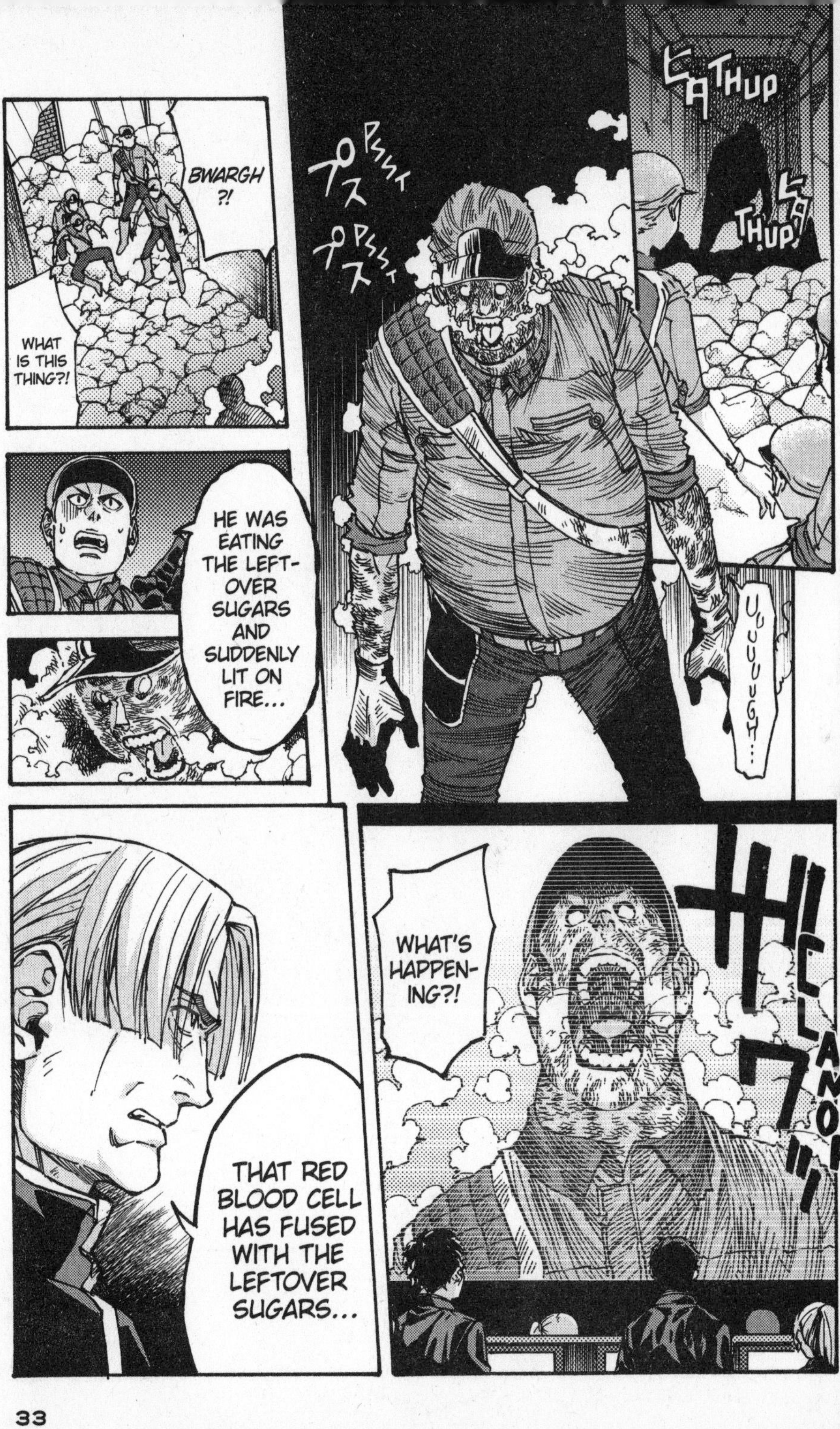

ピタ THUP
ピタ THUP!
プス PSSST
プス PSSST
UUUUUGH...
BWARGH?!
WHAT IS THIS THING?!
HE WAS EATING THE LEFT-OVER SUGARS AND SUDDENLY LIT ON FIRE...
CLAMOR!!!
WHAT'S HAPPEN-ING?!
THAT RED BLOOD CELL HAS FUSED WITH THE LEFTOVER SUGARS...

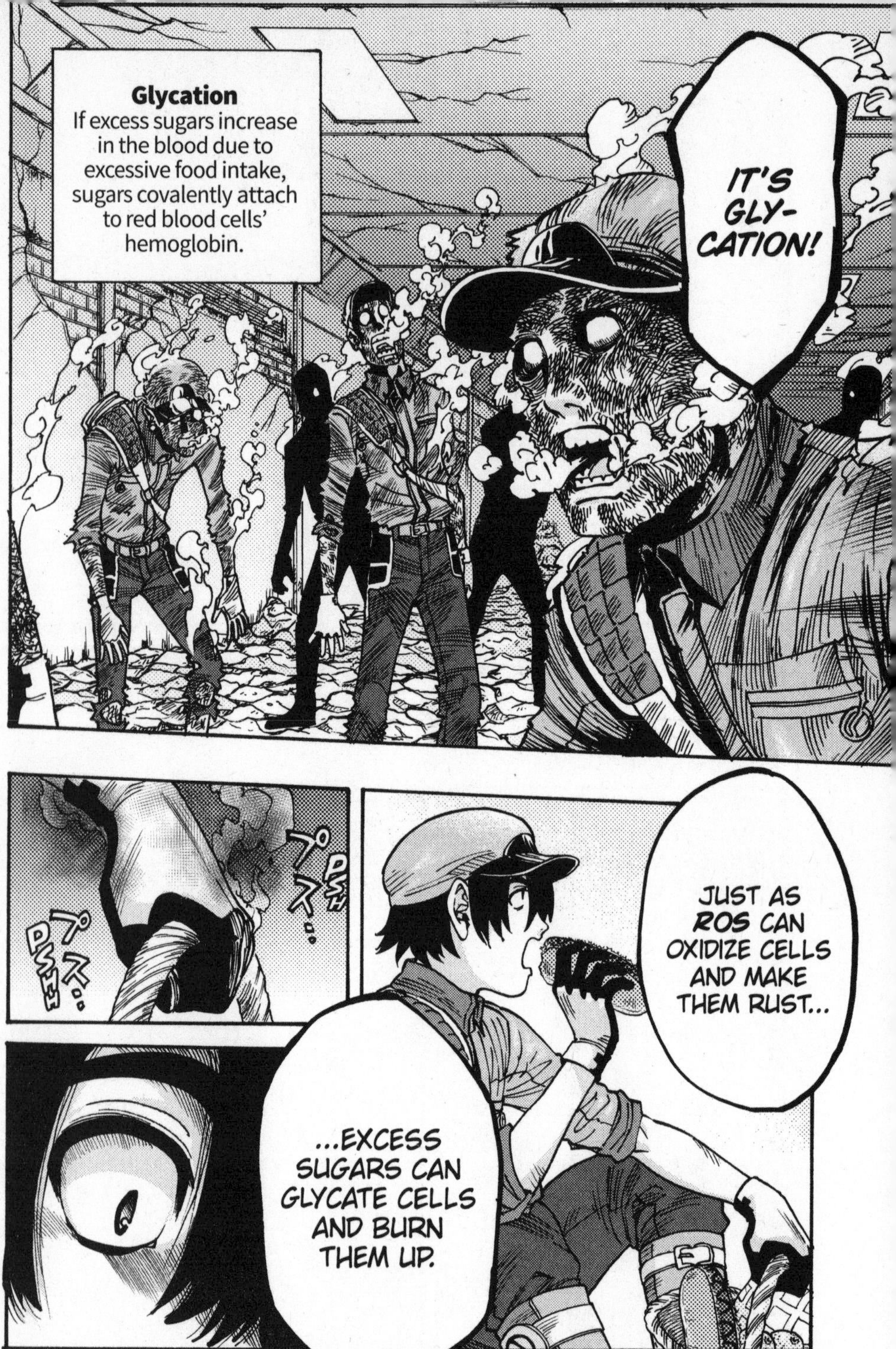
IT'S GLY-CATION!
Glycation
If excess sugars increase in the blood due to excessive food intake, sugars covalently attach to red blood cells' hemoglobin.
JUST AS ROS CAN OXIDIZE CELLS AND MAKE THEM RUST...
...EXCESS SUGARS CAN GLYCATE CELLS AND BURN THEM UP.
プス‥ PSH
プス‥ PSHH

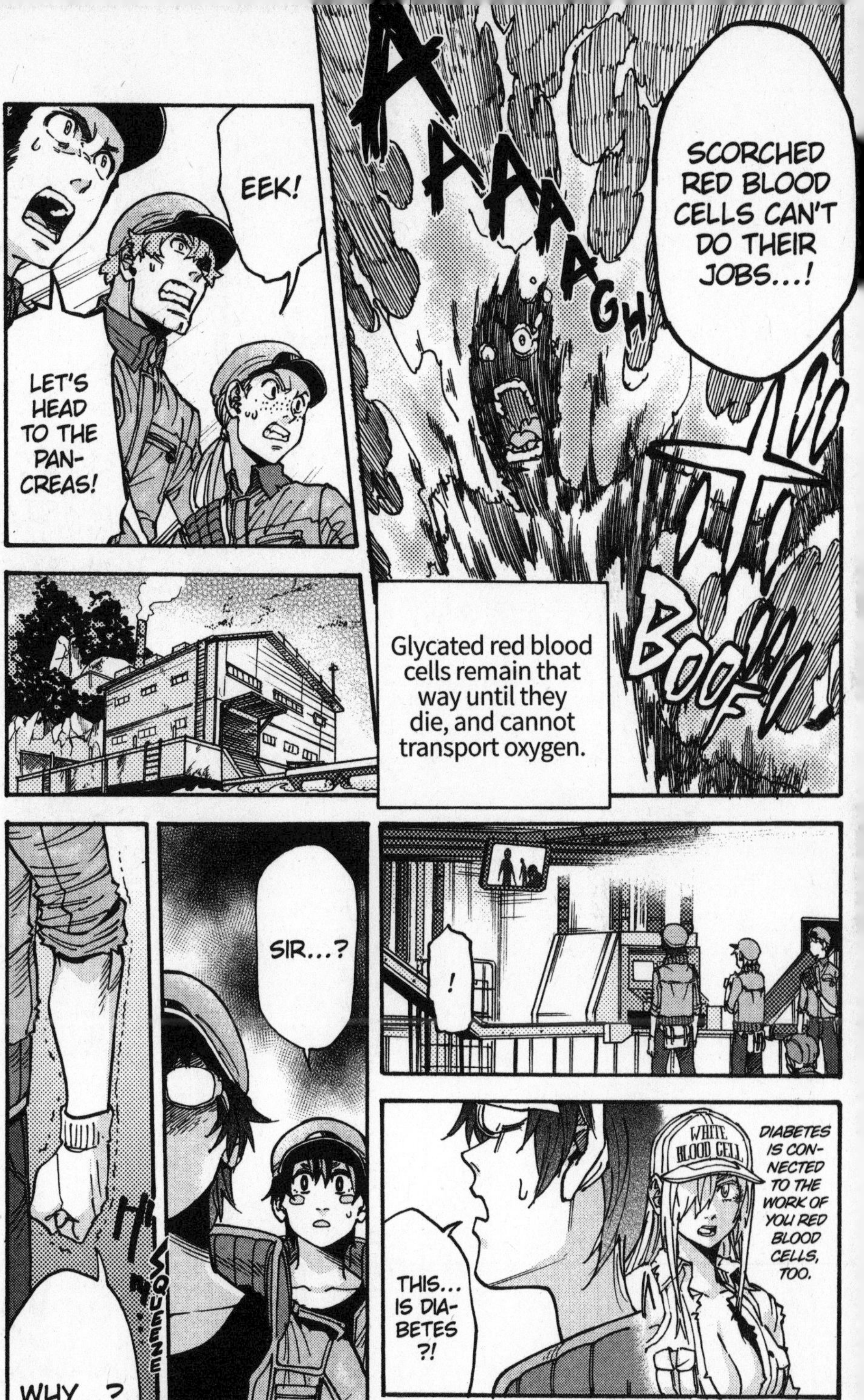
SCORCHED RED BLOOD CELLS CAN'T DO THEIR JOBS...!
AAAAAGH
BOOF
EEK!
LET'S HEAD TO THE PAN-CREAS!
Glycated red blood cells remain that way until they die, and cannot transport oxygen.
!
DIABETES IS CON-NECTED TO THE WORK OF YOU RED BLOOD CELLS, TOO.
THIS... IS DIA-BETES ?!
SIR...?
SQUEEZE
WHY...?

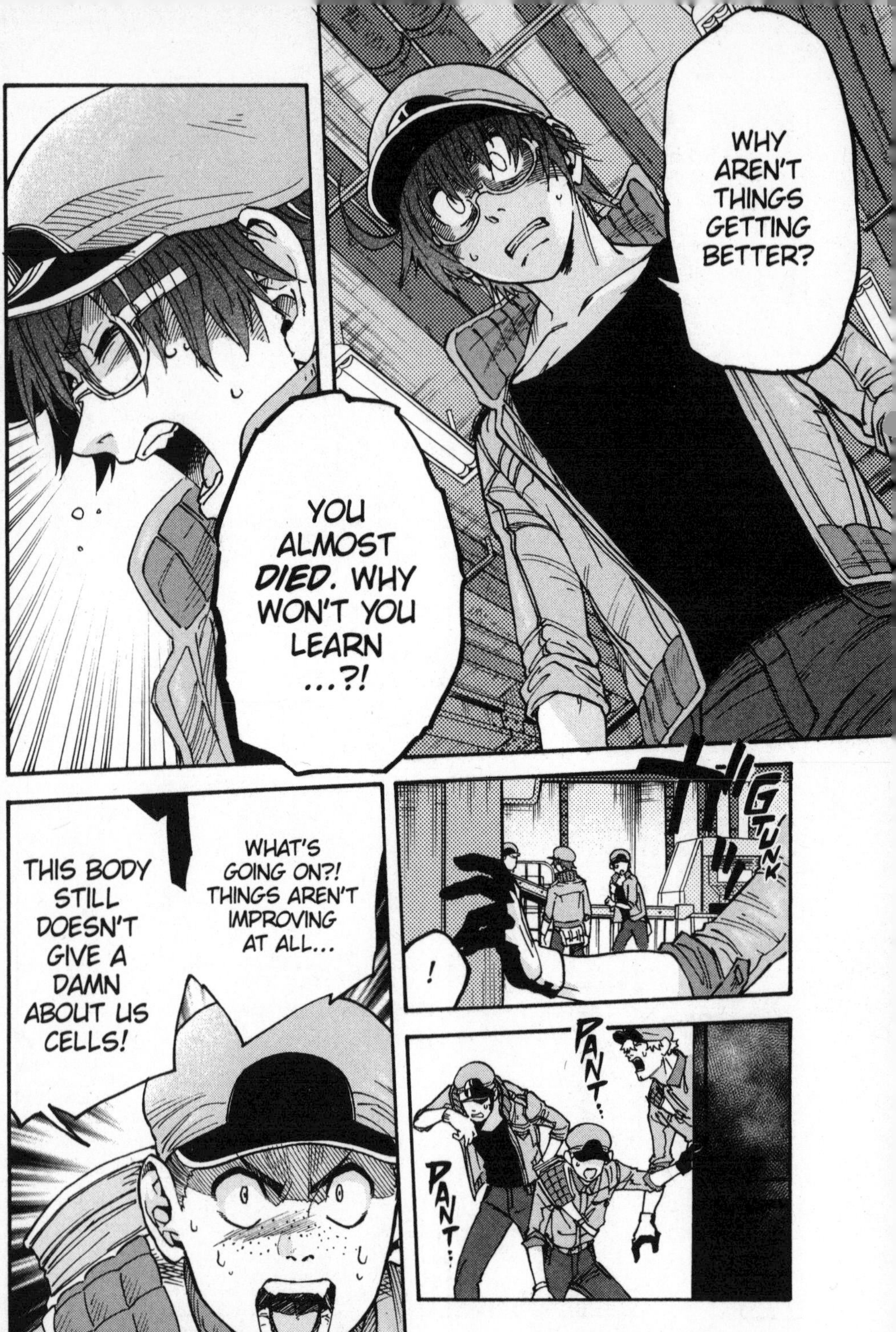
WHY AREN'T THINGS GETTING BETTER?
YOU ALMOST DIED. WHY WON'T YOU LEARN ...?!
GTUNK
!
PANT...
PANT...
WHAT'S GOING ON?! THINGS AREN'T IMPROVING AT ALL...
THIS BODY STILL DOESN'T GIVE A DAMN ABOUT US CELLS!

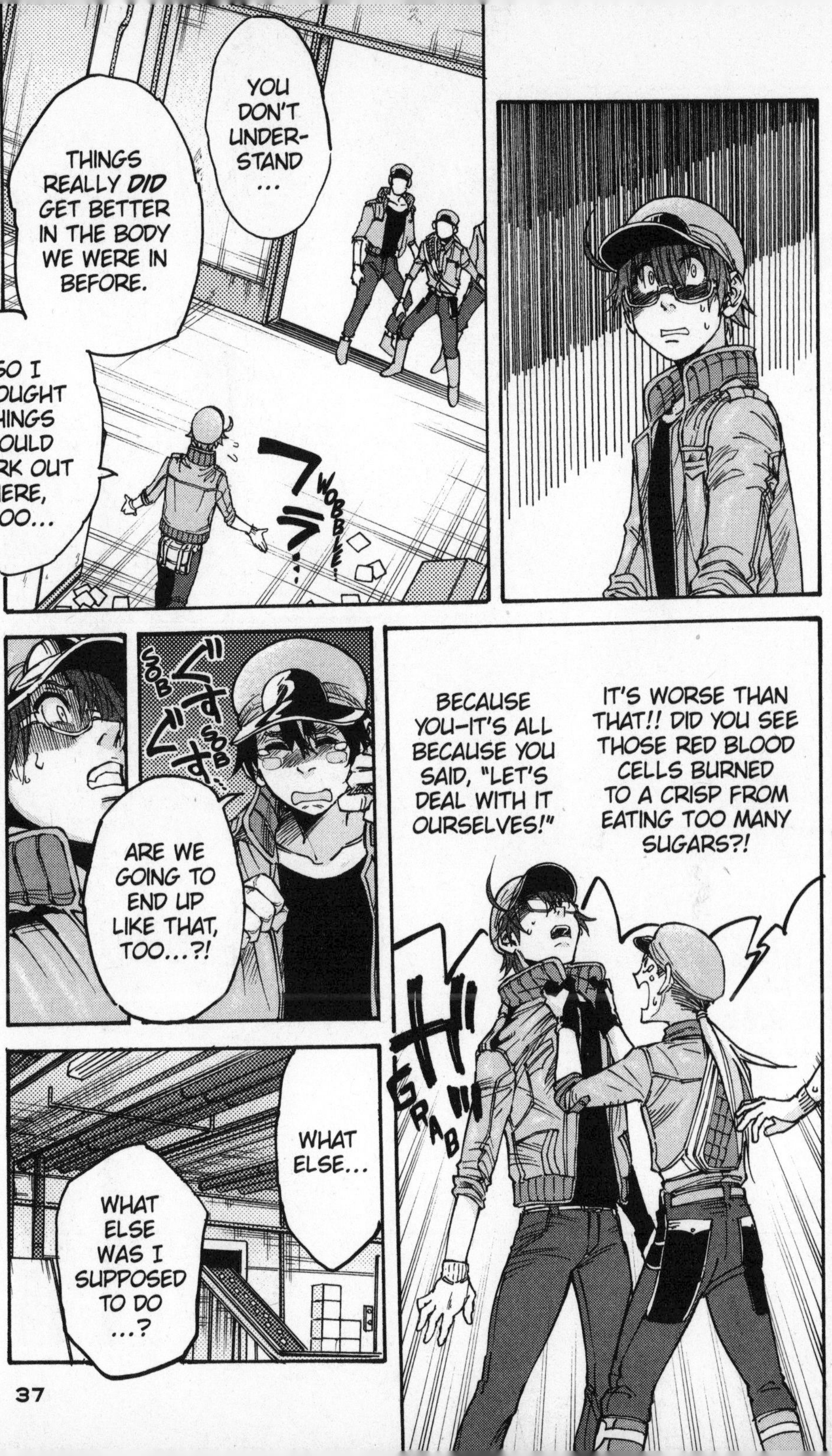
YOU DON'T UNDER-STAND...
THINGS REALLY *DID* GET BETTER IN THE BODY WE WERE IN BEFORE.
SO I THOUGHT THINGS WOULD WORK OUT HERE, TOO...
WOBBLE...
IT'S WORSE THAN THAT!! DID YOU SEE THOSE RED BLOOD CELLS BURNED TO A CRISP FROM EATING TOO MANY SUGARS?!
BECAUSE YOU–IT'S ALL BECAUSE YOU SAID, "LET'S DEAL WITH IT OURSELVES!"
GRAB!!!
SOB SOB
ぐすぐす...
ARE WE GOING TO END UP LIKE THAT, TOO...?!
WHAT ELSE...
WHAT ELSE WAS I SUPPOSED TO DO ...?

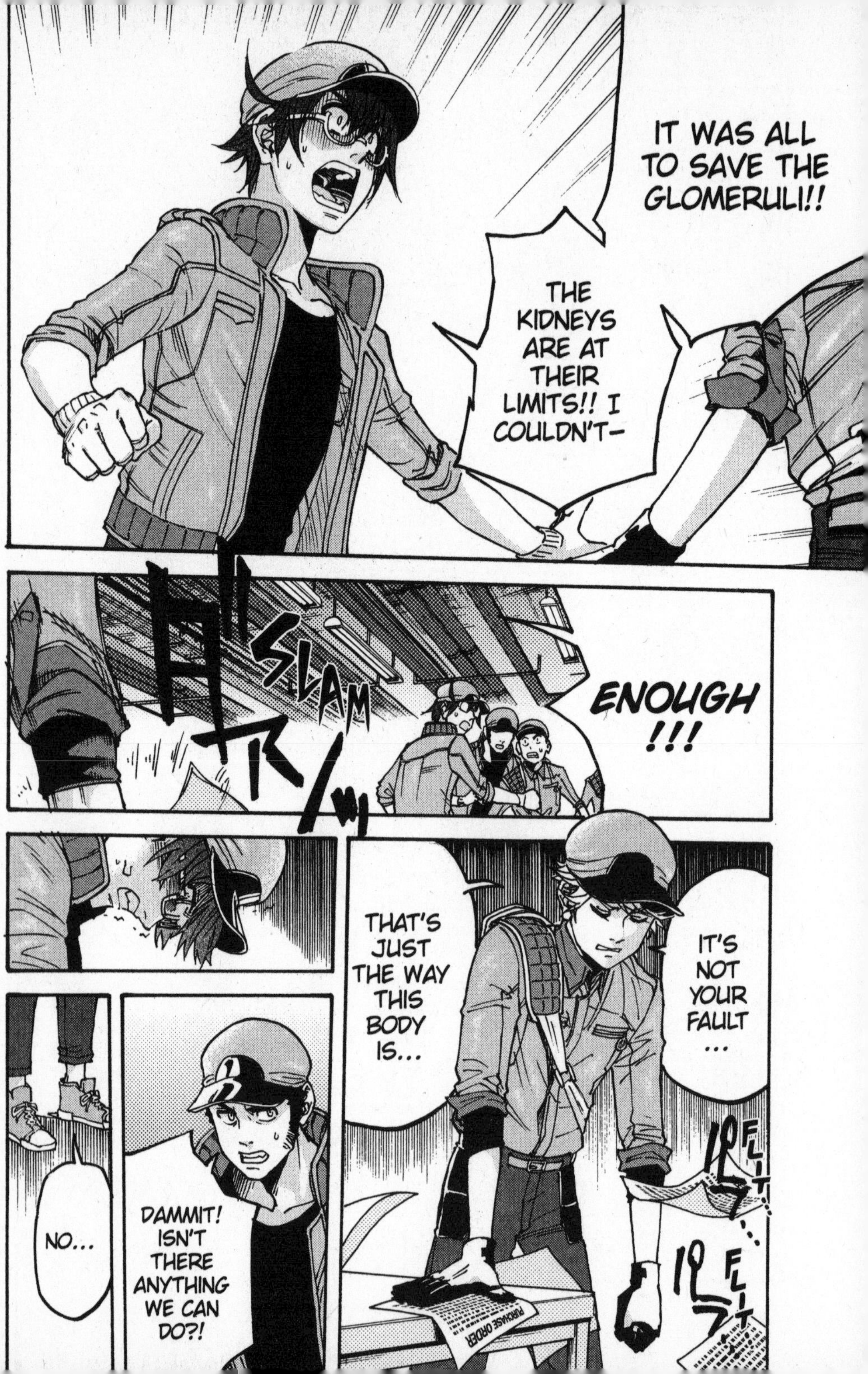
IT WAS ALL TO SAVE THE GLOMERULI!!
THE KIDNEYS ARE AT THEIR LIMITS!! I COULDN'T—
ENOUGH!!!
SLAM
IT'S NOT YOUR FAULT...
THAT'S JUST THE WAY THIS BODY IS...
FLIT
FLIT
PURCHASE ORDER
DAMMIT! ISN'T THERE ANYTHING WE CAN DO?!
NO...

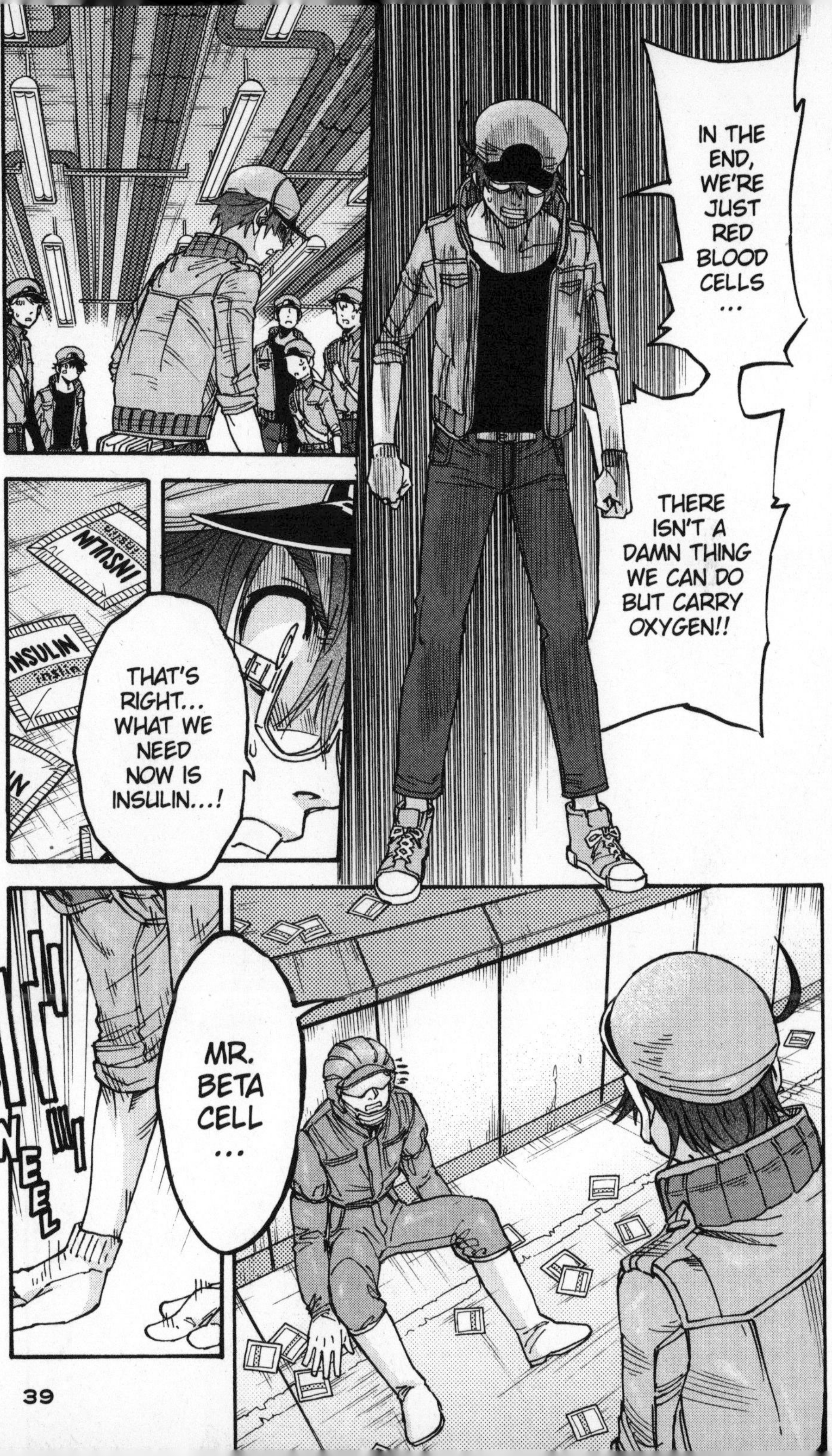
IN THE END, WE'RE JUST RED BLOOD CELLS...
THERE ISN'T A DAMN THING WE CAN DO BUT CARRY OXYGEN!!
THAT'S RIGHT... WHAT WE NEED NOW IS INSULIN...!
INSULIN
INSULIN
MR. BETA CELL...
KNEEL

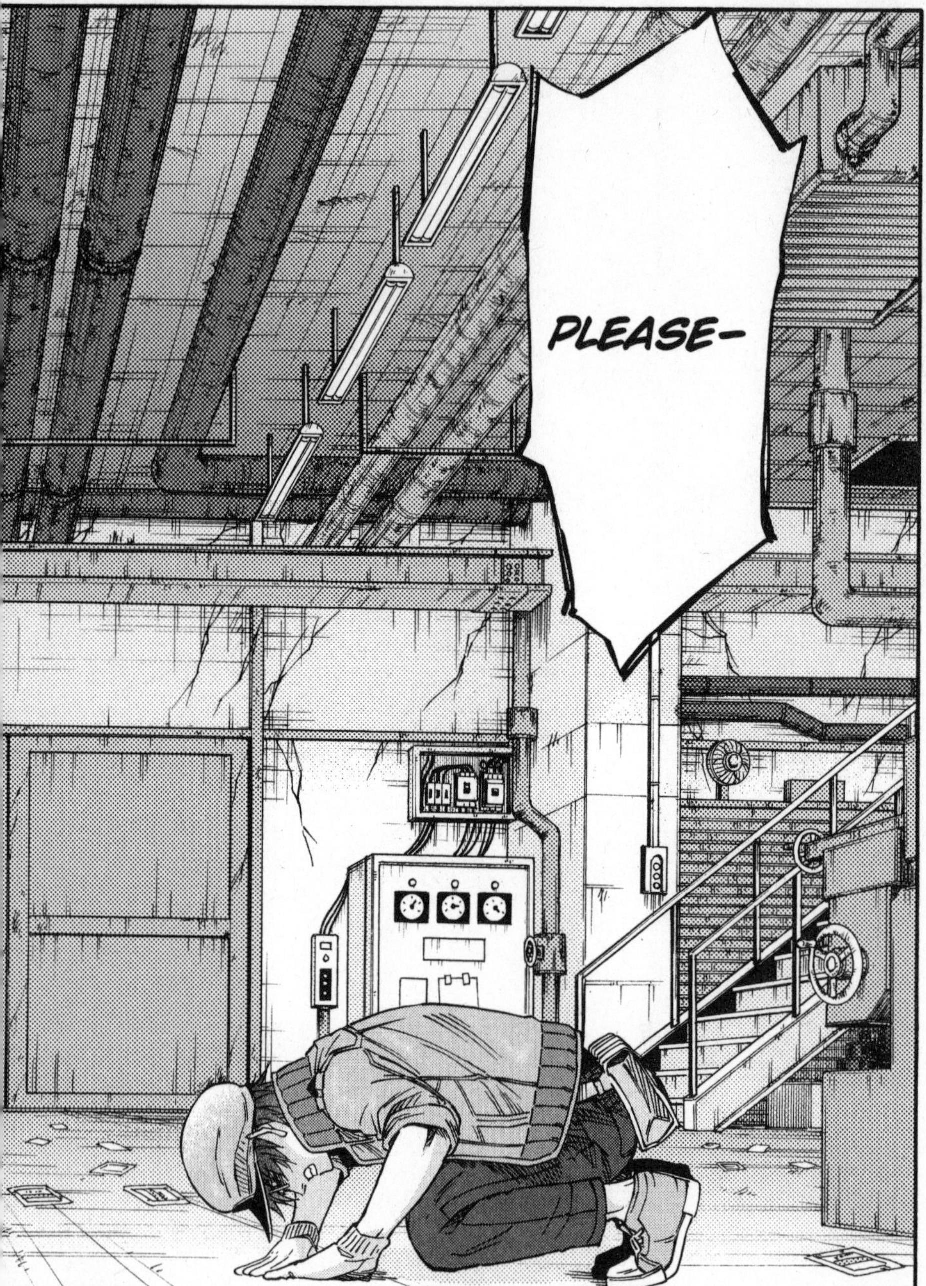
PLEASE-
INSULIN
INSULIN

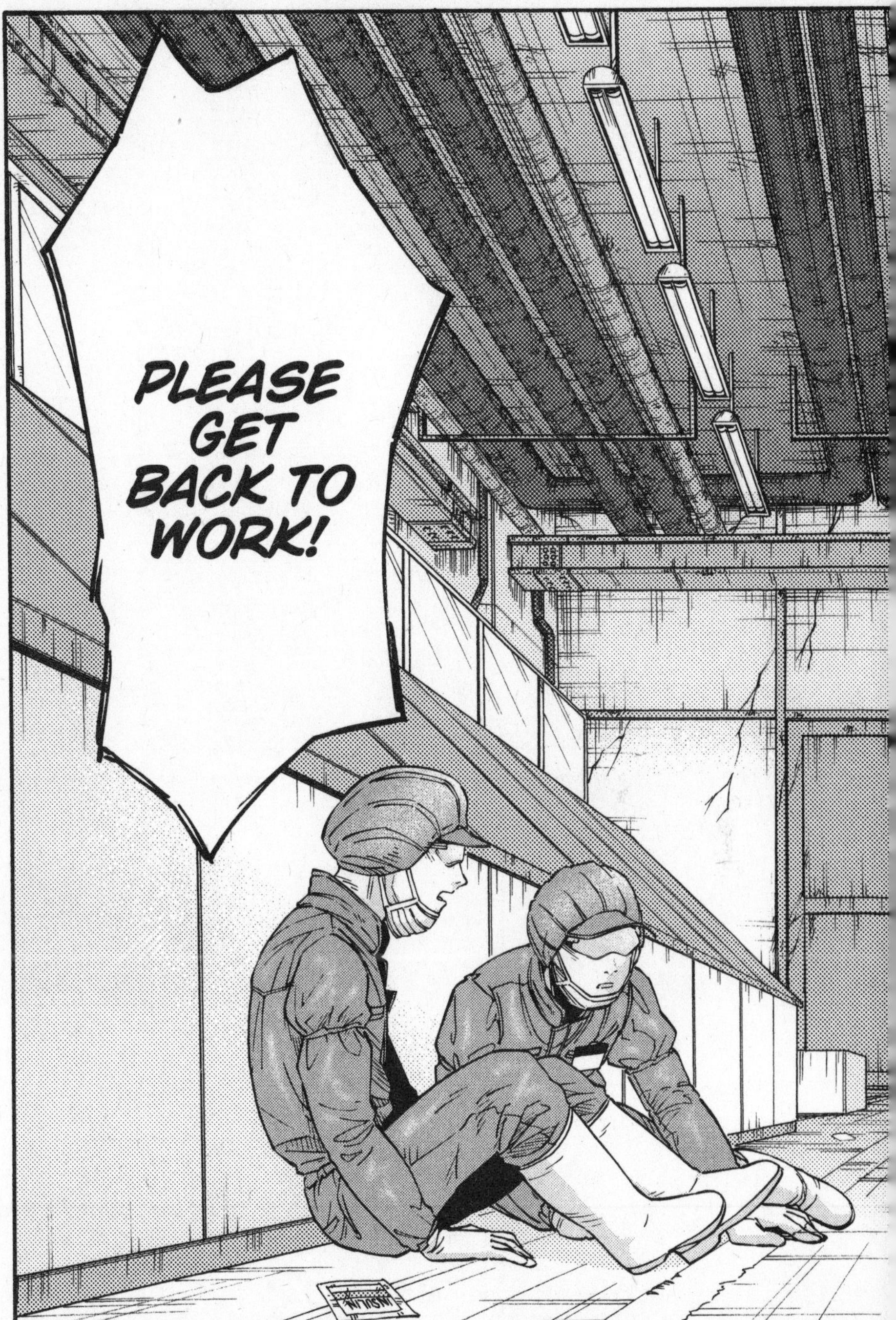
PLEASE GET BACK TO WORK!

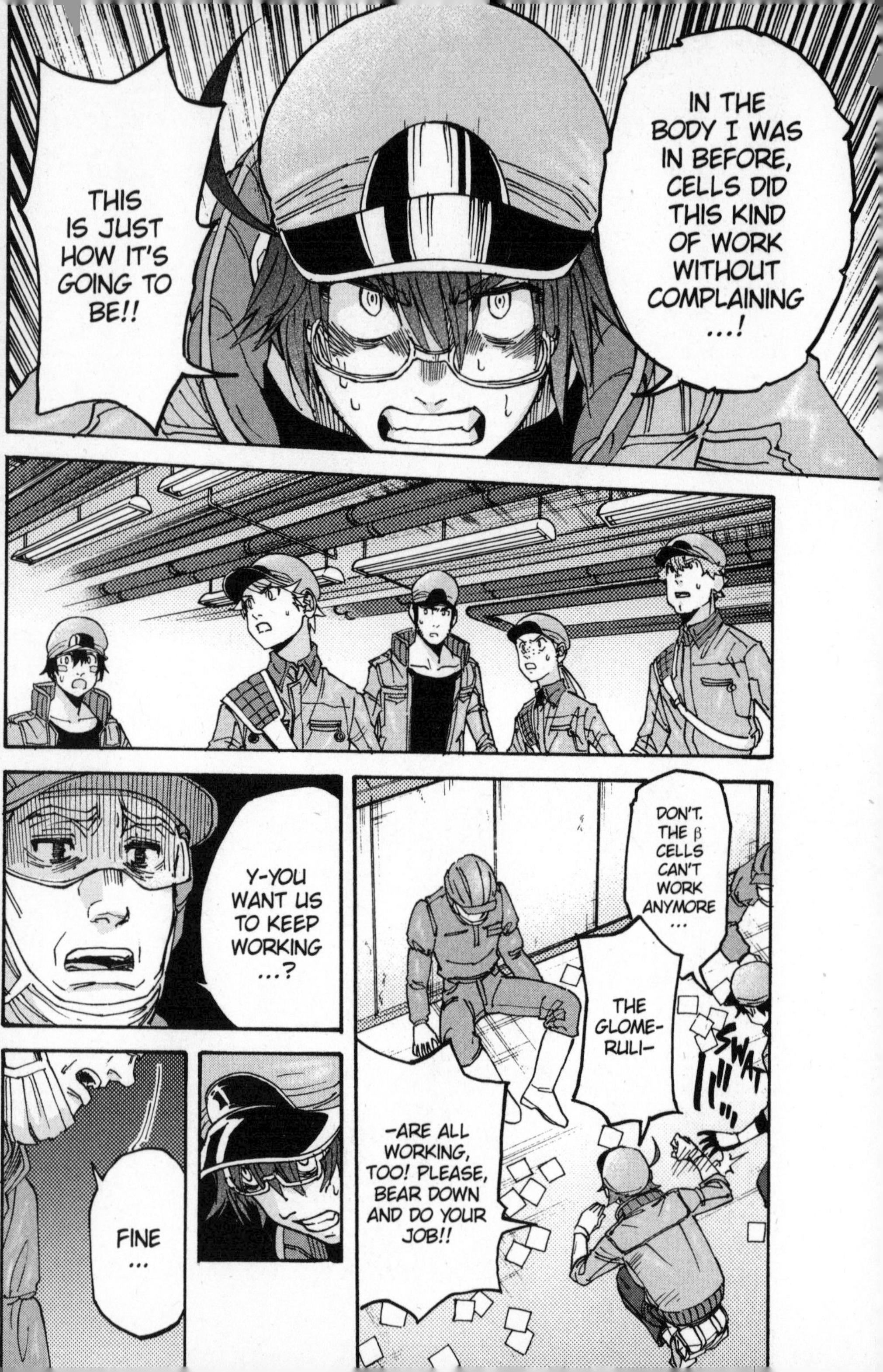
IN THE BODY I WAS IN BEFORE, CELLS DID THIS KIND OF WORK WITHOUT COMPLAINING ...!
THIS IS JUST HOW IT'S GOING TO BE!!
DON'T. THE β CELLS CAN'T WORK ANYMORE ...
THE GLOME-RULI-
-ARE ALL WORKING, TOO! PLEASE, BEAR DOWN AND DO YOUR JOB!!
SWAT!!
Y-YOU WANT US TO KEEP WORKING ...?
FINE ...

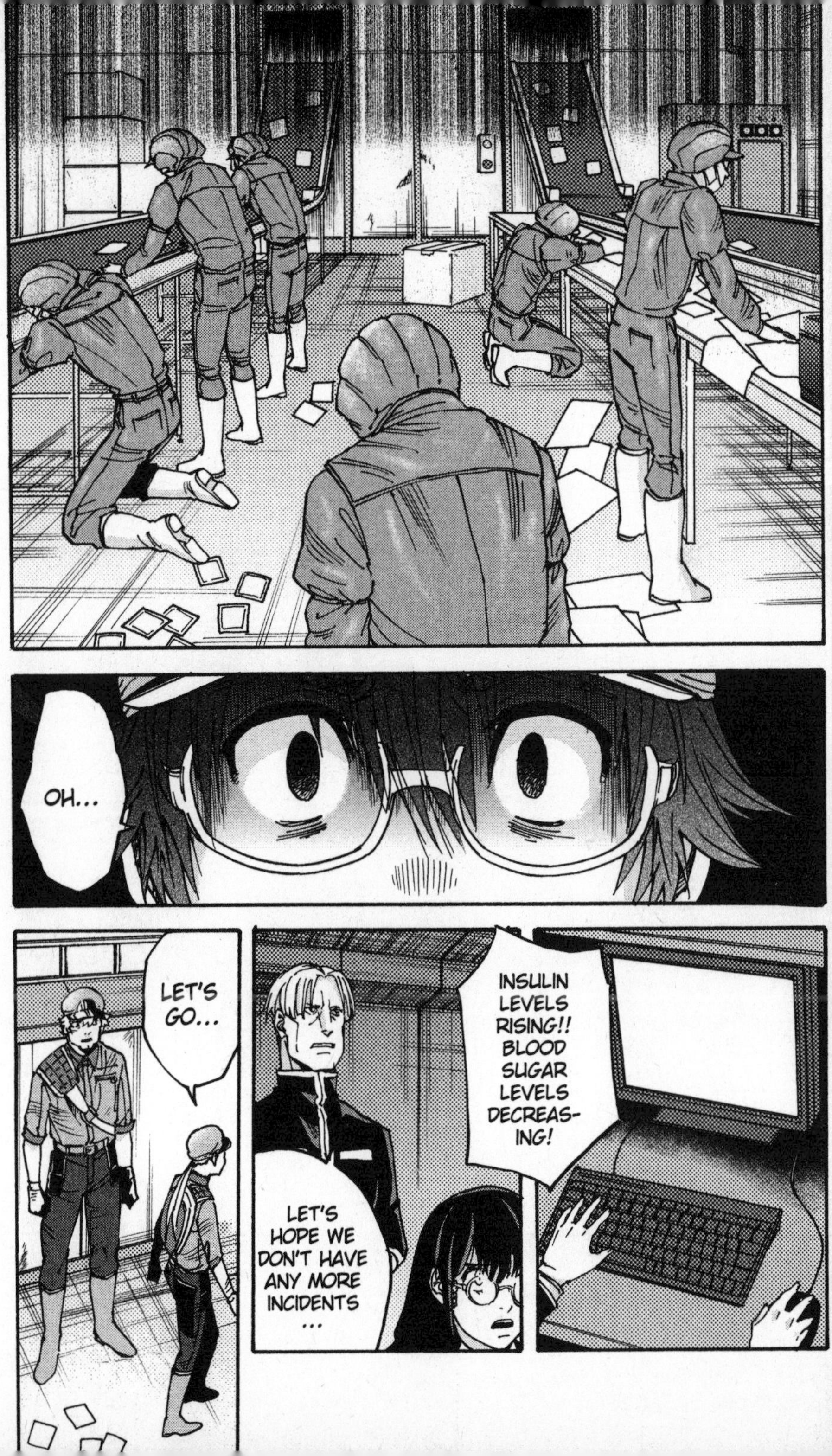
OH...
INSULIN LEVELS RISING!! BLOOD SUGAR LEVELS DECREAS-ING!
LET'S HOPE WE DON'T HAVE ANY MORE INCIDENTS ...
LET'S GO...

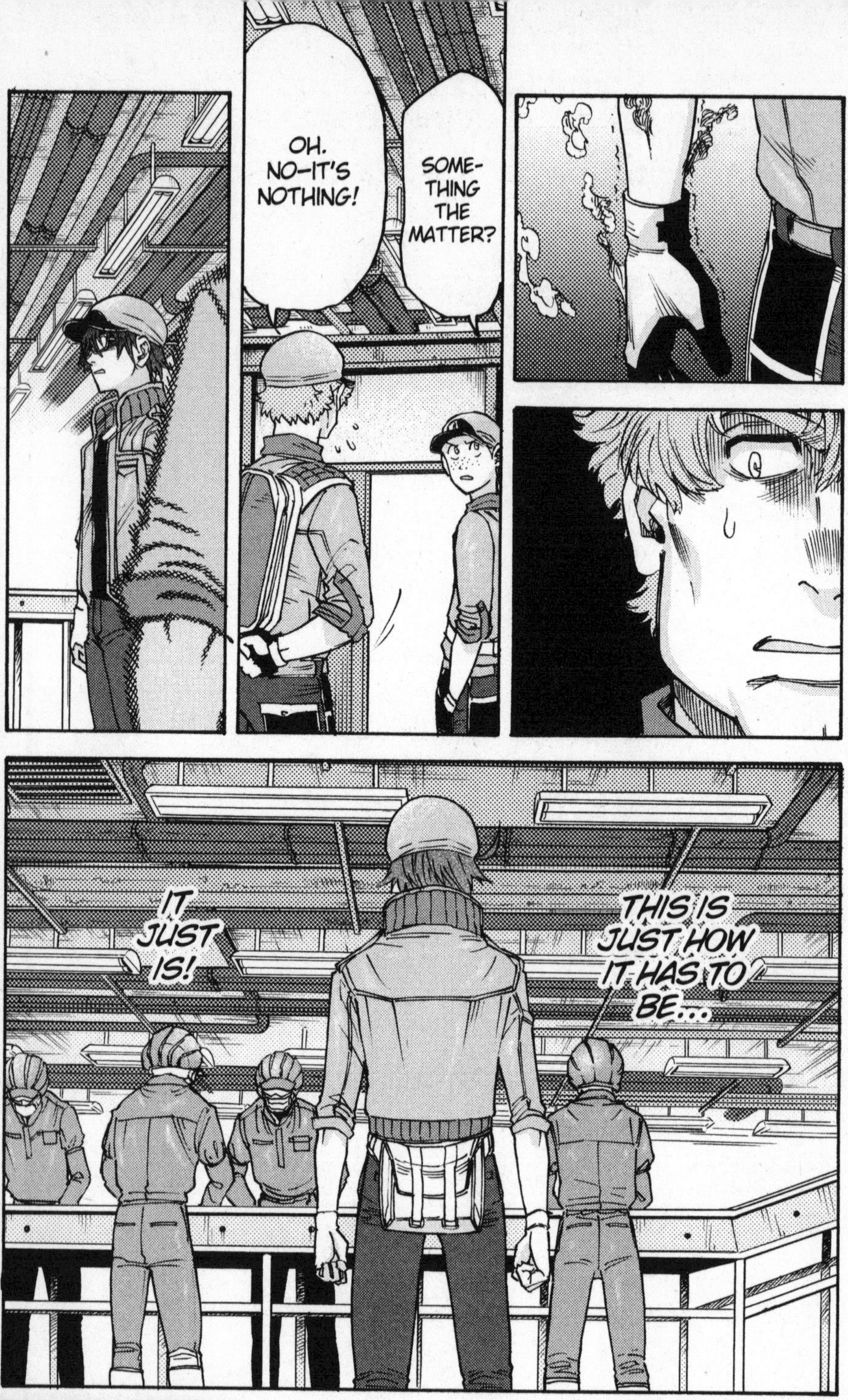
SOME-THING THE MATTER?
OH. NO—IT'S NOTHING!
THIS IS JUST HOW IT HAS TO BE...
IT JUST IS!

CHAPTER 19 - END

20. AGA, SEMEN, AND DISAPPEARING JOBS

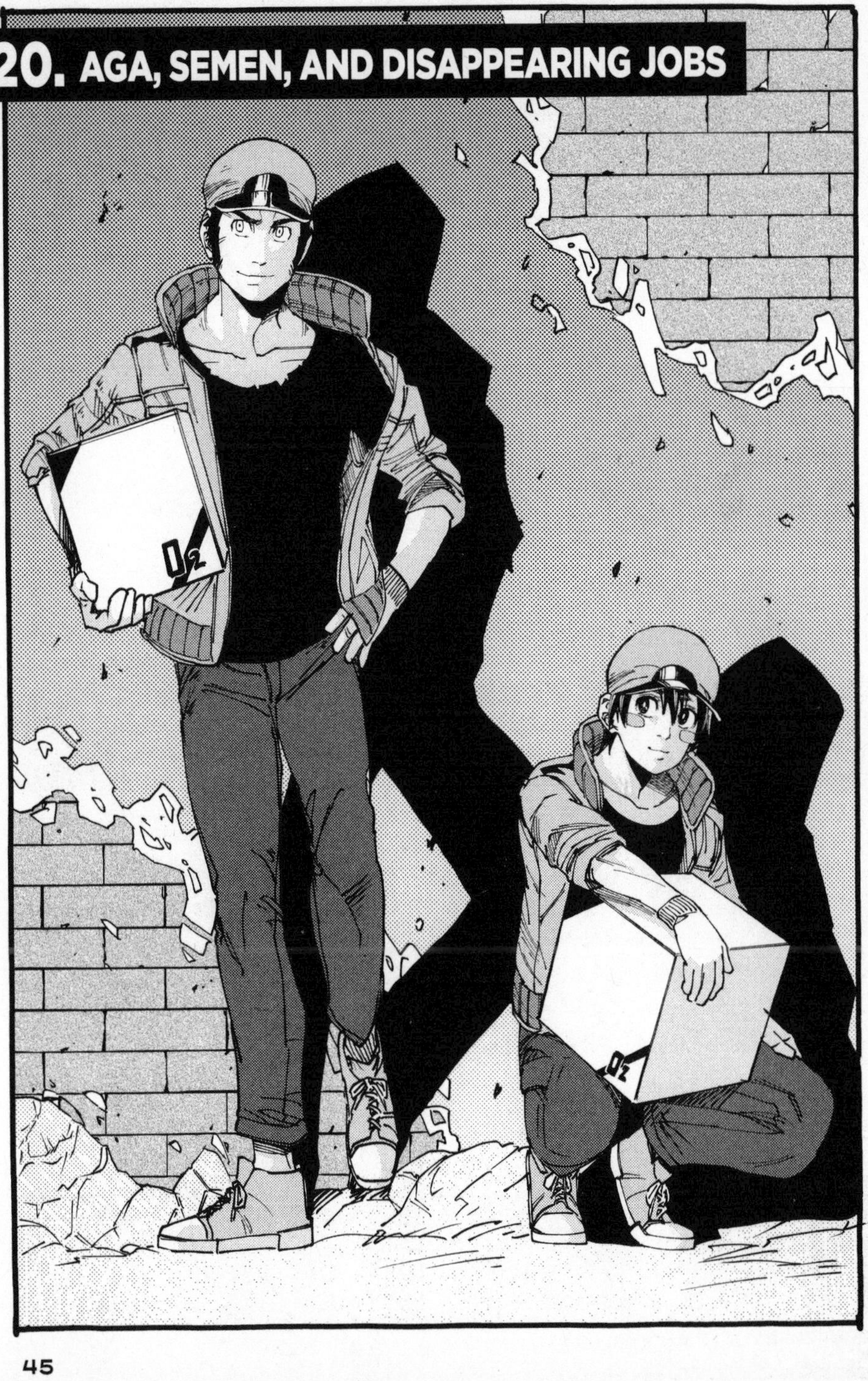

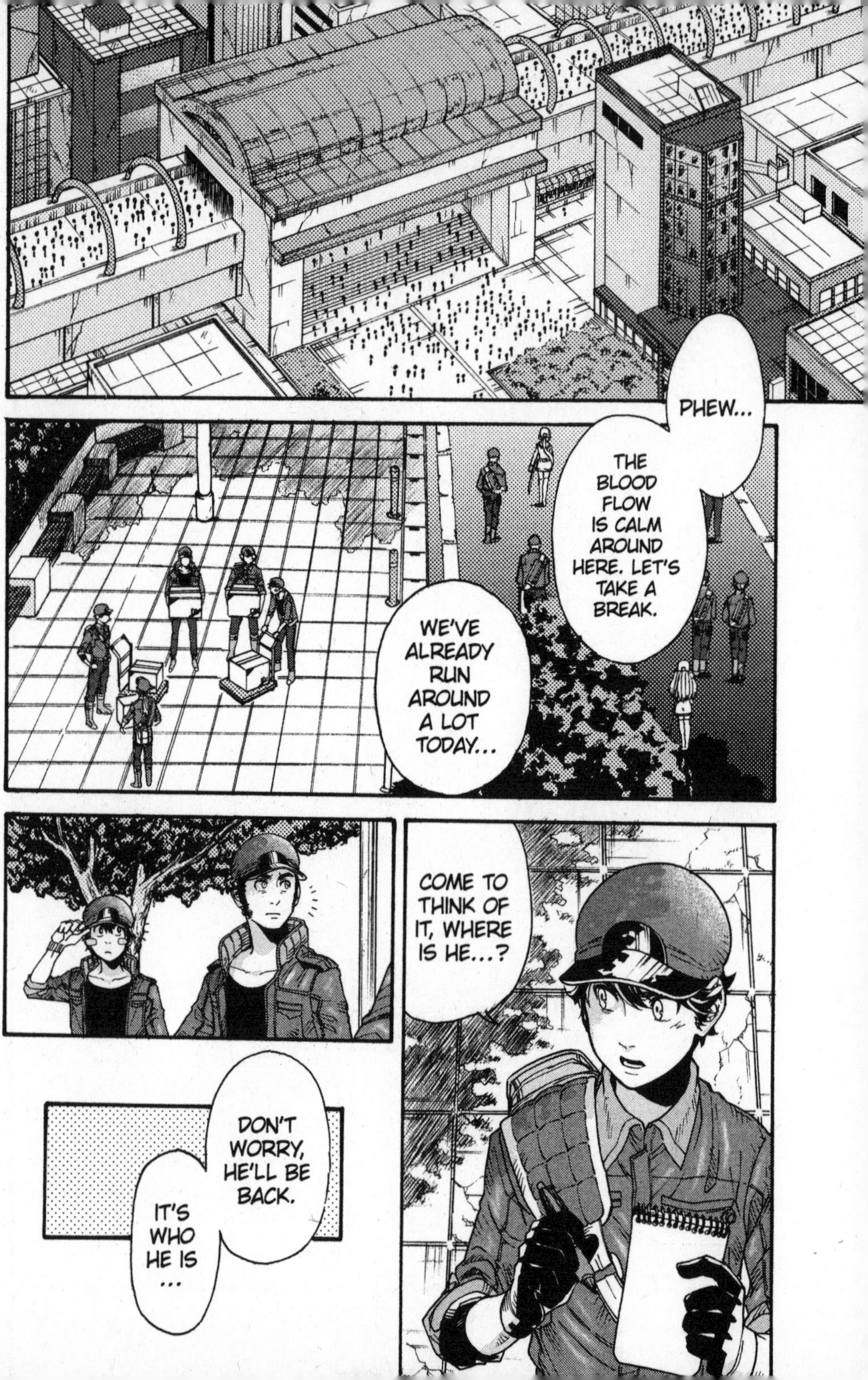
PHEW...
THE BLOOD FLOW IS CALM AROUND HERE. LET'S TAKE A BREAK.
WE'VE ALREADY RUN AROUND A LOT TODAY...
COME TO THINK OF IT, WHERE IS HE...?
DON'T WORRY, HE'LL BE BACK.
IT'S WHO HE IS...

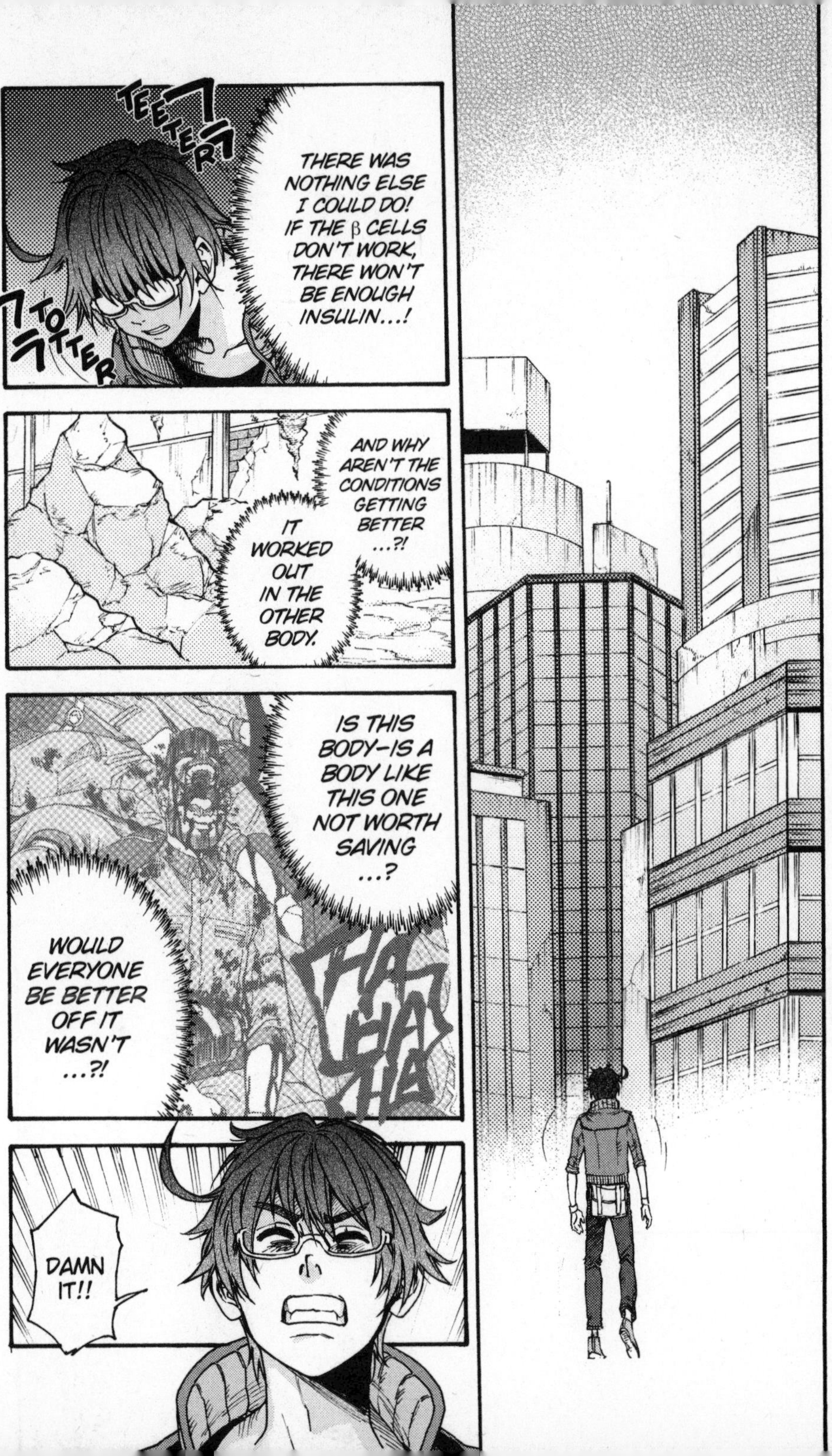
THERE WAS NOTHING ELSE I COULD DO! IF THE β CELLS DON'T WORK, THERE WON'T BE ENOUGH INSULIN...!
TEETER
TOTTER
AND WHY AREN'T THE CONDITIONS GETTING BETTER ...?!
IT WORKED OUT IN THE OTHER BODY.
IS THIS BODY—IS A BODY LIKE THIS ONE NOT WORTH SAVING ...?
HA HA HA
WOULD EVERYONE BE BETTER OFF IT WASN'T ...?!
DAMN IT!!

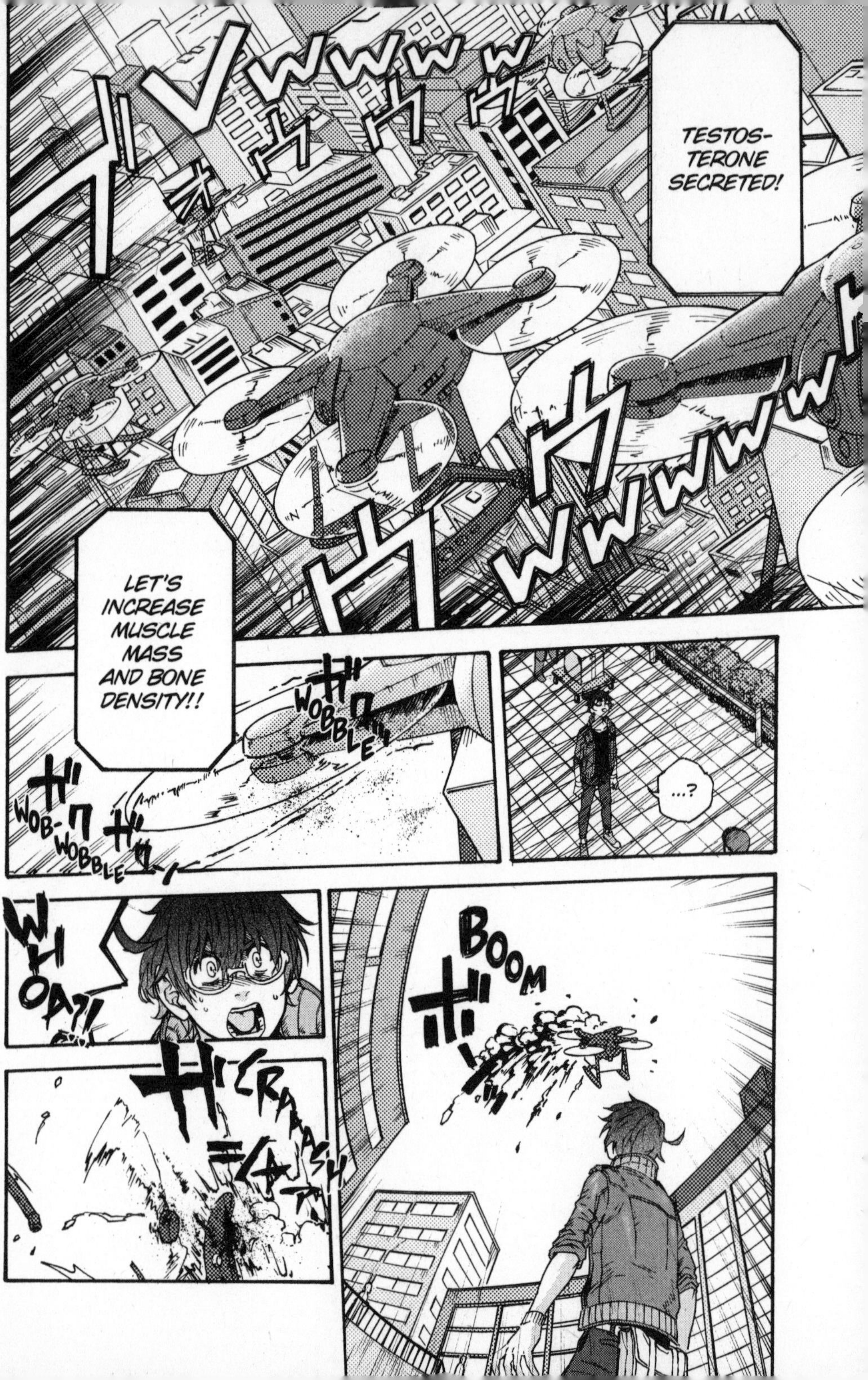
TESTOS-TERONE SECRETED!
VWWWWW
WWWWWWWW
LET'S INCREASE MUSCLE MASS AND BONE DENSITY!!
...?
WOBBLE
WOB-WOBBLE
BOOM
WHOA?!
CRAAASH

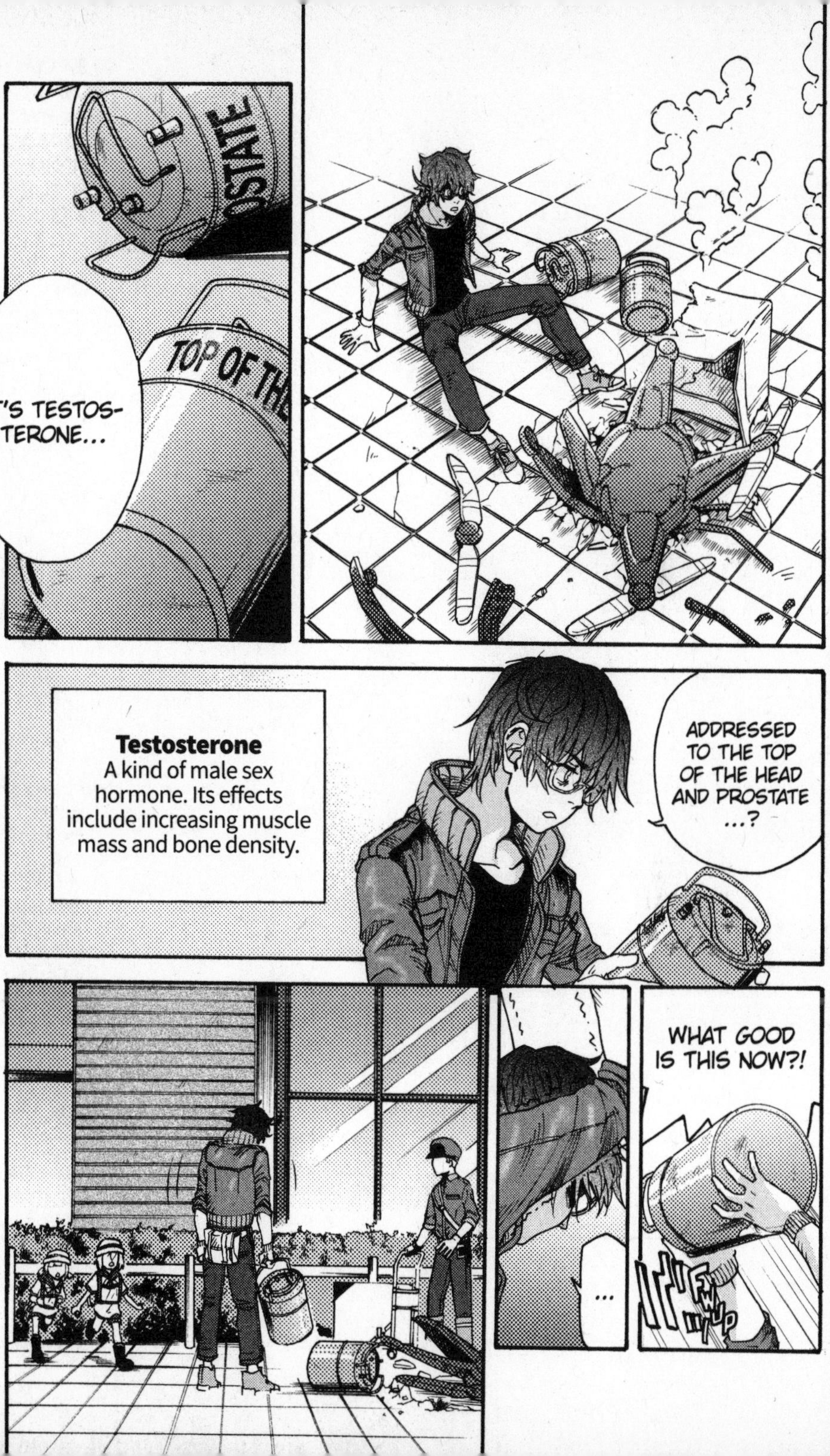
IT'S TESTOS-TERONE...
ADDRESSED TO THE TOP OF THE HEAD AND PROSTATE ...?
Testosterone
A kind of male sex hormone. Its effects include increasing muscle mass and bone density.
WHAT GOOD IS THIS NOW?!
FWUP
...

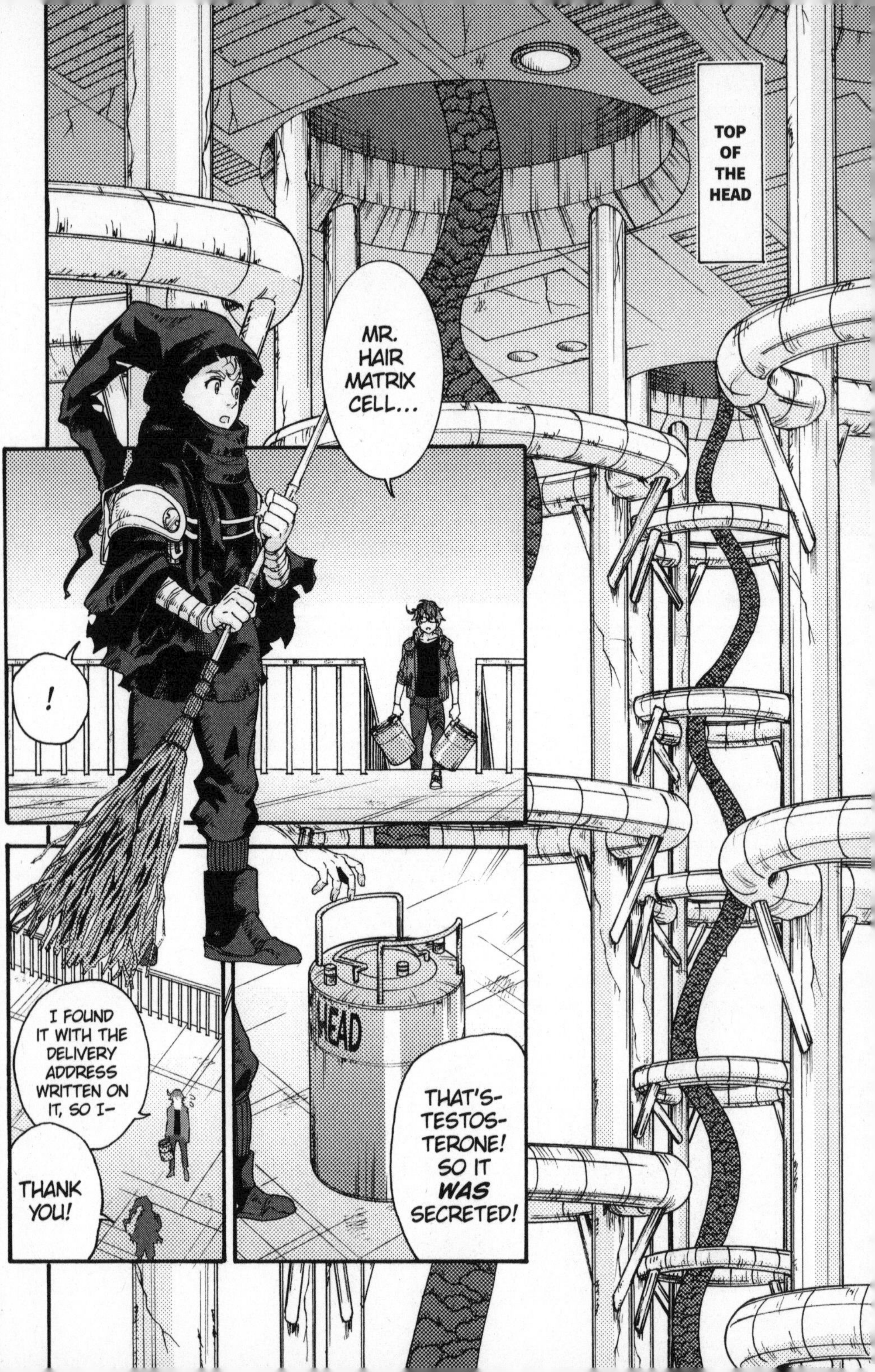
TOP OF THE HEAD
MR. HAIR MATRIX CELL...
!
THAT'S- TESTOSTERONE! SO IT ***WAS*** SECRETED!
I FOUND IT WITH THE DELIVERY ADDRESS WRITTEN ON IT, SO I-
THANK YOU!

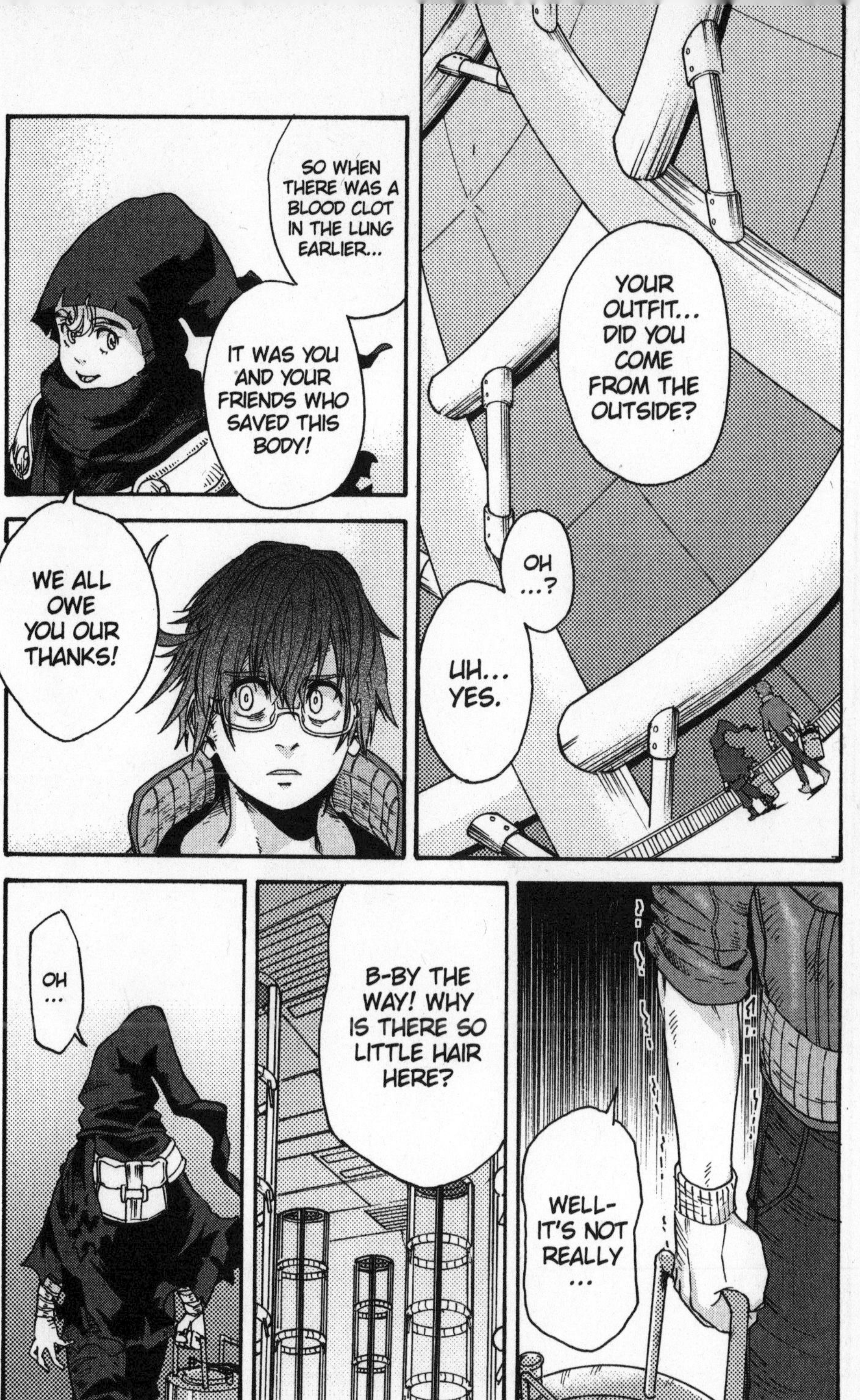
YOUR OUTFIT... DID YOU COME FROM THE OUTSIDE?
OH ...?
UH... YES.
SO WHEN THERE WAS A BLOOD CLOT IN THE LUNG EARLIER...
IT WAS YOU AND YOUR FRIENDS WHO SAVED THIS BODY!
WE ALL OWE YOU OUR THANKS!
WELL- IT'S NOT REALLY ...
B-BY THE WAY! WHY IS THERE SO LITTLE HAIR HERE?
OH ...

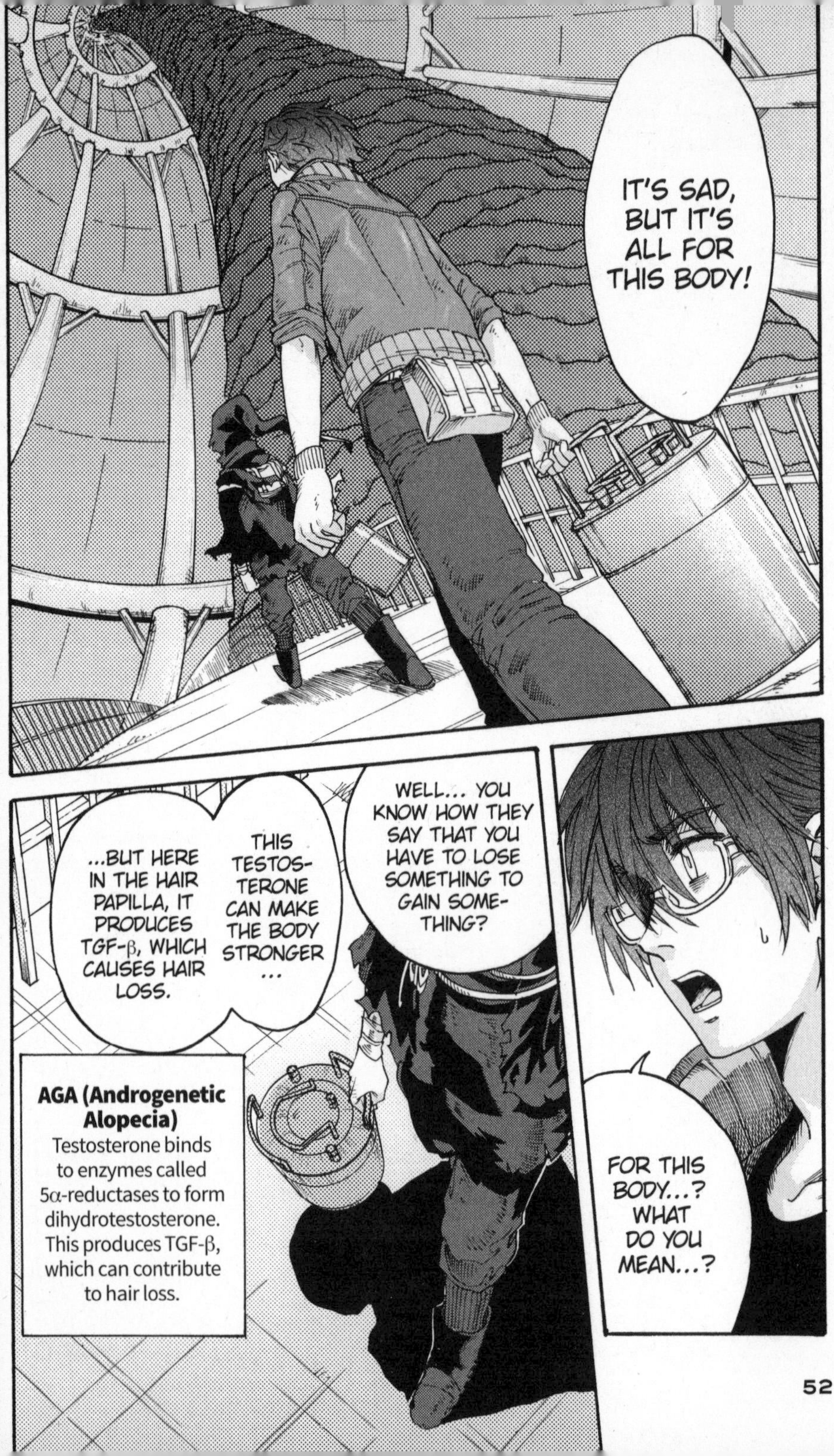
IT'S SAD, BUT IT'S ALL FOR THIS BODY!
FOR THIS BODY...? WHAT DO YOU MEAN...?
WELL... YOU KNOW HOW THEY SAY THAT YOU HAVE TO LOSE SOMETHING TO GAIN SOME-THING?
THIS TESTOS-TERONE CAN MAKE THE BODY STRONGER ...
...BUT HERE IN THE HAIR PAPILLA, IT PRODUCES TGF-β, WHICH CAUSES HAIR LOSS.
AGA (Androgenetic Alopecia)
Testosterone binds to enzymes called 5α-reductases to form dihydrotestosterone. This produces TGF-β, which can contribute to hair loss.

BUT... THAT'S–
THUD...!!
THERE ARE HAIRS THAT I'VE CARED FOR SINCE THEY WERE JUST STRANDS OF BABY FUZZ ...
I WATCHED OVER THEM AS THEY GREW FROM THIN, WEAK THINGS...AND NOW I HAVE TO SEE THEM GO.
TO BE HONEST, THERE'S A PART OF ME THAT'S FRUSTRATED.
BUT TGF-β IS A NECESSARY SUBSTANCE FOR BUILDING MUSCLE AND BONE...
WHEN YOU THINK ABOUT THIS BODY AS A WHOLE, IT'S IMPORTANT ...!
PSSHH
KACHAK!!!
YOU SAY THE BODY AS A WHOLE ...!
MR. HAIR MATRIX CELL, ARE YOU OKAY WITH THAT?
NO, I'M NOT... BUT ISN'T THAT HOW WORK IS?
GRIP

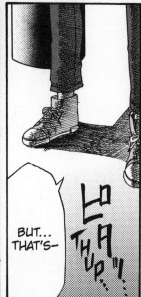

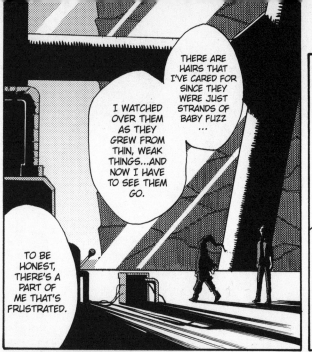

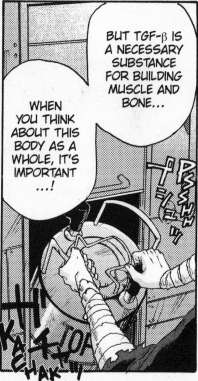

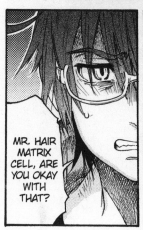

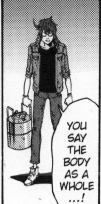

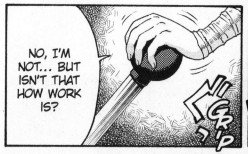

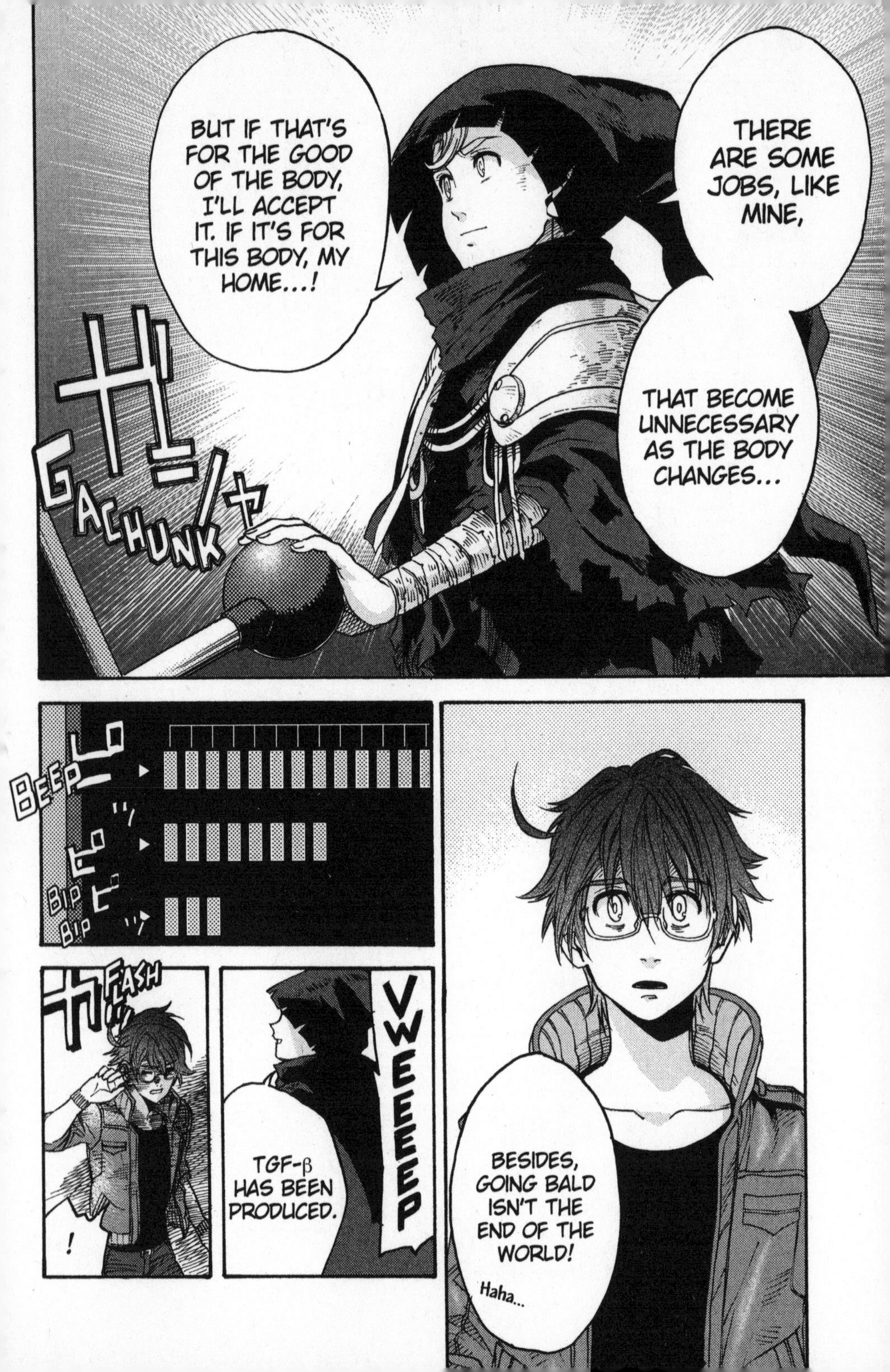
THERE ARE SOME JOBS, LIKE MINE,
THAT BECOME UNNECESSARY AS THE BODY CHANGES...
BUT IF THAT'S FOR THE GOOD OF THE BODY, I'LL ACCEPT IT. IF IT'S FOR THIS BODY, MY HOME...!
GACHUNK
BESIDES, GOING BALD ISN'T THE END OF THE WORLD!
Haha...
BEEP
BIP BIP
VWEEEEP
TGF-β HAS BEEN PRODUCED.
FLASH
!

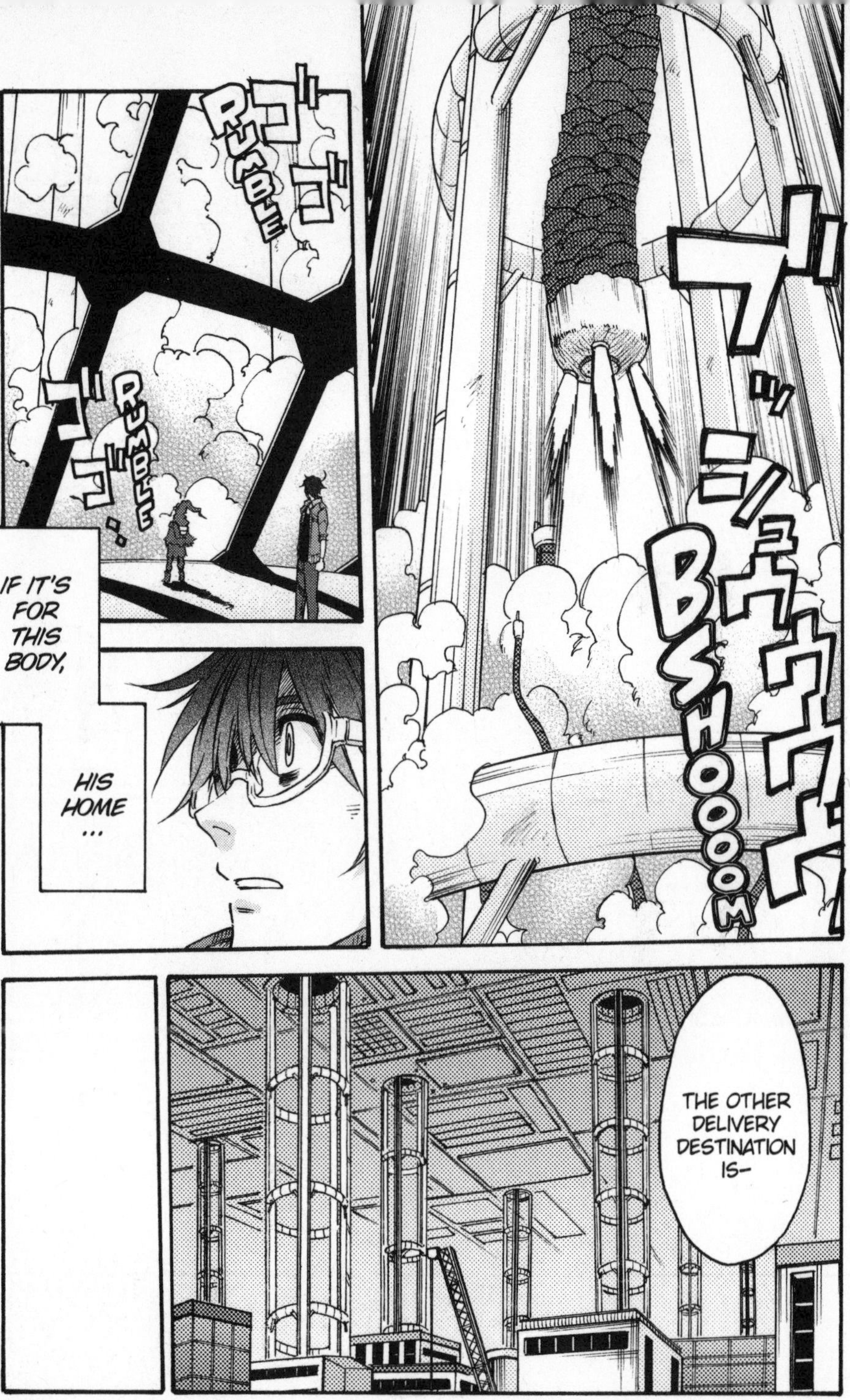
BSHOOOOM
RUMBLE
RUMBLE
IF IT'S FOR THIS BODY,
HIS HOME ...
THE OTHER DELIVERY DESTINATION IS–

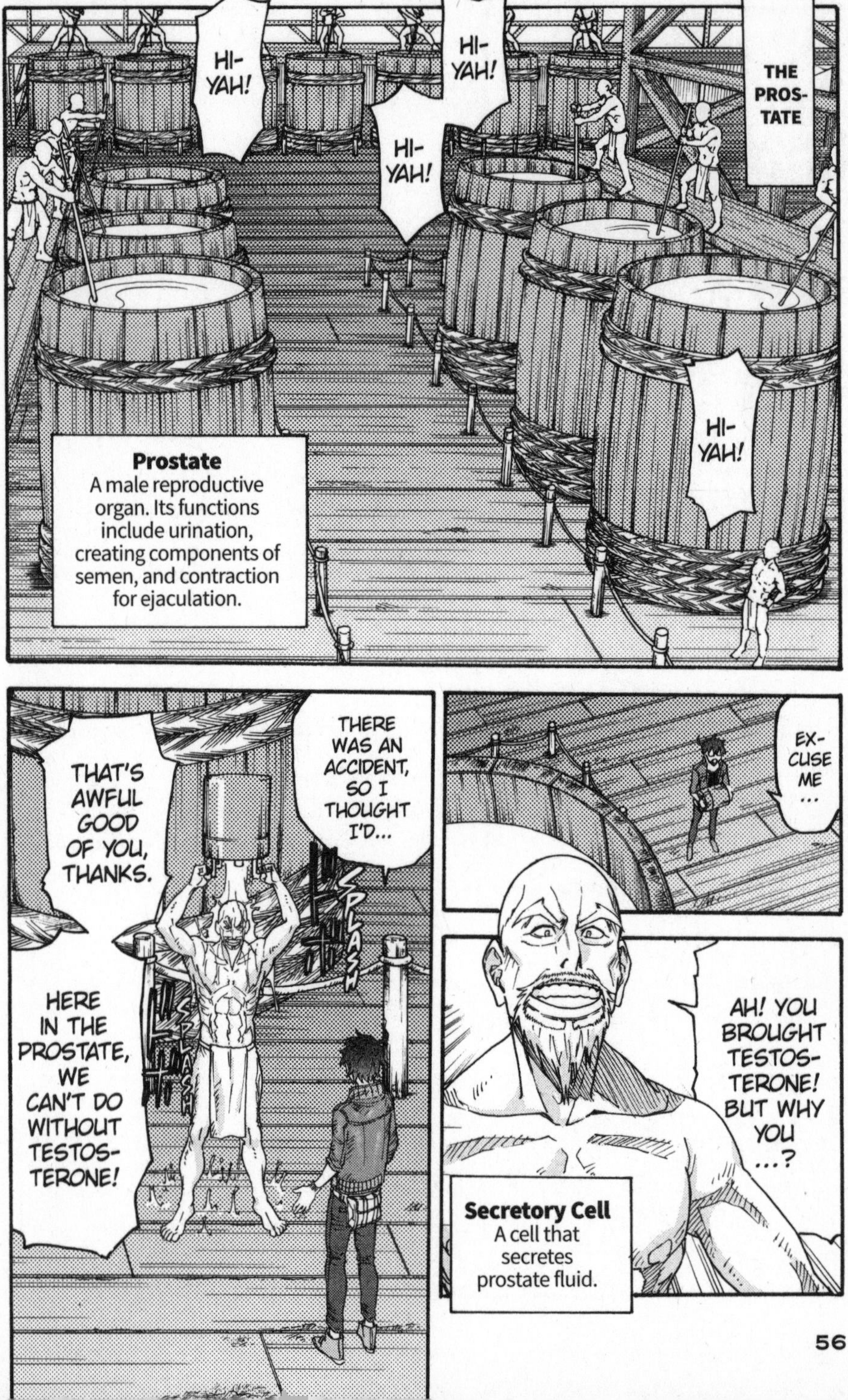
THE PROS-TATE
HI-YAH!
HI-YAH!
HI-YAH!
HI-YAH!
Prostate
A male reproductive organ. Its functions include urination, creating components of semen, and contraction for ejaculation.
EX-CUSE ME...
AH! YOU BROUGHT TESTOS-TERONE! BUT WHY YOU...?
Secretory Cell
A cell that secretes prostate fluid.
THERE WAS AN ACCIDENT, SO I THOUGHT I'D...
SPLASH
THAT'S AWFUL GOOD OF YOU, THANKS.
SPLASH
HERE IN THE PROSTATE, WE CAN'T DO WITHOUT TESTOS-TERONE!

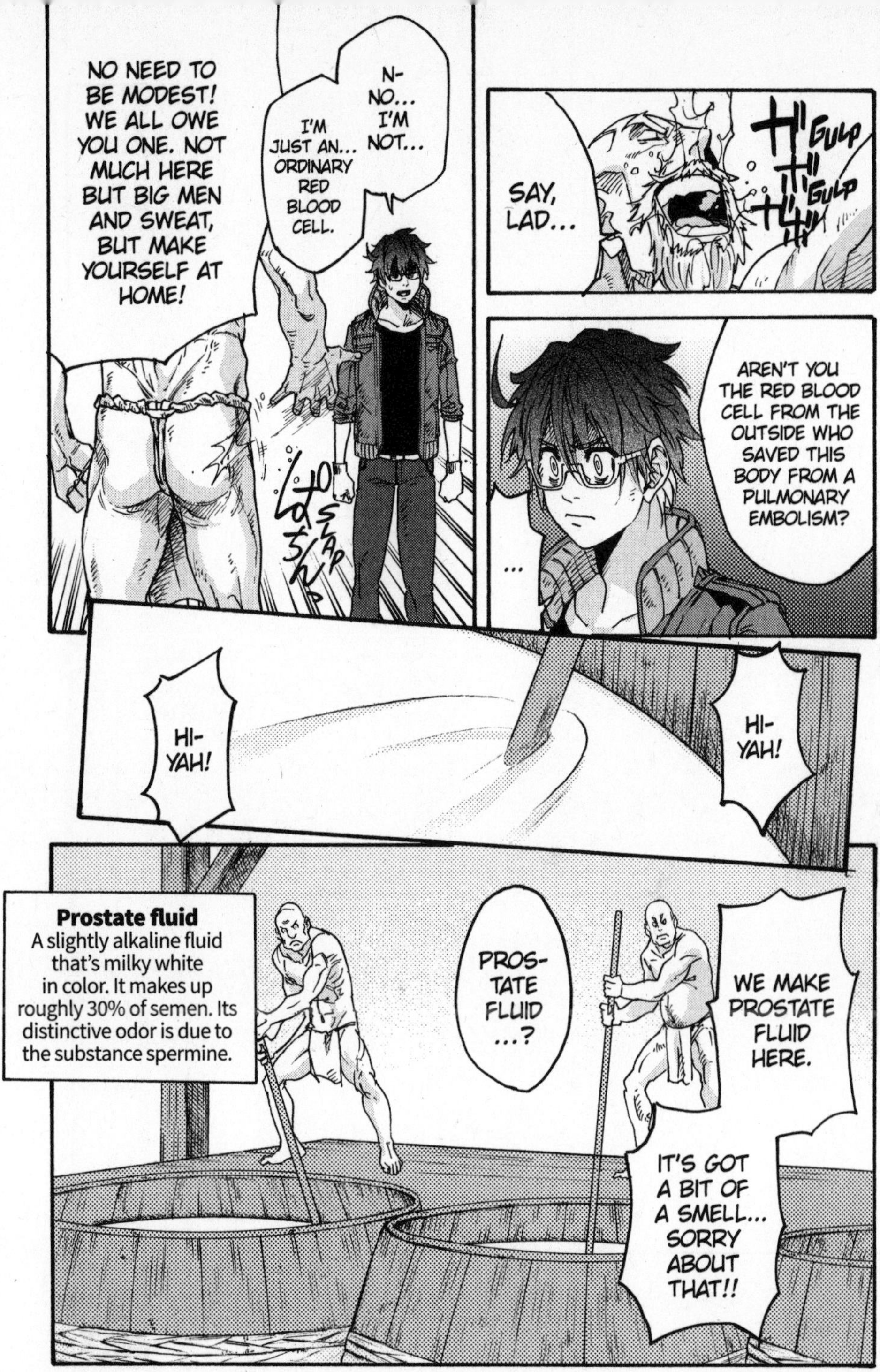
SAY, LAD...
GULP GULP
AREN'T YOU THE RED BLOOD CELL FROM THE OUTSIDE WHO SAVED THIS BODY FROM A PULMONARY EMBOLISM?
...
N-NO... I'M NOT...
I'M JUST AN... ORDINARY RED BLOOD CELL.
NO NEED TO BE MODEST! WE ALL OWE YOU ONE. NOT MUCH HERE BUT BIG MEN AND SWEAT, BUT MAKE YOURSELF AT HOME!
SLAP
HI-YAH!
HI-YAH!
WE MAKE PROSTATE FLUID HERE.
PROS-TATE FLUID ...?
IT'S GOT A BIT OF A SMELL... SORRY ABOUT THAT!!
Prostate fluid
A slightly alkaline fluid that's milky white in color. It makes up roughly 30% of semen. Its distinctive odor is due to the substance spermine.

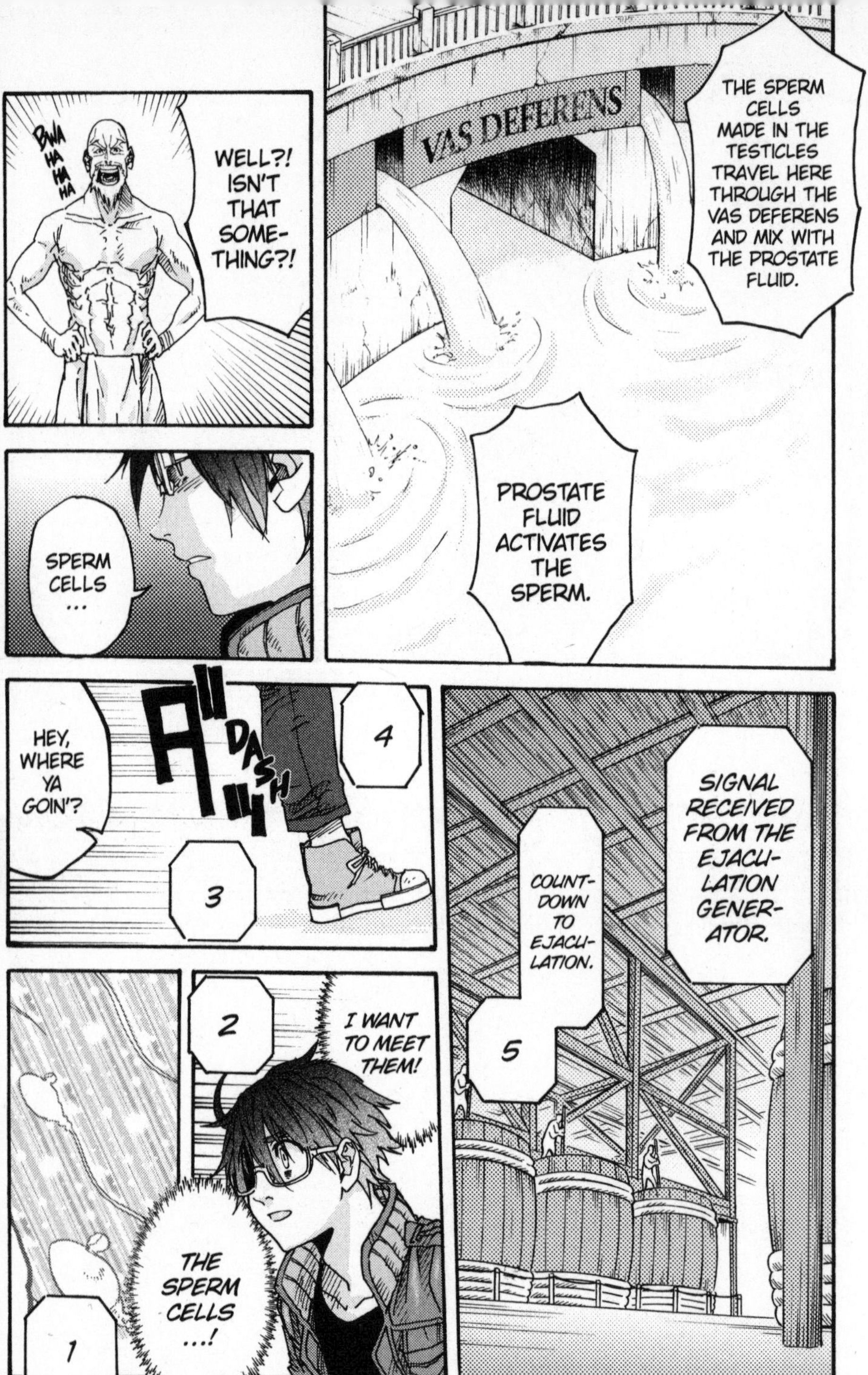
VAS DEFERENS
THE SPERM CELLS MADE IN THE TESTICLES TRAVEL HERE THROUGH THE VAS DEFERENS AND MIX WITH THE PROSTATE FLUID.
PROSTATE FLUID ACTIVATES THE SPERM.
BWA HA HA HA
WELL?! ISN'T THAT SOME-THING?!
SPERM CELLS ...
SIGNAL RECEIVED FROM THE EJACU-LATION GENER-ATOR.
COUNT-DOWN TO EJACU-LATION.
5
4
HEY, WHERE YA GOIN'?
DASH
3
2
I WANT TO MEET THEM!
THE SPERM CELLS ...!
1

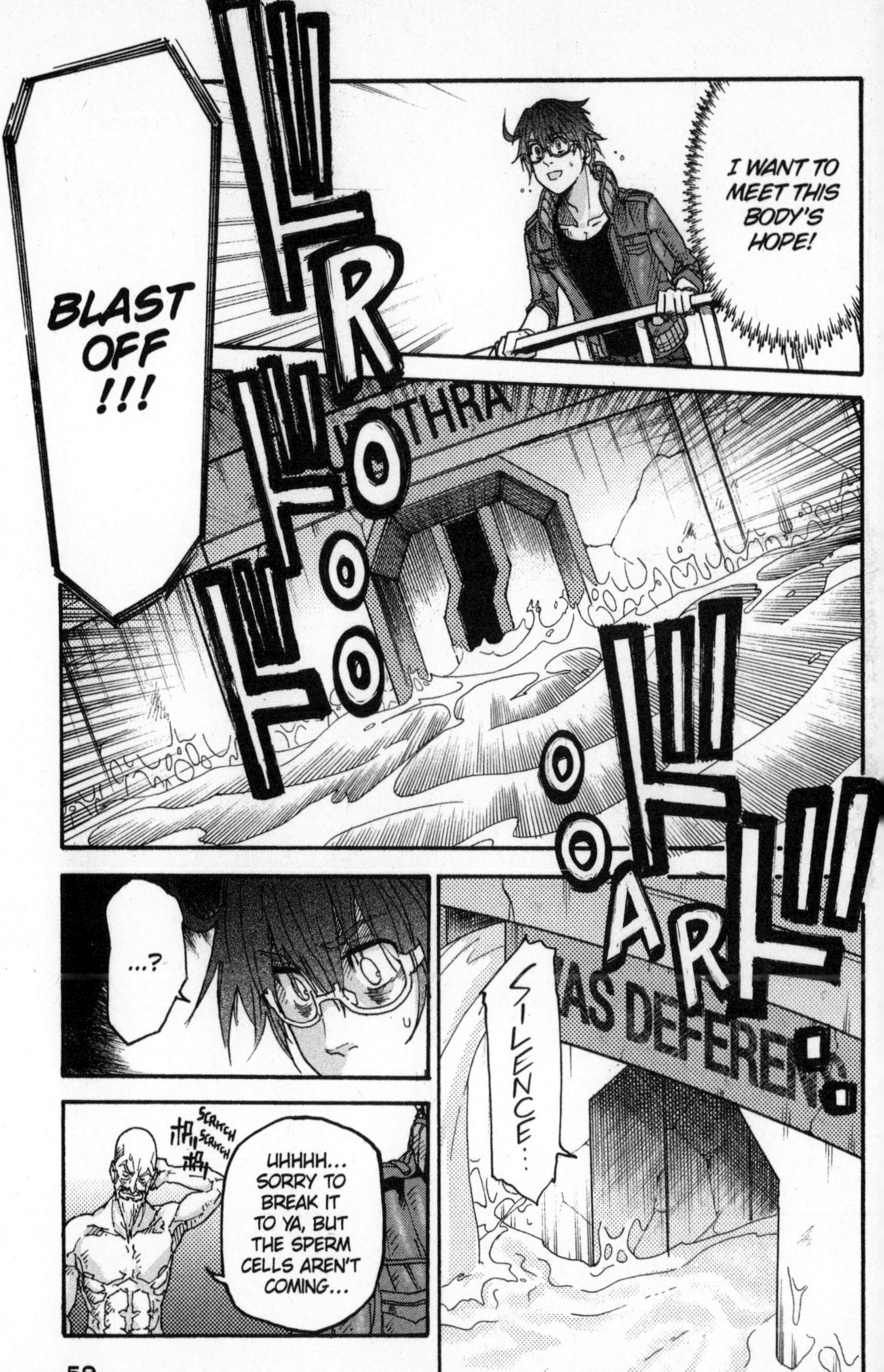
I WANT TO MEET THIS BODY'S HOPE!
BLAST OFF !!!
ROOOOOOAR!!
SILENCE...
...?
SCRATCH SCRATCH
UHHHH... SORRY TO BREAK IT TO YA, BUT THE SPERM CELLS AREN'T COMING...

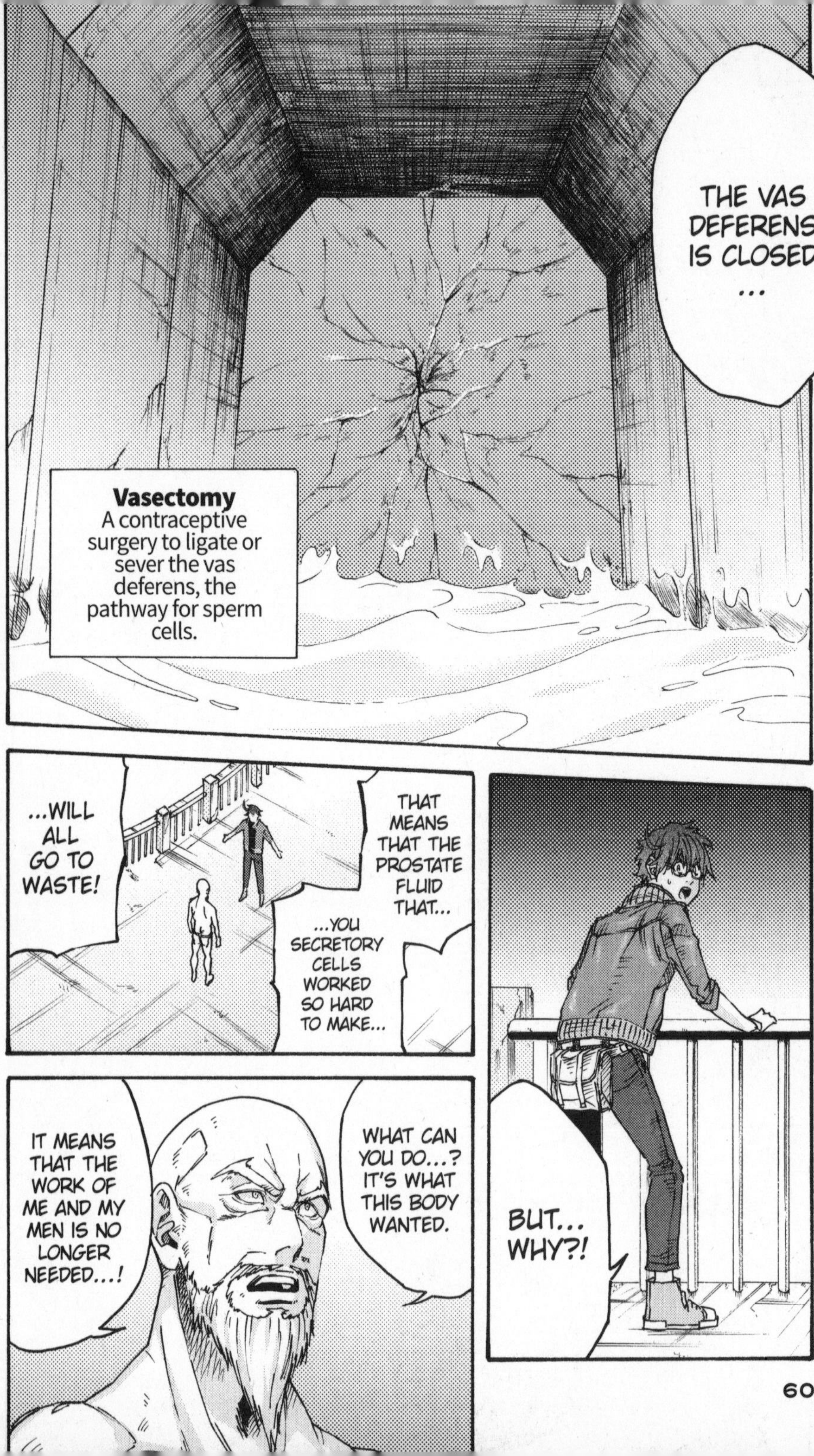
THE VAS DEFERENS IS CLOSED ...
Vasectomy
A contraceptive surgery to ligate or sever the vas deferens, the pathway for sperm cells.
BUT... WHY?!
THAT MEANS THAT THE PROSTATE FLUID THAT...
...YOU SECRETORY CELLS WORKED SO HARD TO MAKE...
...WILL ALL GO TO WASTE!
WHAT CAN YOU DO...? IT'S WHAT THIS BODY WANTED.
IT MEANS THAT THE WORK OF ME AND MY MEN IS NO LONGER NEEDED...!

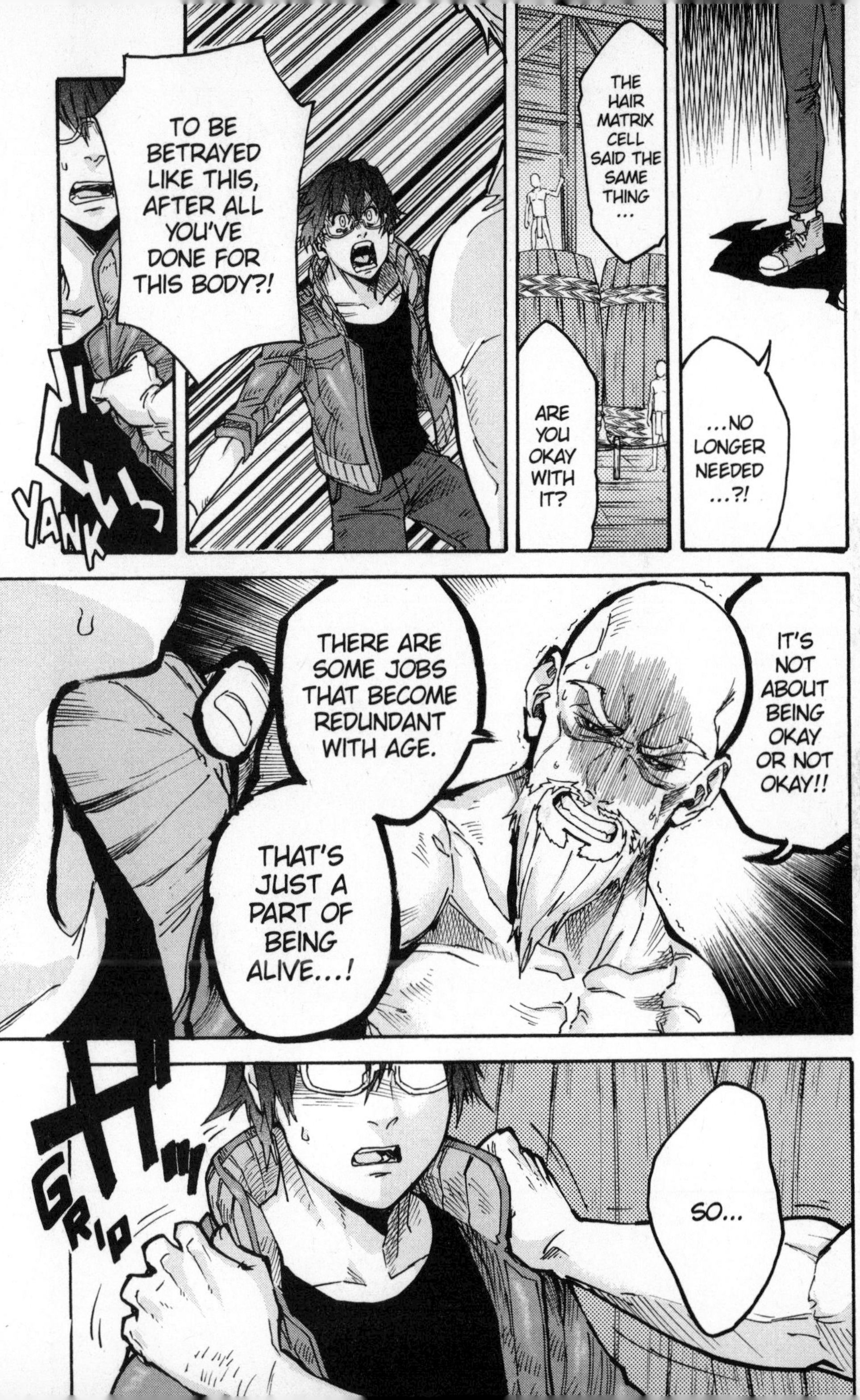
...NO LONGER NEEDED ...?!
THE HAIR MATRIX CELL SAID THE SAME THING ...
ARE YOU OKAY WITH IT?
TO BE BETRAYED LIKE THIS, AFTER ALL YOU'VE DONE FOR THIS BODY?!
YANK
IT'S NOT ABOUT BEING OKAY OR NOT OKAY!!
THERE ARE SOME JOBS THAT BECOME REDUNDANT WITH AGE.
THAT'S JUST A PART OF BEING ALIVE...!
SO...
GRIP

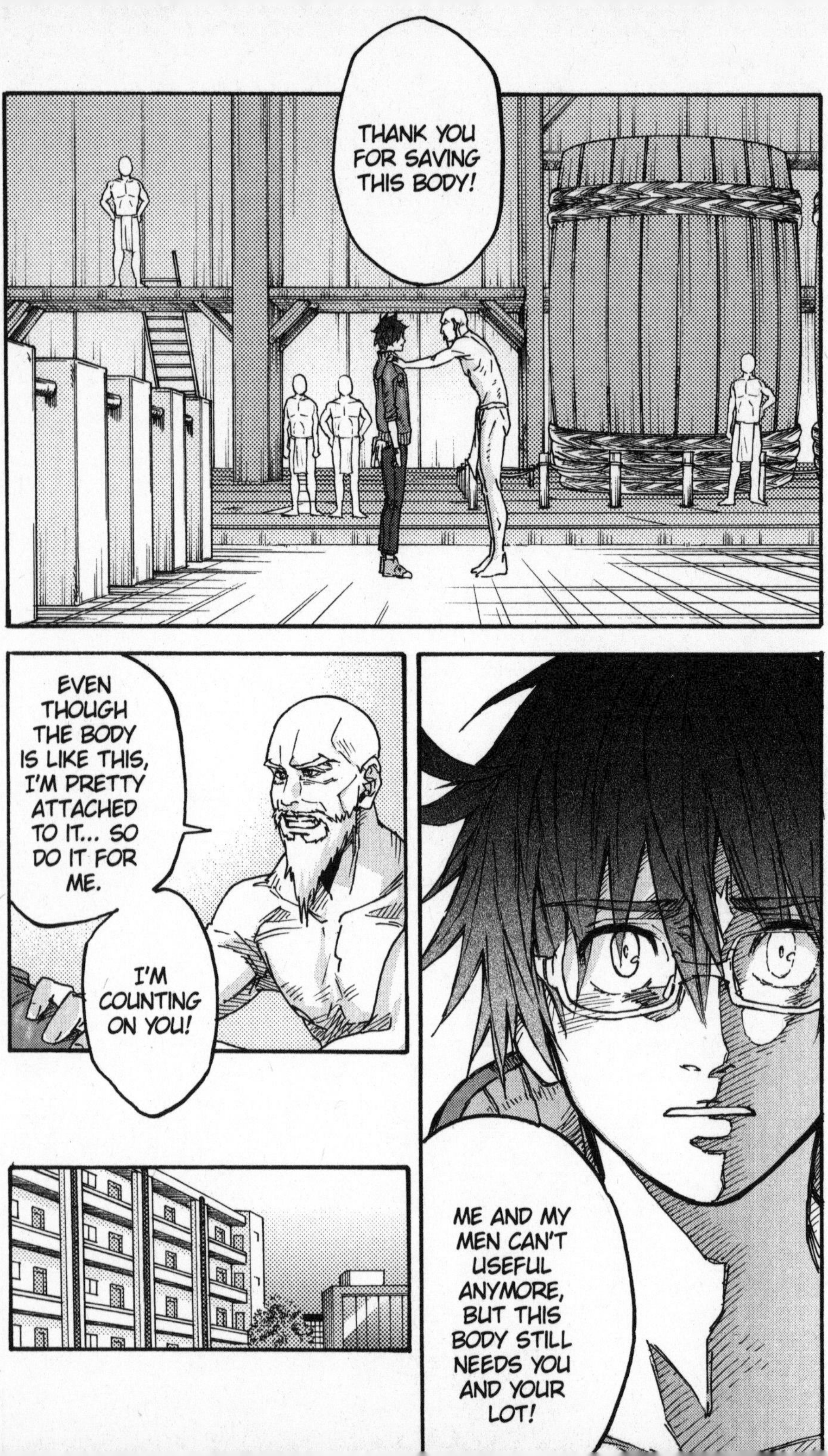
THANK YOU FOR SAVING THIS BODY!
ME AND MY MEN CAN'T USEFUL ANYMORE, BUT THIS BODY STILL NEEDS YOU AND YOUR LOT!
EVEN THOUGH THE BODY IS LIKE THIS, I'M PRETTY ATTACHED TO IT... SO DO IT FOR ME.
I'M COUNTING ON YOU!

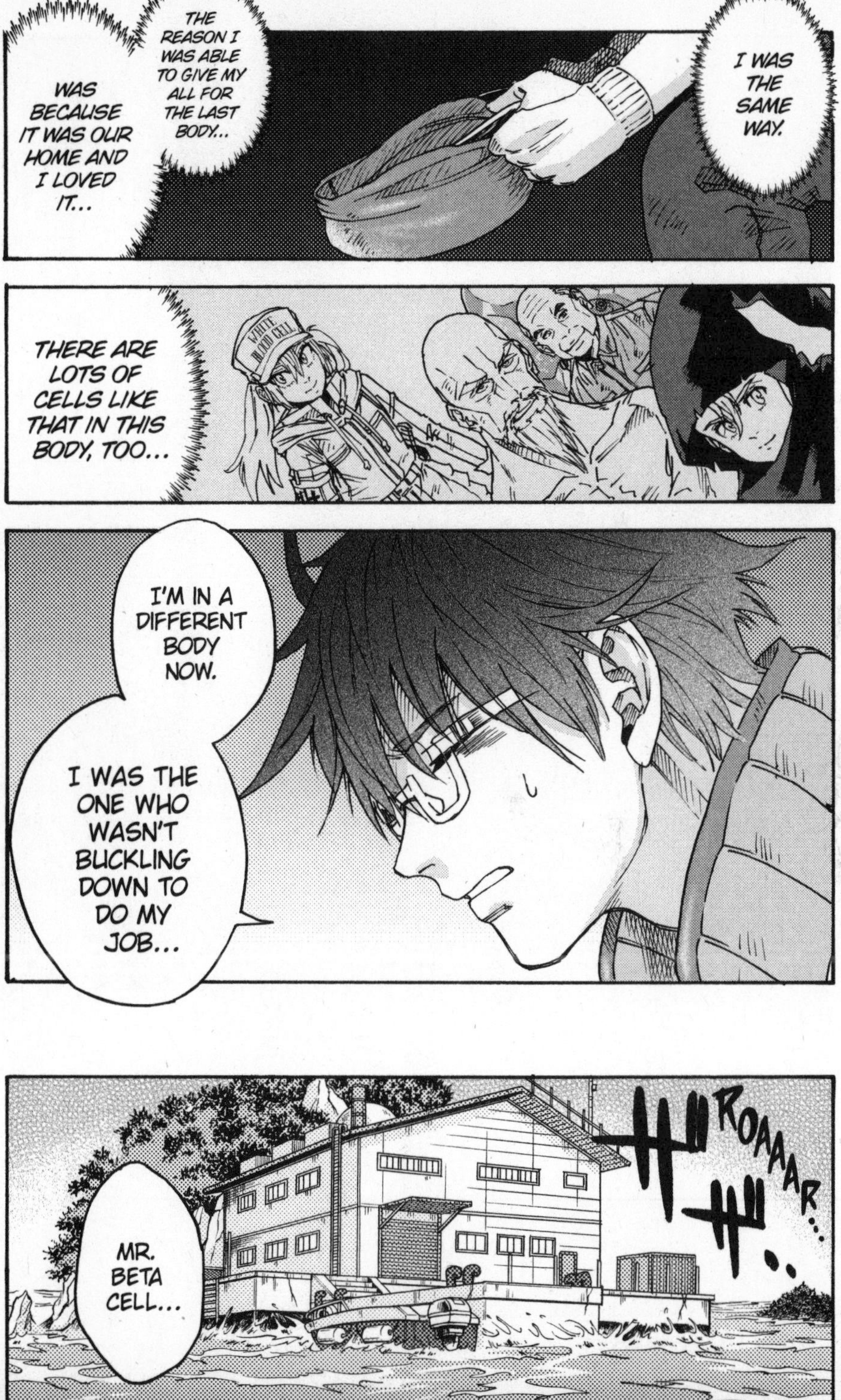
I WAS THE SAME WAY.
THE REASON I WAS ABLE TO GIVE MY ALL FOR THE LAST BODY...
WAS BECAUSE IT WAS OUR HOME AND I LOVED IT...
THERE ARE LOTS OF CELLS LIKE THAT IN THIS BODY, TOO...
I'M IN A DIFFERENT BODY NOW.
I WAS THE ONE WHO WASN'T BUCKLING DOWN TO DO MY JOB...
ROAAAAR...
MR. BETA CELL...

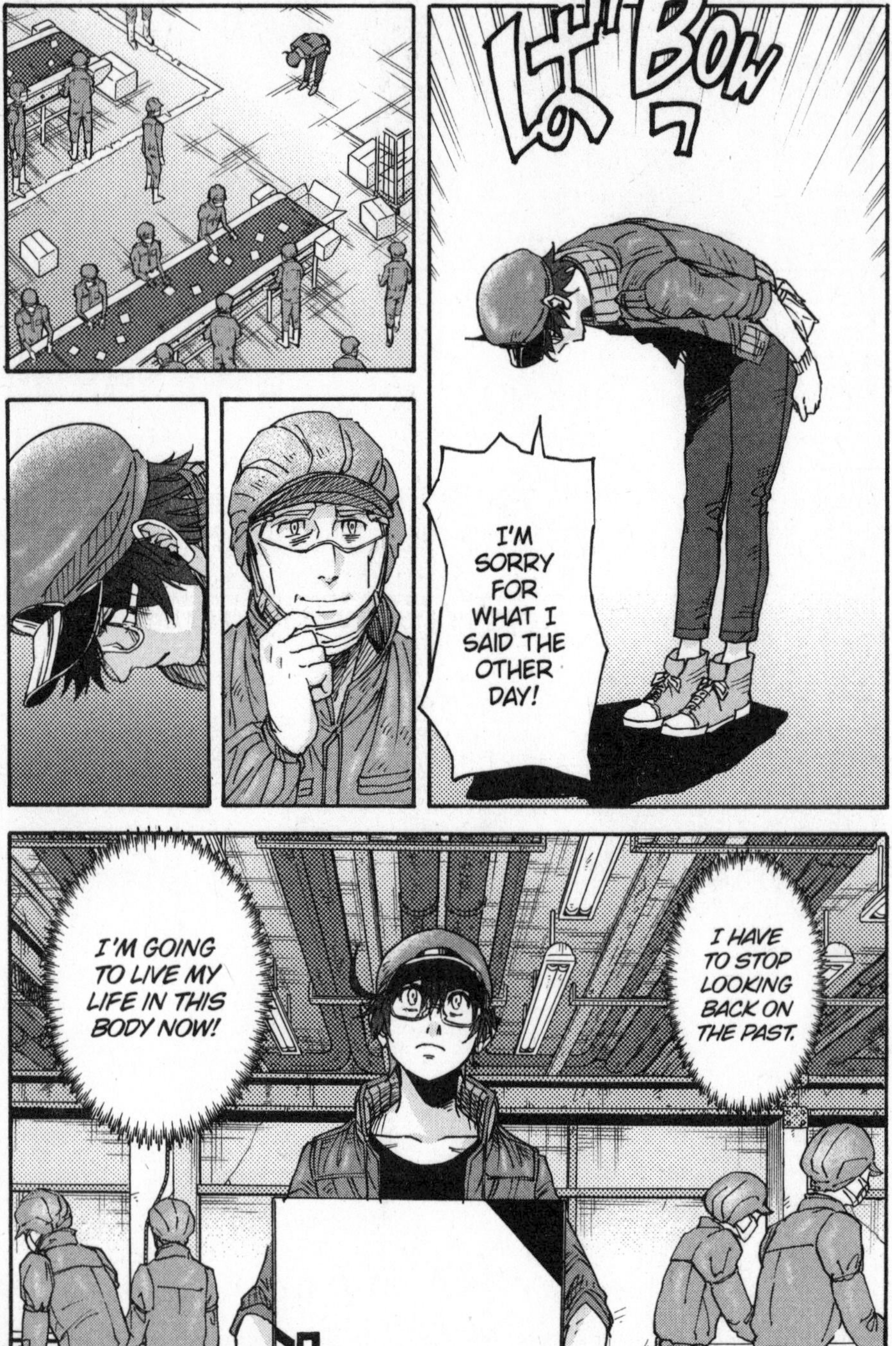
BOW
I'M SORRY FOR WHAT I SAID THE OTHER DAY!
I HAVE TO STOP LOOKING BACK ON THE PAST.
I'M GOING TO LIVE MY LIFE IN THIS BODY NOW!

CHAPTER 20 - END

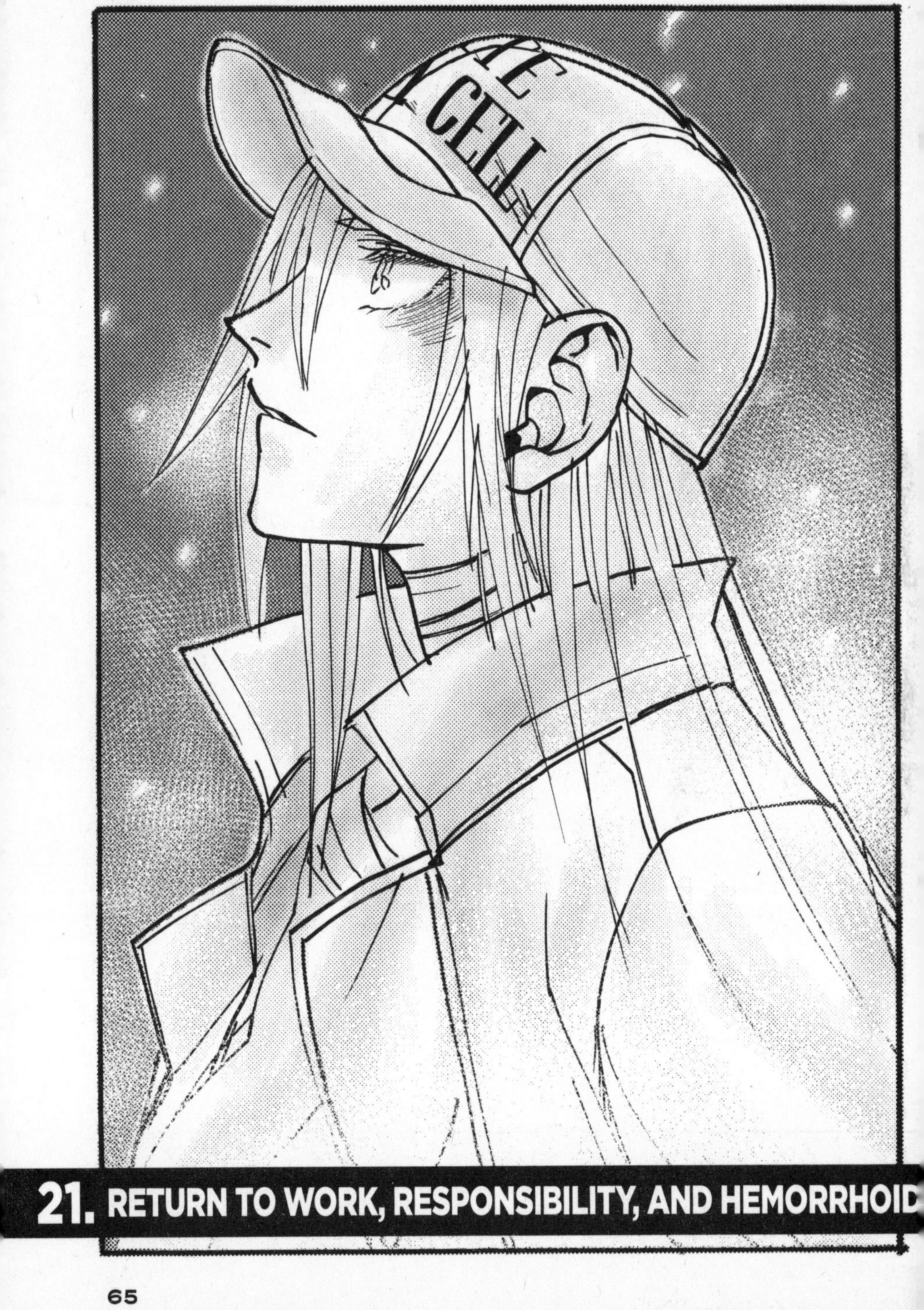

21. RETURN TO WORK, RESPONSIBILITY, AND HEMORRHOID

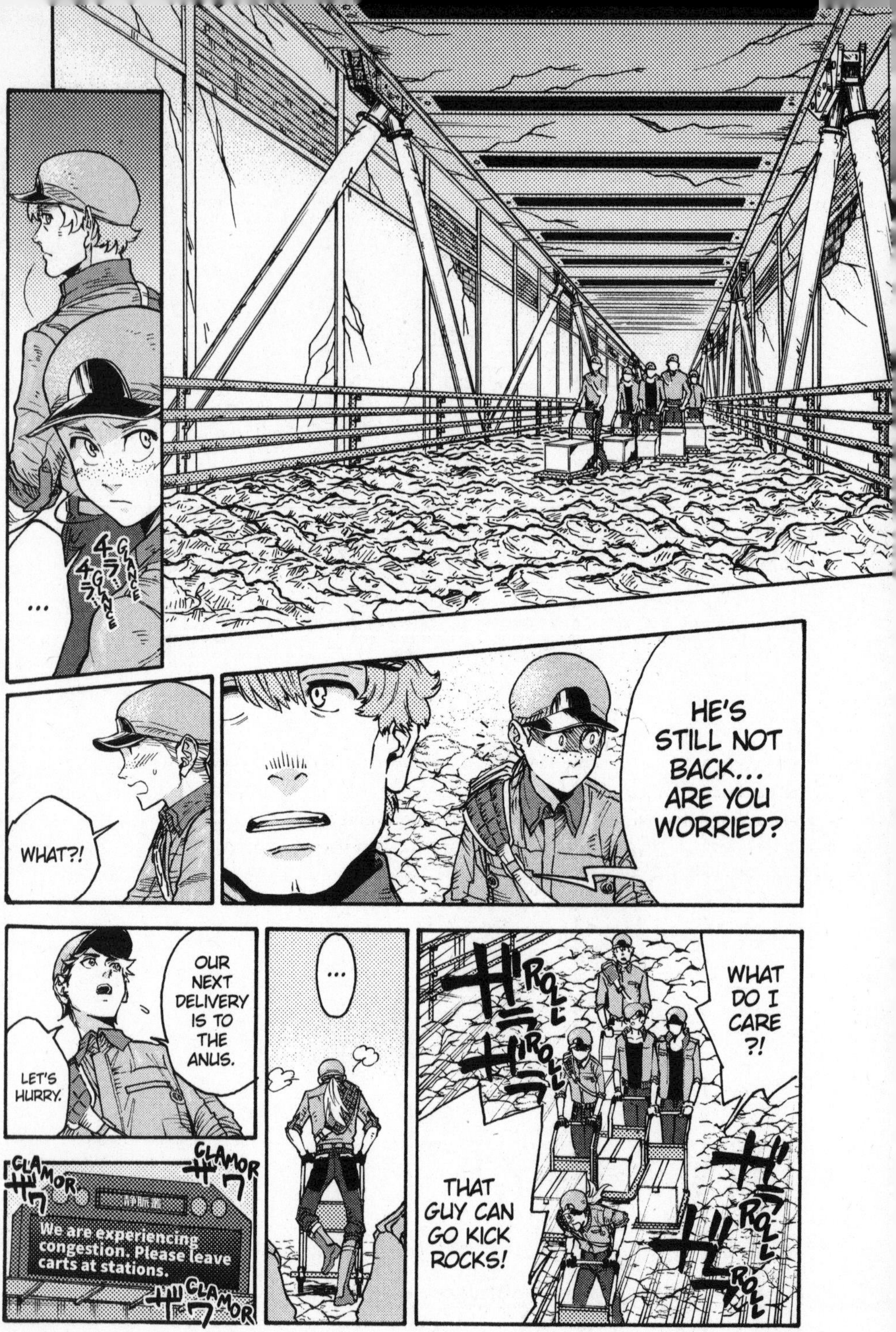
GLANCE GLANCE
...
HE'S STILL NOT BACK... ARE YOU WORRIED?
WHAT?!
WHAT DO I CARE?!
ROLL ROLL
THAT GUY CAN GO KICK ROCKS!
ROLL ROLL
...
OUR NEXT DELIVERY IS TO THE ANUS.
LET'S HURRY.
CLAMOR CLAMOR
We are experiencing congestion. Please leave carts at stations.
CLAMOR

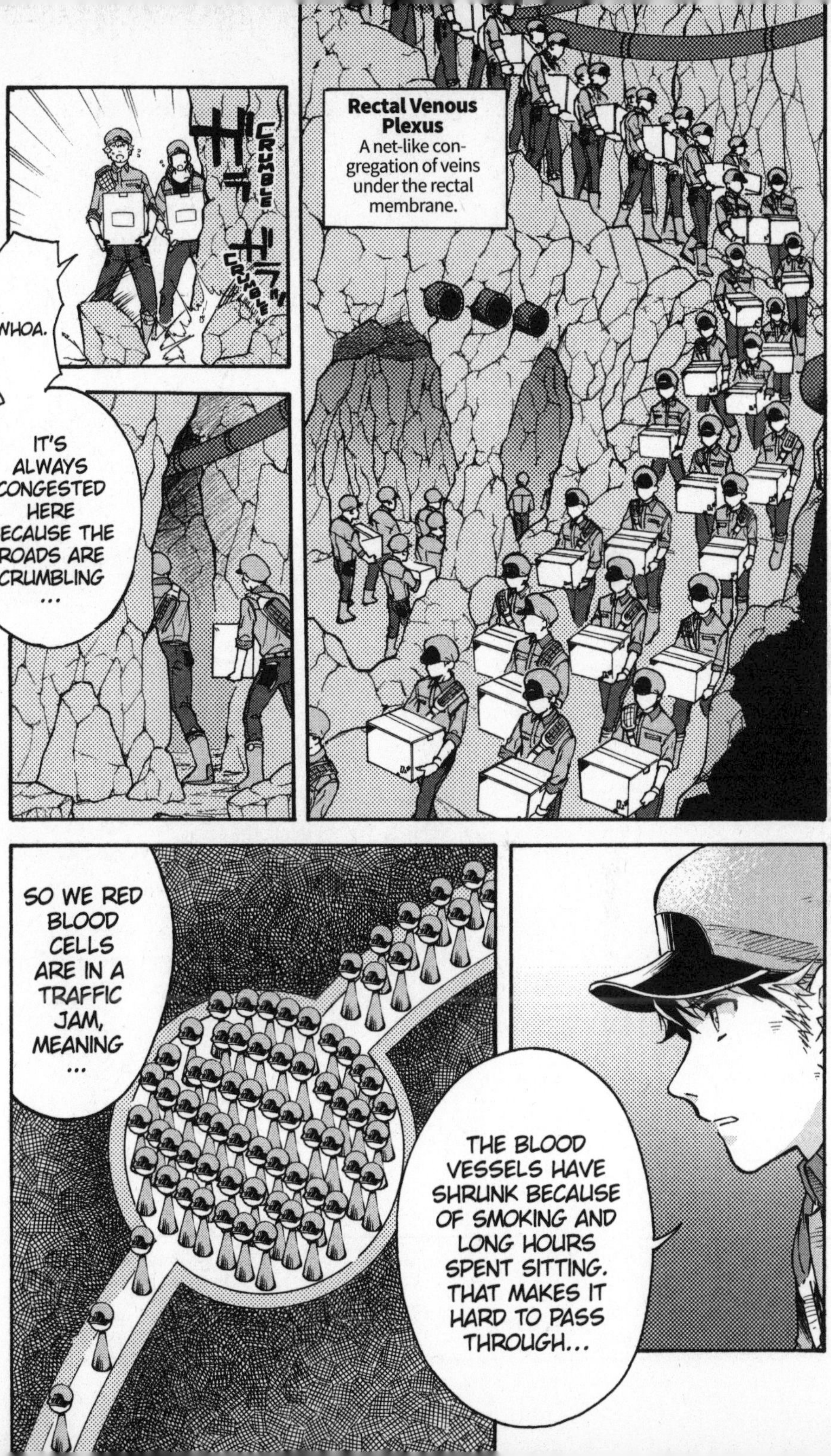

Rectal Venous Plexus
A net-like congregation of veins under the rectal membrane.
CRUMBLE
CRUMBLE
WHOA.
IT'S ALWAYS CONGESTED HERE BECAUSE THE ROADS ARE CRUMBLING ...
THE BLOOD VESSELS HAVE SHRUNK BECAUSE OF SMOKING AND LONG HOURS SPENT SITTING. THAT MAKES IT HARD TO PASS THROUGH...
SO WE RED BLOOD CELLS ARE IN A TRAFFIC JAM, MEANING ...

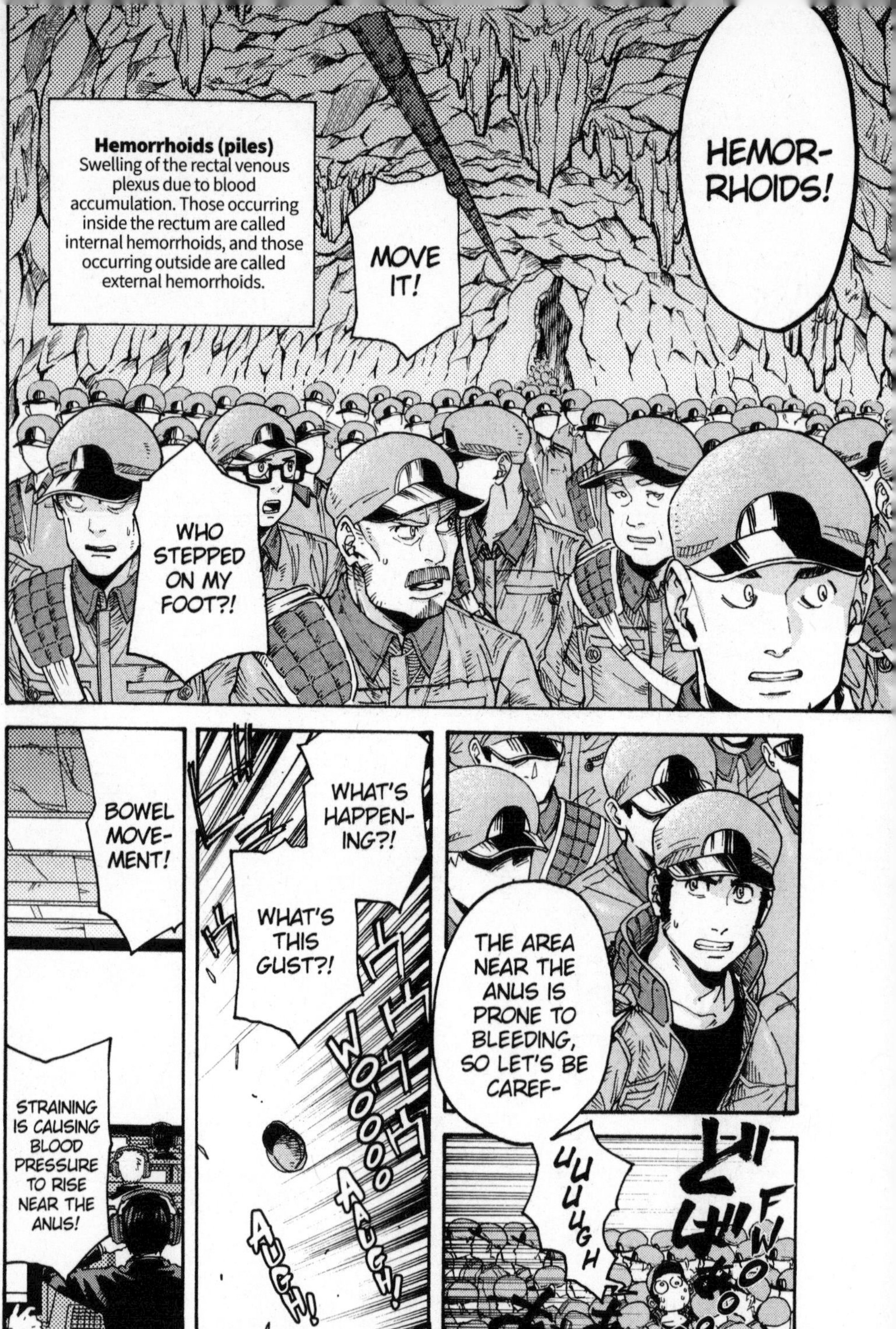
HEMORRHOIDS!
MOVE IT!
Hemorrhoids (piles)
Swelling of the rectal venous plexus due to blood accumulation. Those occurring inside the rectum are called internal hemorrhoids, and those occurring outside are called external hemorrhoids.
WHO STEPPED ON MY FOOT?!
THE AREA NEAR THE ANUS IS PRONE TO BLEEDING, SO LET'S BE CAREF-
UUUUUGH
FWOOOOSH
WHAT'S HAPPENING?!
WHAT'S THIS GUST?!
WOOOOOO
AAUGH!
AUGH!
BOWEL MOVEMENT!
STRAINING IS CAUSING BLOOD PRESSURE TO RISE NEAR THE ANUS!

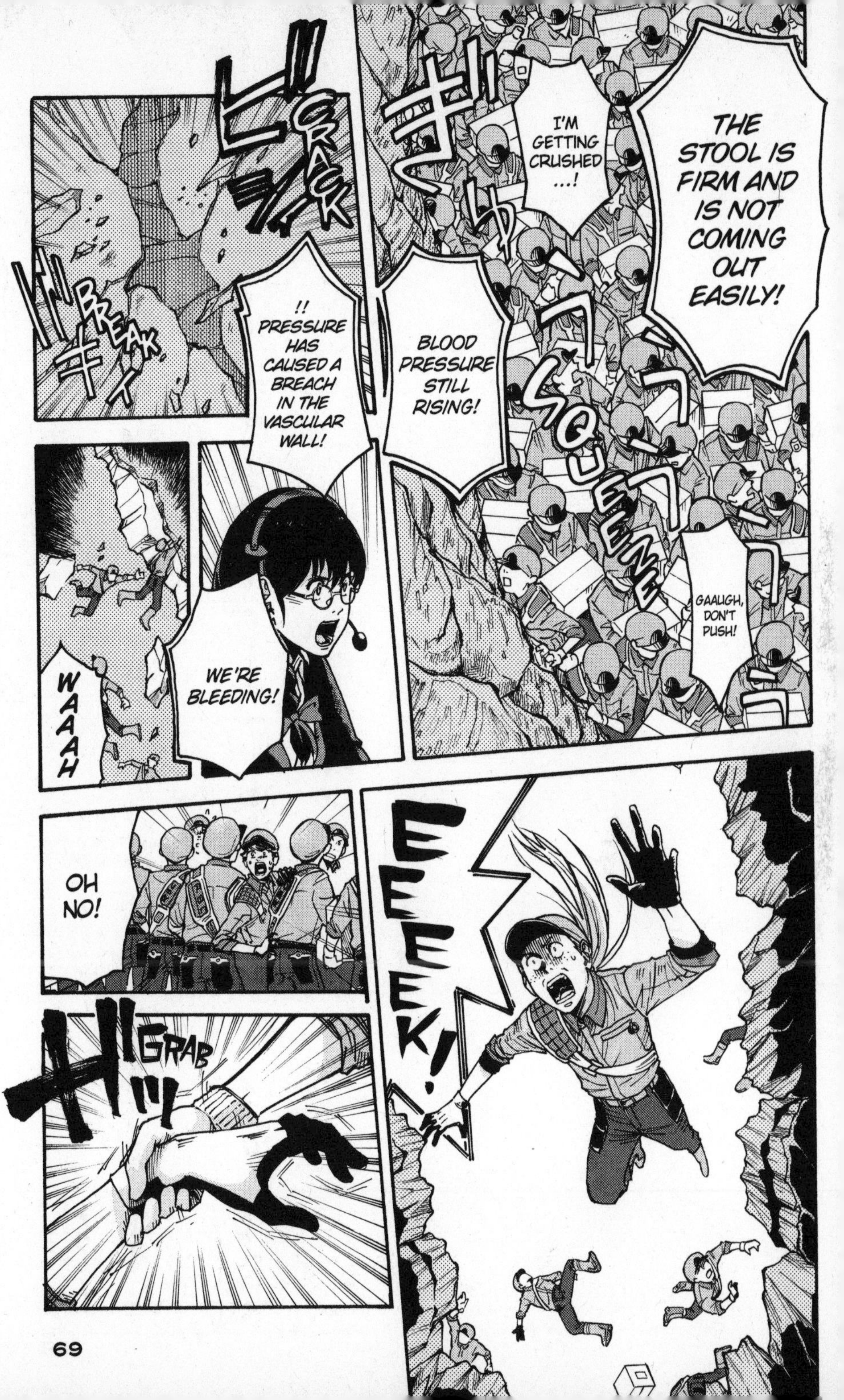
THE STOOL IS FIRM AND IS NOT COMING OUT EASILY!
I'M GETTING CRUSHED ...!
SQUEEEZE
BLOOD PRESSURE STILL RISING!
GAAUGH, DON'T PUSH!
CRACK
BREAK
!! PRESSURE HAS CAUSED A BREACH IN THE VASCULAR WALL!
WE'RE BLEEDING!
WAAAAH
EEEEK!
OH NO!
GRAB

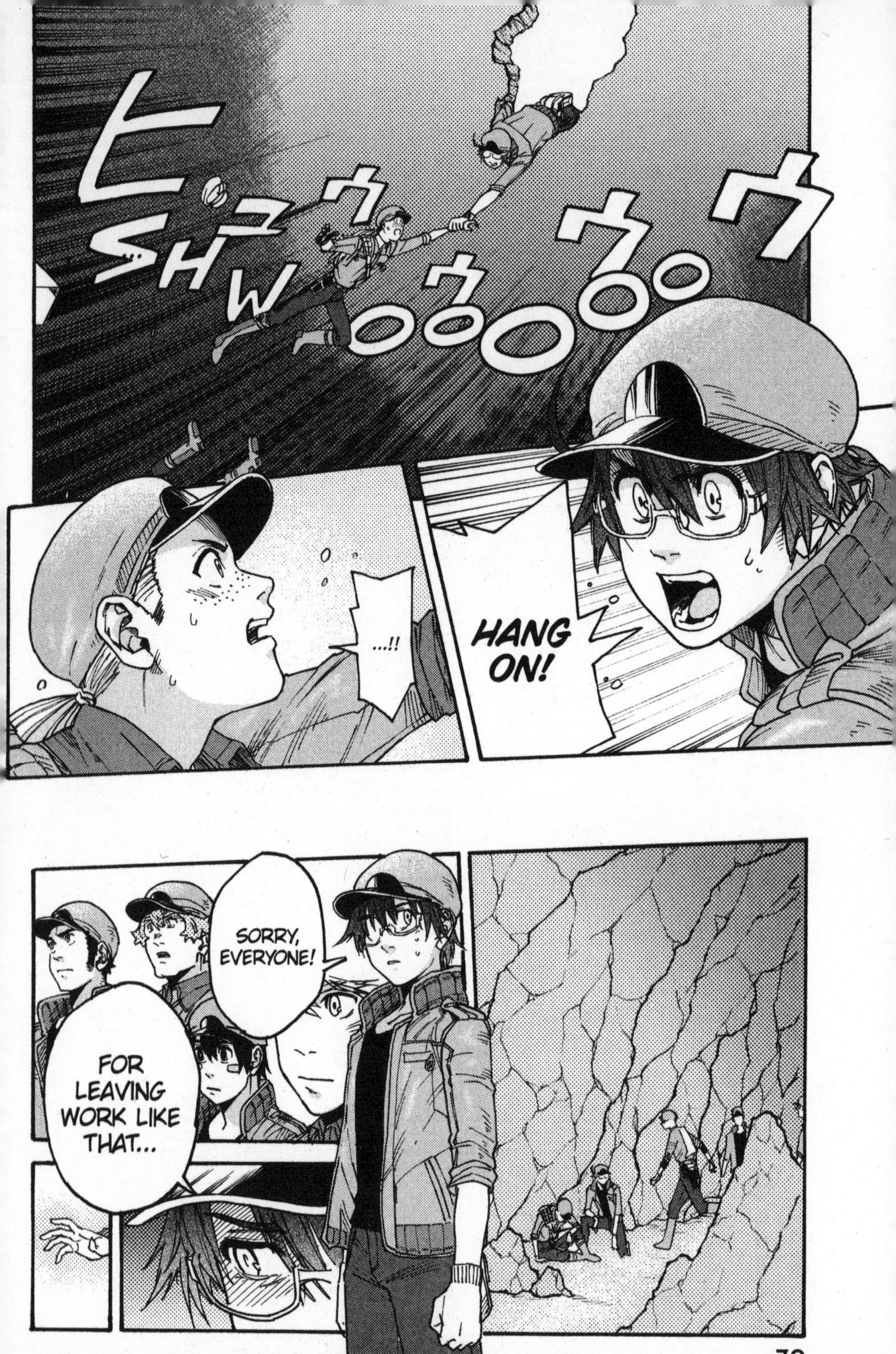
SHWOOOOO
HANG ON!
...!!
SORRY, EVERYONE!
FOR LEAVING WORK LIKE THAT...

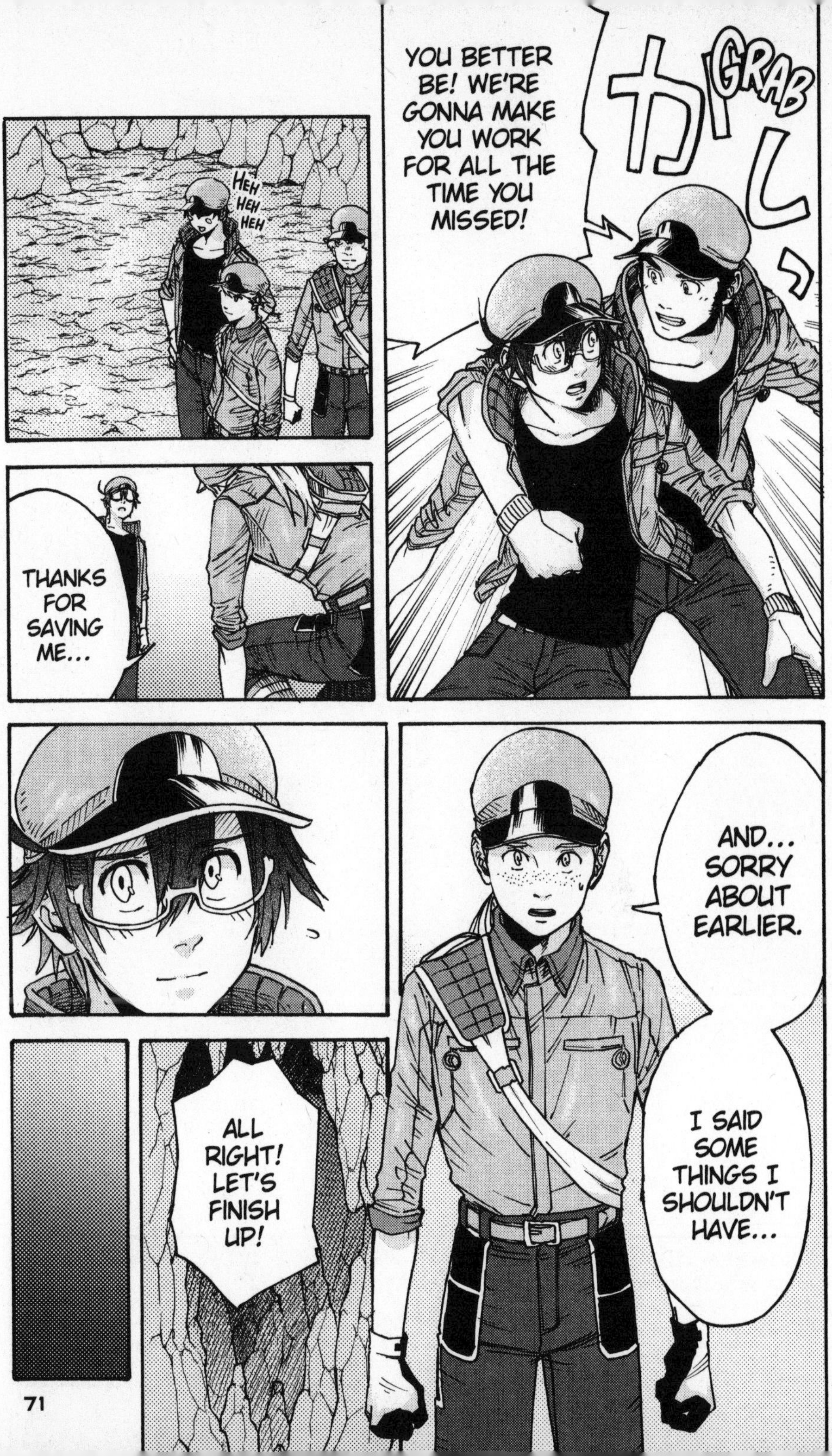
YOU BETTER BE! WE'RE GONNA MAKE YOU WORK FOR ALL THE TIME YOU MISSED!
わしっ
GRAB
HEH HEH HEH
THANKS FOR SAVING ME...
AND... SORRY ABOUT EARLIER.
I SAID SOME THINGS I SHOULDN'T HAVE...
ALL RIGHT! LET'S FINISH UP!

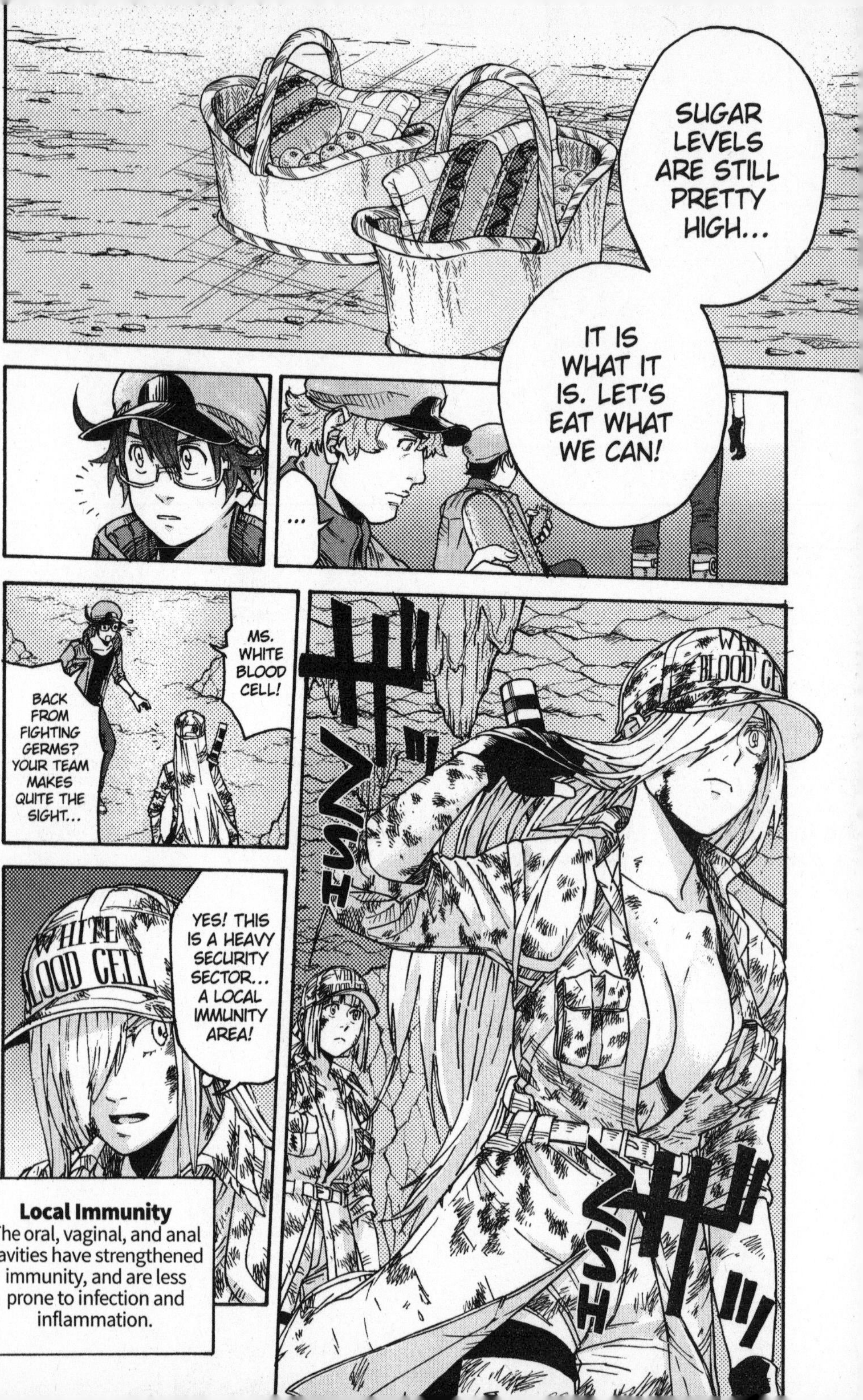
SUGAR LEVELS ARE STILL PRETTY HIGH...
IT IS WHAT IT IS. LET'S EAT WHAT WE CAN!
...
WHSH!!
BLOOD CELL
WHITE
WHSH!!
MS. WHITE BLOOD CELL!
BACK FROM FIGHTING GERMS? YOUR TEAM MAKES QUITE THE SIGHT...
YES! THIS IS A HEAVY SECURITY SECTOR... A LOCAL IMMUNITY AREA!
WHITE BLOOD CELL
Local Immunity
The oral, vaginal, and anal cavities have strengthened immunity, and are less prone to infection and inflammation.

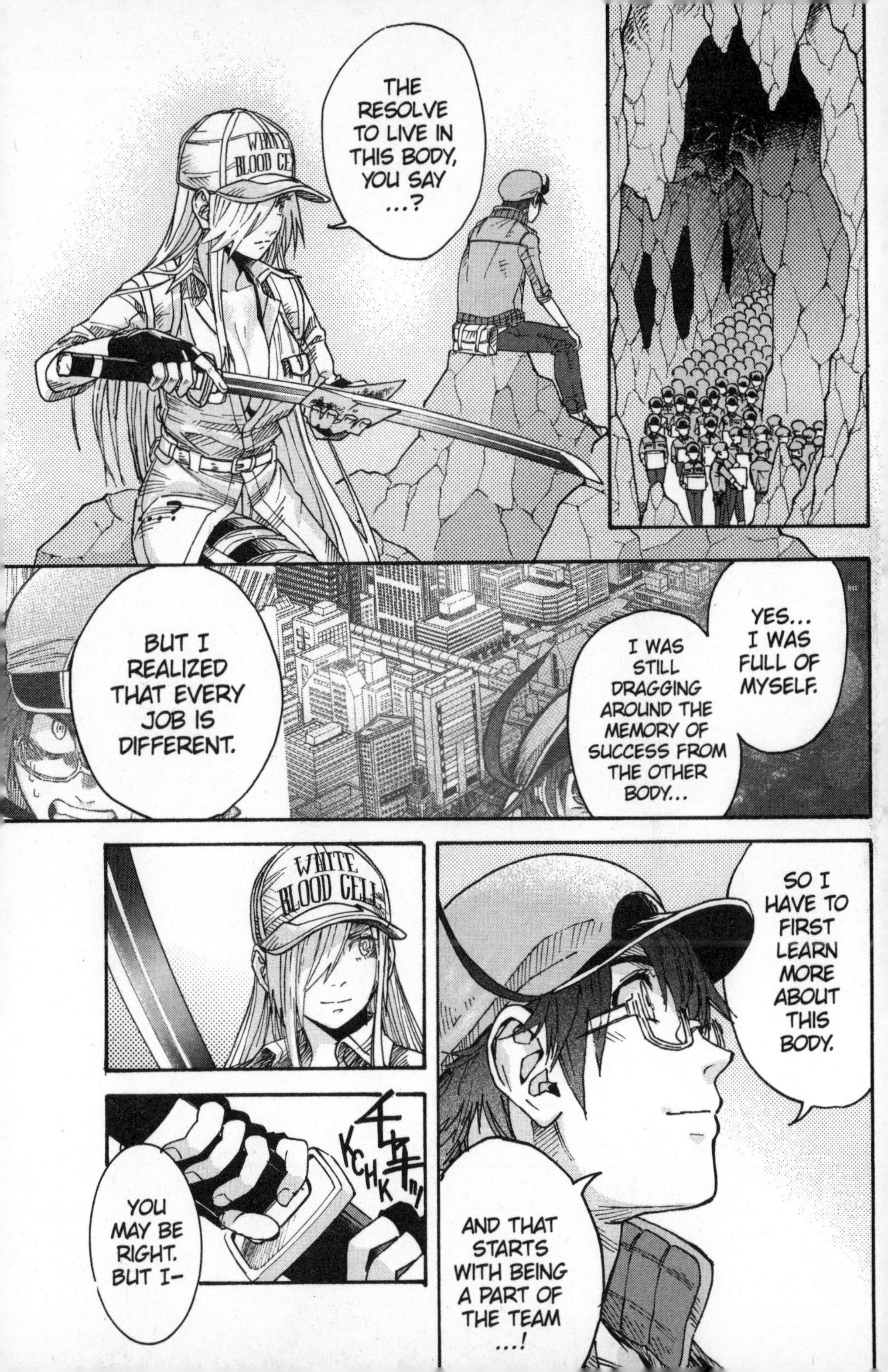
THE RESOLVE TO LIVE IN THIS BODY, YOU SAY ...?
YES... I WAS FULL OF MYSELF.
I WAS STILL DRAGGING AROUND THE MEMORY OF SUCCESS FROM THE OTHER BODY...
BUT I REALIZED THAT EVERY JOB IS DIFFERENT.
SO I HAVE TO FIRST LEARN MORE ABOUT THIS BODY.
AND THAT STARTS WITH BEING A PART OF THE TEAM ...!
WHITE BLOOD CELL
KCHK
YOU MAY BE RIGHT. BUT I-

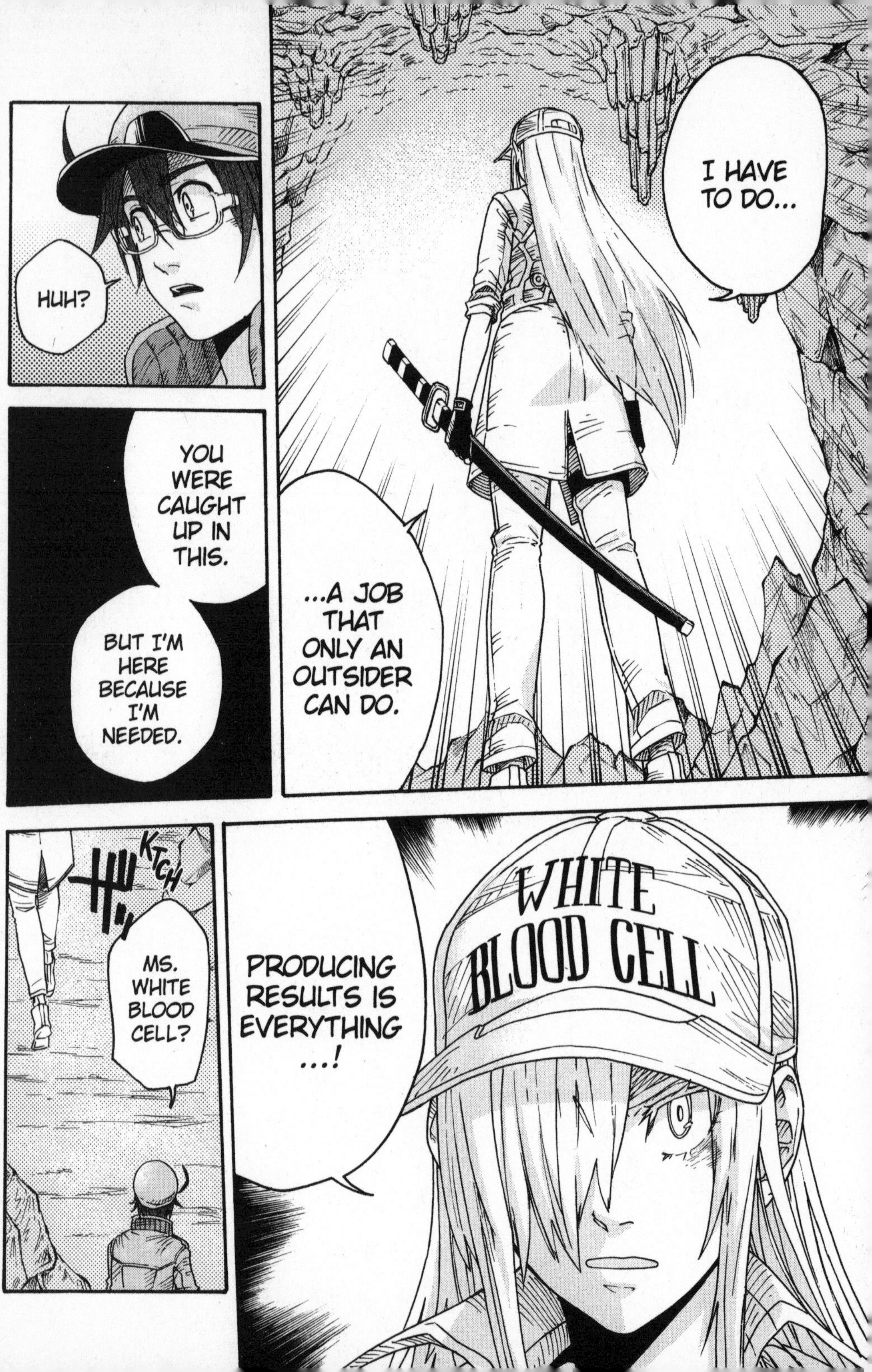
I HAVE TO DO...
...A JOB THAT ONLY AN OUTSIDER CAN DO.
HUH?
YOU WERE CAUGHT UP IN THIS.
BUT I'M HERE BECAUSE I'M NEEDED.
WHITE BLOOD CELL
PRODUCING RESULTS IS EVERYTHING ...!
KTCH
MS. WHITE BLOOD CELL?

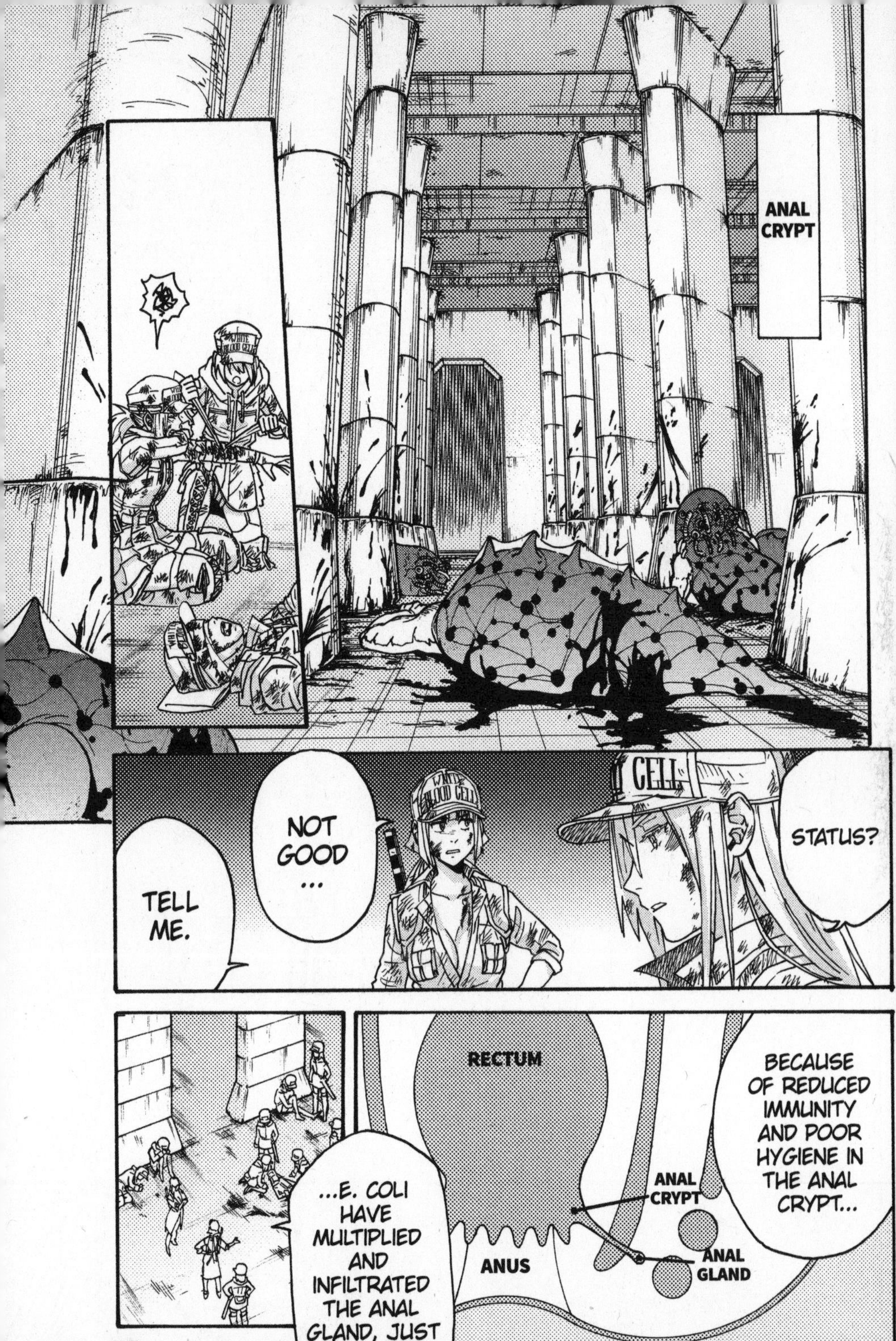
ANAL CRYPT
STATUS?
NOT GOOD ...
TELL ME.
BECAUSE OF REDUCED IMMUNITY AND POOR HYGIENE IN THE ANAL CRYPT...
RECTUM
ANAL CRYPT
ANAL GLAND
ANUS
...E. COLI HAVE MULTIPLIED AND INFILTRATED THE ANAL GLAND, JUST PAST HERE.

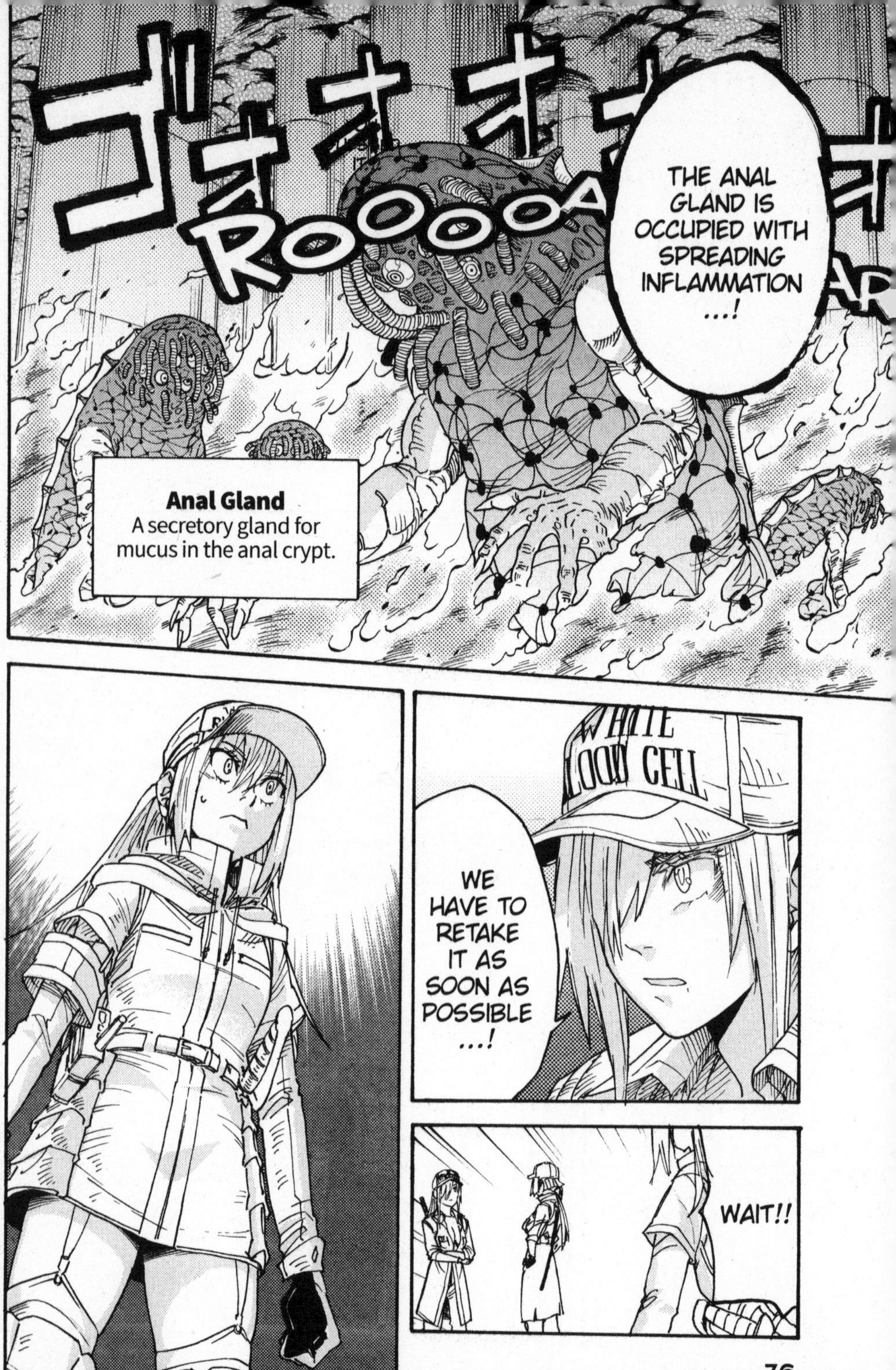
ROOOOA
AR
THE ANAL GLAND IS OCCUPIED WITH SPREADING INFLAMMATION ...!
Anal Gland
A secretory gland for mucus in the anal crypt.
WE HAVE TO RETAKE IT AS SOON AS POSSIBLE ...!
WAIT!!

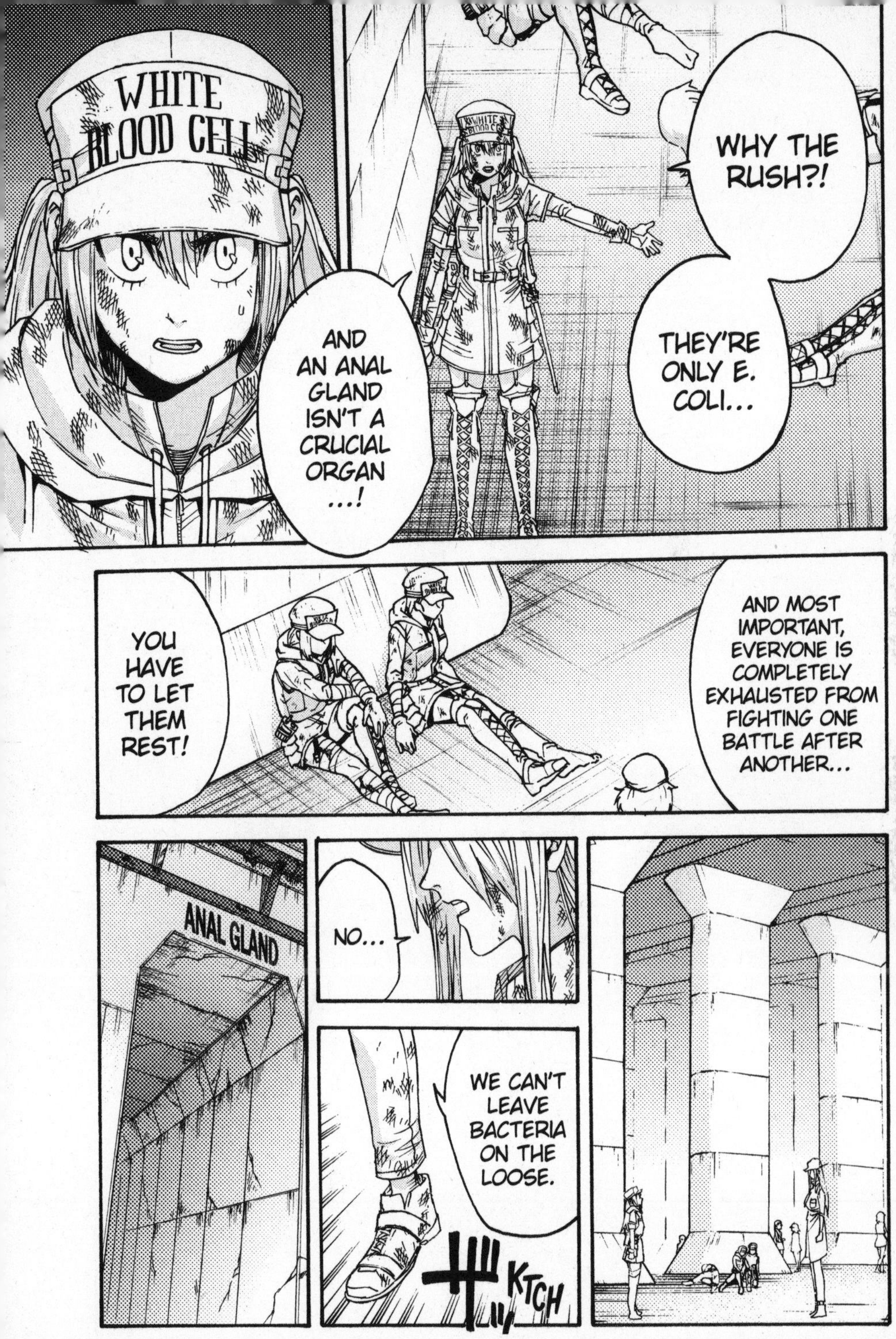
WHY THE RUSH?!
THEY'RE ONLY E. COLI...
AND AN ANAL GLAND ISN'T A CRUCIAL ORGAN...!
WHITE BLOOD CELL
AND MOST IMPORTANT, EVERYONE IS COMPLETELY EXHAUSTED FROM FIGHTING ONE BATTLE AFTER ANOTHER...
YOU HAVE TO LET THEM REST!
NO...
WE CAN'T LEAVE BACTERIA ON THE LOOSE.
KTCH
ANAL GLAND

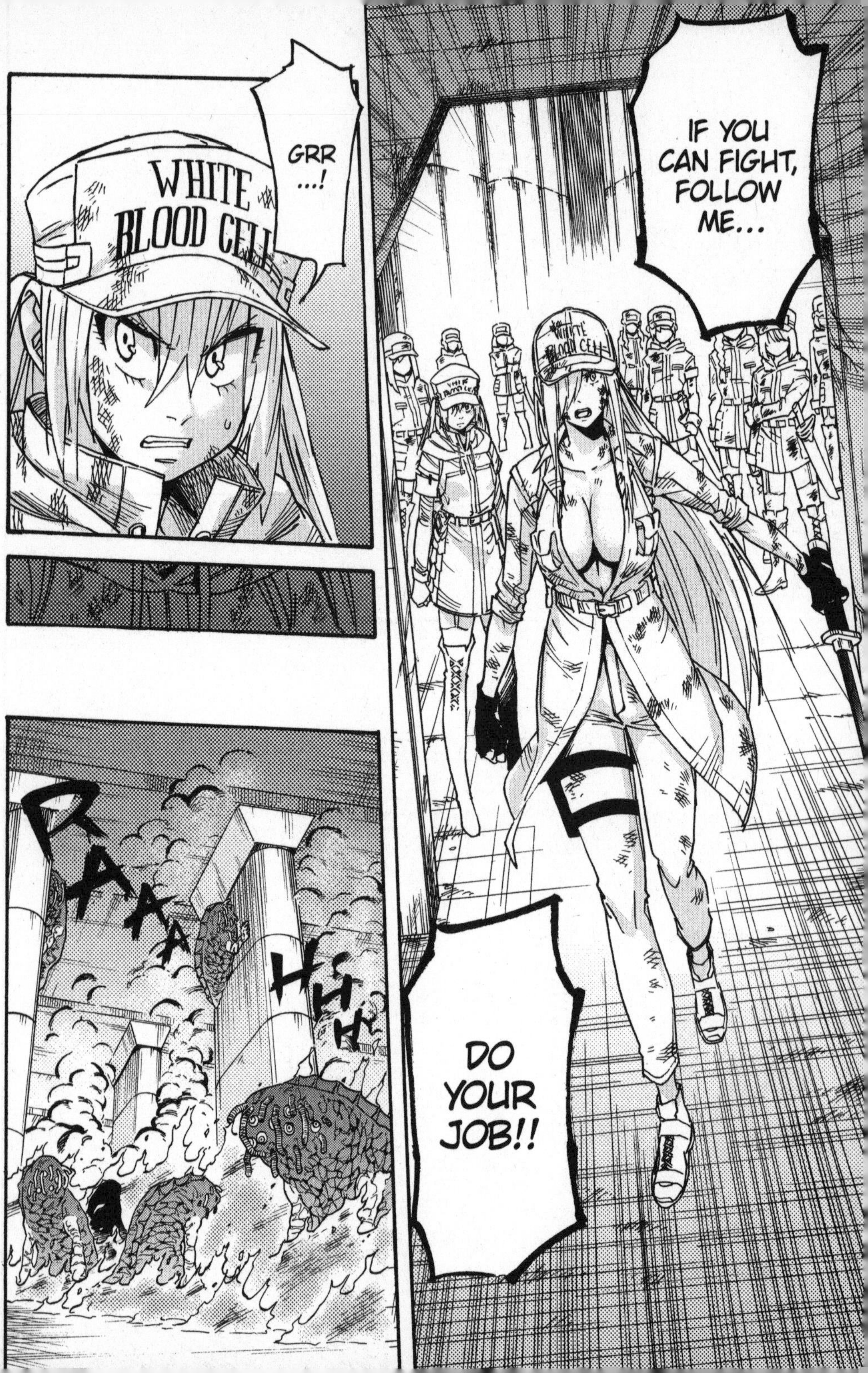
IF YOU CAN FIGHT, FOLLOW ME...
DO YOUR JOB!!
WHITE BLOOD CELL
GRR ...!
RAAAHHH

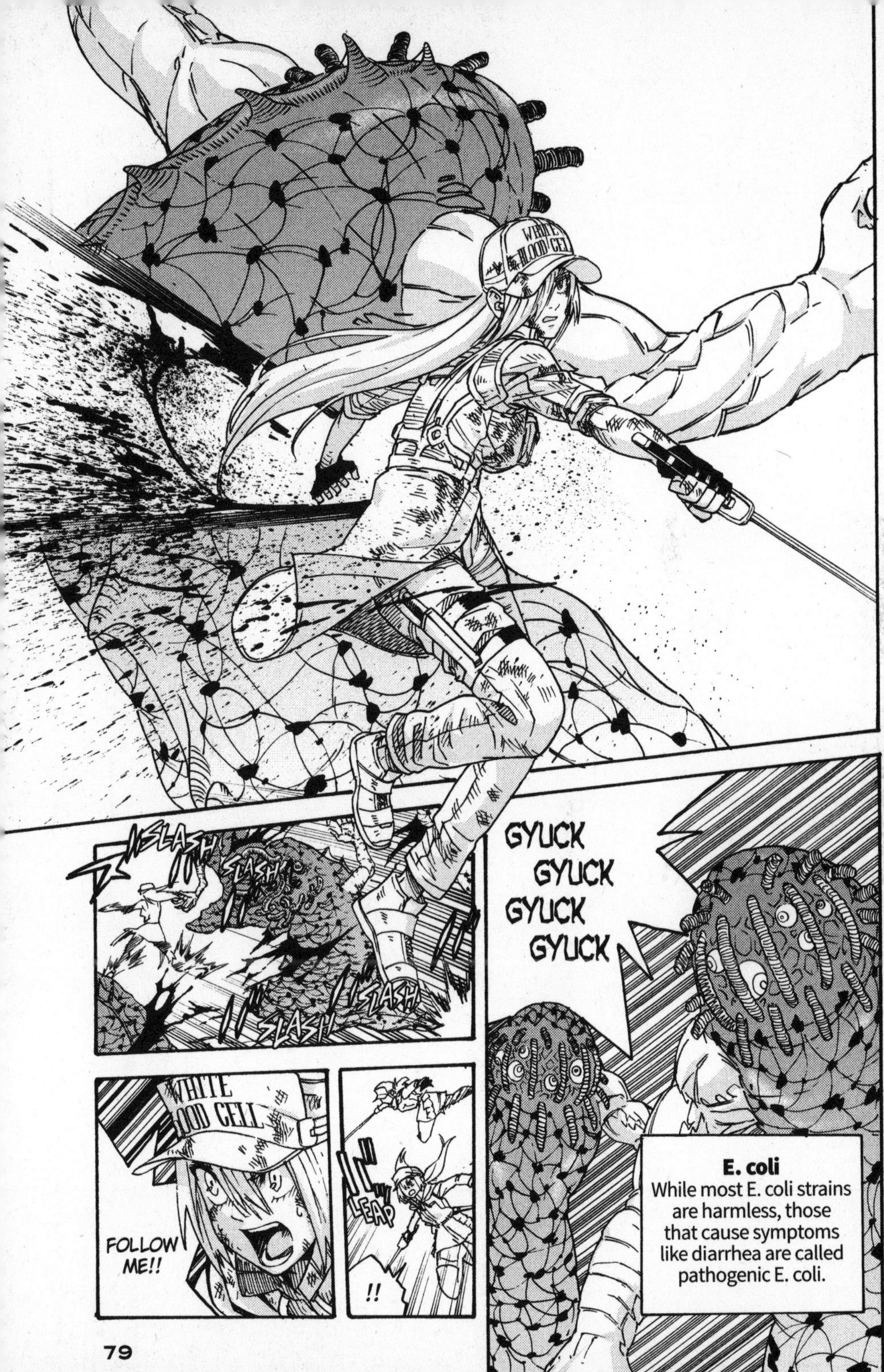
GYUCK
GYUCK
GYUCK
GYUCK
E. coli
While most E. coli strains are harmless, those that cause symptoms like diarrhea are called pathogenic E. coli.
SLASH
SLASH
SLASH
SLASH
LEAP
!!
FOLLOW ME!!

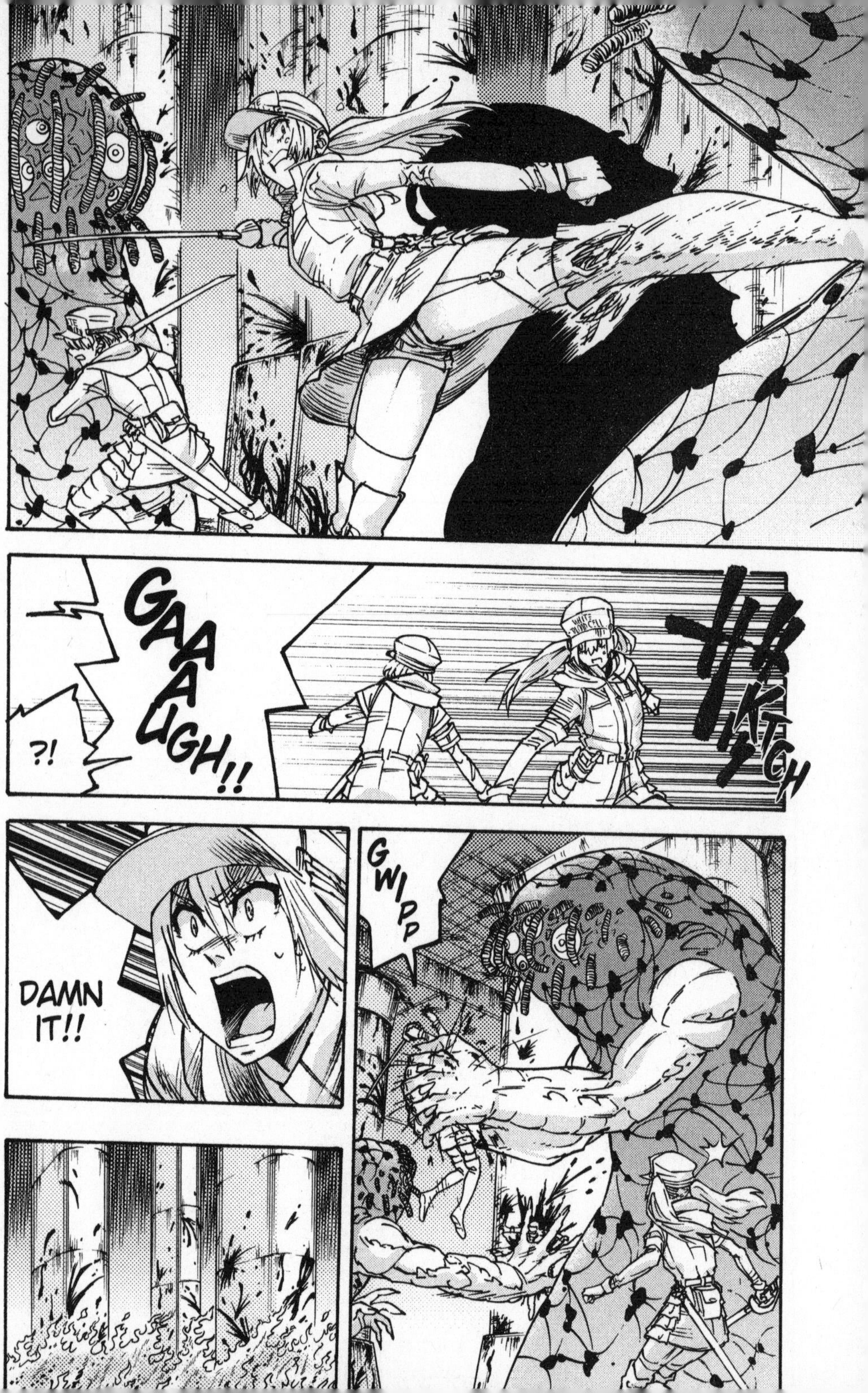
KKTCH
GAAAAUGH!!
?!
GWIPP
DAMN IT!!

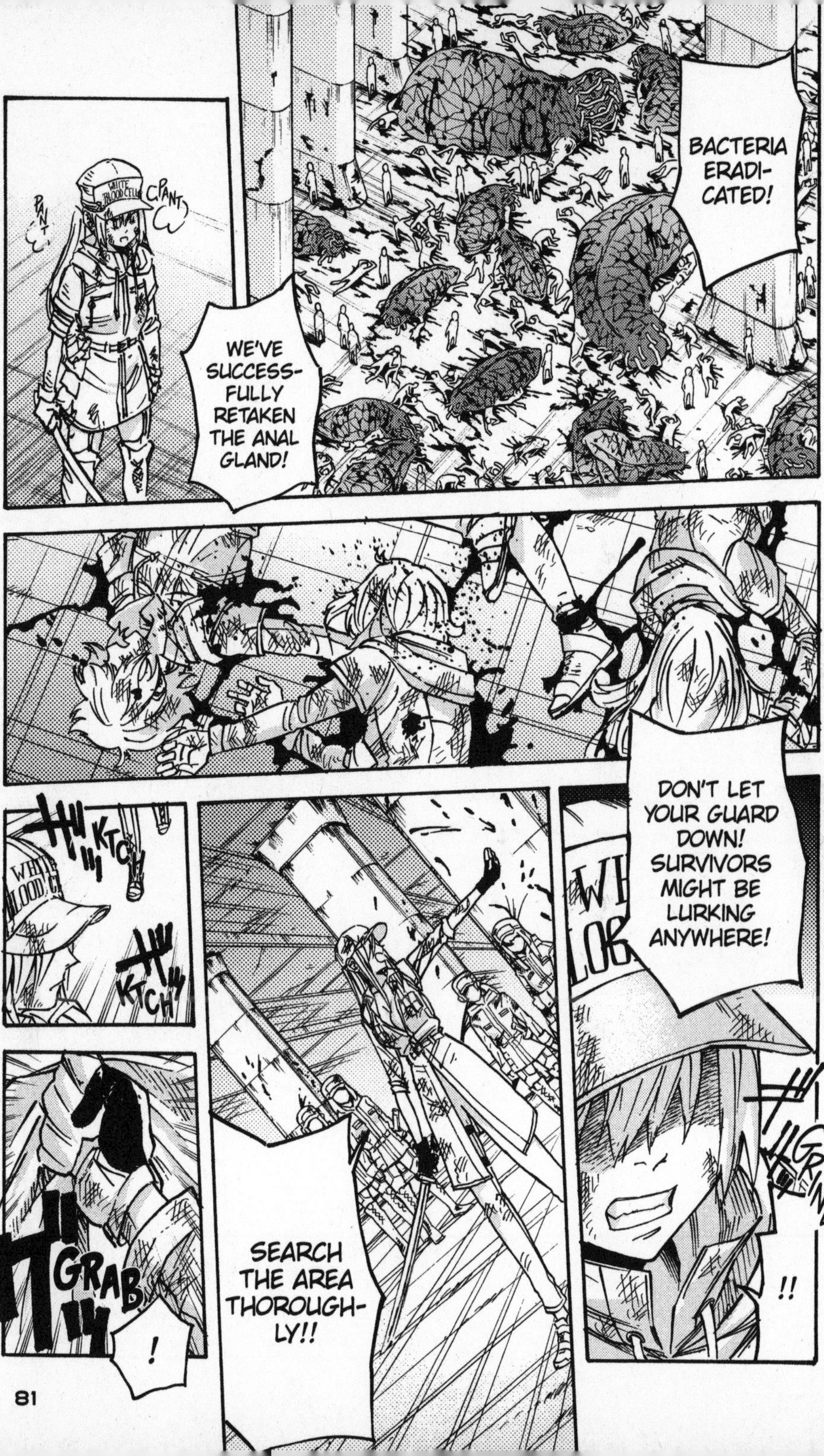

BACTERIA ERADICATED!
WE'VE SUCCESSFULLY RETAKEN THE ANAL GLAND!
PANT
PANT
DON'T LET YOUR GUARD DOWN! SURVIVORS MIGHT BE LURKING ANYWHERE!
GRIND
!!
SEARCH THE AREA THOROUGHLY!!
KTCH
KTCH
GRAB
!

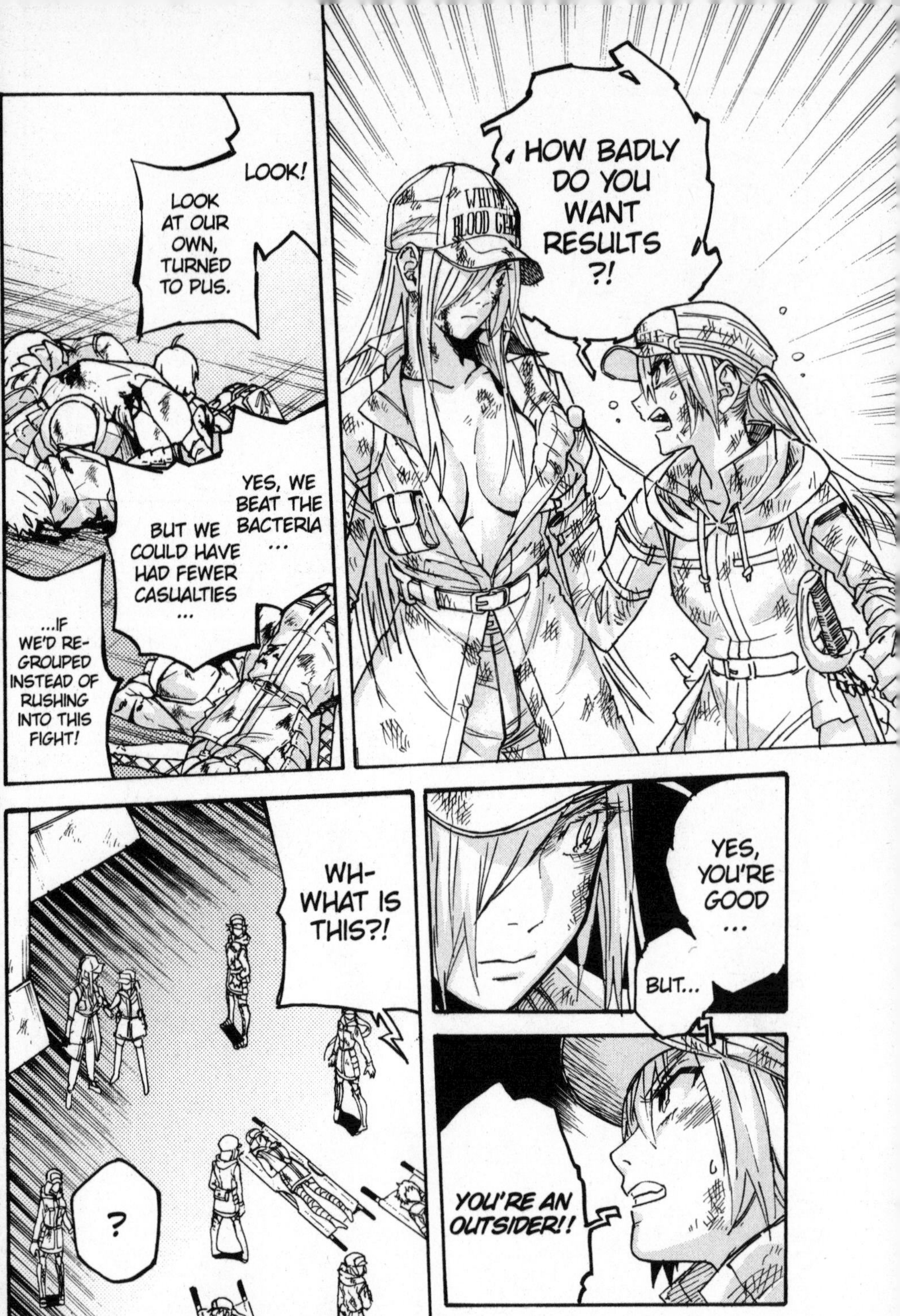
HOW BADLY DO YOU WANT RESULTS?!
LOOK!
LOOK AT OUR OWN, TURNED TO PUS.
YES, WE BEAT THE BACTERIA...
BUT WE COULD HAVE HAD FEWER CASUALTIES...
...IF WE'D RE-GROUPED INSTEAD OF RUSHING INTO THIS FIGHT!
YES, YOU'RE GOOD...
BUT...
YOU'RE AN OUTSIDER!!
WH-WHAT IS THIS?!
?

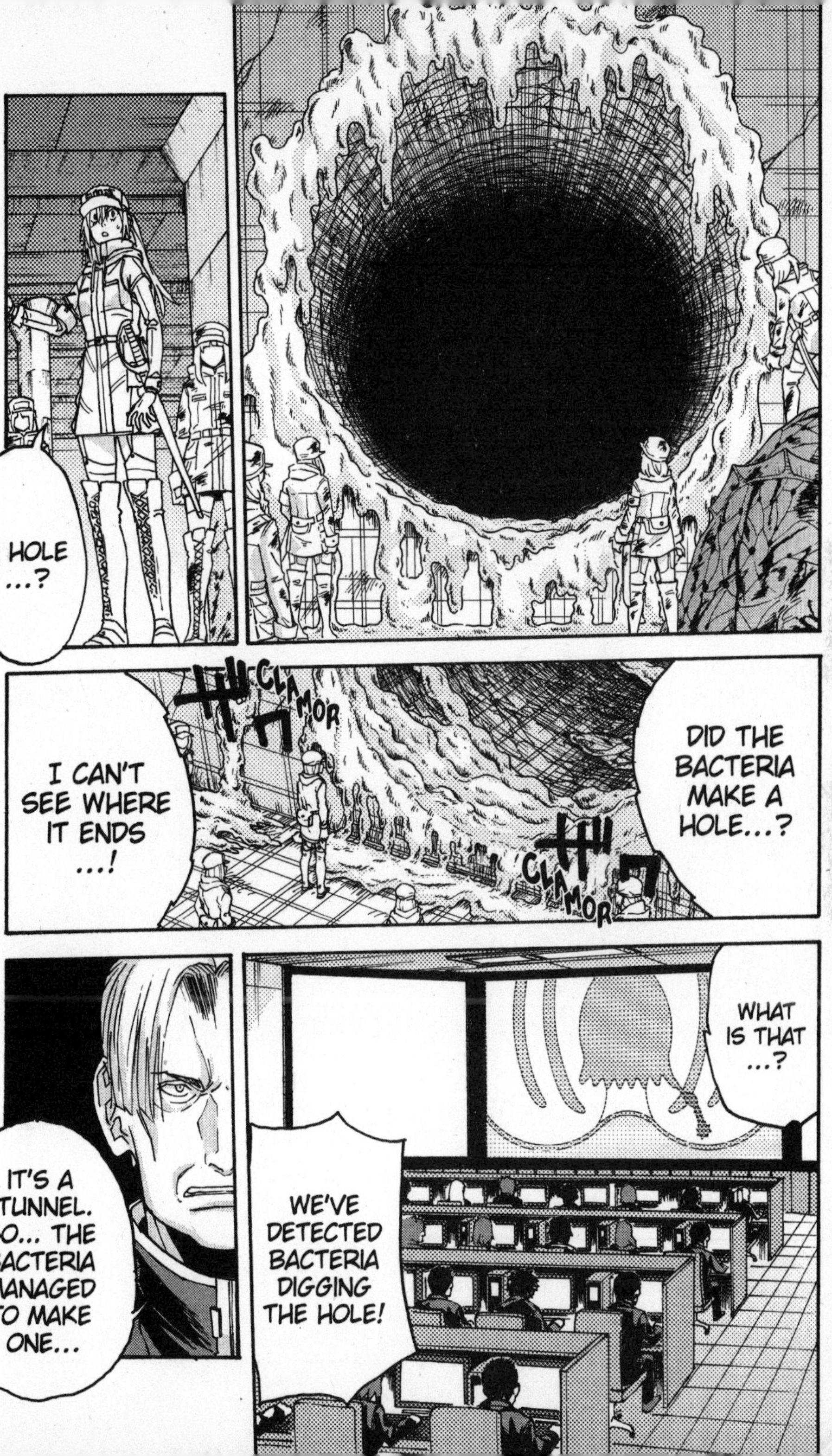
A HOLE ...?
DID THE BACTERIA MAKE A HOLE...?
CLAMOR
CLAMOR
I CAN'T SEE WHERE IT ENDS ...!
WHAT IS THAT ...?
WE'VE DETECTED BACTERIA DIGGING THE HOLE!
IT'S A TUNNEL. SO... THE BACTERIA MANAGED TO MAKE ONE...

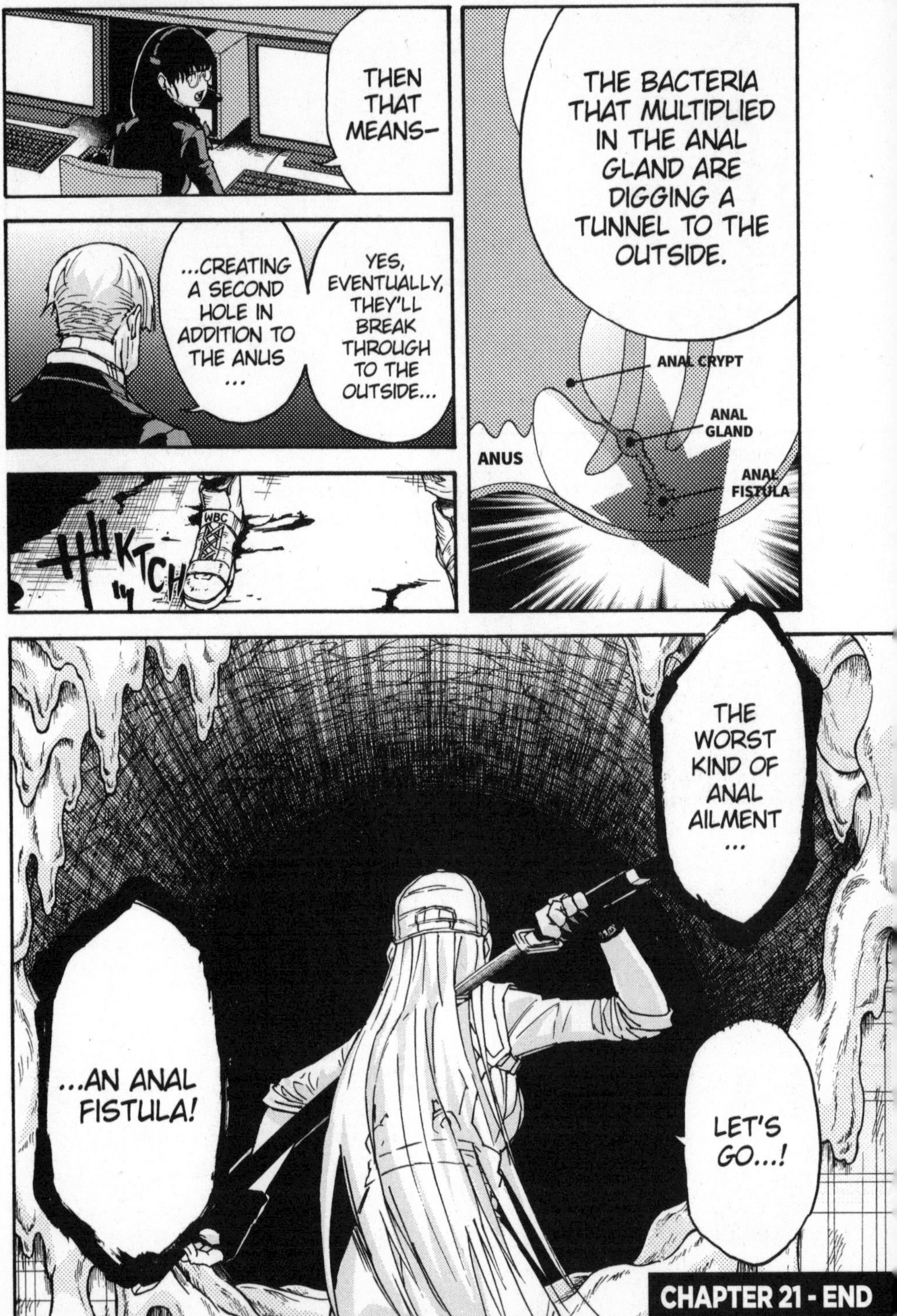
THE BACTERIA THAT MULTIPLIED IN THE ANAL GLAND ARE DIGGING A TUNNEL TO THE OUTSIDE.
ANAL CRYPT
ANAL GLAND
ANUS
ANAL FISTULA
THEN THAT MEANS—
YES, EVENTUALLY, THEY'LL BREAK THROUGH TO THE OUTSIDE...
...CREATING A SECOND HOLE IN ADDITION TO THE ANUS ...
WBC
HUKTCH
THE WORST KIND OF ANAL AILMENT ...
...AN ANAL FISTULA!
LET'S GO...!
CHAPTER 21 - END

22. ANAL FISTULA, FAULT, AND RESULTS

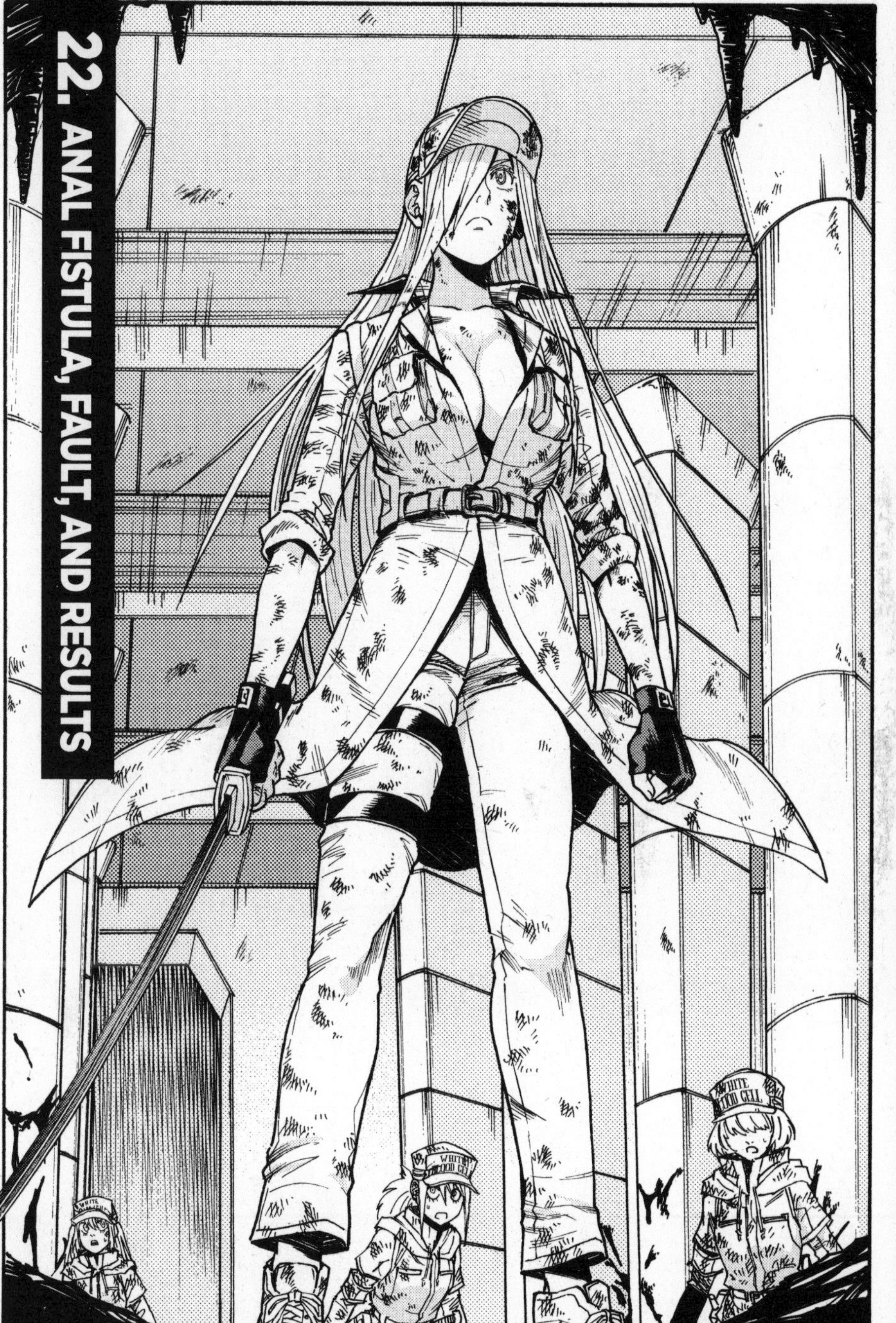

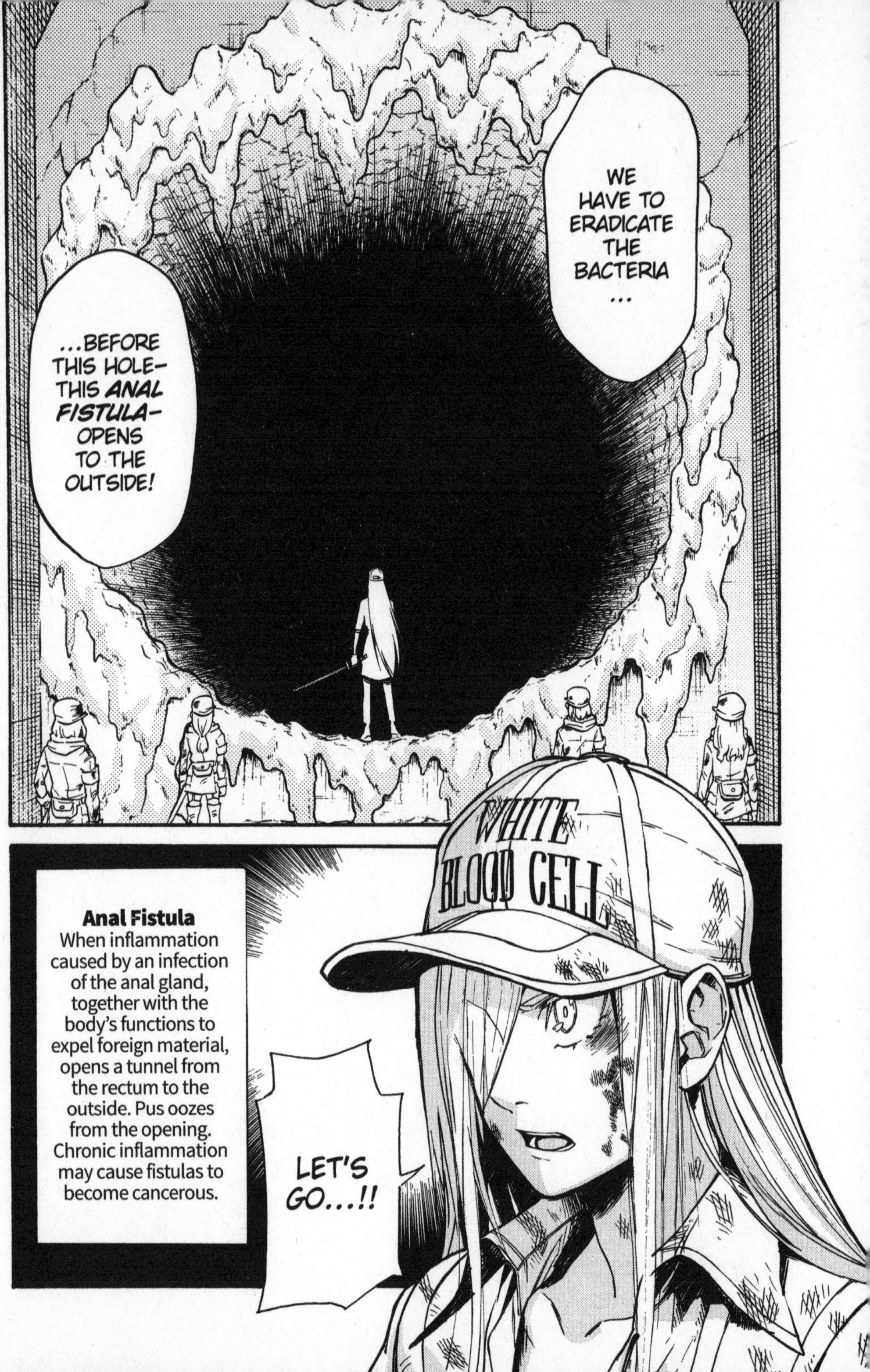

WE HAVE TO ERADICATE THE BACTERIA...
...BEFORE THIS HOLE- THIS *ANAL FISTULA*- OPENS TO THE OUTSIDE!
WHITE BLOOD CELL
LET'S GO...!!
Anal Fistula
When inflammation caused by an infection of the anal gland, together with the body's functions to expel foreign material, opens a tunnel from the rectum to the outside. Pus oozes from the opening. Chronic inflammation may cause fistulas to become cancerous.

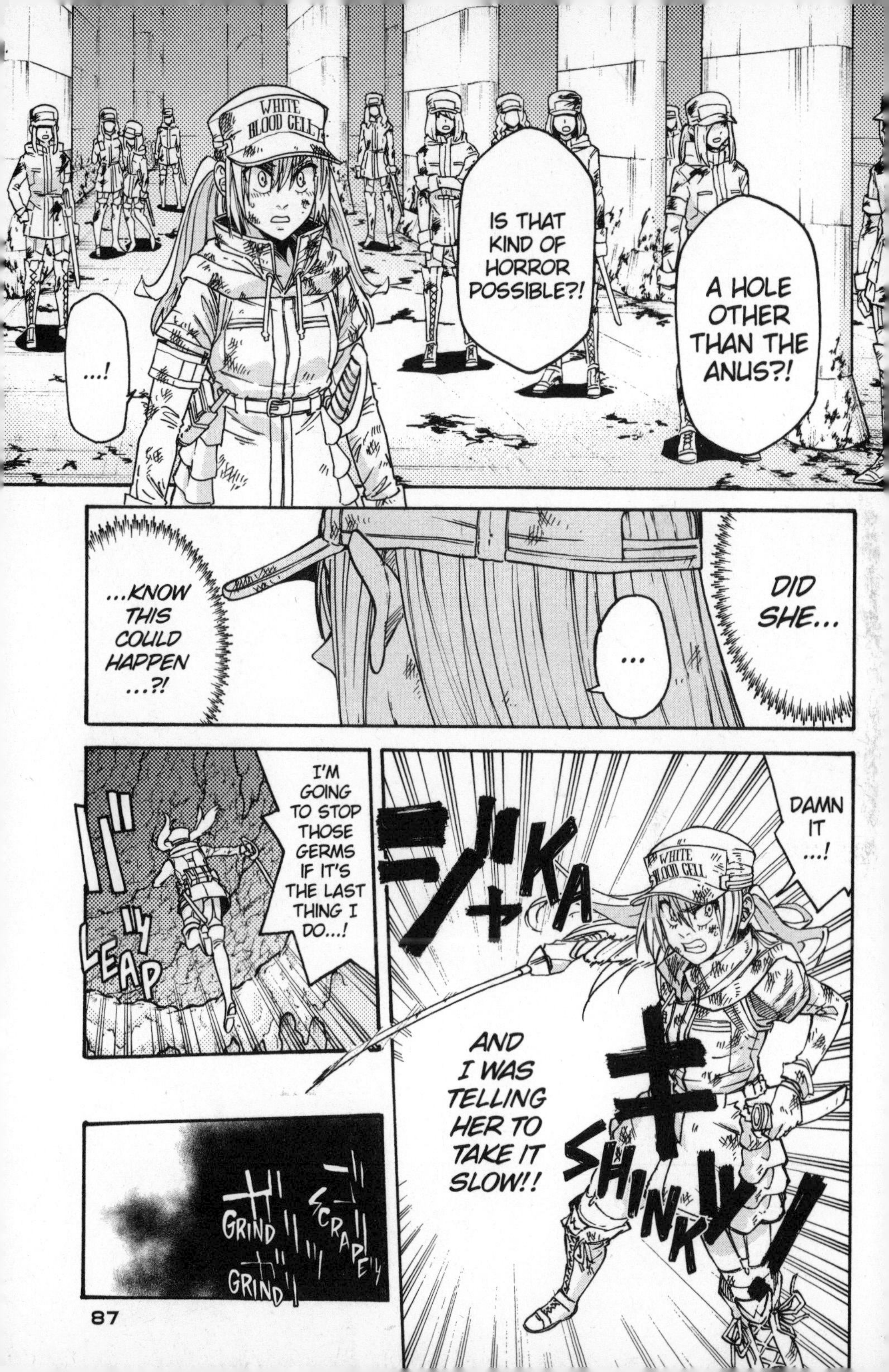
A HOLE OTHER THAN THE ANUS?!
IS THAT KIND OF HORROR POSSIBLE?!
...!
DID SHE...
...
...KNOW THIS COULD HAPPEN...?!
DAMN IT ...!
KA
AND I WAS TELLING HER TO TAKE IT SLOW!!
SHINK
I'M GOING TO STOP THOSE GERMS IF IT'S THE LAST THING I DO...!
LEAP
SCRAPE
GRIND
GRIND

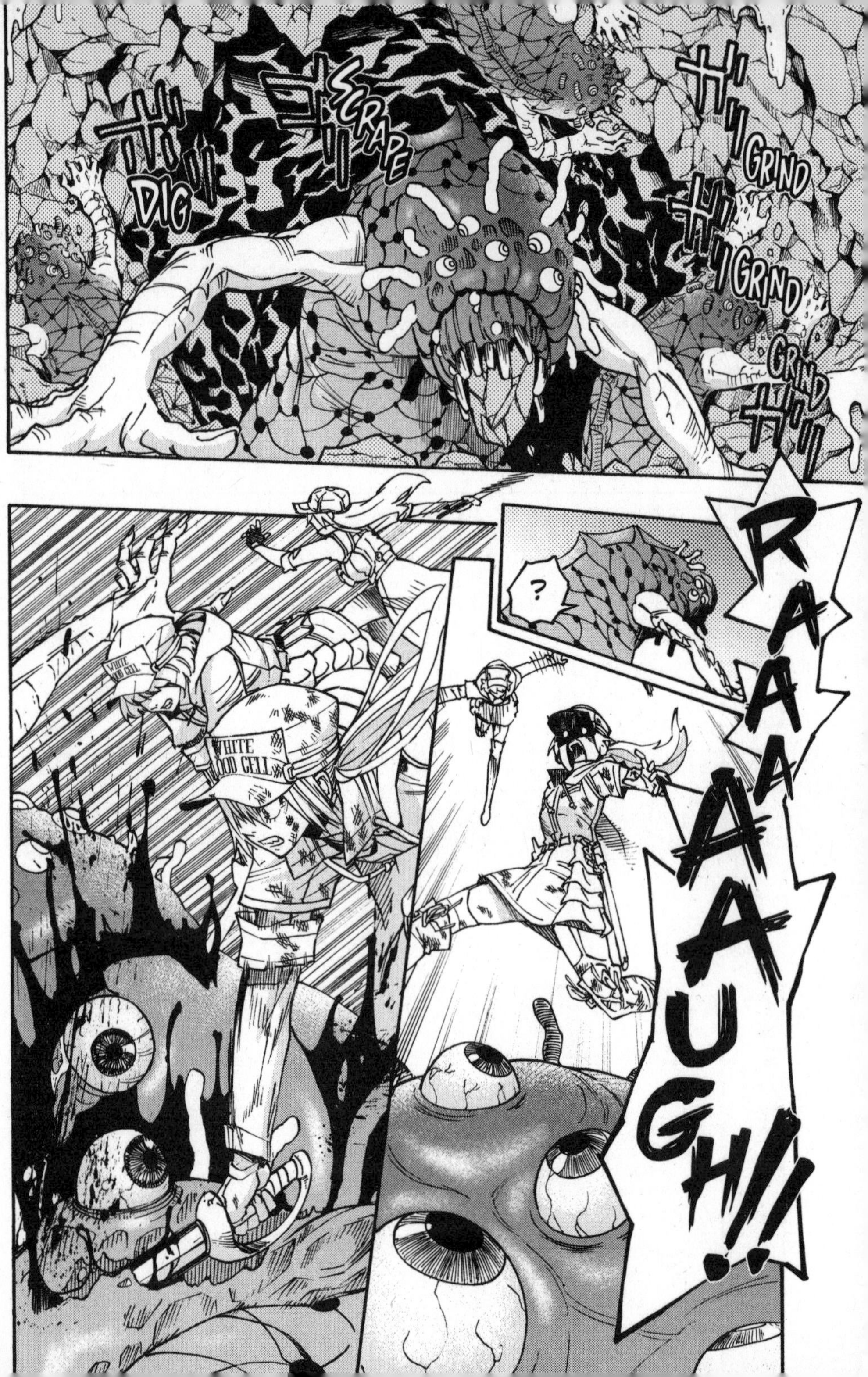
GRIND
GRIND
GRIND
SCRAPE
DIG
RAAAAAUGH!!
?

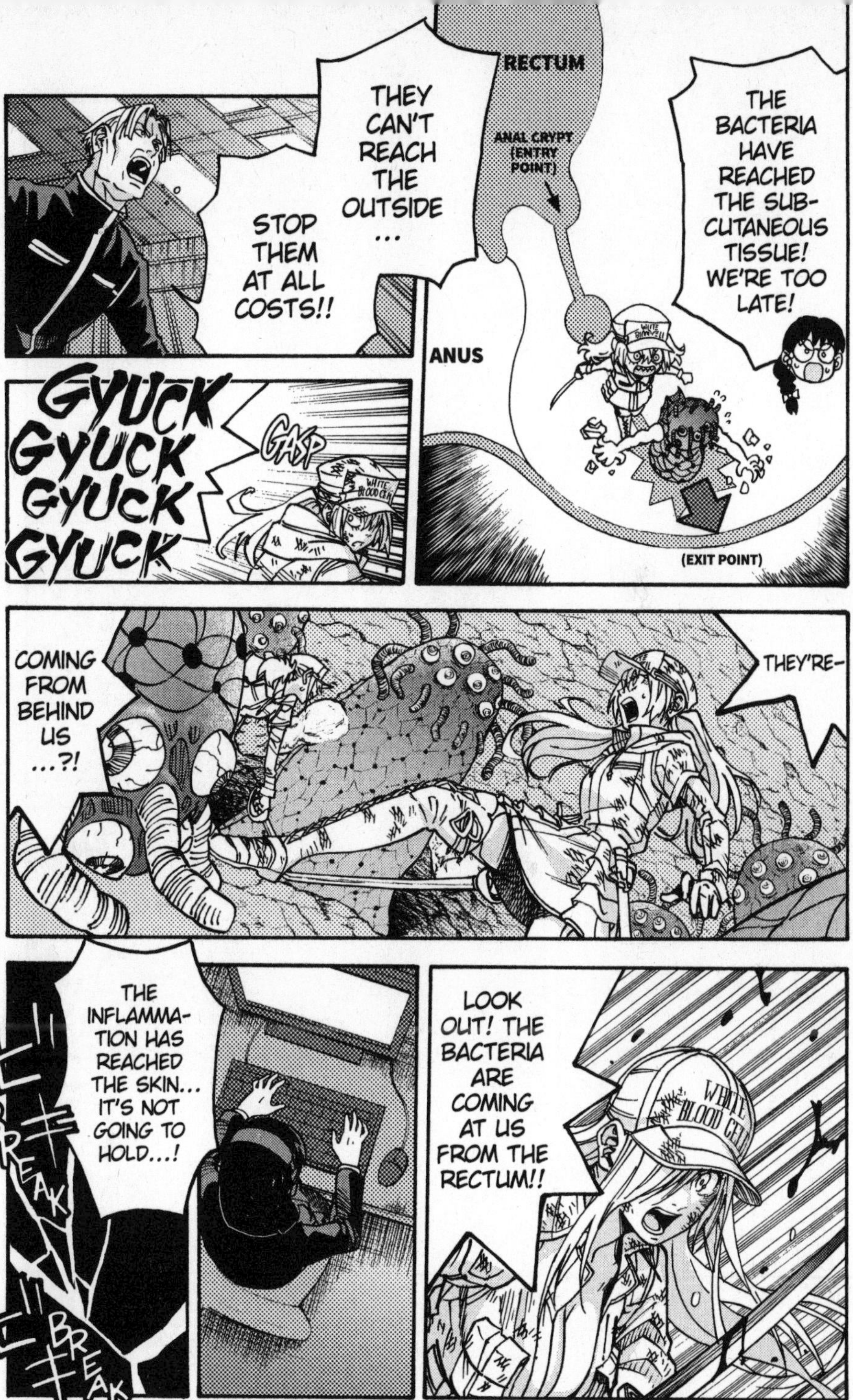
RECTUM
ANAL CRYPT (ENTRY POINT)
THE BACTERIA HAVE REACHED THE SUB-CUTANEOUS TISSUE! WE'RE TOO LATE!
ANUS
(EXIT POINT)
THEY CAN'T REACH THE OUTSIDE...
STOP THEM AT ALL COSTS!!
GASP
GYUCK GYUCK GYUCK GYUCK
THEY'RE-
COMING FROM BEHIND US...?!
LOOK OUT! THE BACTERIA ARE COMING AT US FROM THE RECTUM!!
THE INFLAMMATION HAS REACHED THE SKIN... IT'S NOT GOING TO HOLD...!
BREAK
BREAK

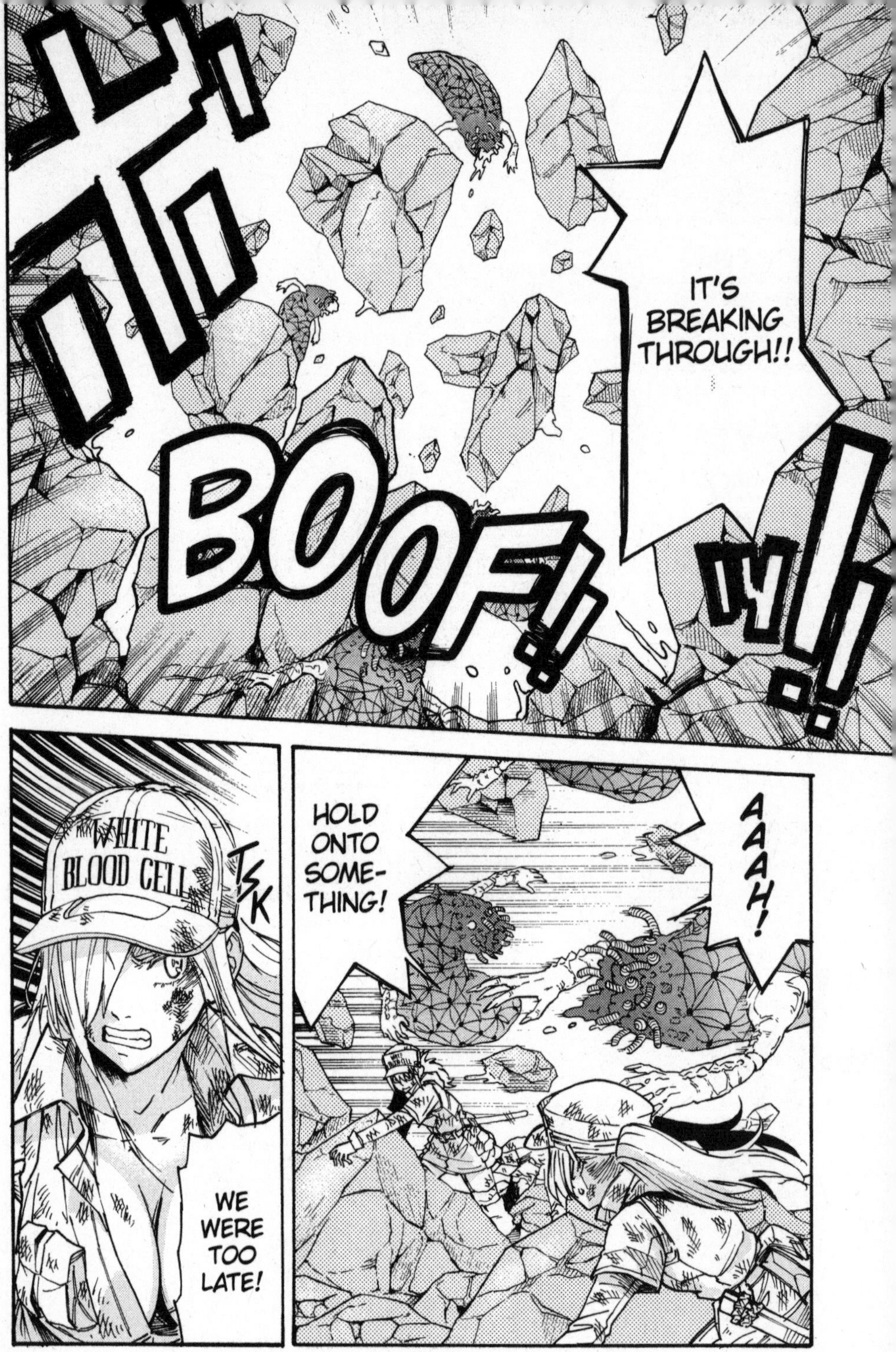
IT'S BREAKING THROUGH!!
BOOF!!
AAAAH!
HOLD ONTO SOME-THING!
WHITE BLOOD CELL
TSK
WE WERE TOO LATE!

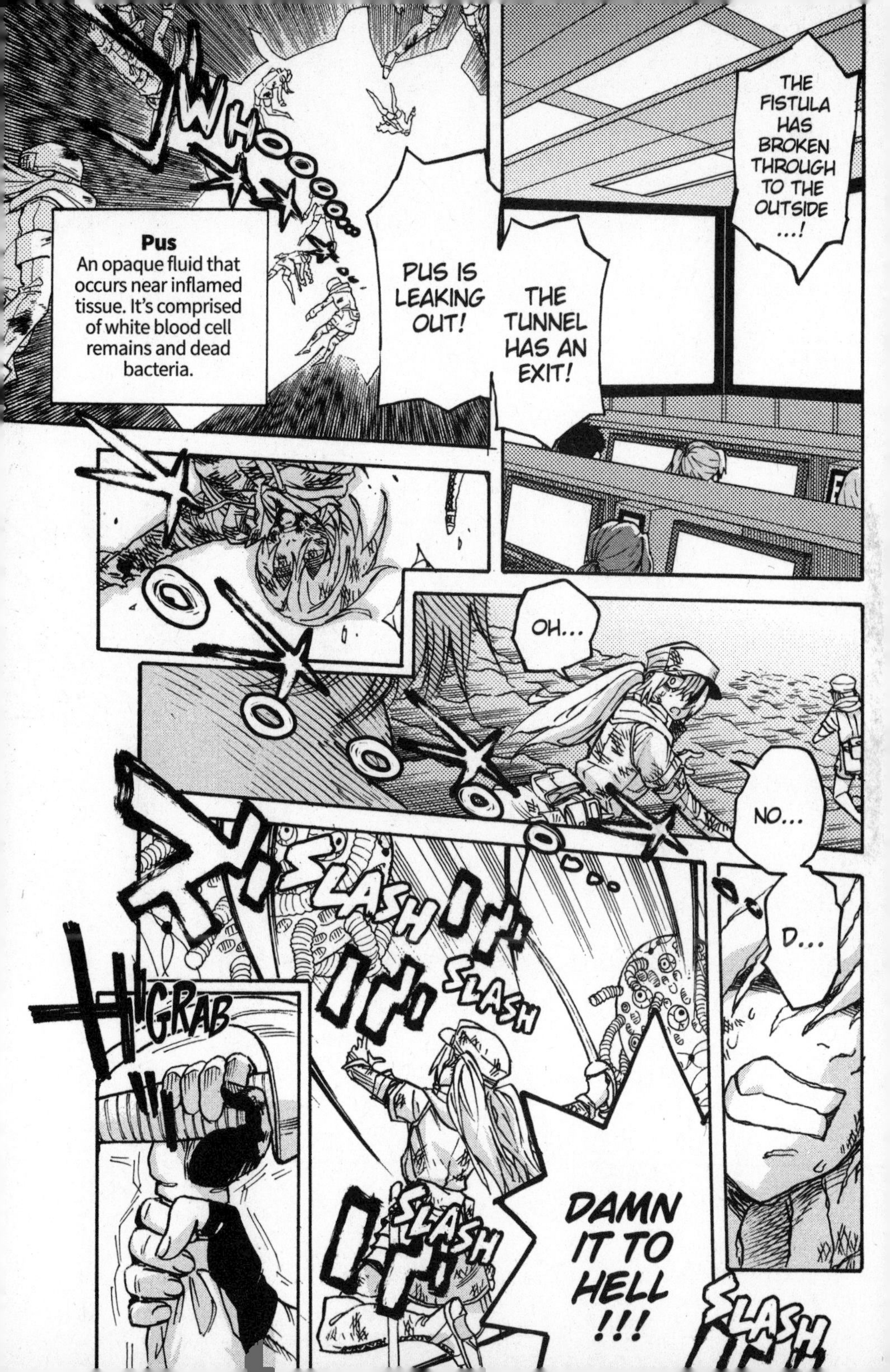
THE FISTULA HAS BROKEN THROUGH TO THE OUTSIDE...!
THE TUNNEL HAS AN EXIT!
PUS IS LEAKING OUT!
WHOOOOO...
Pus
An opaque fluid that occurs near inflamed tissue. It's comprised of white blood cell remains and dead bacteria.
OH...
NO...
D...
DAMN IT TO HELL!!!
SLASH
SLASH
SLASH
SLASH
GRAB

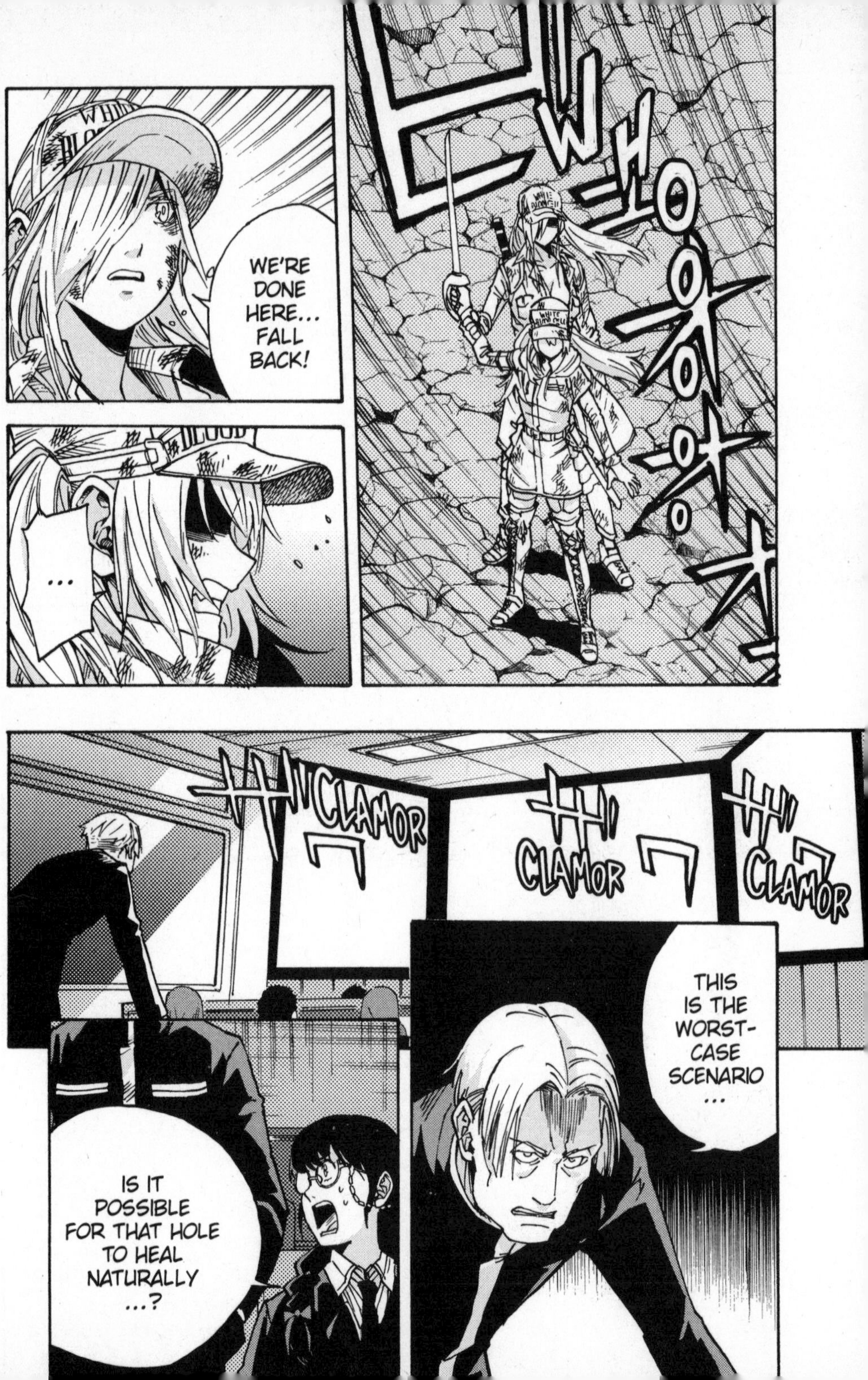
WHOOOOOOO
WE'RE DONE HERE... FALL BACK!
...
CLAMOR
CLAMOR
CLAMOR
THIS IS THE WORST-CASE SCENARIO...
IS IT POSSIBLE FOR THAT HOLE TO HEAL NATURALLY...?

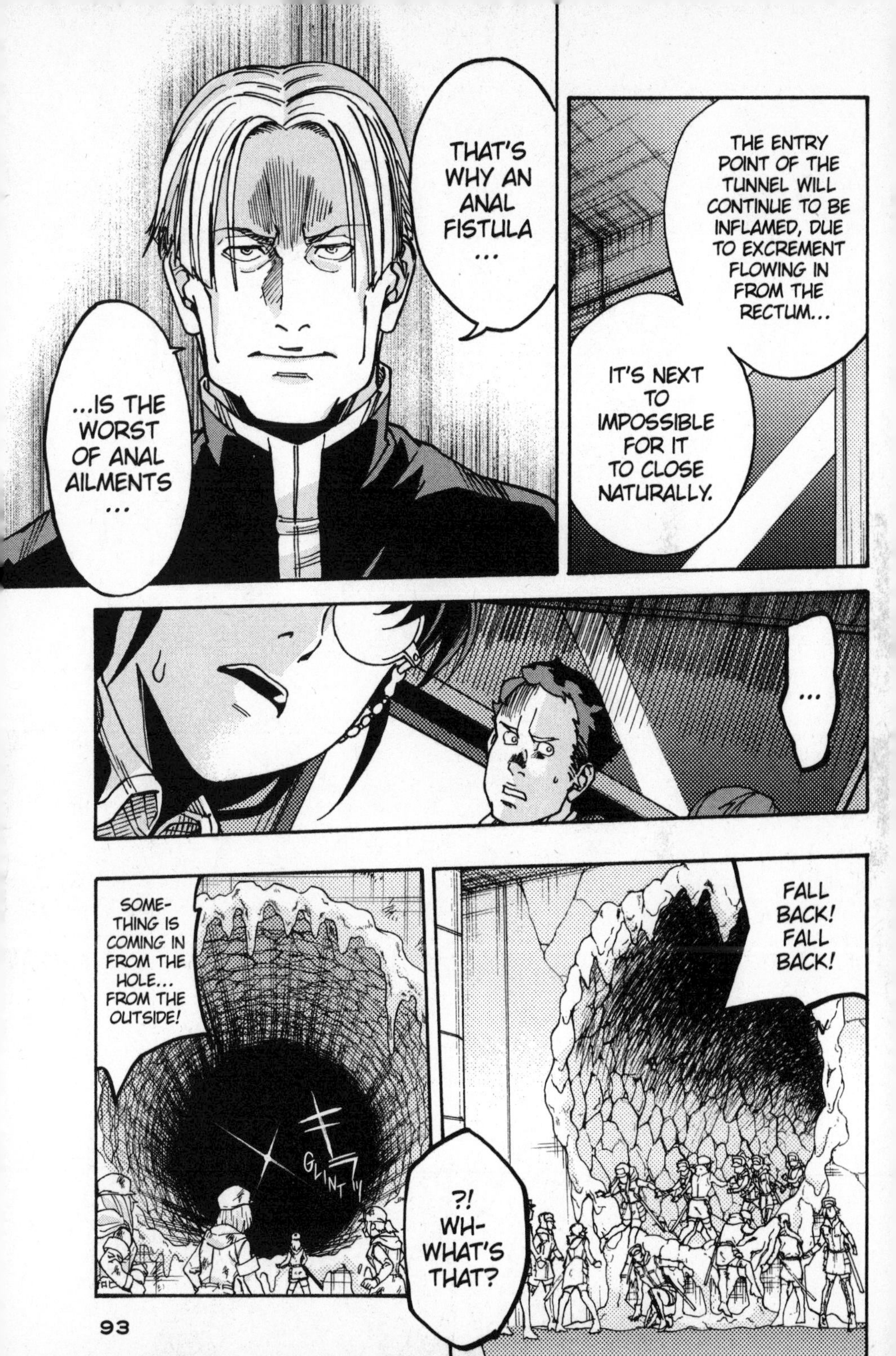
THE ENTRY POINT OF THE TUNNEL WILL CONTINUE TO BE INFLAMED, DUE TO EXCREMENT FLOWING IN FROM THE RECTUM...
IT'S NEXT TO IMPOSSIBLE FOR IT TO CLOSE NATURALLY.
THAT'S WHY AN ANAL FISTULA ...
...IS THE WORST OF ANAL AILMENTS ...
...
FALL BACK! FALL BACK!
?! WH- WHAT'S THAT?
SOME- THING IS COMING IN FROM THE HOLE... FROM THE OUTSIDE!
GLINT

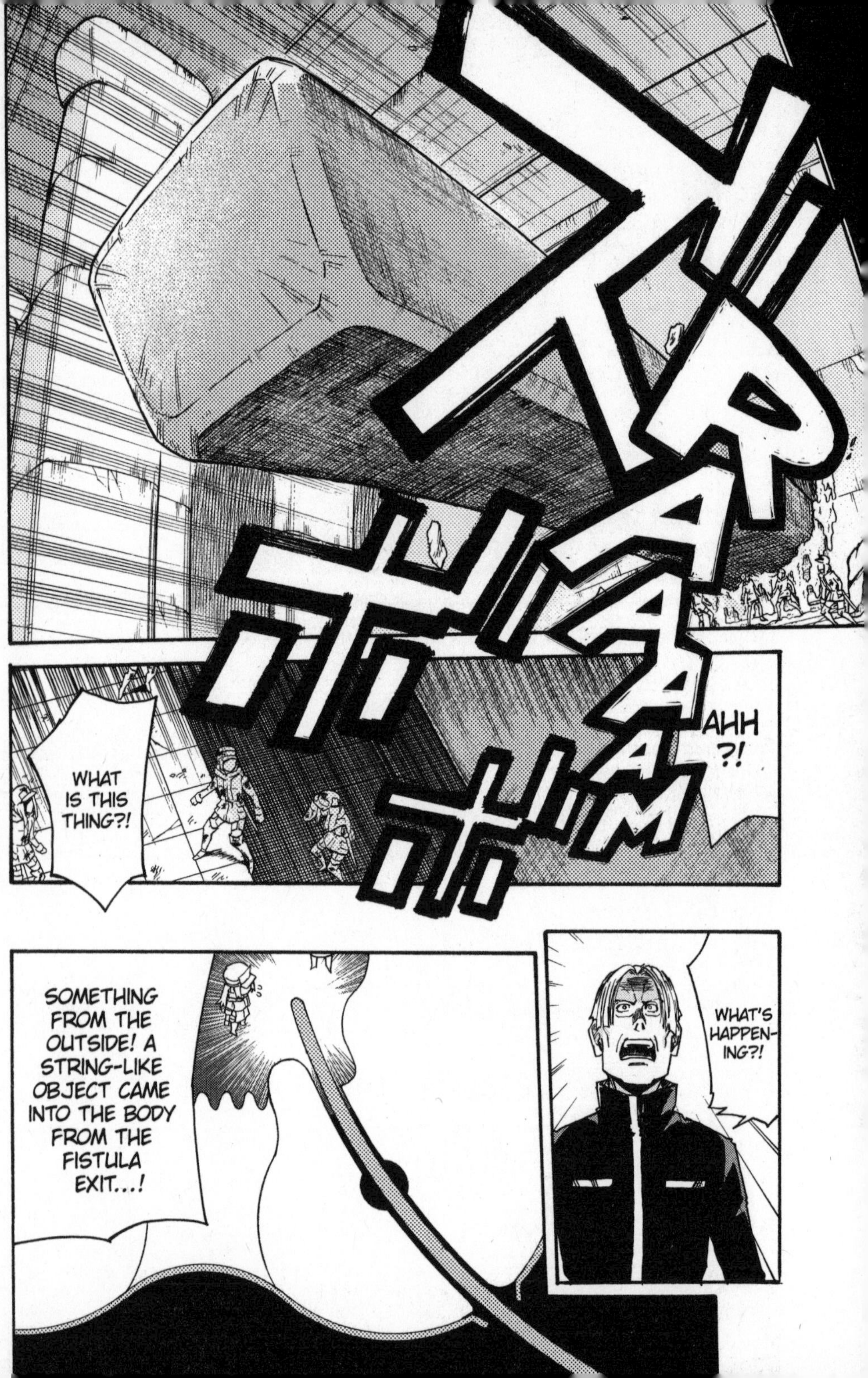
VRAAAM
AHH ?!
WHAT IS THIS THING?!
WHAT'S HAPPENING?!
SOMETHING FROM THE OUTSIDE! A STRING-LIKE OBJECT CAME INTO THE BODY FROM THE FISTULA EXIT...!

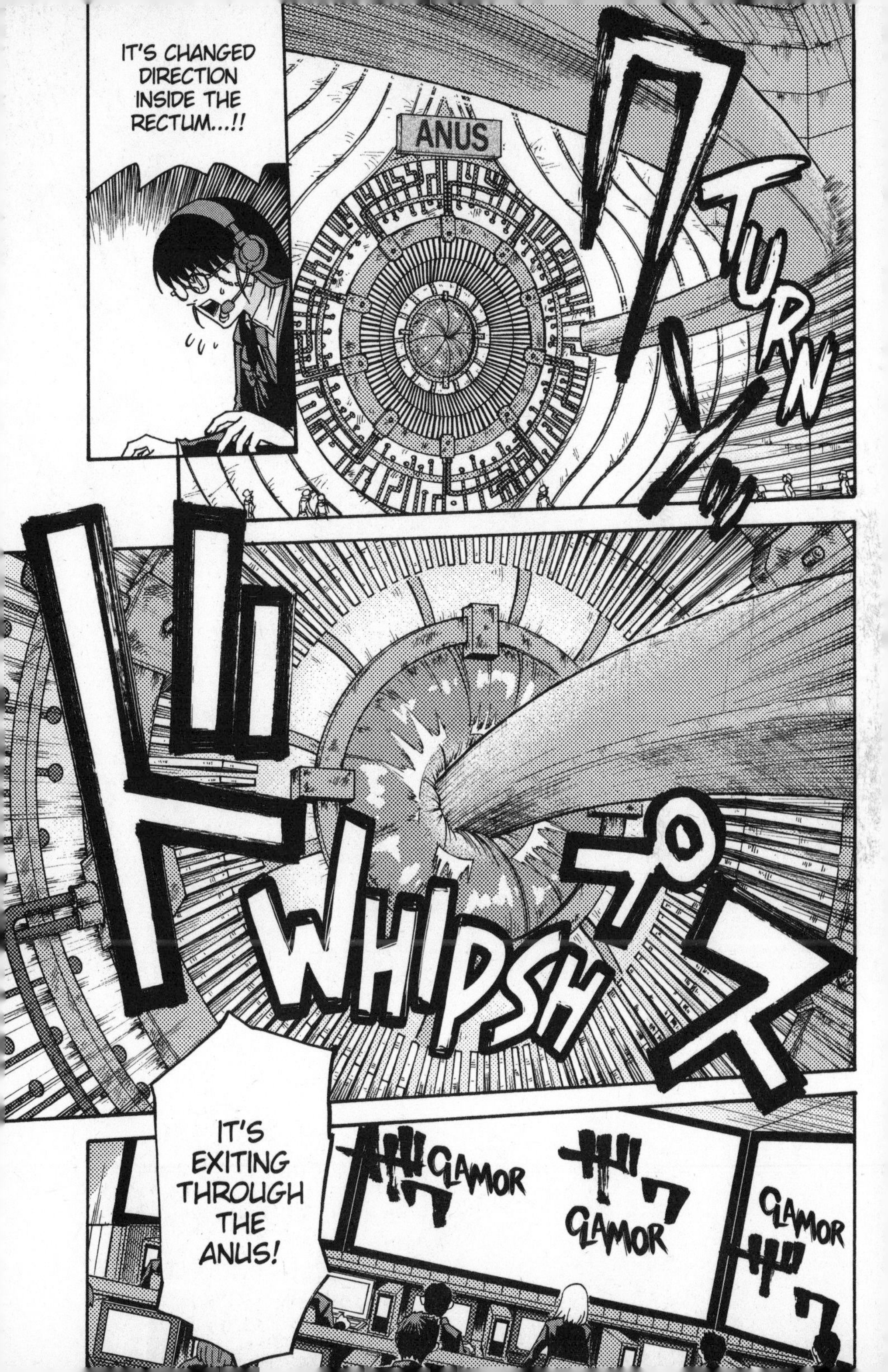
ANUS
TURN
IT'S CHANGED DIRECTION INSIDE THE RECTUM...!!
WHIPSH
GLAMOR
GLAMOR
GLAMOR
IT'S EXITING THROUGH THE ANUS!

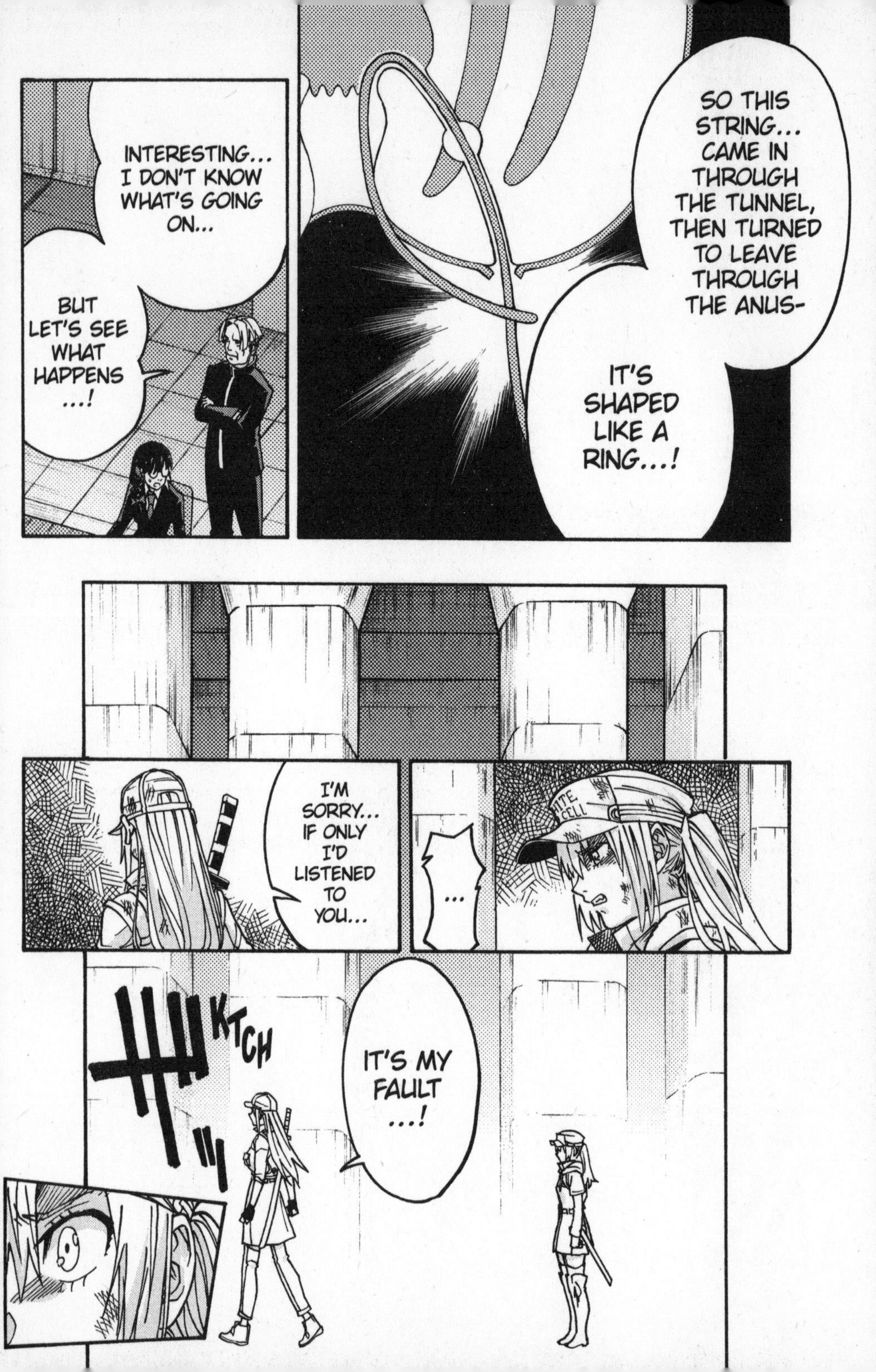
SO THIS STRING... CAME IN THROUGH THE TUNNEL, THEN TURNED TO LEAVE THROUGH THE ANUS-
IT'S SHAPED LIKE A RING...!
INTERESTING... I DON'T KNOW WHAT'S GOING ON...
BUT LET'S SEE WHAT HAPPENS ...!
...
I'M SORRY... IF ONLY I'D LISTENED TO YOU...
IT'S MY FAULT ...!
KTCH

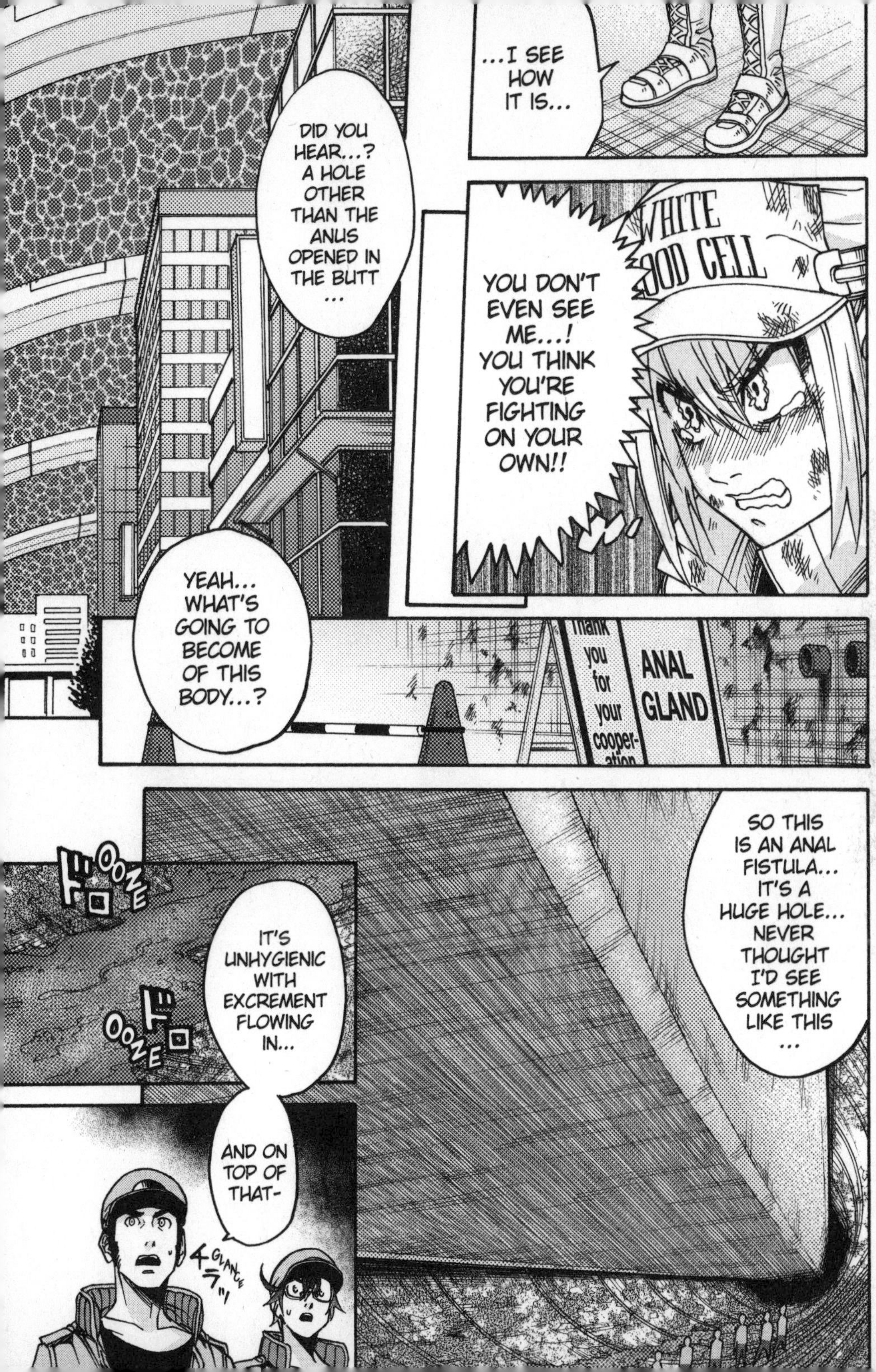
...I SEE HOW IT IS...
WHITE
YOU DON'T EVEN SEE ME...! YOU THINK YOU'RE FIGHTING ON YOUR OWN!!
DID YOU HEAR...? A HOLE OTHER THAN THE ANUS OPENED IN THE BUTT...
YEAH... WHAT'S GOING TO BECOME OF THIS BODY...?
Thank you for your cooper-ation
ANAL GLAND
SO THIS IS AN ANAL FISTULA... IT'S A HUGE HOLE... NEVER THOUGHT I'D SEE SOMETHING LIKE THIS...
OOZE
OOZE
IT'S UNHYGIENIC WITH EXCREMENT FLOWING IN...
AND ON TOP OF THAT-
GLANCE

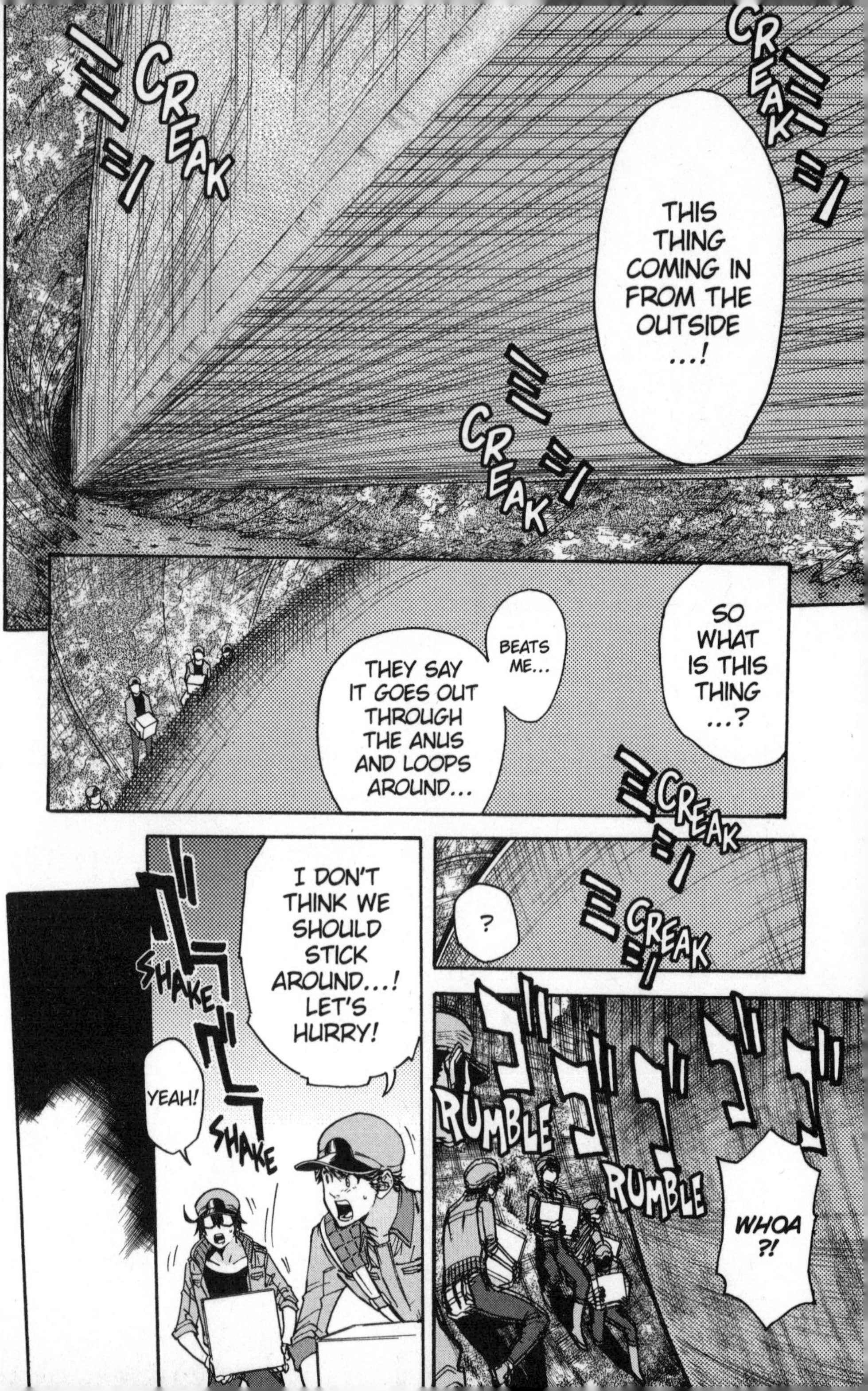
CREAK
THIS THING COMING IN FROM THE OUTSIDE ...!
CREAK
CREAK
SO WHAT IS THIS THING ...?
BEATS ME...
THEY SAY IT GOES OUT THROUGH THE ANUS AND LOOPS AROUND...
CREAK
?
CREAK
RUMBLE
RUMBLE
WHOA ?!
I DON'T THINK WE SHOULD STICK AROUND...! LET'S HURRY!
SHAKE
YEAH!
SHAKE

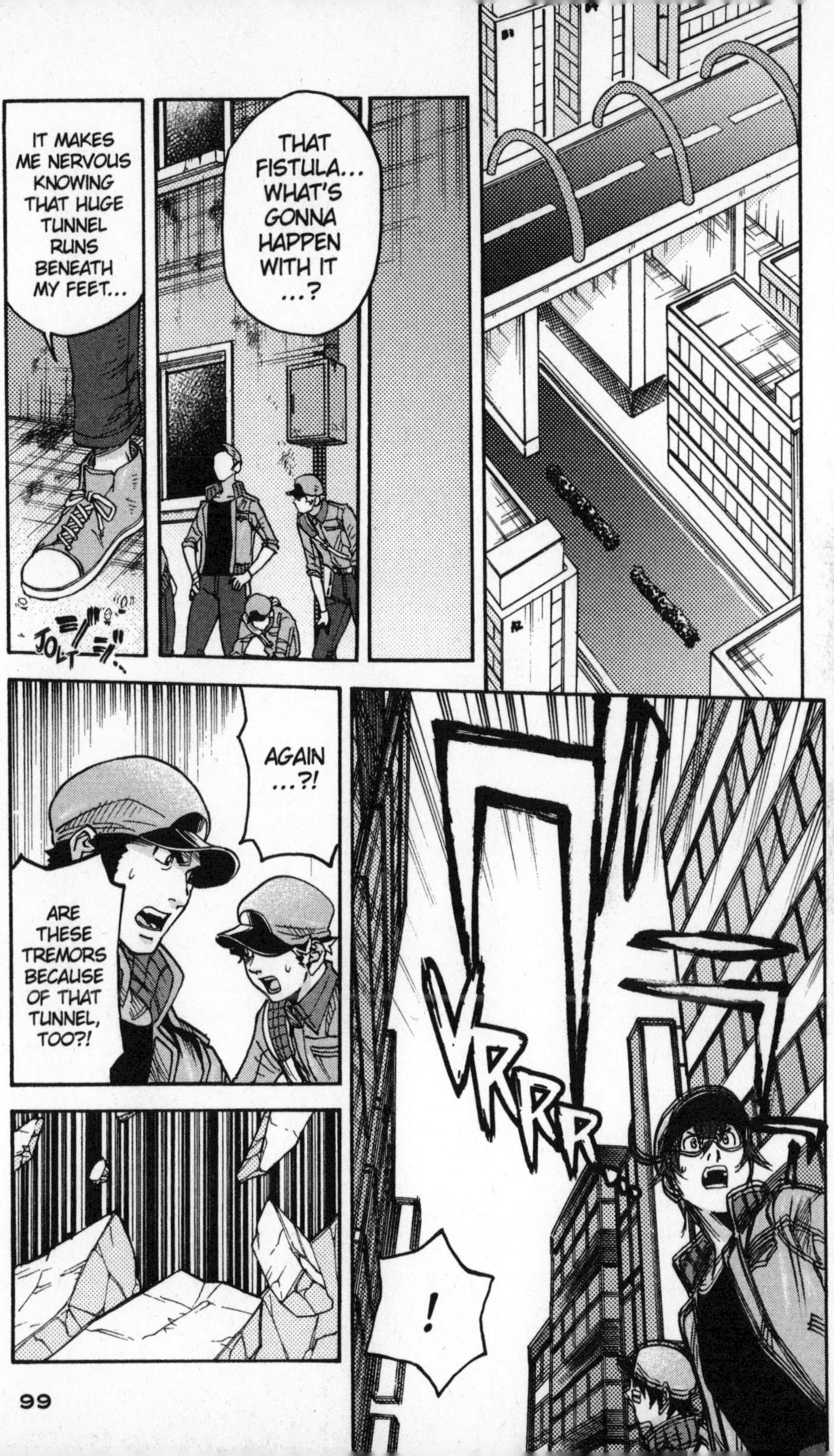
THAT FISTULA... WHAT'S GONNA HAPPEN WITH IT ...?
IT MAKES ME NERVOUS KNOWING THAT HUGE TUNNEL RUNS BENEATH MY FEET...
JOLT
VRRR
!
AGAIN ...?!
ARE THESE TREMORS BECAUSE OF THAT TUNNEL, TOO?!

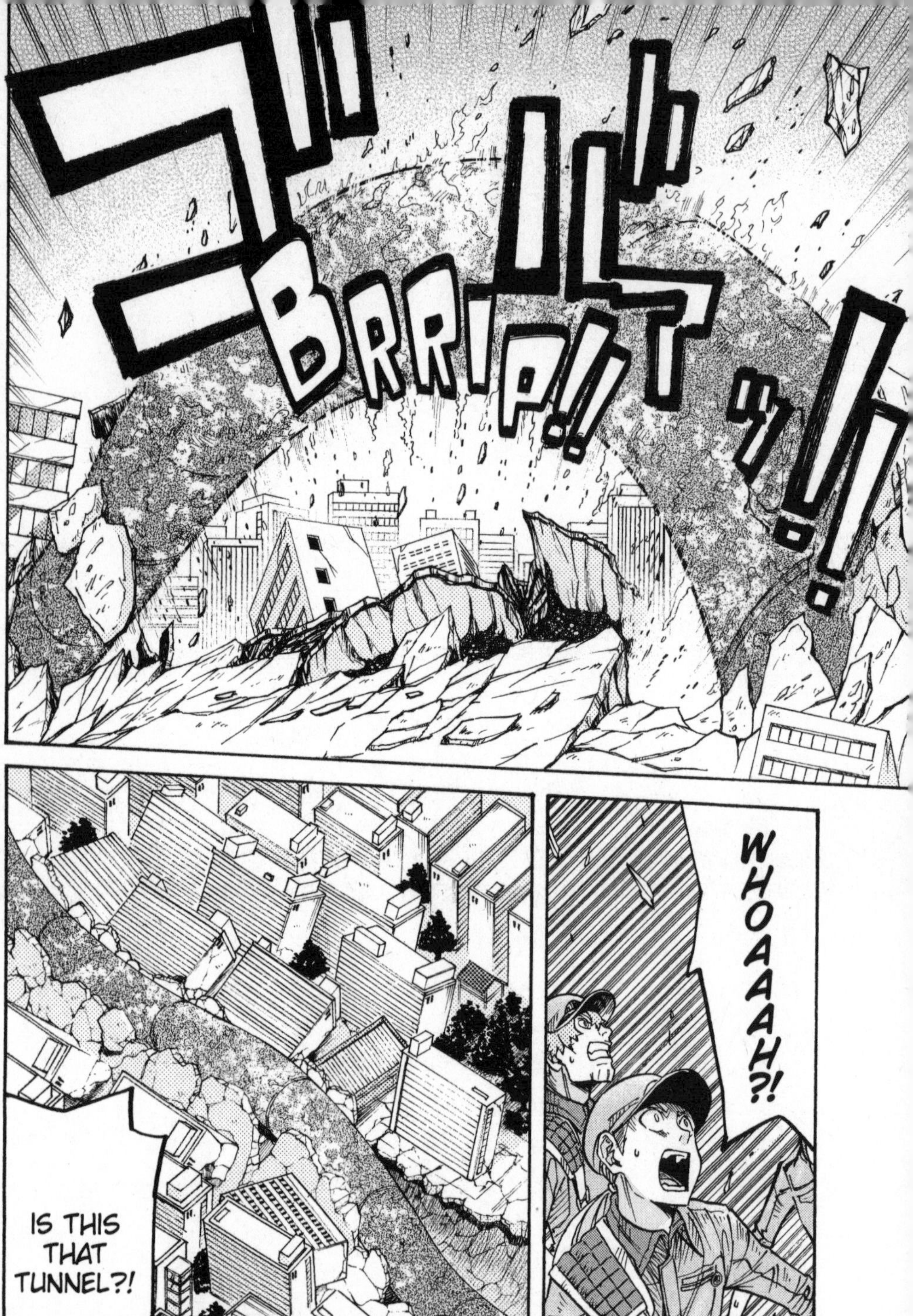
BRRIP!!
WHOAAAAH?!
IS THIS THAT TUNNEL?!

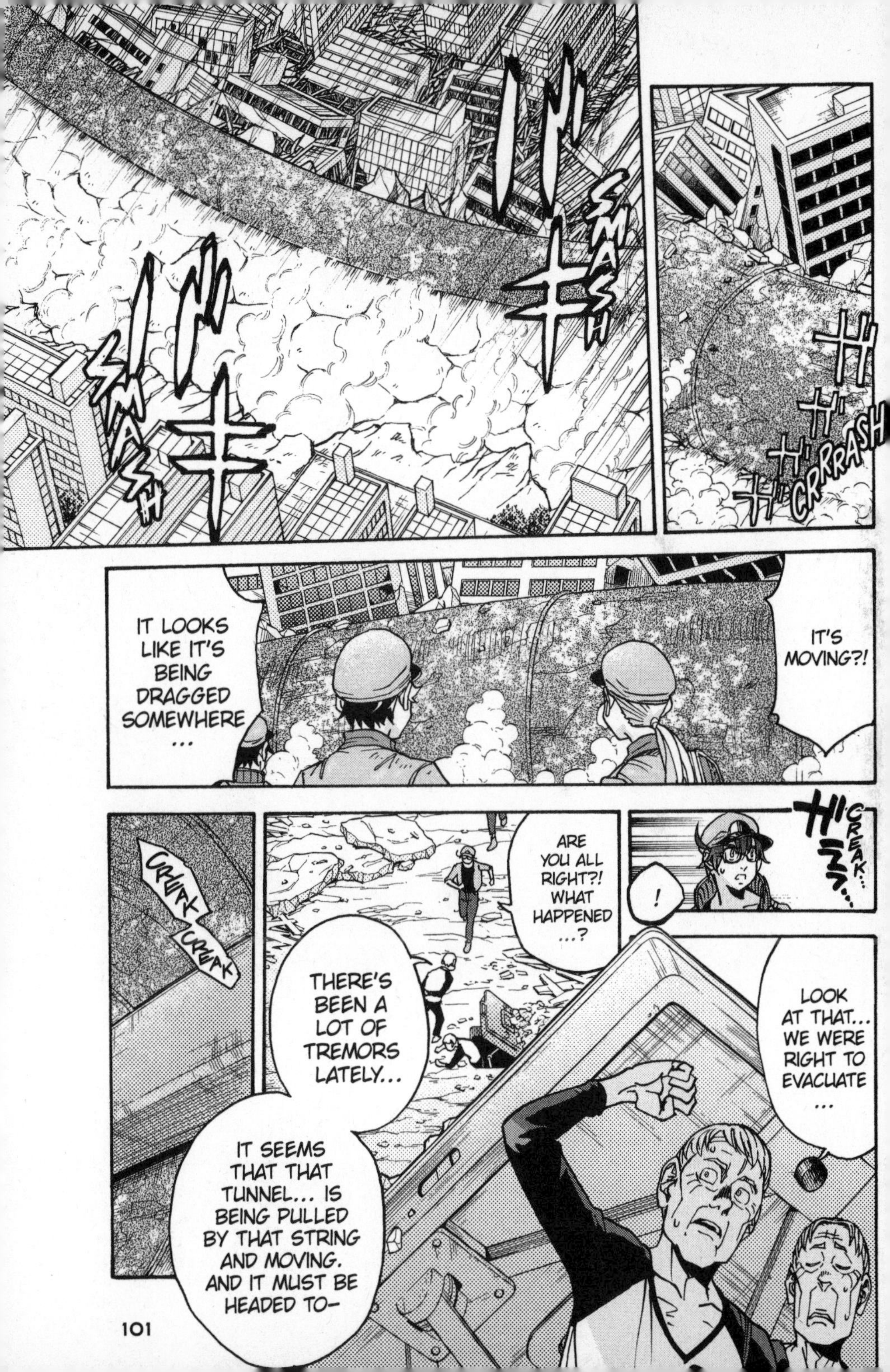
CRRRASH
SMASH
SMASH
IT'S MOVING?!
IT LOOKS LIKE IT'S BEING DRAGGED SOMEWHERE...
CREAK...
!
ARE YOU ALL RIGHT?! WHAT HAPPENED...?
CREAK CREAK
LOOK AT THAT... WE WERE RIGHT TO EVACUATE...
THERE'S BEEN A LOT OF TREMORS LATELY...
IT SEEMS THAT THAT TUNNEL... IS BEING PULLED BY THAT STRING AND MOVING. AND IT MUST BE HEADED TO-

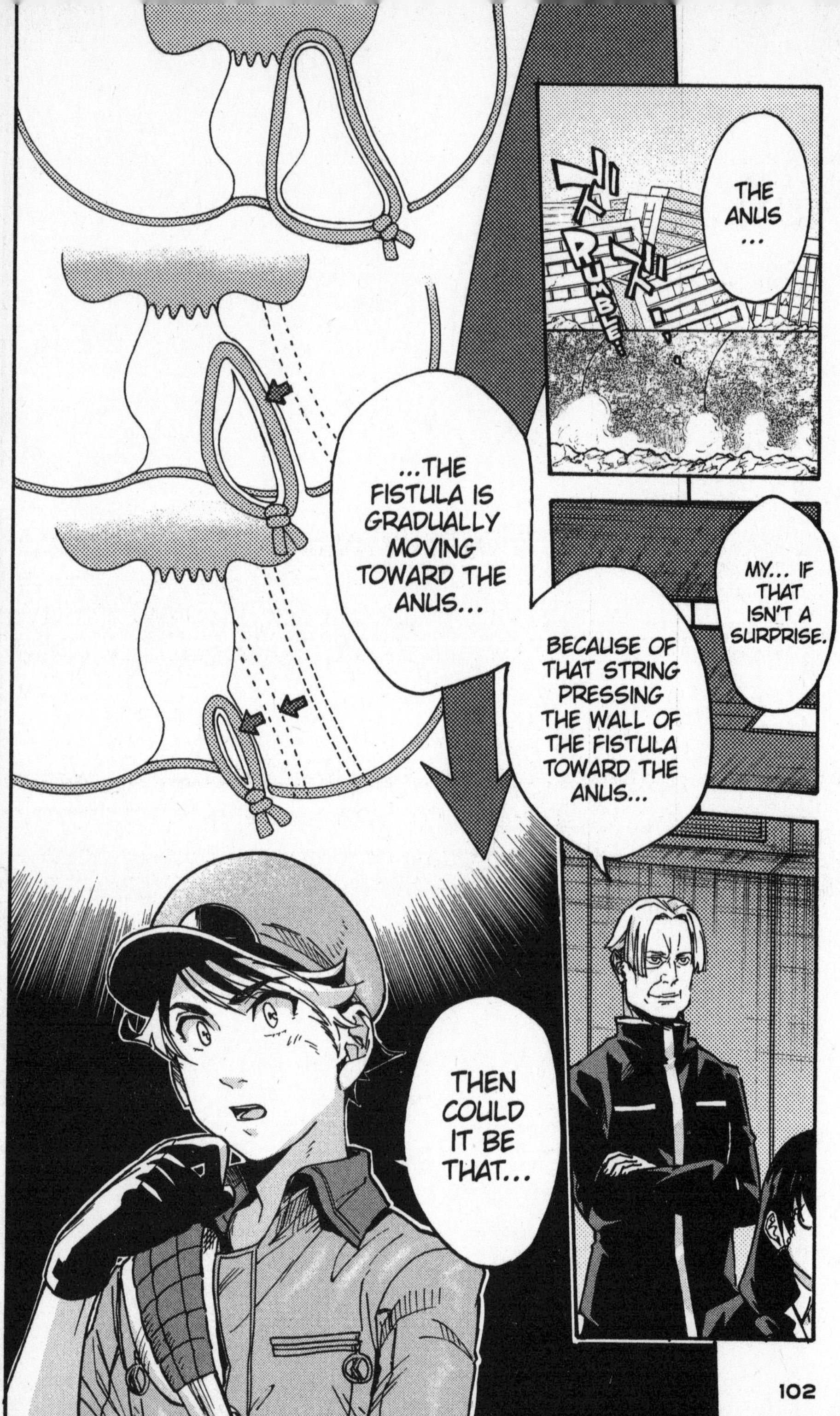
THE ANUS ...
RUMBLE
...THE FISTULA IS GRADUALLY MOVING TOWARD THE ANUS...
BECAUSE OF THAT STRING PRESSING THE WALL OF THE FISTULA TOWARD THE ANUS...
MY... IF THAT ISN'T A SURPRISE.
THEN COULD IT BE THAT...

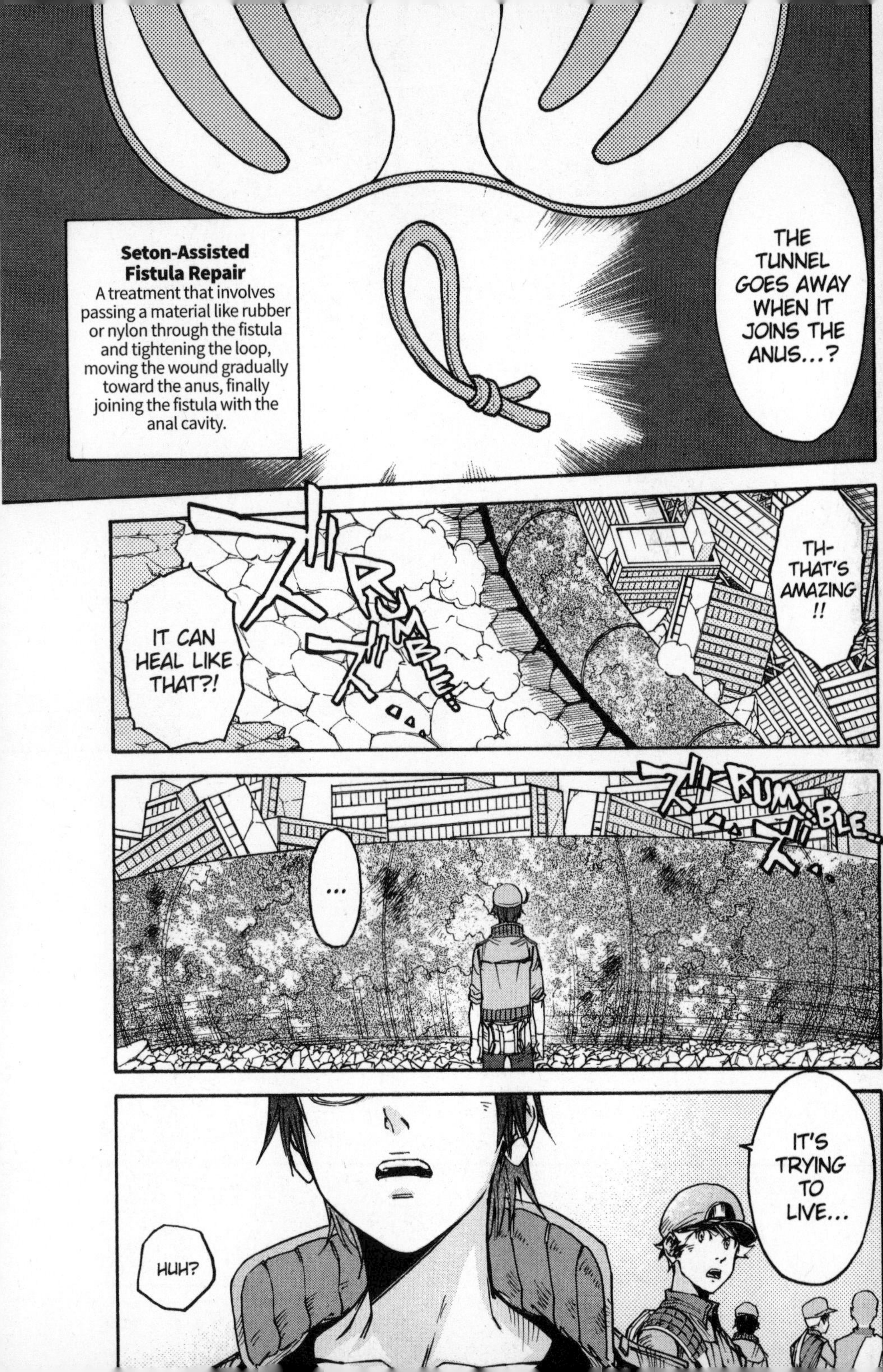
THE TUNNEL GOES AWAY WHEN IT JOINS THE ANUS...?
Seton-Assisted Fistula Repair
A treatment that involves passing a material like rubber or nylon through the fistula and tightening the loop, moving the wound gradually toward the anus, finally joining the fistula with the anal cavity.
RUMBLE...
TH-THAT'S AMAZING!!
IT CAN HEAL LIKE THAT?!
RUMBLE...
...
IT'S TRYING TO LIVE...
HUH?

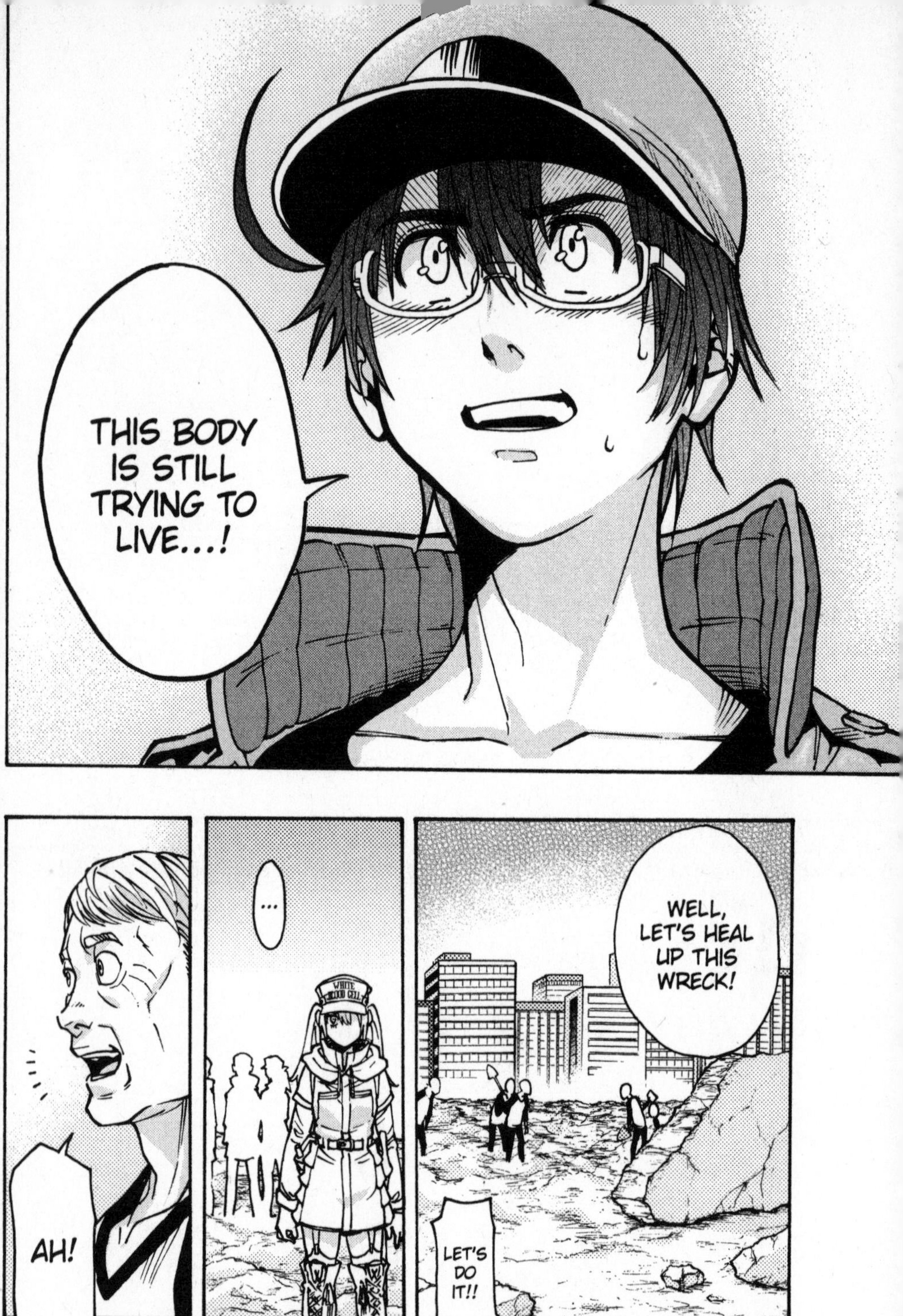
THIS BODY IS STILL TRYING TO LIVE...!
WELL, LET'S HEAL UP THIS WRECK!
LET'S DO IT!!
...
AH!

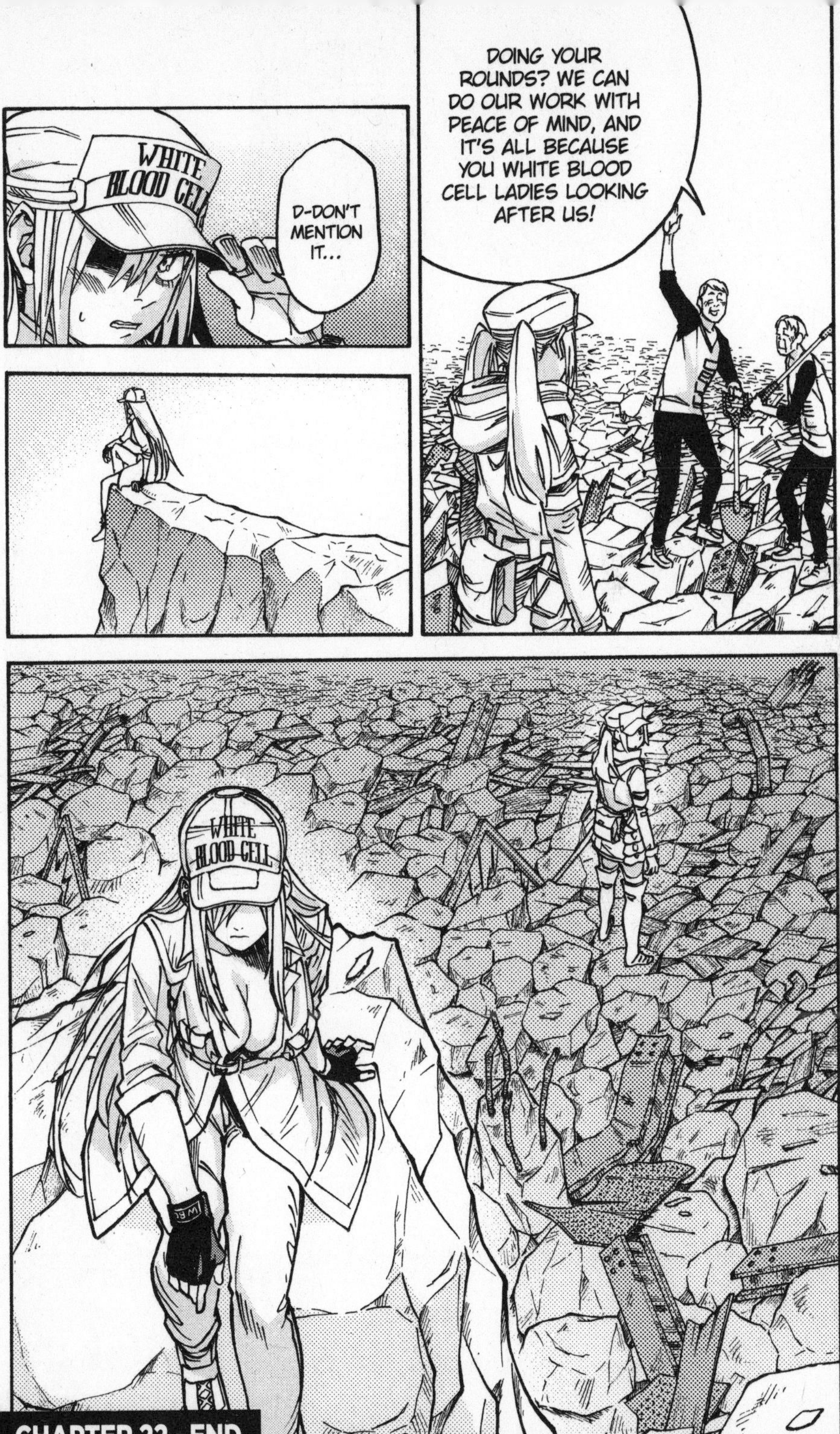
DOING YOUR ROUNDS? WE CAN DO OUR WORK WITH PEACE OF MIND, AND IT'S ALL BECAUSE YOU WHITE BLOOD CELL LADIES LOOKING AFTER US!
WHITE BLOOD CELL
D-DON'T MENTION IT...
WHITE BLOOD CELL

CHAPTER 22 - END

Cells at Work!
はたらく細胞
CODE BLACK

23. SHINGLES, DUTY, AND TEAMMATES

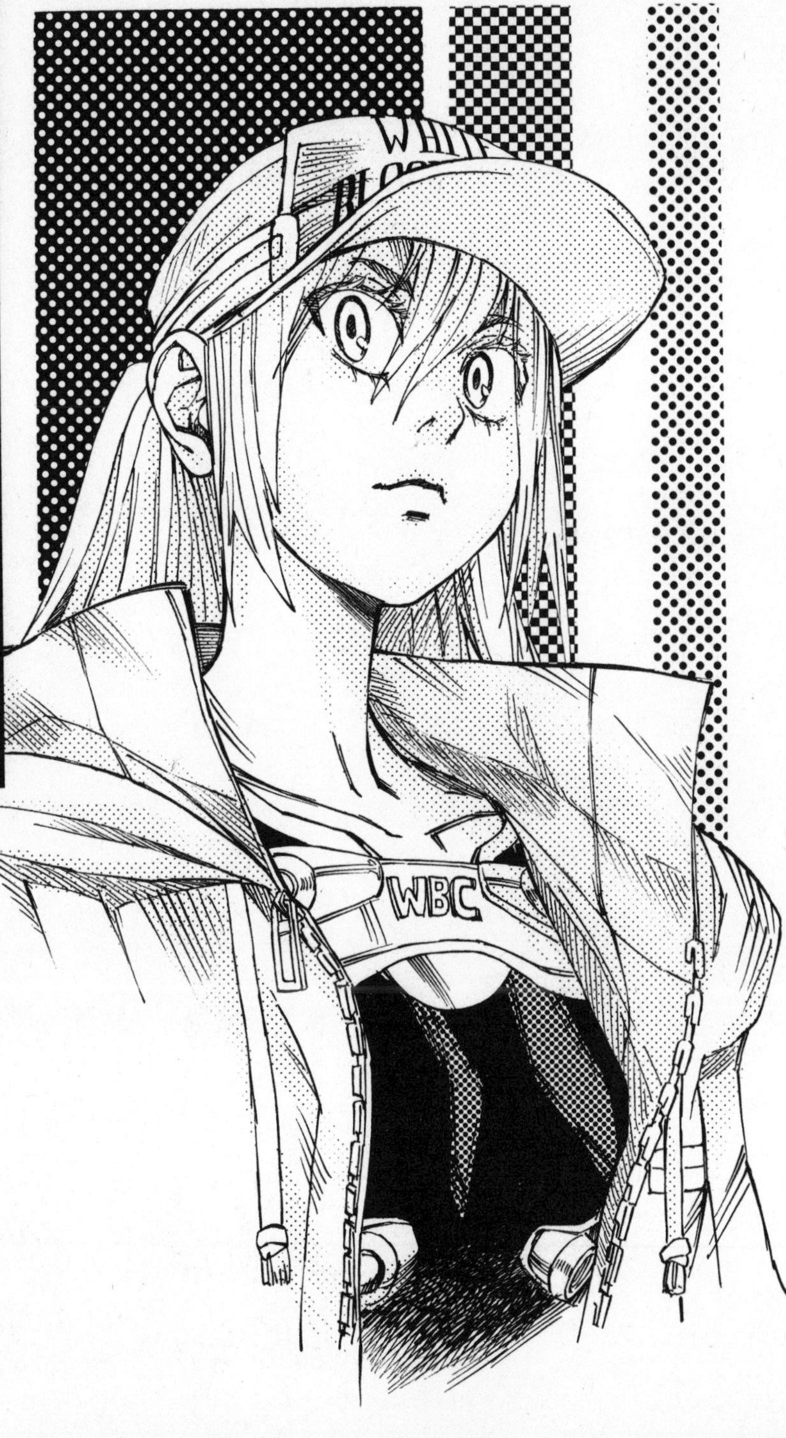
WBC

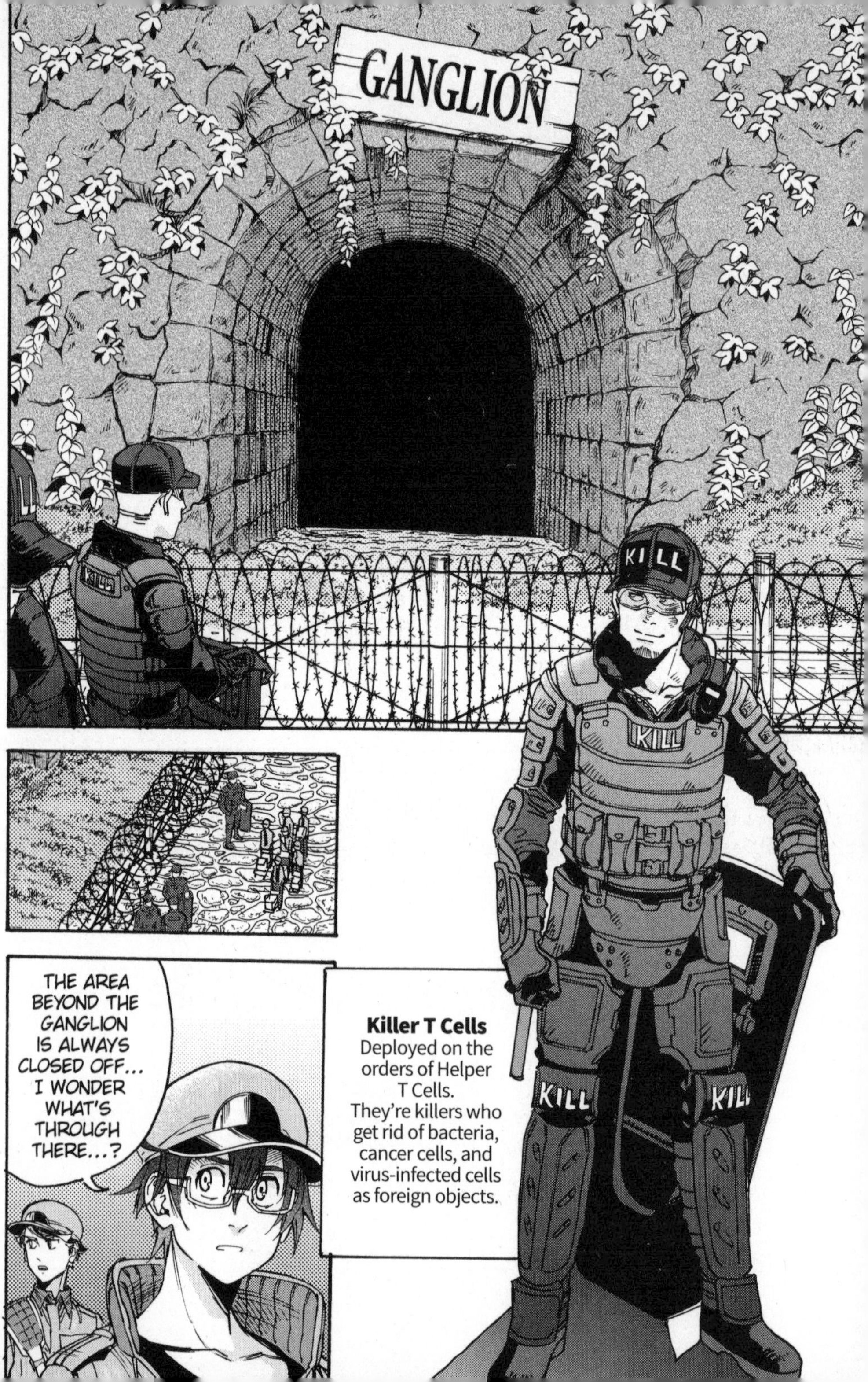
GANGLION
Killer T Cells
Deployed on the orders of Helper T Cells.
They're killers who get rid of bacteria, cancer cells, and virus-infected cells as foreign objects.
THE AREA BEYOND THE GANGLION IS ALWAYS CLOSED OFF... I WONDER WHAT'S THROUGH THERE...?

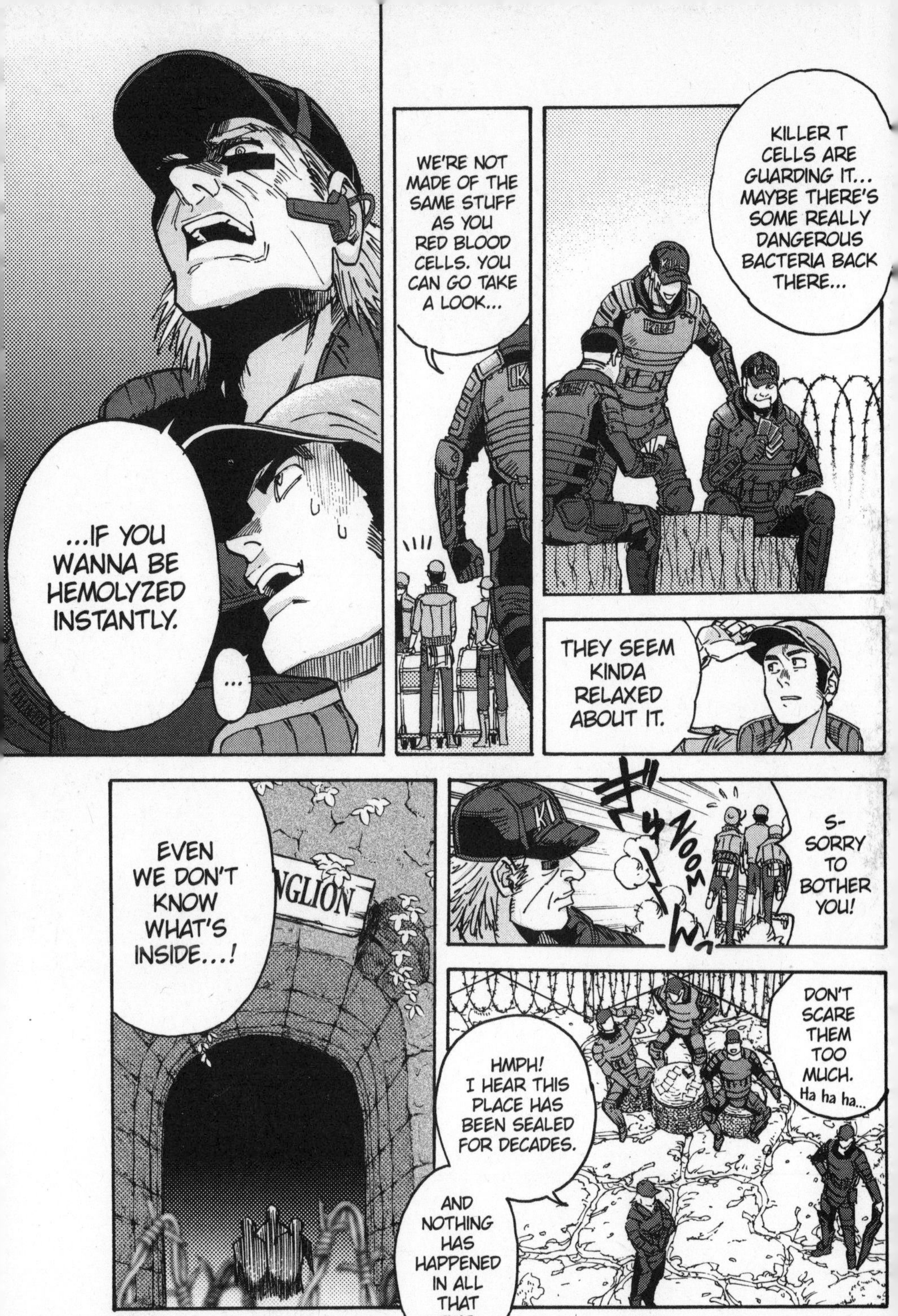
KILLER T CELLS ARE GUARDING IT... MAYBE THERE'S SOME REALLY DANGEROUS BACTERIA BACK THERE...
THEY SEEM KINDA RELAXED ABOUT IT.
WE'RE NOT MADE OF THE SAME STUFF AS YOU RED BLOOD CELLS. YOU CAN GO TAKE A LOOK...
...IF YOU WANNA BE HEMOLYZED INSTANTLY.
...
S-SORRY TO BOTHER YOU!
NOOM
DON'T SCARE THEM TOO MUCH. Ha ha ha...
HMPH! I HEAR THIS PLACE HAS BEEN SEALED FOR DECADES.
AND NOTHING HAS HAPPENED IN ALL THAT TIME.
EVEN WE DON'T KNOW WHAT'S INSIDE...!
NGLION

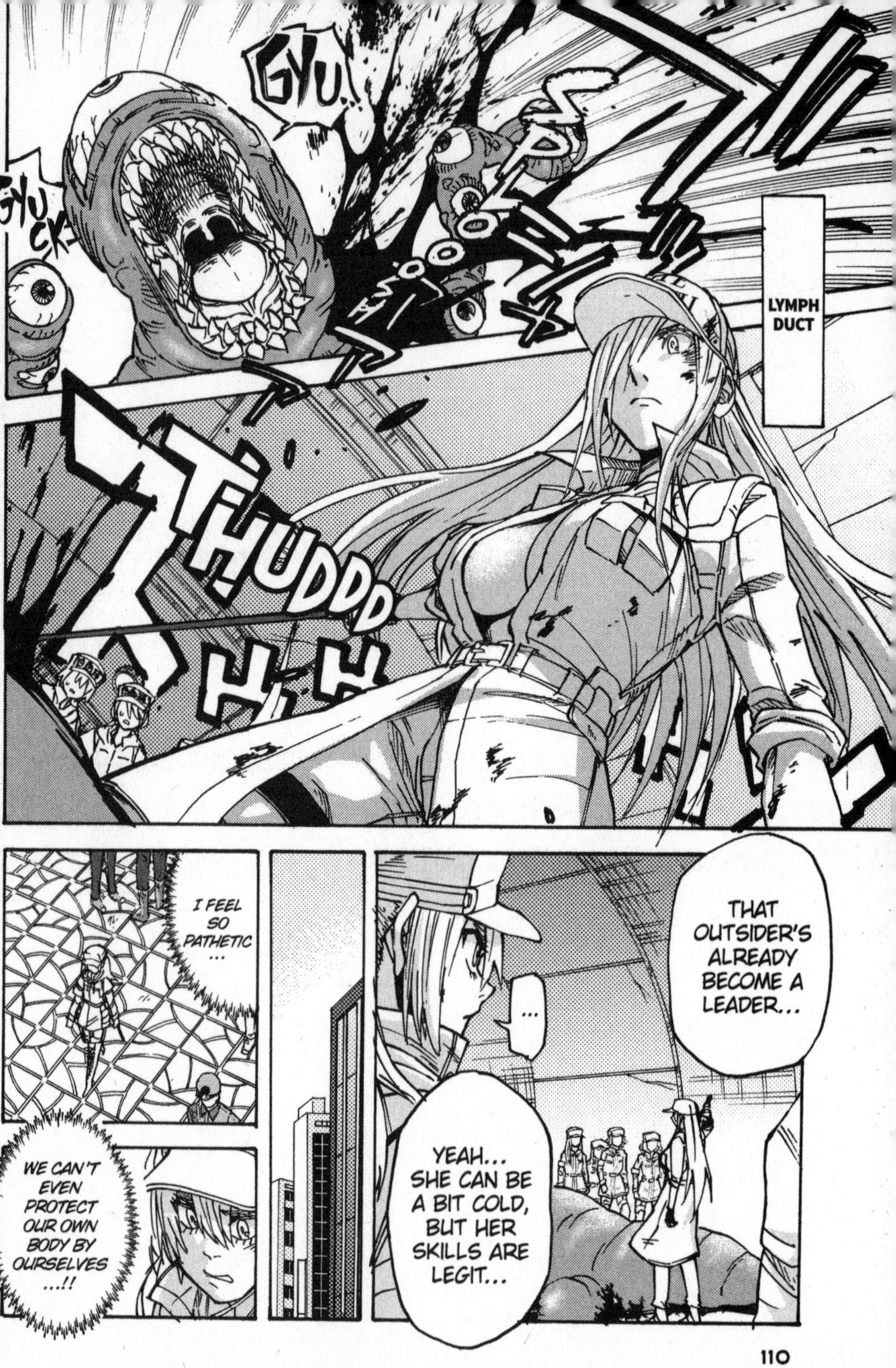
LYMPH DUCT
GYU
GYUCK
THUDDD
THAT OUTSIDER'S ALREADY BECOME A LEADER...
...
YEAH... SHE CAN BE A BIT COLD, BUT HER SKILLS ARE LEGIT...
I FEEL SO PATHETIC ...
WE CAN'T EVEN PROTECT OUR OWN BODY BY OURSELVES ...!!

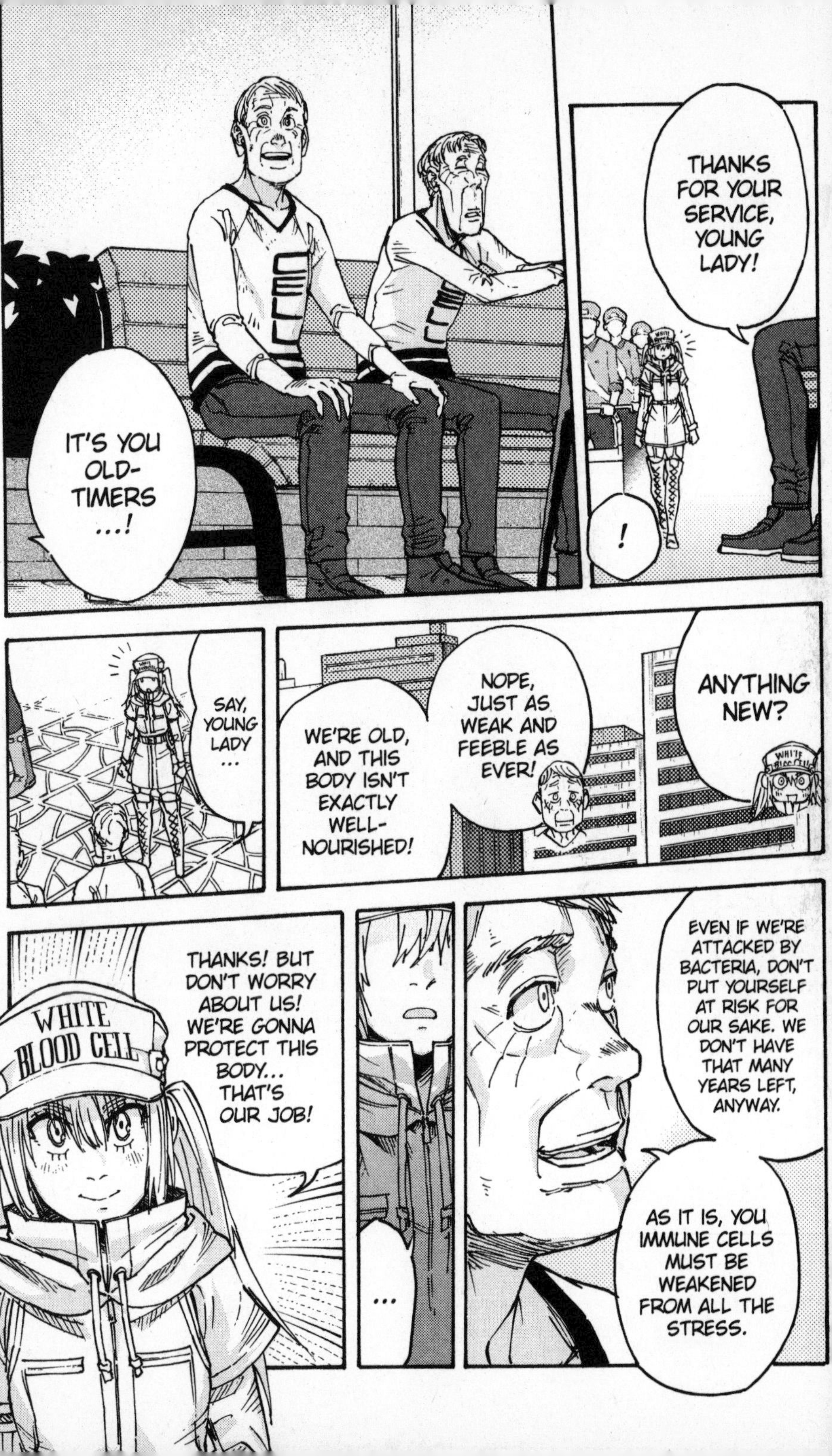
THANKS FOR YOUR SERVICE, YOUNG LADY!
!
IT'S YOU OLD-TIMERS ...!
ANYTHING NEW?
NOPE, JUST AS WEAK AND FEEBLE AS EVER!
WE'RE OLD, AND THIS BODY ISN'T EXACTLY WELL-NOURISHED!
SAY, YOUNG LADY ...
EVEN IF WE'RE ATTACKED BY BACTERIA, DON'T PUT YOURSELF AT RISK FOR OUR SAKE. WE DON'T HAVE THAT MANY YEARS LEFT, ANYWAY.
AS IT IS, YOU IMMUNE CELLS MUST BE WEAKENED FROM ALL THE STRESS.
...
THANKS! BUT DON'T WORRY ABOUT US! WE'RE GONNA PROTECT THIS BODY... THAT'S OUR JOB!
WHITE BLOOD CELL

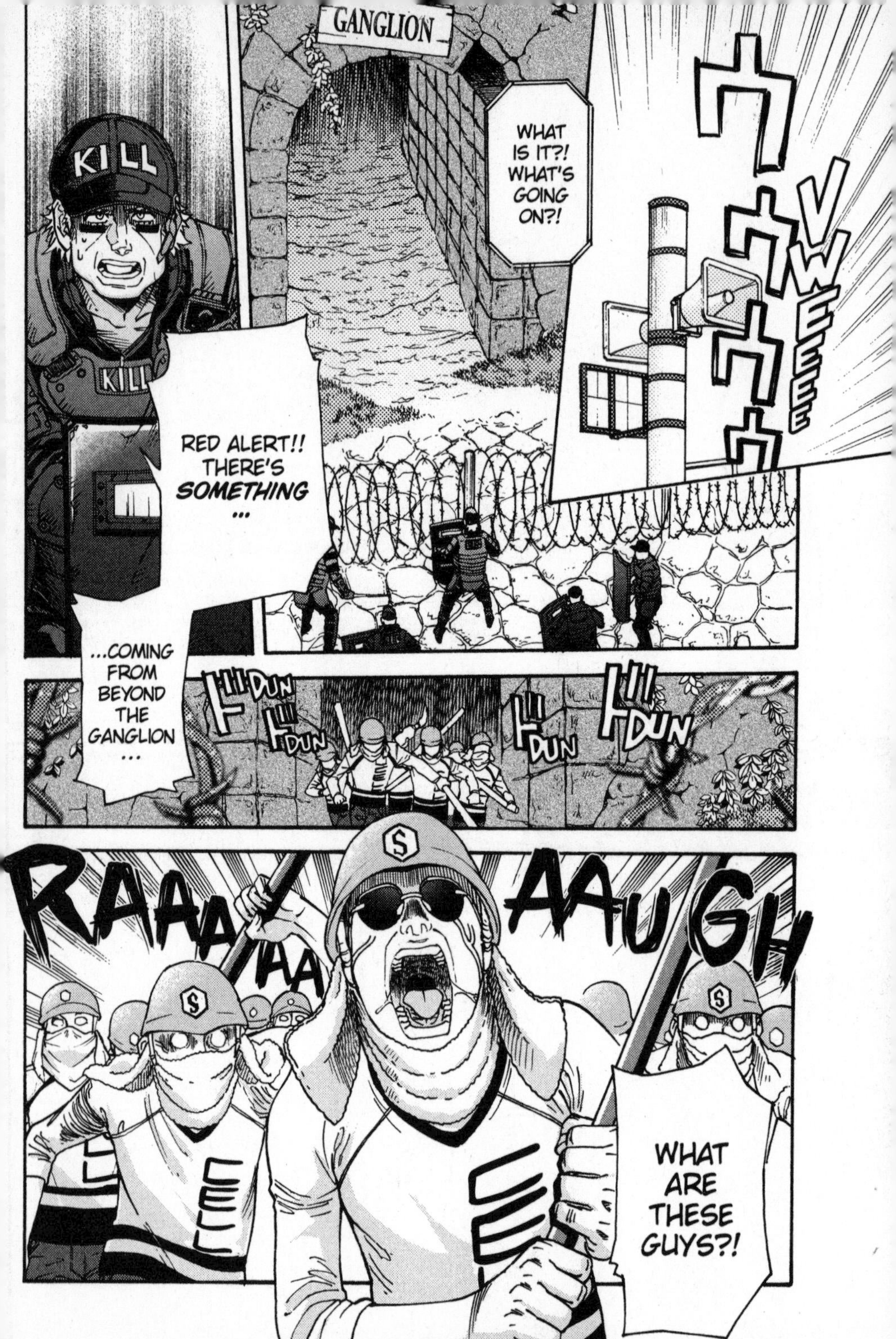
ウウウウ
VWEEEE
GANGLION
WHAT IS IT?! WHAT'S GOING ON?!
RED ALERT!! THERE'S *SOMETHING* ...
...COMING FROM BEYOND THE GANGLION ...
ド DUN
ド DUN
ド DUN
ド DUN
RAAAAAAAAUGH
WHAT ARE THESE GUYS?!

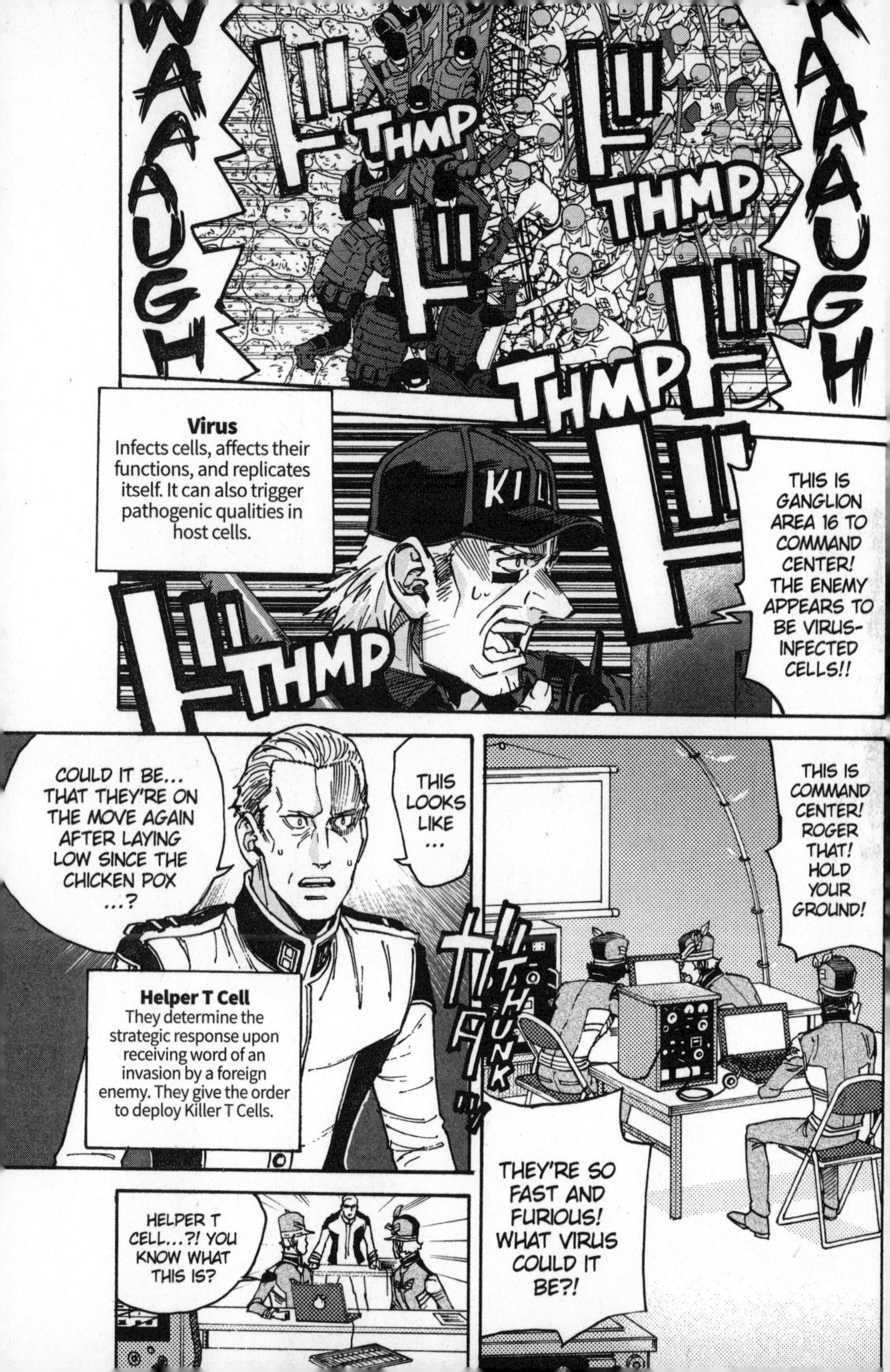
KAAAUGH
THMP
THMP
THMP
WAAUGH
THIS IS GANGLION AREA 16 TO COMMAND CENTER! THE ENEMY APPEARS TO BE VIRUS-INFECTED CELLS!!
THMP
KILL
Virus
Infects cells, affects their functions, and replicates itself. It can also trigger pathogenic qualities in host cells.
THIS IS COMMAND CENTER! ROGER THAT! HOLD YOUR GROUND!
THUNK
THEY'RE SO FAST AND FURIOUS! WHAT VIRUS COULD IT BE?!
THIS LOOKS LIKE ...
COULD IT BE... THAT THEY'RE ON THE MOVE AGAIN AFTER LAYING LOW SINCE THE CHICKEN POX ...?
Helper T Cell
They determine the strategic response upon receiving word of an invasion by a foreign enemy. They give the order to deploy Killer T Cells.
HELPER T CELL...?! YOU KNOW WHAT THIS IS?

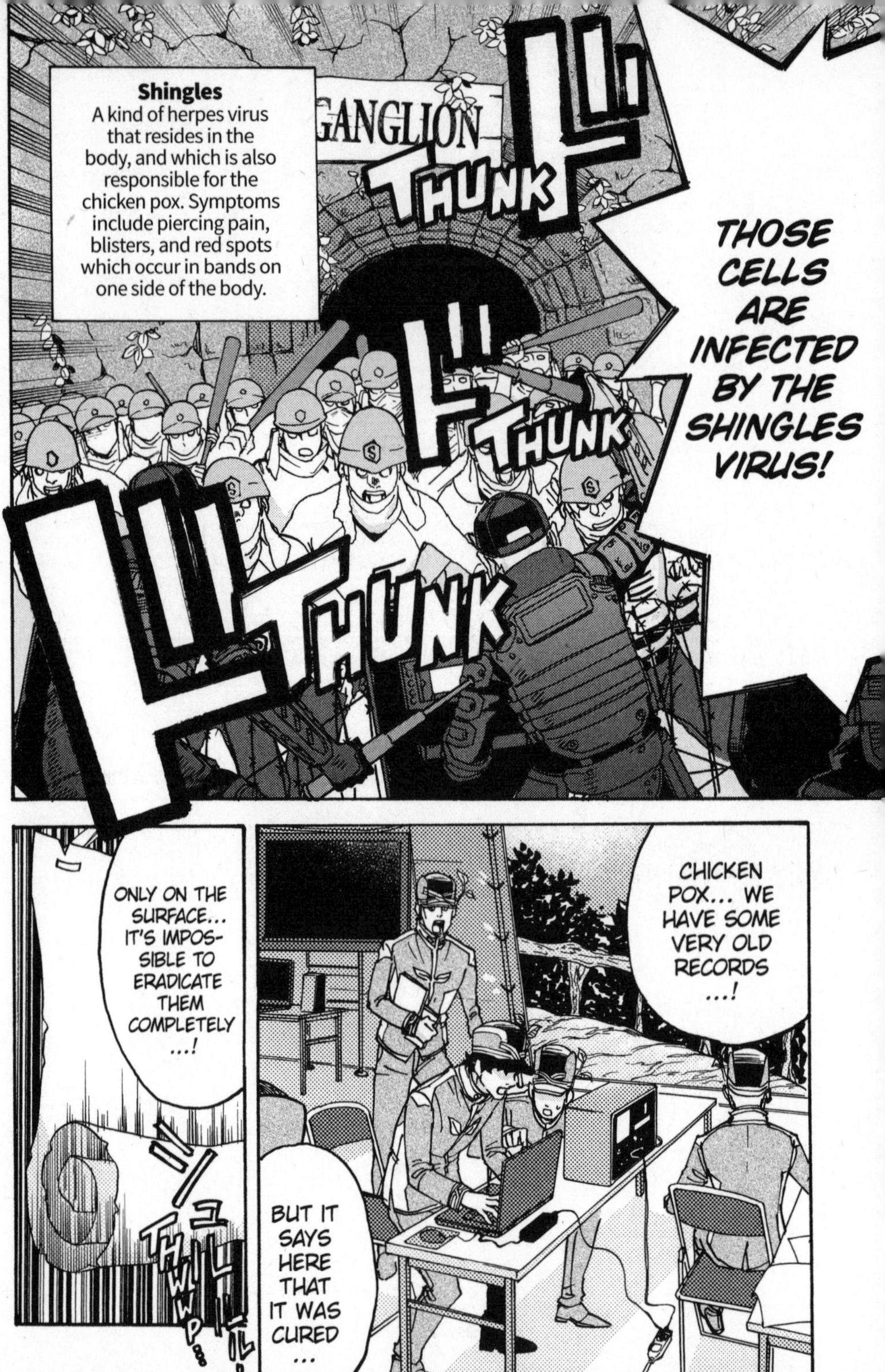
Shingles
A kind of herpes virus that resides in the body, and which is also responsible for the chicken pox. Symptoms include piercing pain, blisters, and red spots which occur in bands on one side of the body.
GANGLION
THUNK
THOSE CELLS ARE INFECTED BY THE SHINGLES VIRUS!
THUNK
THUNK
CHICKEN POX... WE HAVE SOME VERY OLD RECORDS ...!
BUT IT SAYS HERE THAT IT WAS CURED ...
ONLY ON THE SURFACE... IT'S IMPOSSIBLE TO ERADICATE THEM COMPLETELY ...!
THWWP..

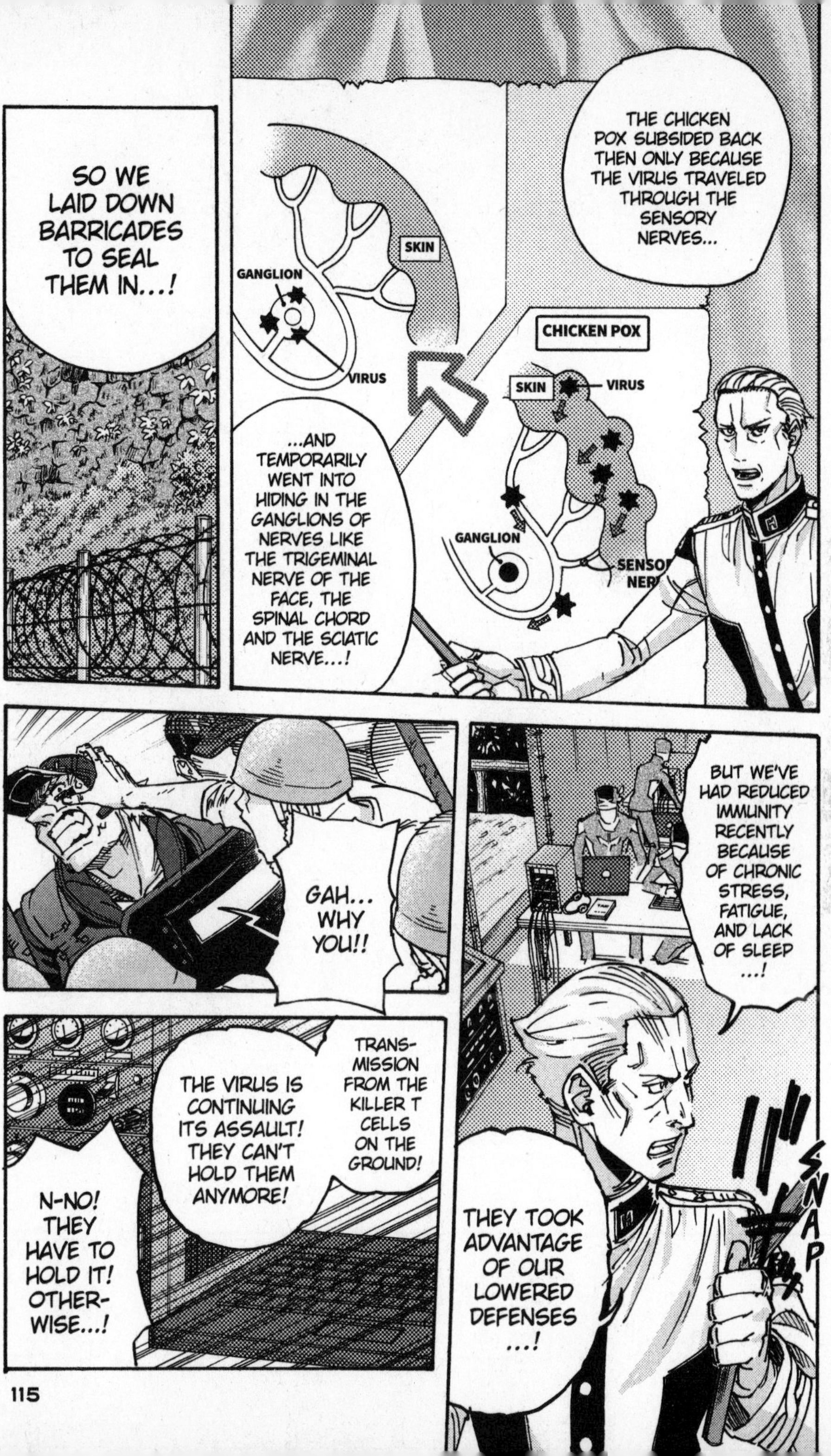
THE CHICKEN POX SUBSIDED BACK THEN ONLY BECAUSE THE VIRUS TRAVELED THROUGH THE SENSORY NERVES...
SKIN
GANGLION
VIRUS
CHICKEN POX
SKIN
VIRUS
GANGLION
...AND TEMPORARILY WENT INTO HIDING IN THE GANGLIONS OF NERVES LIKE THE TRIGEMINAL NERVE OF THE FACE, THE SPINAL CHORD AND THE SCIATIC NERVE...!
SO WE LAID DOWN BARRICADES TO SEAL THEM IN...!
BUT WE'VE HAD REDUCED IMMUNITY RECENTLY BECAUSE OF CHRONIC STRESS, FATIGUE, AND LACK OF SLEEP ...!
THEY TOOK ADVANTAGE OF OUR LOWERED DEFENSES ...!
SNAP
GAH... WHY YOU!!
TRANS-MISSION FROM THE KILLER T CELLS ON THE GROUND!
THE VIRUS IS CONTINUING ITS ASSAULT! THEY CAN'T HOLD THEM ANYMORE!
N-NO! THEY HAVE TO HOLD IT! OTHER-WISE...!

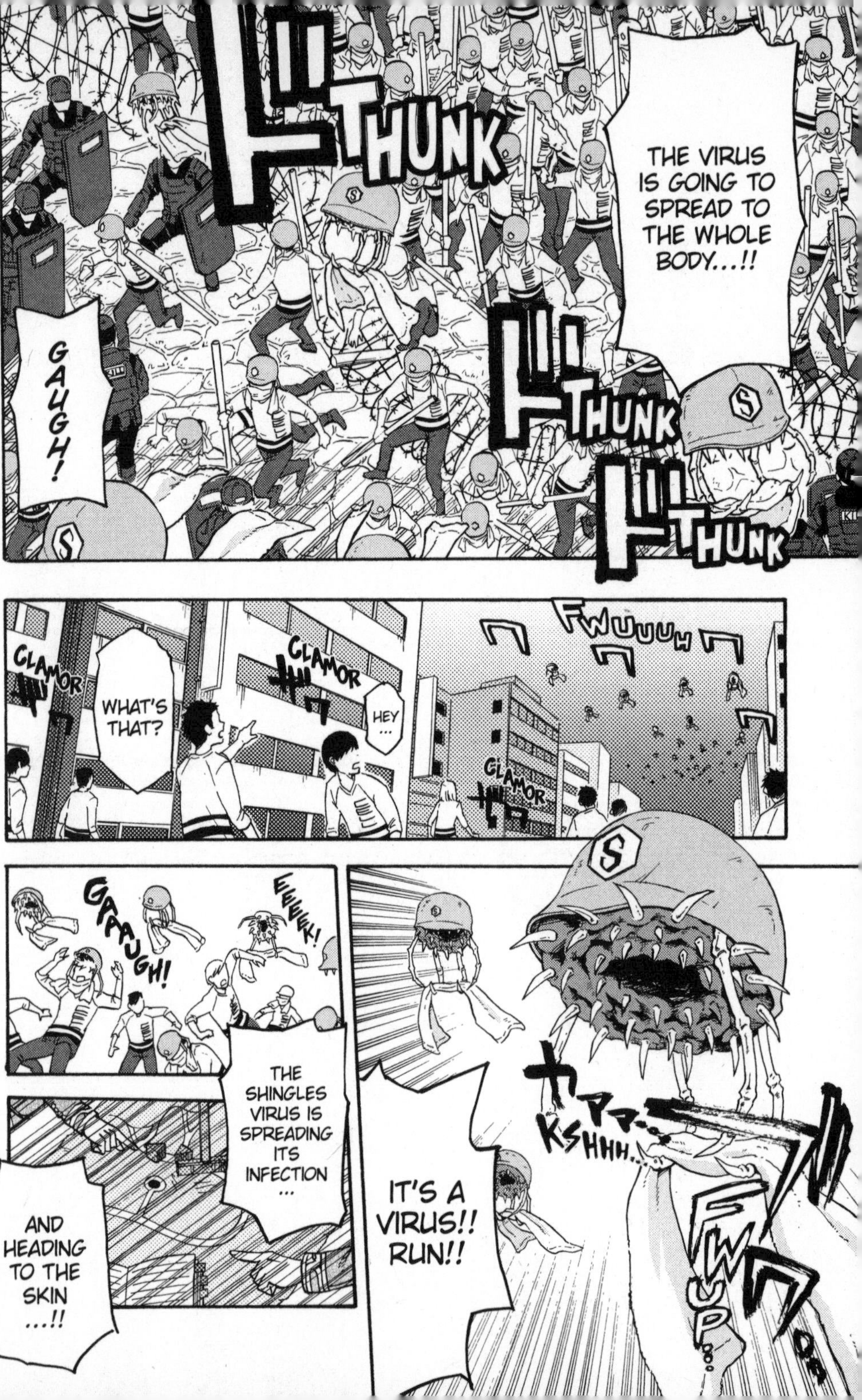
THE VIRUS IS GOING TO SPREAD TO THE WHOLE BODY...!!
THUNK
THUNK
THUNK
GAUGH!
FWUUUH
HEY...
CLAMOR
WHAT'S THAT?
CLAMOR
CLAMOR
KSHHH...
FWUP
IT'S A VIRUS!! RUN!!
EEEEK!
GAAAUGH!
THE SHINGLES VIRUS IS SPREADING ITS INFECTION...
AND HEADING TO THE SKIN...!!

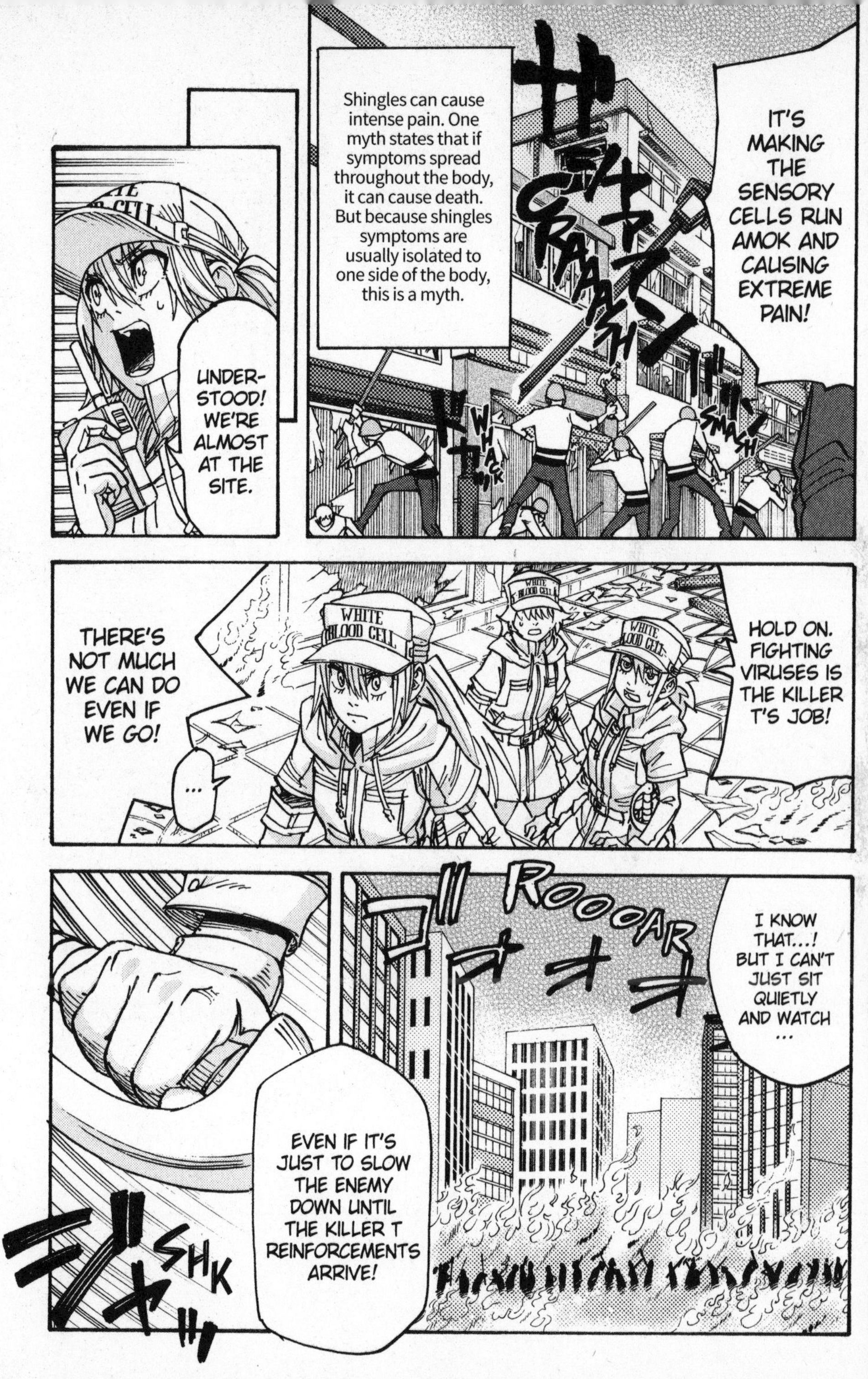
IT'S MAKING THE SENSORY CELLS RUN AMOK AND CAUSING EXTREME PAIN!
CRAAASH
Shingles can cause intense pain. One myth states that if symptoms spread throughout the body, it can cause death. But because shingles symptoms are usually isolated to one side of the body, this is a myth.
SMASH
WHACK
UNDER-STOOD! WE'RE ALMOST AT THE SITE.
HOLD ON. FIGHTING VIRUSES IS THE KILLER T'S JOB!
THERE'S NOT MUCH WE CAN DO EVEN IF WE GO!
...
ROOOAR
I KNOW THAT...! BUT I CAN'T JUST SIT QUIETLY AND WATCH...
EVEN IF IT'S JUST TO SLOW THE ENEMY DOWN UNTIL THE KILLER T REINFORCEMENTS ARRIVE!
SHK

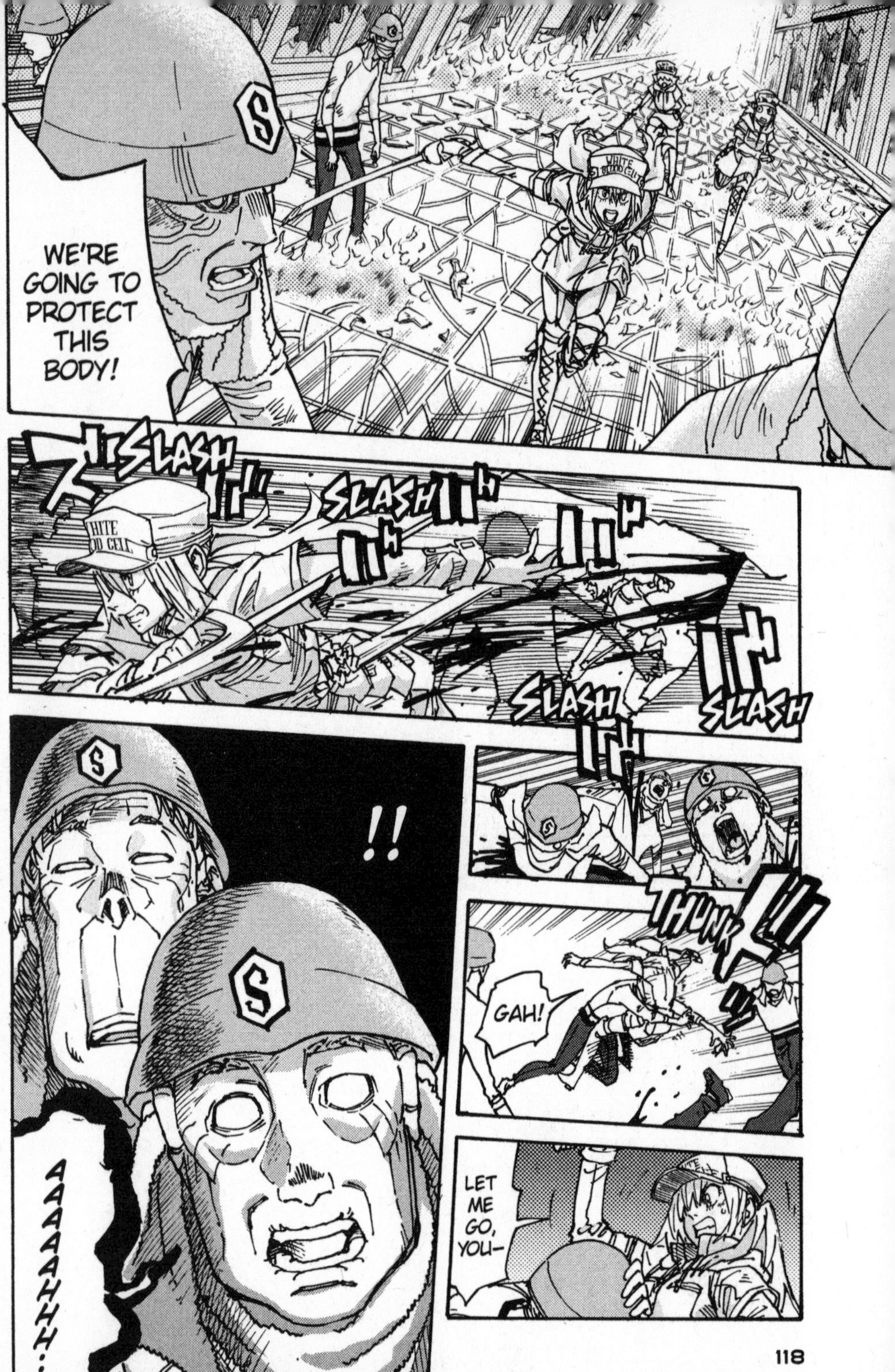

WE'RE GOING TO PROTECT THIS BODY!
SLASH
SLASH
SLASH
SLASH
THUNK
GAH!
LET ME GO, YOU-
!!
AAAAAAHHH...

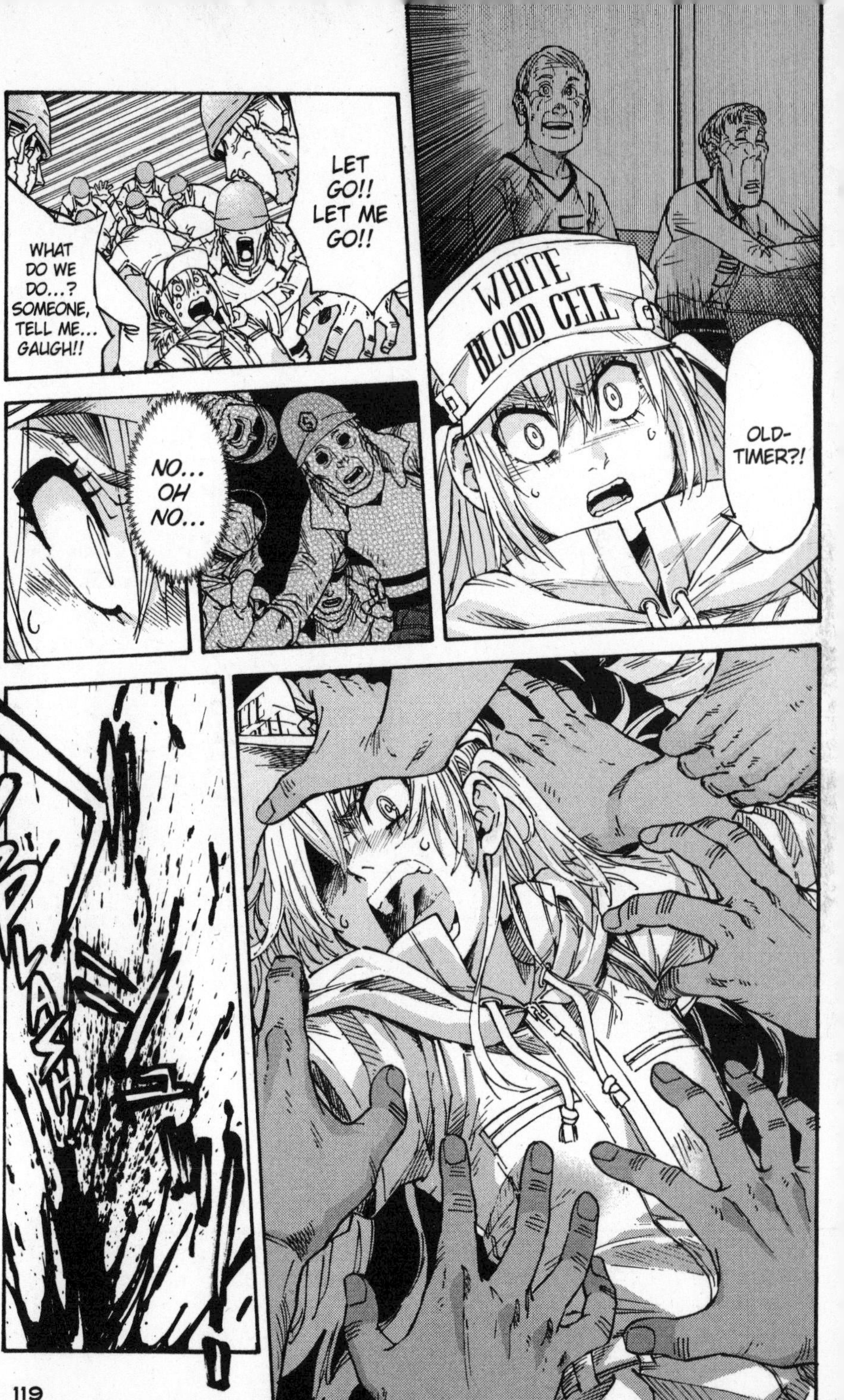
OLD-TIMER?!
LET GO!! LET ME GO!!
WHAT DO WE DO...? SOMEONE, TELL ME... GAUGH!!
NO... OH NO...
SPLASH!!

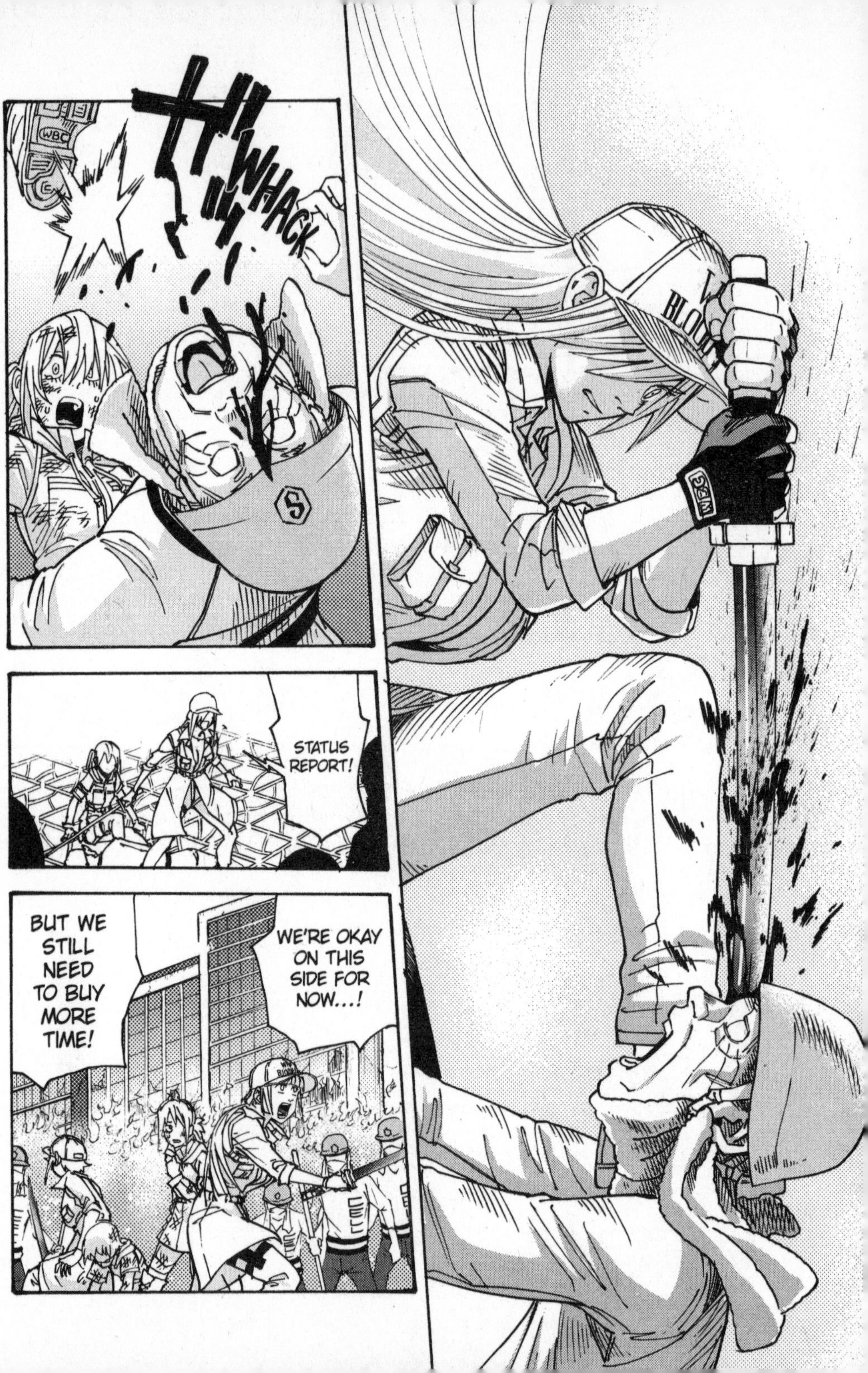
WHACK
STATUS REPORT!
WE'RE OKAY ON THIS SIDE FOR NOW...!
BUT WE STILL NEED TO BUY MORE TIME!

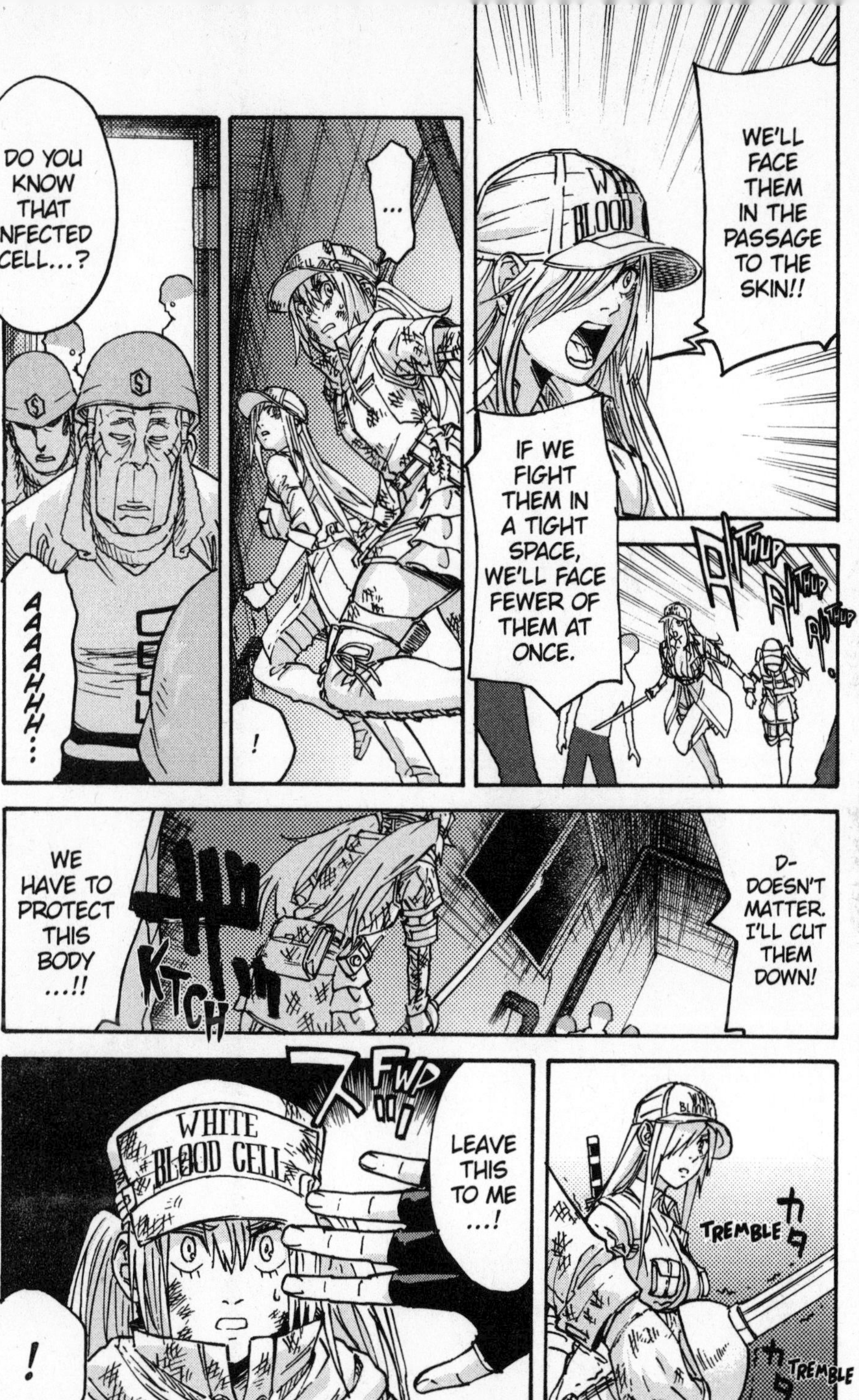
WE'LL FACE THEM IN THE PASSAGE TO THE SKIN!!
IF WE FIGHT THEM IN A TIGHT SPACE, WE'LL FACE FEWER OF THEM AT ONCE.
THUP THUP THUP
...
!
DO YOU KNOW THAT INFECTED CELL...?
AAAAHHH...
D-DOESN'T MATTER. I'LL CUT THEM DOWN!
KTCH
WE HAVE TO PROTECT THIS BODY ...!!
TREMBLE
TREMBLE
FWD
LEAVE THIS TO ME ...!
!

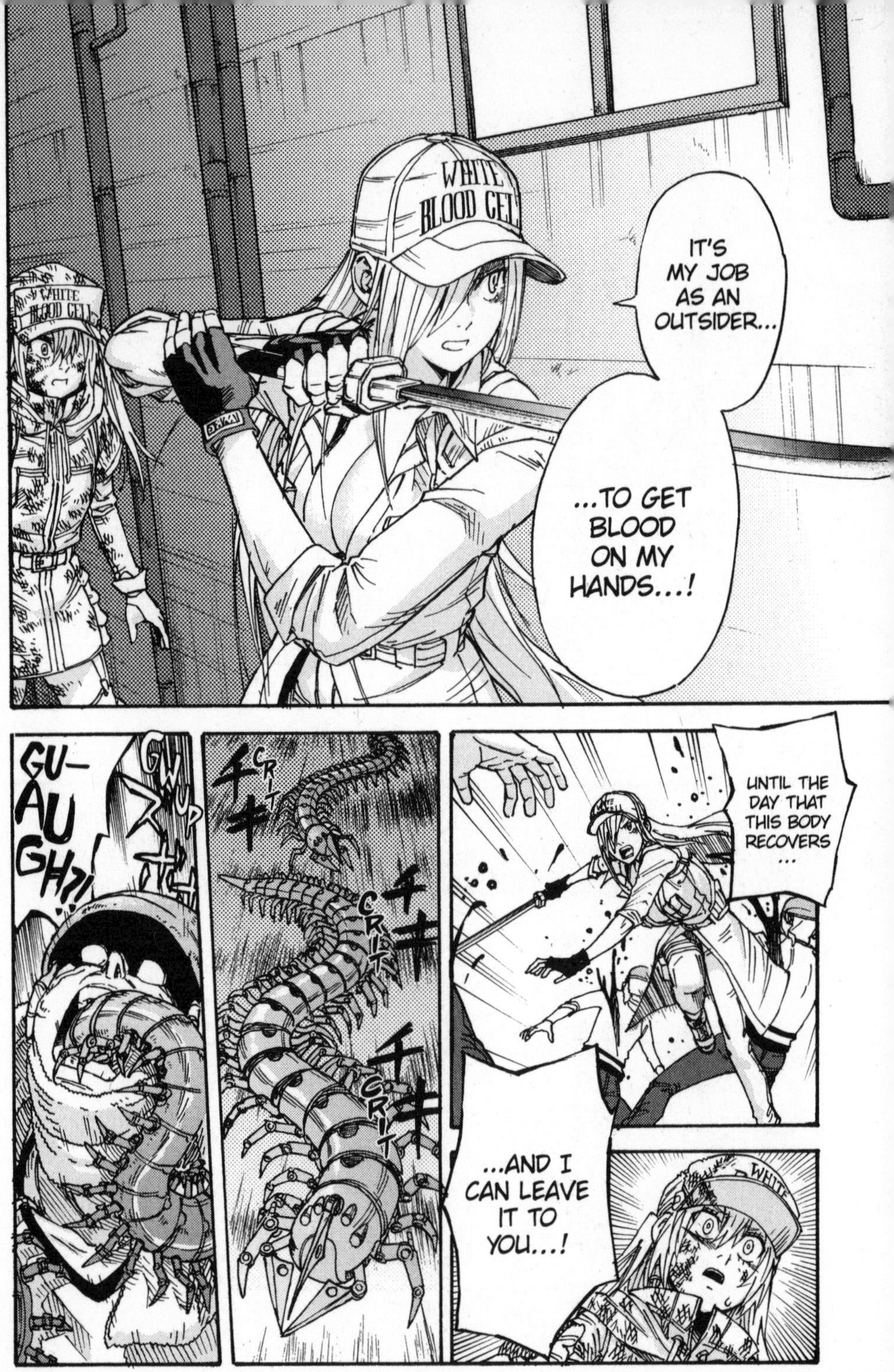
IT'S MY JOB AS AN OUTSIDER...
...TO GET BLOOD ON MY HANDS...!
UNTIL THE DAY THAT THIS BODY RECOVERS ...
...AND I CAN LEAVE IT TO YOU...!
CRIT
CRIT
CRIT
GWUP
GU-AUGH?!

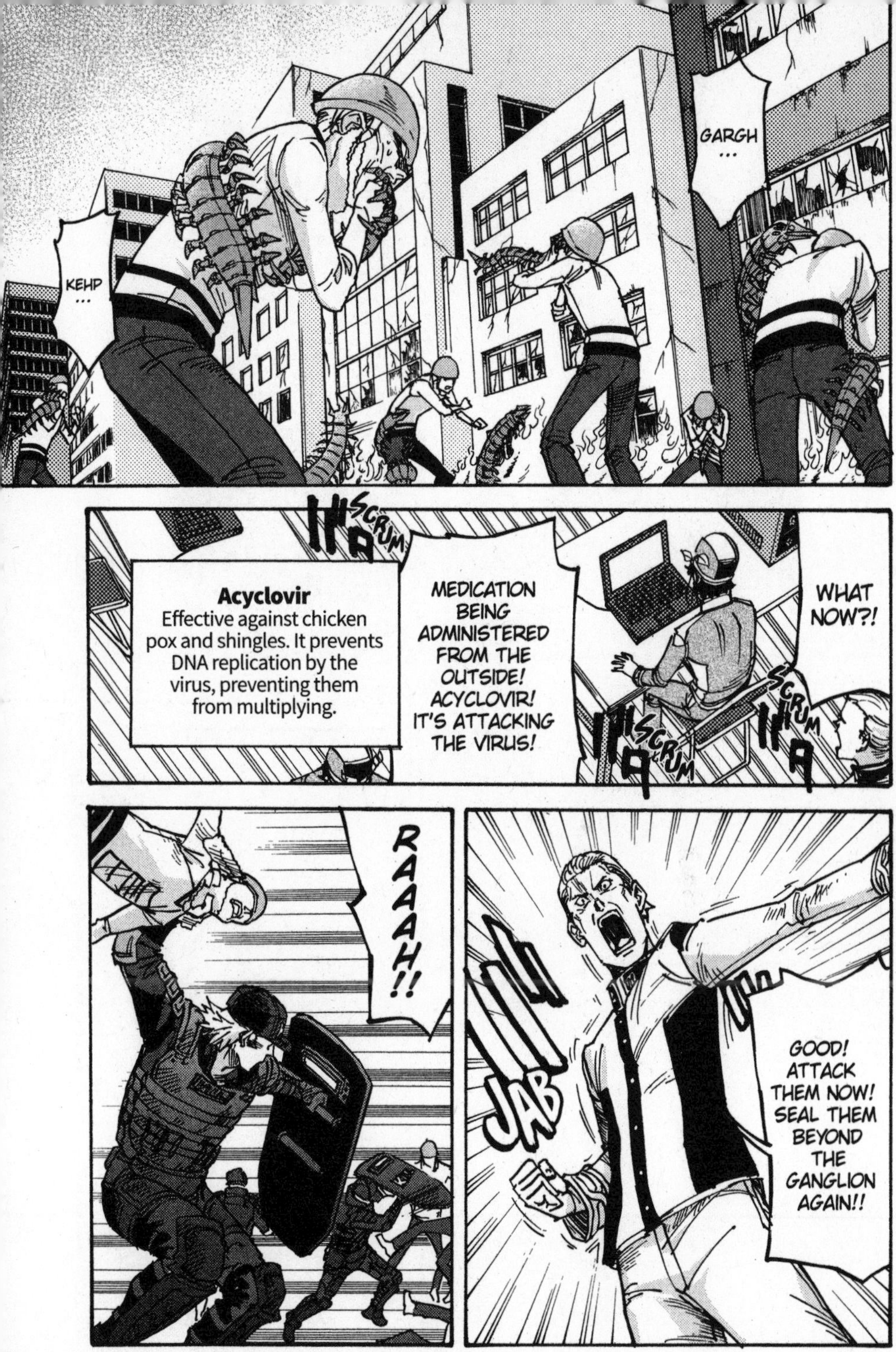
GARGH ...
KEHP ...
WHAT NOW?!
SCRUM
SCRUM
SCRUM
SCRUM
MEDICATION BEING ADMINISTERED FROM THE OUTSIDE! ACYCLOVIR! IT'S ATTACKING THE VIRUS!
Acyclovir
Effective against chicken pox and shingles. It prevents DNA replication by the virus, preventing them from multiplying.
GOOD! ATTACK THEM NOW! SEAL THEM BEYOND THE GANGLION AGAIN!!
JAB
RAAAAH!!

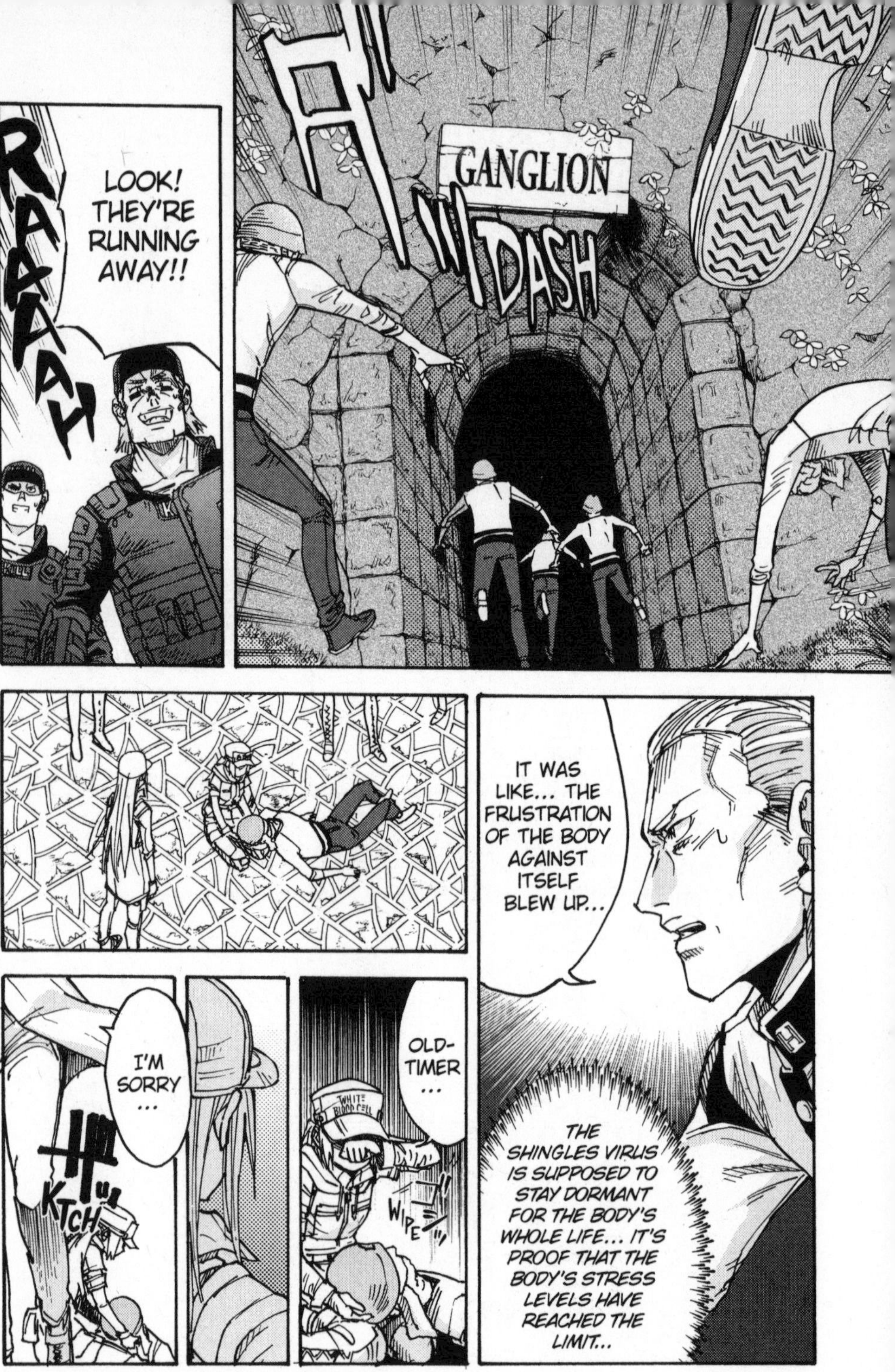
GANGLION
DASH
RAAAAH
LOOK! THEY'RE RUNNING AWAY!!
IT WAS LIKE... THE FRUSTRATION OF THE BODY AGAINST ITSELF BLEW UP...
THE SHINGLES VIRUS IS SUPPOSED TO STAY DORMANT FOR THE BODY'S WHOLE LIFE... IT'S PROOF THAT THE BODY'S STRESS LEVELS HAVE REACHED THE LIMIT...
OLD-TIMER...
WHITE BLOOD CELL
WIPE
I'M SORRY...
KTCH

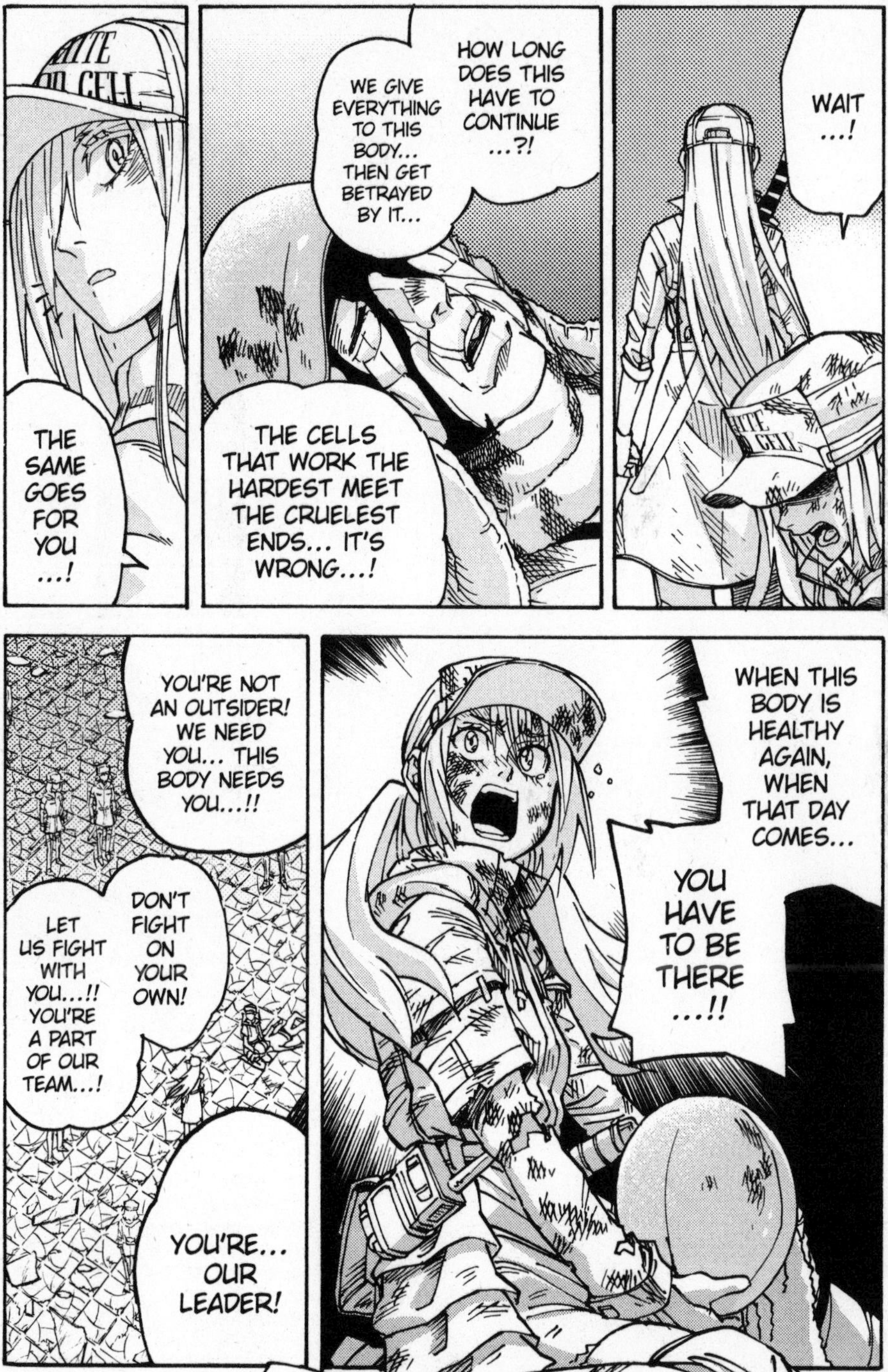
WAIT ...!
HOW LONG DOES THIS HAVE TO CONTINUE ...?!
WE GIVE EVERYTHING TO THIS BODY... THEN GET BETRAYED BY IT...
THE CELLS THAT WORK THE HARDEST MEET THE CRUELEST ENDS... IT'S WRONG...!
THE SAME GOES FOR YOU ...!
WHEN THIS BODY IS HEALTHY AGAIN, WHEN THAT DAY COMES...
YOU HAVE TO BE THERE ...!!
YOU'RE NOT AN OUTSIDER! WE NEED YOU... THIS BODY NEEDS YOU...!!
DON'T FIGHT ON YOUR OWN!
LET US FIGHT WITH YOU...!! YOU'RE A PART OF OUR TEAM...!
YOU'RE... OUR LEADER!

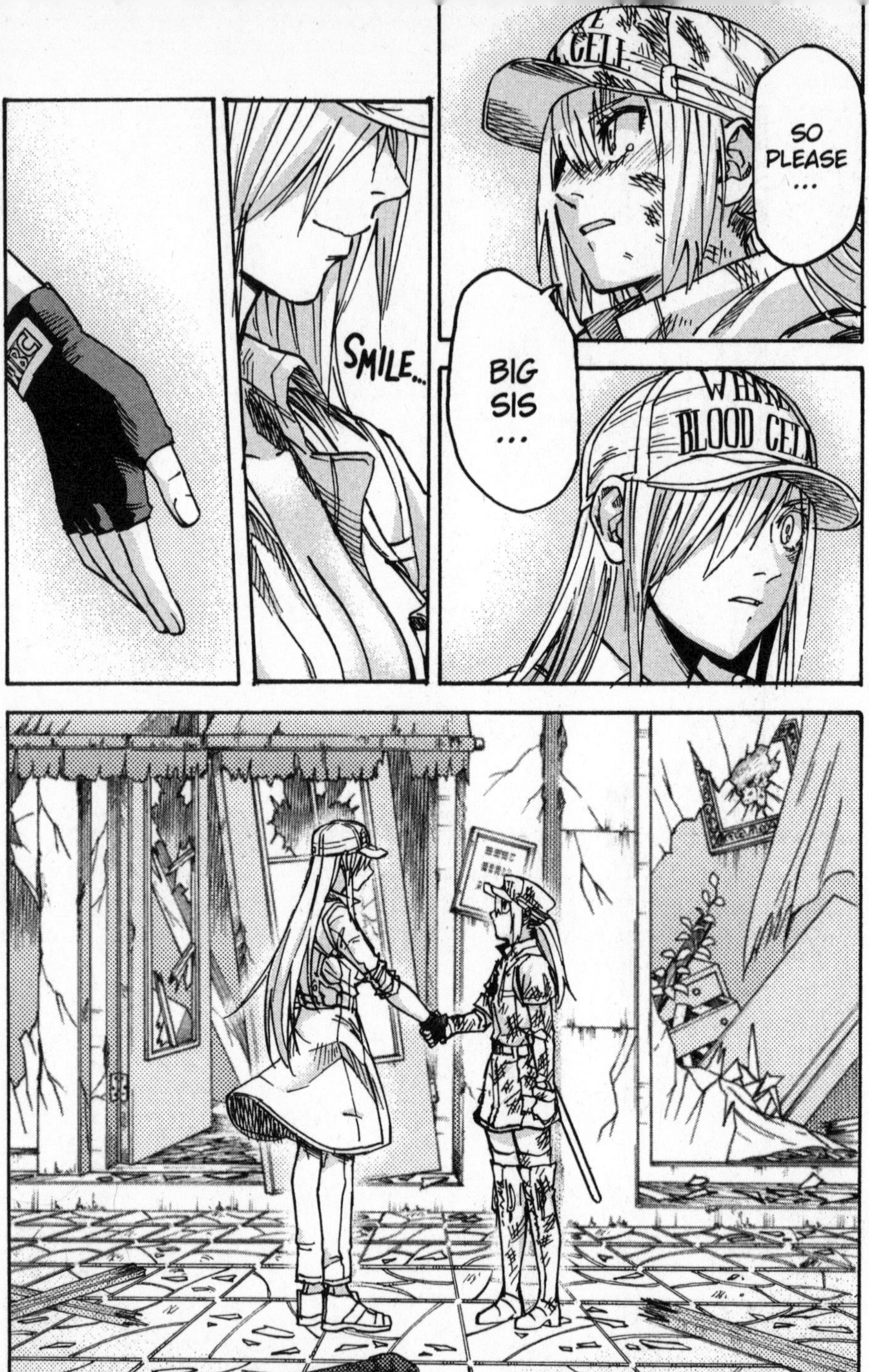
SO PLEASE ...
BIG SIS ...
SMILE...
WHITE BLOOD CELL

CHAPTER 23 - END

24. SUGARS, BLOOD VESSELS, AND CATASTROPHE

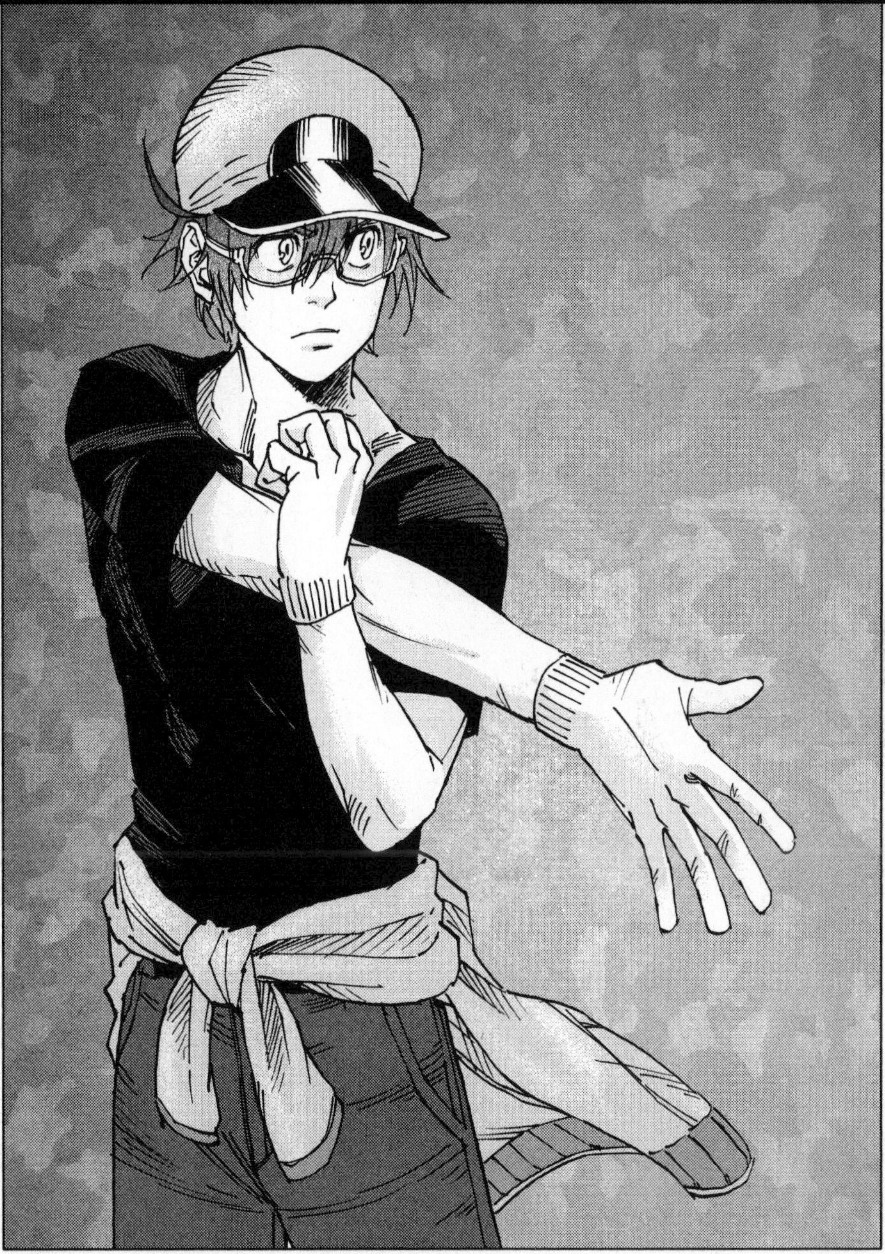

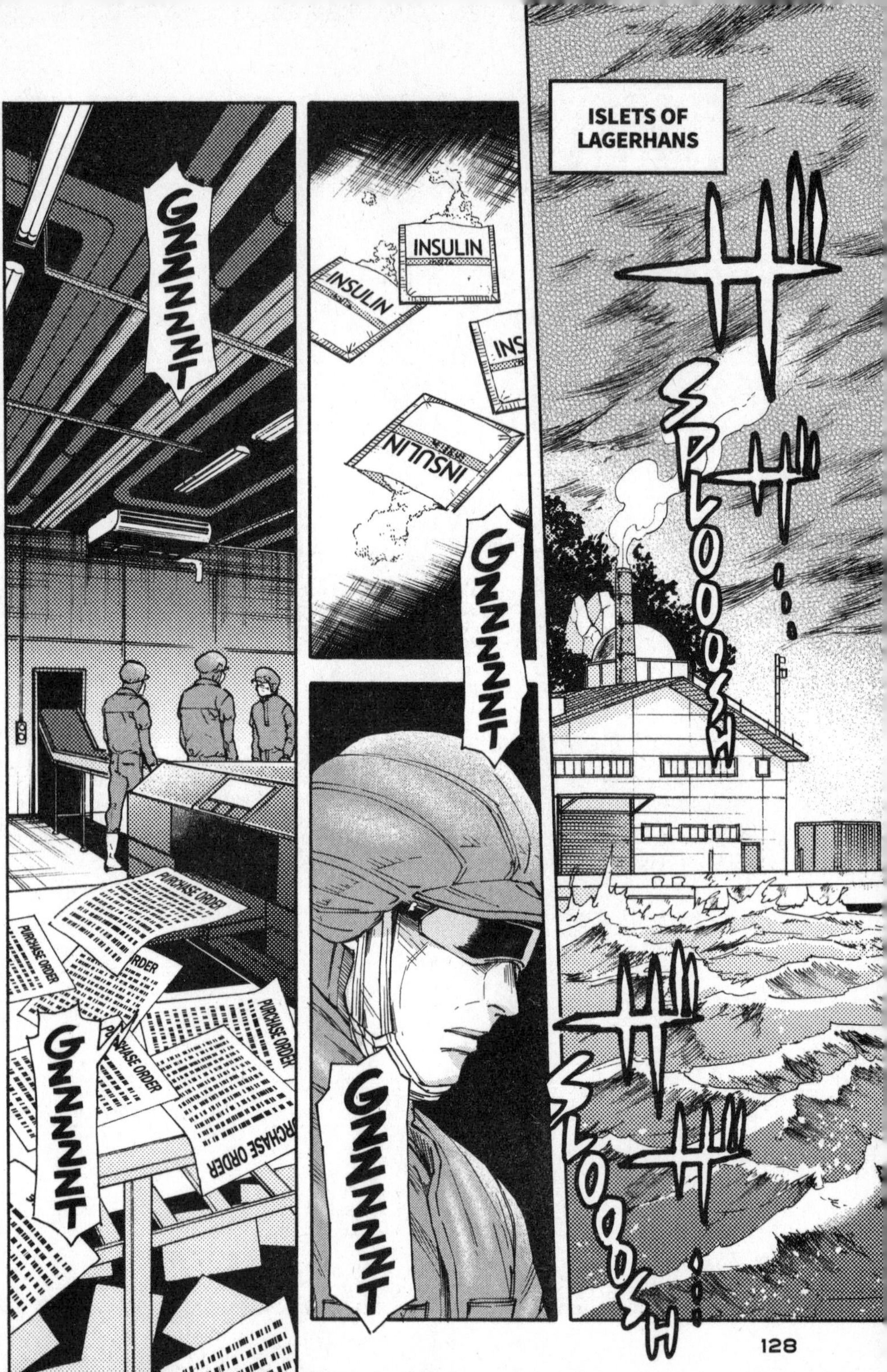
ISLETS OF LAGERHANS
SPLOOOOSH...
SLOOOOSH...
INSULIN
INSULIN
INSULIN
GNNZZZZT
GNNZZZZT
GNNZZZZT
PURCHASE ORDER
PURCHASE ORDER
PURCHASE ORDER
PURCHASE ORDER
GNNZZZZT

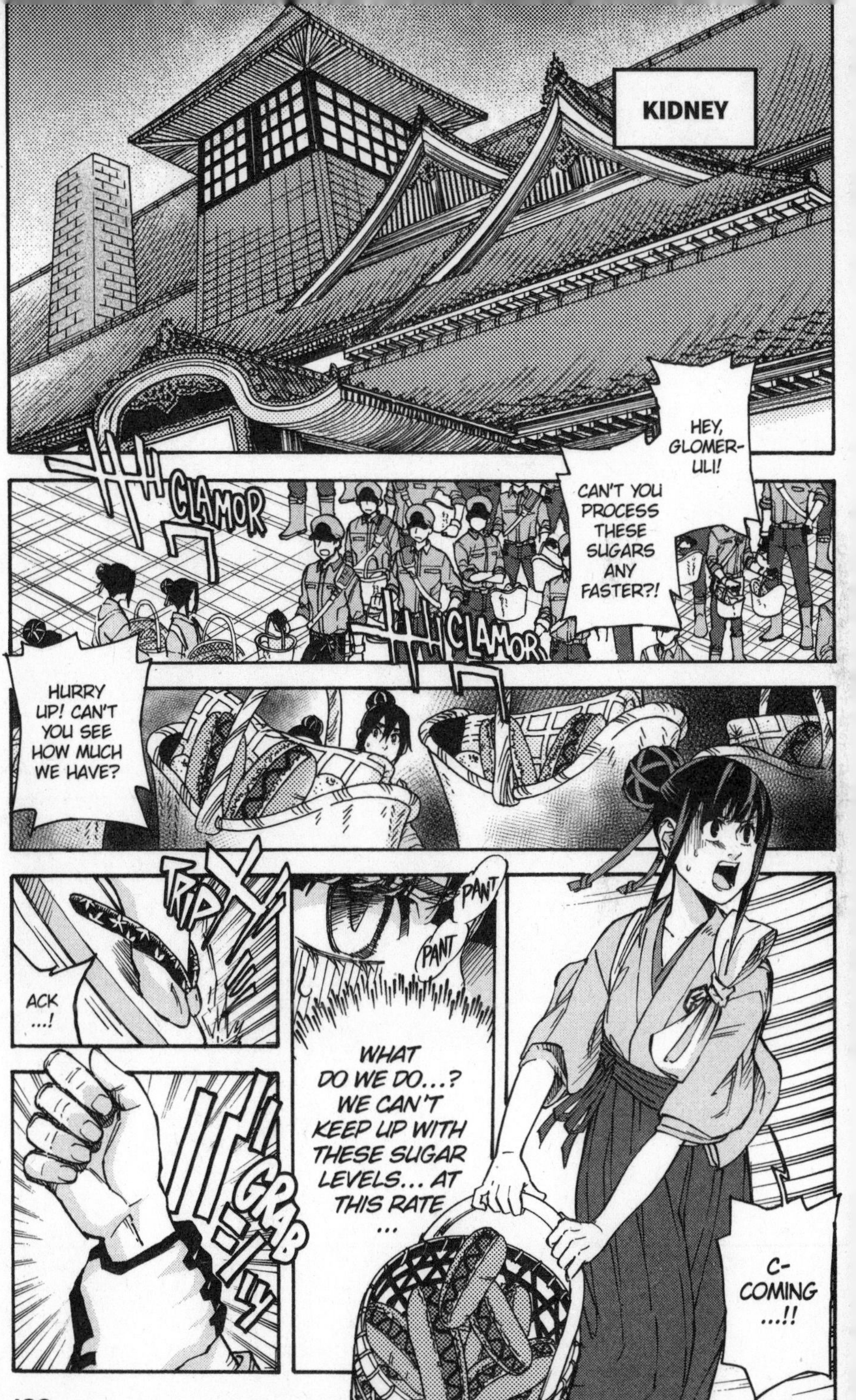
KIDNEY
HEY, GLOMER-ULI!
CAN'T YOU PROCESS THESE SUGARS ANY FASTER?!
CLAMOR
CLAMOR
HURRY UP! CAN'T YOU SEE HOW MUCH WE HAVE?
C-COMING ...!!
PANT
PANT
TRIP
ACK ...!
WHAT DO WE DO...? WE CAN'T KEEP UP WITH THESE SUGAR LEVELS... AT THIS RATE ...
GRAB

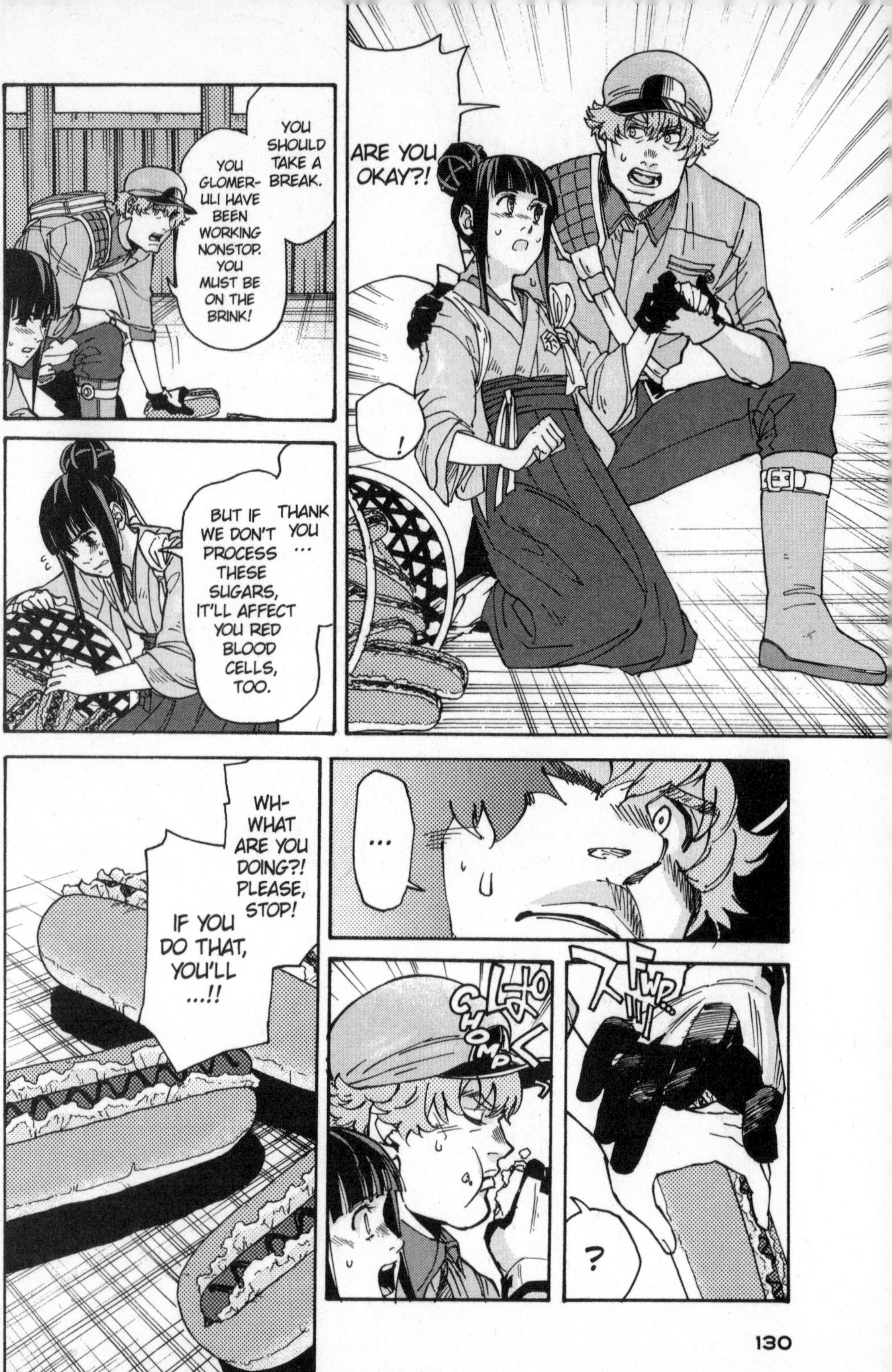
ARE YOU OKAY?!
!
YOU GLOMER-ULI HAVE BEEN WORKING NONSTOP. YOU MUST BE ON THE BRINK!
YOU SHOULD TAKE A BREAK.
THANK YOU ...
BUT IF WE DON'T PROCESS THESE SUGARS, IT'LL AFFECT YOU RED BLOOD CELLS, TOO.
...
FWP...
?
CHOMP
WH-WHAT ARE YOU DOING?! PLEASE, STOP!
IF YOU DO THAT, YOU'LL ...!!

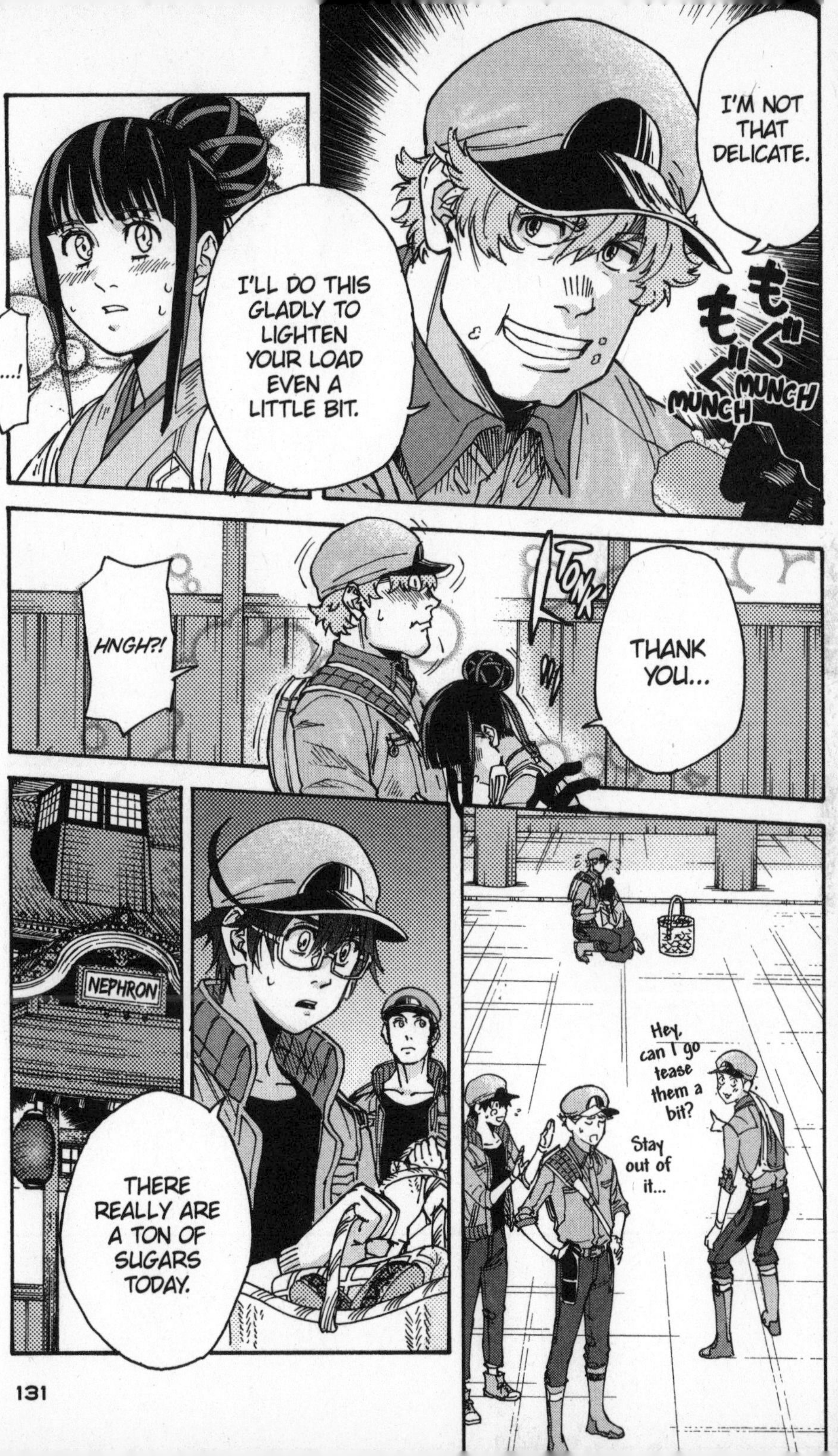
I'M NOT THAT DELICATE.
もぐもぐ
MUNCH MUNCH
I'LL DO THIS GLADLY TO LIGHTEN YOUR LOAD EVEN A LITTLE BIT.
...!
THANK YOU...
TONK
HNGH?!
Hey, can I go tease them a bit?
Stay out of it...
THERE REALLY ARE A TON OF SUGARS TODAY.
NEPHRON

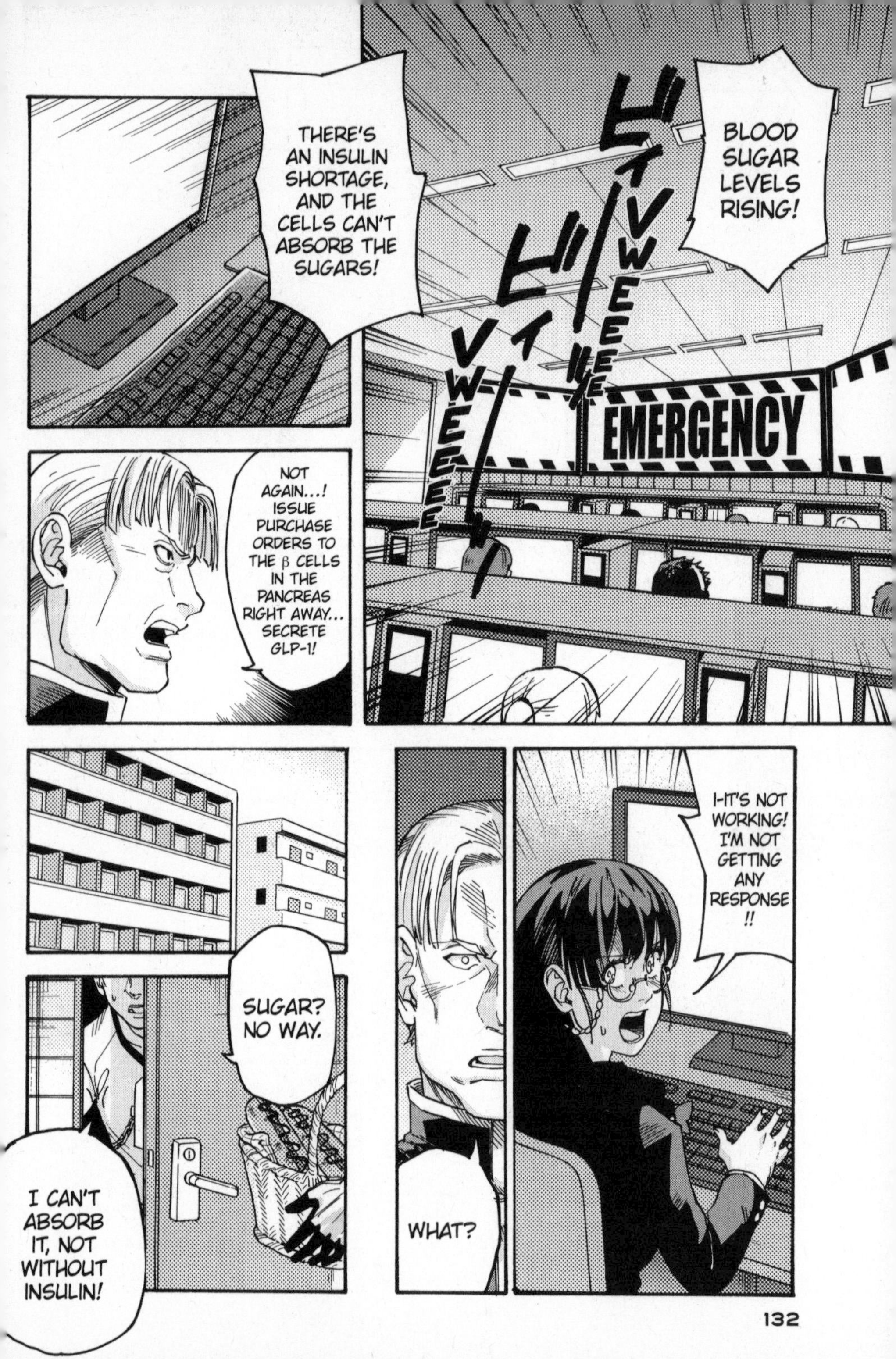
BLOOD SUGAR LEVELS RISING!
VWEEEEE
VWEEEEE
EMERGENCY
THERE'S AN INSULIN SHORTAGE, AND THE CELLS CAN'T ABSORB THE SUGARS!
NOT AGAIN...! ISSUE PURCHASE ORDERS TO THE β CELLS IN THE PANCREAS RIGHT AWAY... SECRETE GLP-1!
I-IT'S NOT WORKING! I'M NOT GETTING ANY RESPONSE!!
WHAT?
SUGAR? NO WAY.
I CAN'T ABSORB IT, NOT WITHOUT INSULIN!

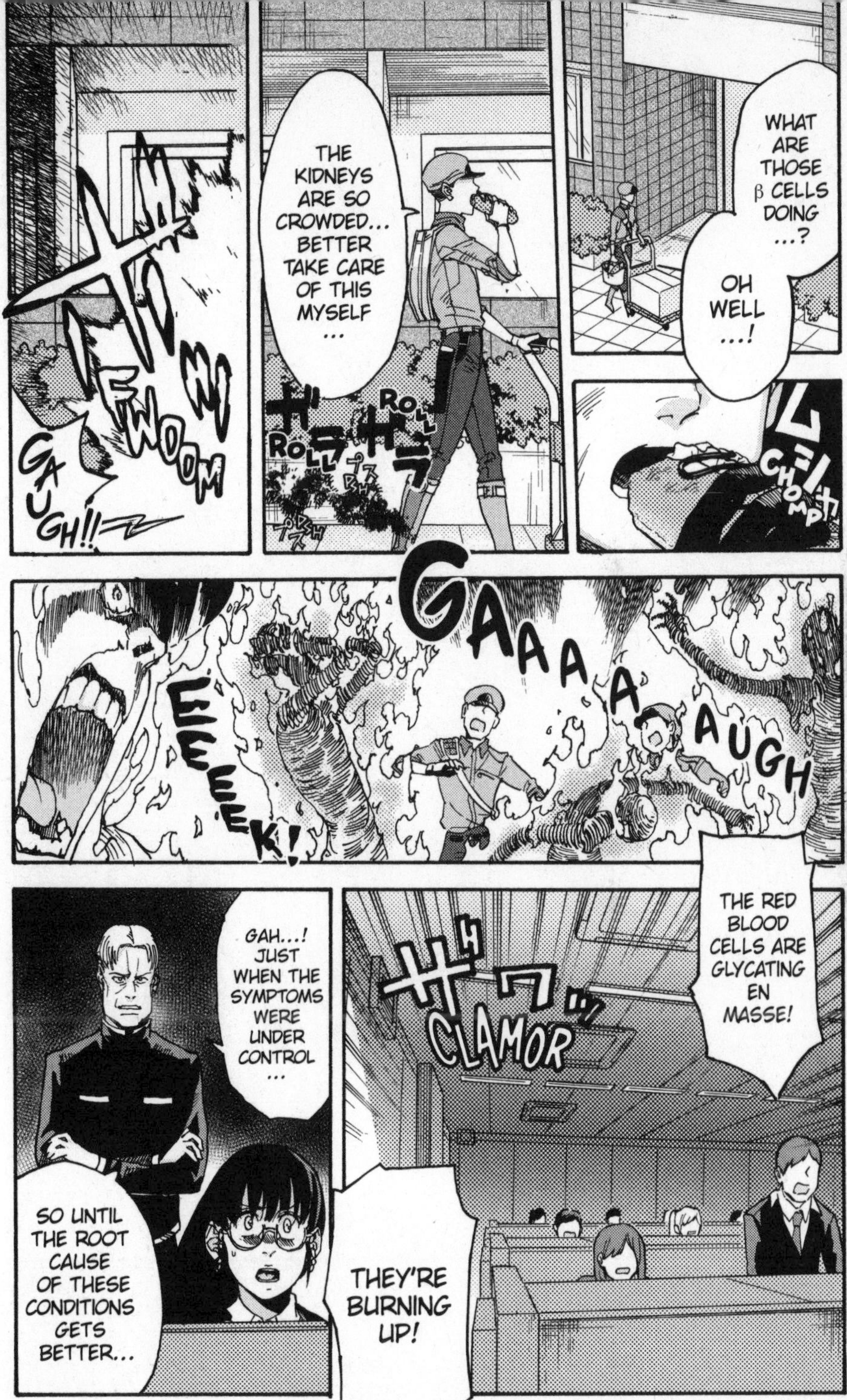

WHAT ARE THOSE β CELLS DOING ...?
OH WELL ...!
CHOMP
THE KIDNEYS ARE SO CROWDED... BETTER TAKE CARE OF THIS MYSELF ...
ROLL
ROLL
PSH
PSH
FWOOM
GAUGH!!
GAAAAAUGH
EEEEEK!
THE RED BLOOD CELLS ARE GLYCATING EN MASSE!
CLAMOR
THEY'RE BURNING UP!
GAH...! JUST WHEN THE SYMPTOMS WERE UNDER CONTROL ...
SO UNTIL THE ROOT CAUSE OF THESE CONDITIONS GETS BETTER...

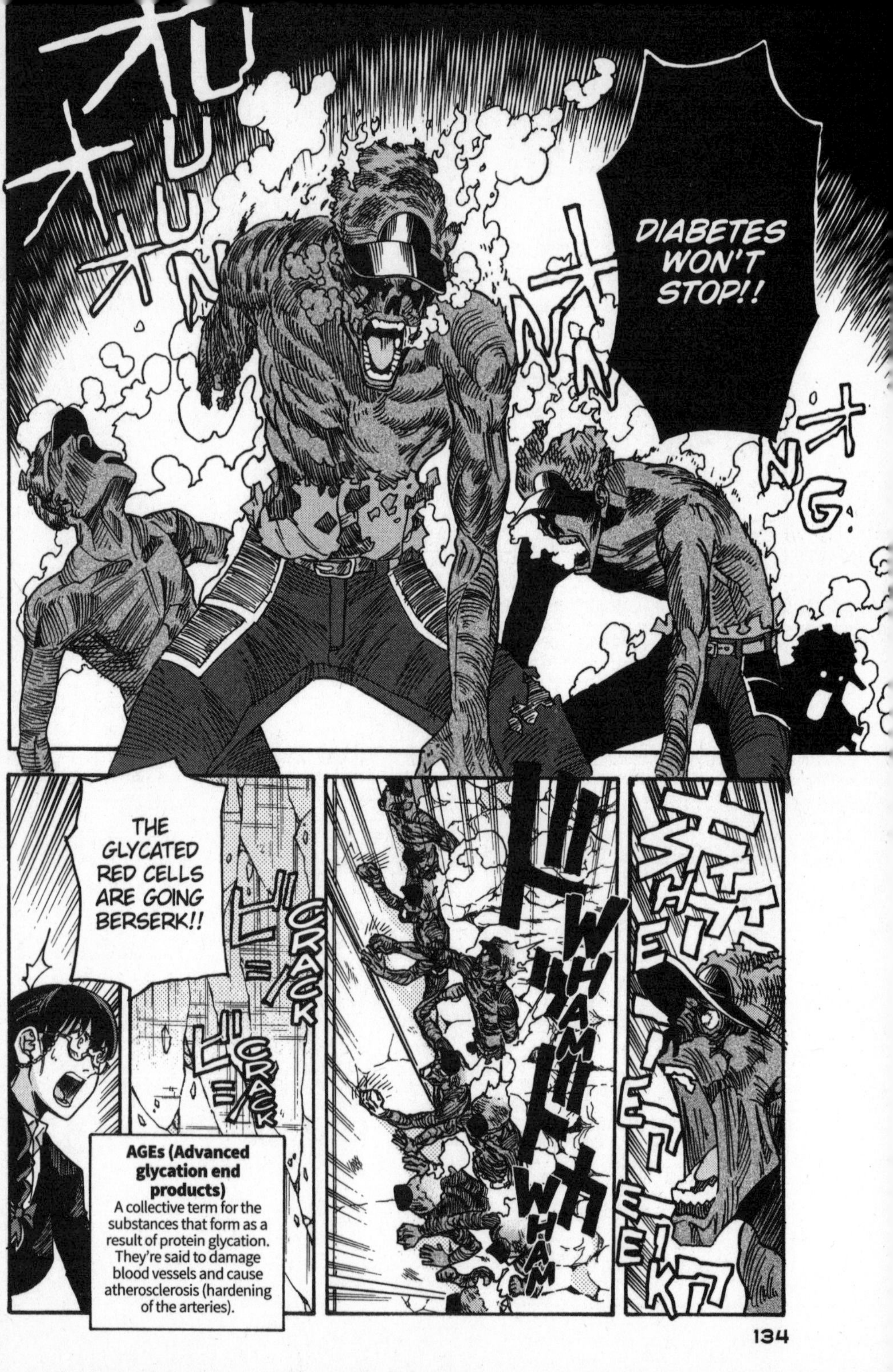

DIABETES WON'T STOP!!
WHAM
WHAM
THE GLYCATED RED CELLS ARE GOING BERSERK!!
CRACK
CRACK
AGEs (Advanced glycation end products)
A collective term for the substances that form as a result of protein glycation. They're said to damage blood vessels and cause atherosclerosis (hardening of the arteries).

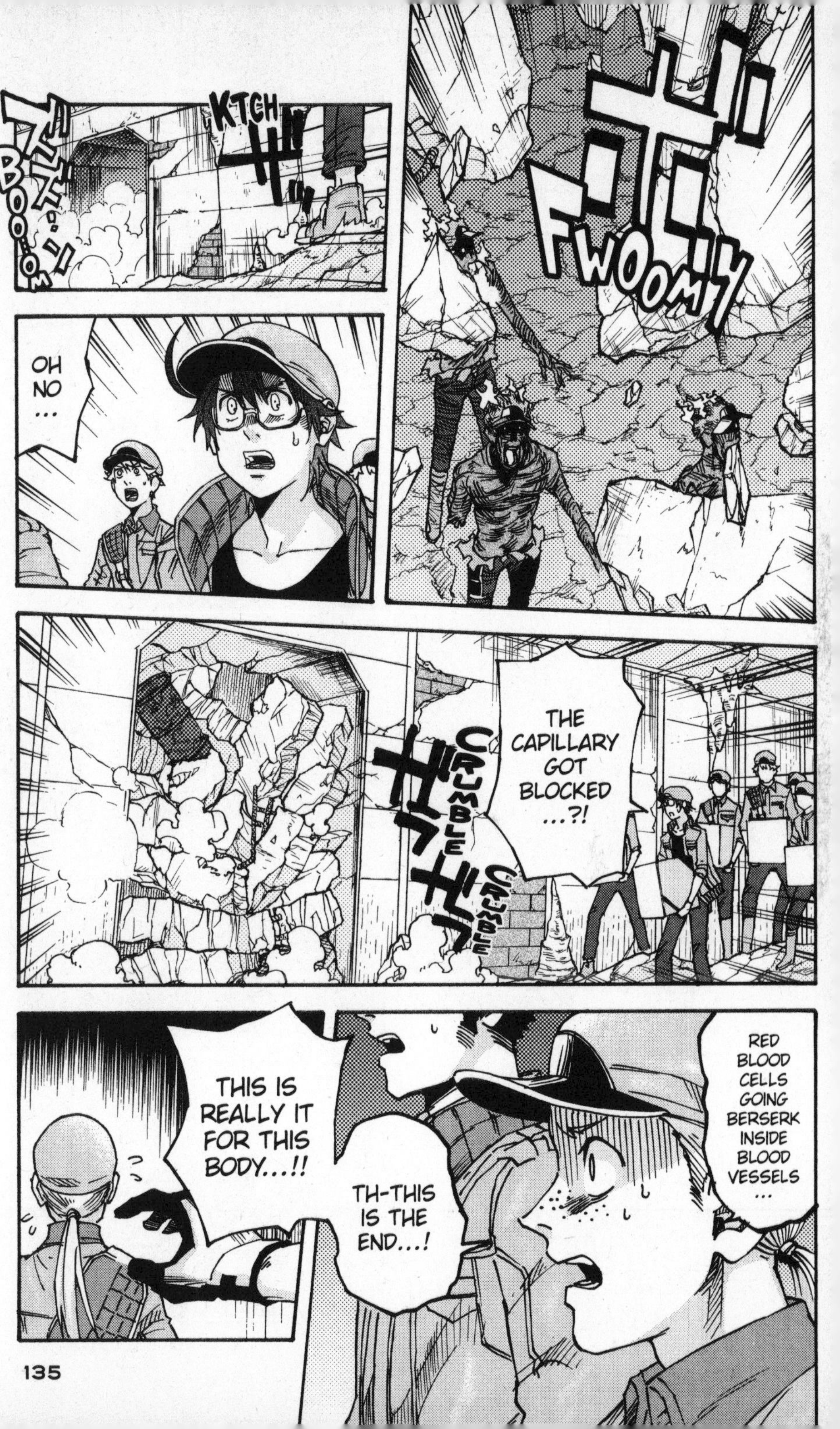
FWOOM
KTCH
BOOOOOM
OH NO ...
THE CAPILLARY GOT BLOCKED ...?!
CRUMBLE
CRUMBLE
RED BLOOD CELLS GOING BERSERK INSIDE BLOOD VESSELS ...
TH-THIS IS THE END...!
THIS IS REALLY IT FOR THIS BODY...!!

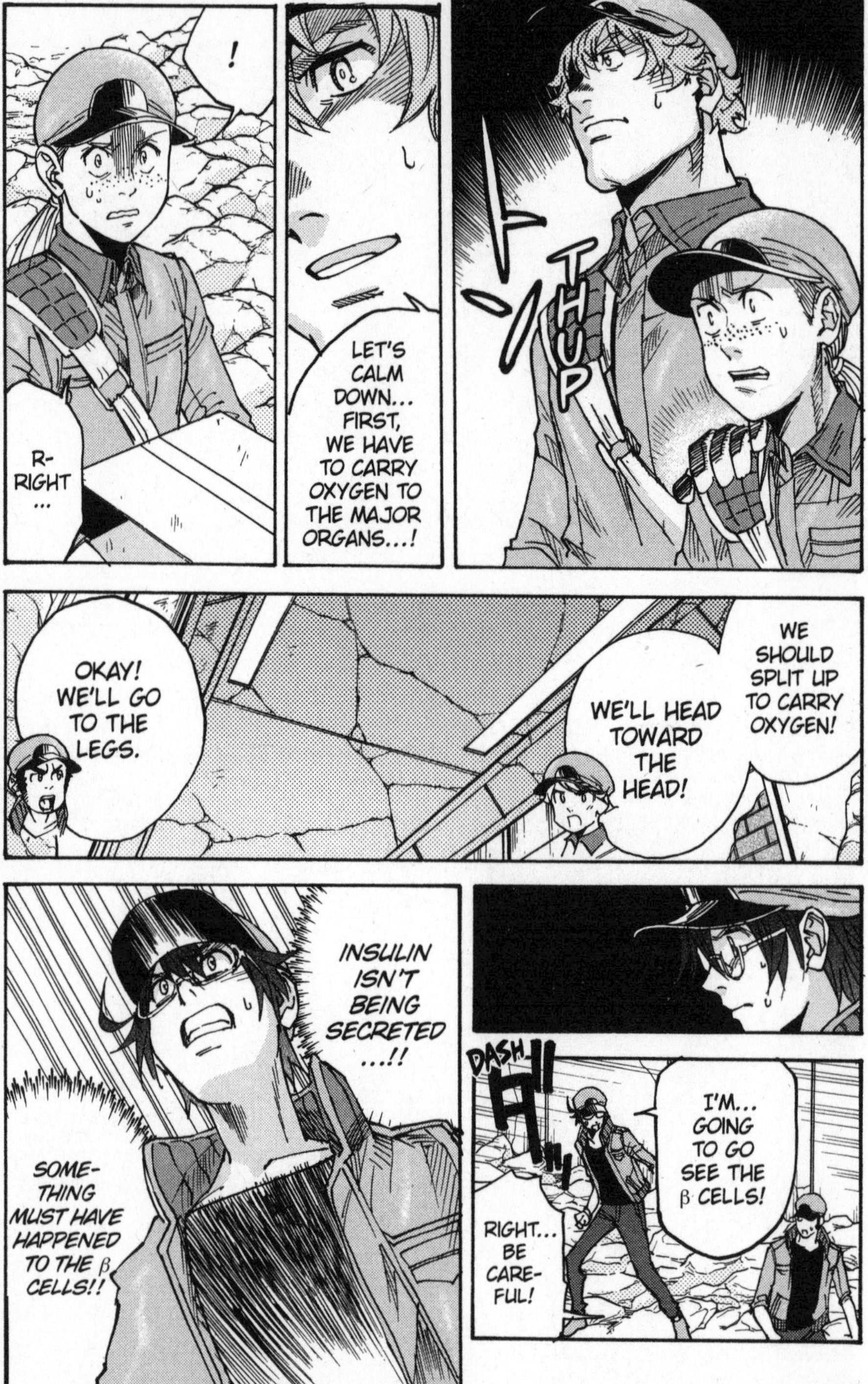
THUP
LET'S CALM DOWN... FIRST, WE HAVE TO CARRY OXYGEN TO THE MAJOR ORGANS...!
!
R-RIGHT ...
WE SHOULD SPLIT UP TO CARRY OXYGEN!
WE'LL HEAD TOWARD THE HEAD!
OKAY! WE'LL GO TO THE LEGS.
DASH
I'M... GOING TO GO SEE THE β CELLS!
RIGHT... BE CARE-FUL!
INSULIN ISN'T BEING SECRETED ...!!
SOME-THING MUST HAVE HAPPENED TO THE β CELLS!!

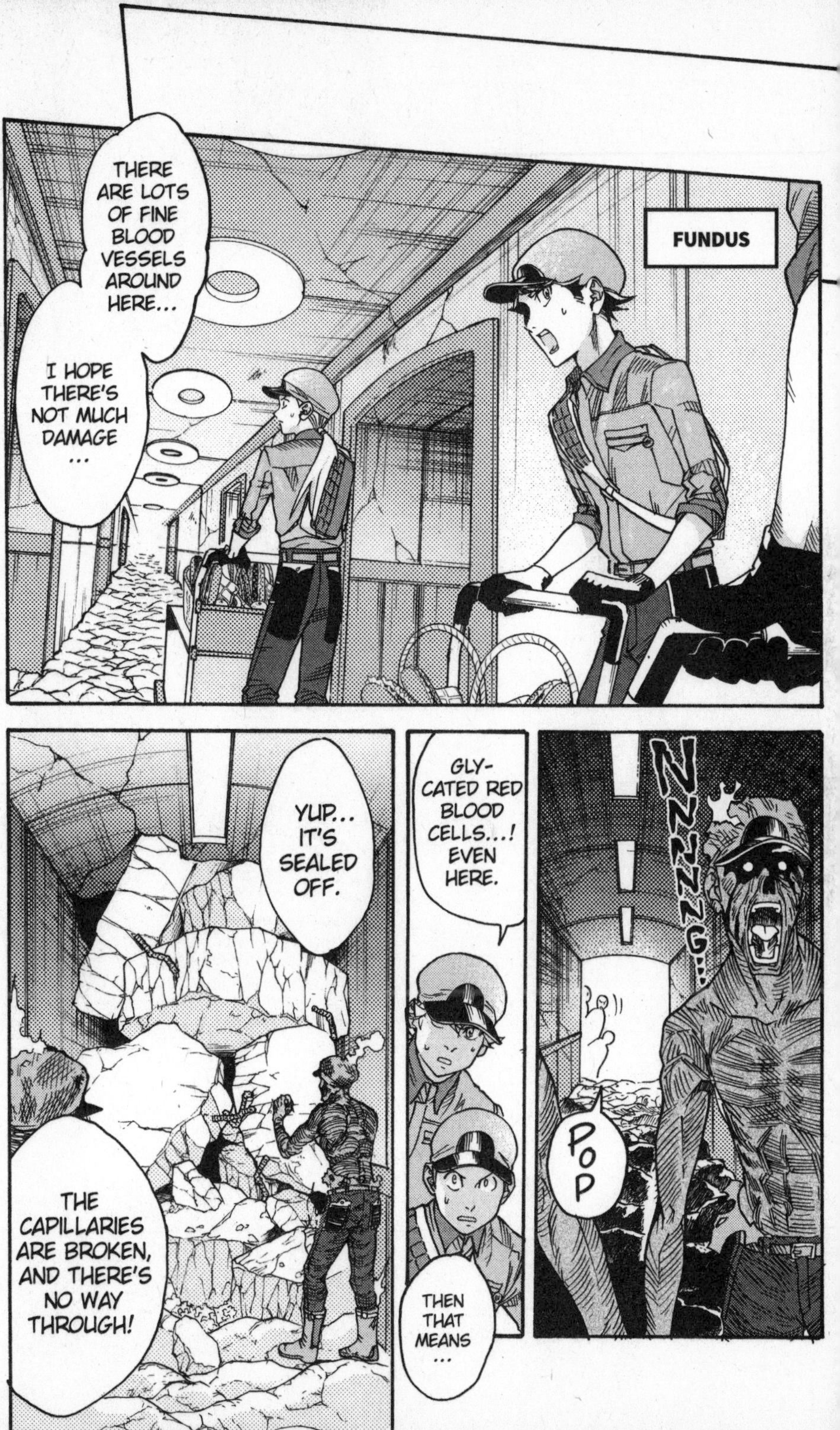
FUNDUS
THERE ARE LOTS OF FINE BLOOD VESSELS AROUND HERE...
I HOPE THERE'S NOT MUCH DAMAGE...
NNNNNG...
POP
GLY-CATED RED BLOOD CELLS...! EVEN HERE.
THEN THAT MEANS...
YUP... IT'S SEALED OFF.
THE CAPILLARIES ARE BROKEN, AND THERE'S NO WAY THROUGH!

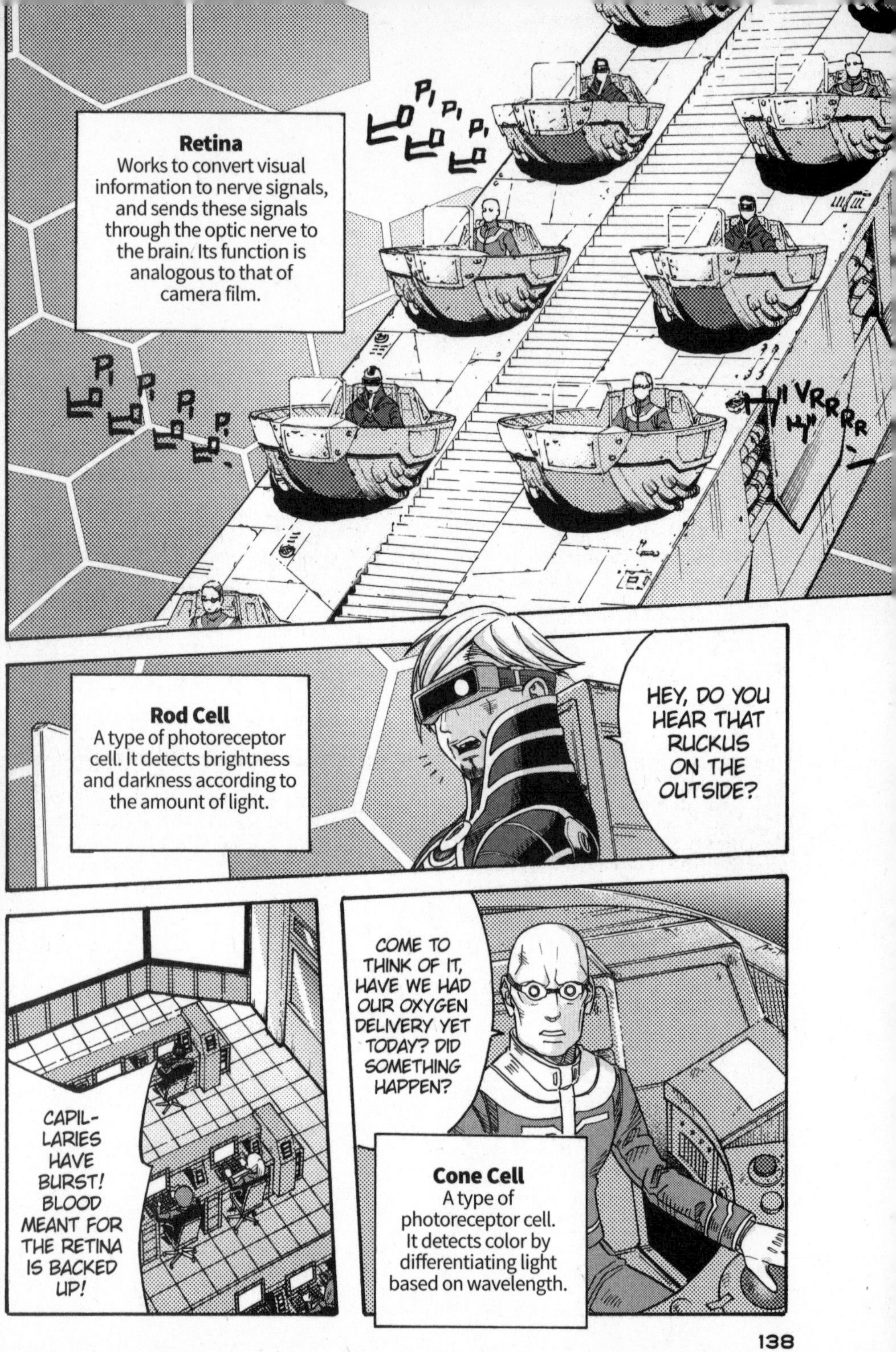
PI PI PI
Retina
Works to convert visual information to nerve signals, and sends these signals through the optic nerve to the brain. Its function is analogous to that of camera film.
VRRRRR
PI PI PI PI
HEY, DO YOU HEAR THAT RUCKUS ON THE OUTSIDE?
Rod Cell
A type of photoreceptor cell. It detects brightness and darkness according to the amount of light.
COME TO THINK OF IT, HAVE WE HAD OUR OXYGEN DELIVERY YET TODAY? DID SOMETHING HAPPEN?
Cone Cell
A type of photoreceptor cell. It detects color by differentiating light based on wavelength.
CAPIL-LARIES HAVE BURST! BLOOD MEANT FOR THE RETINA IS BACKED UP!

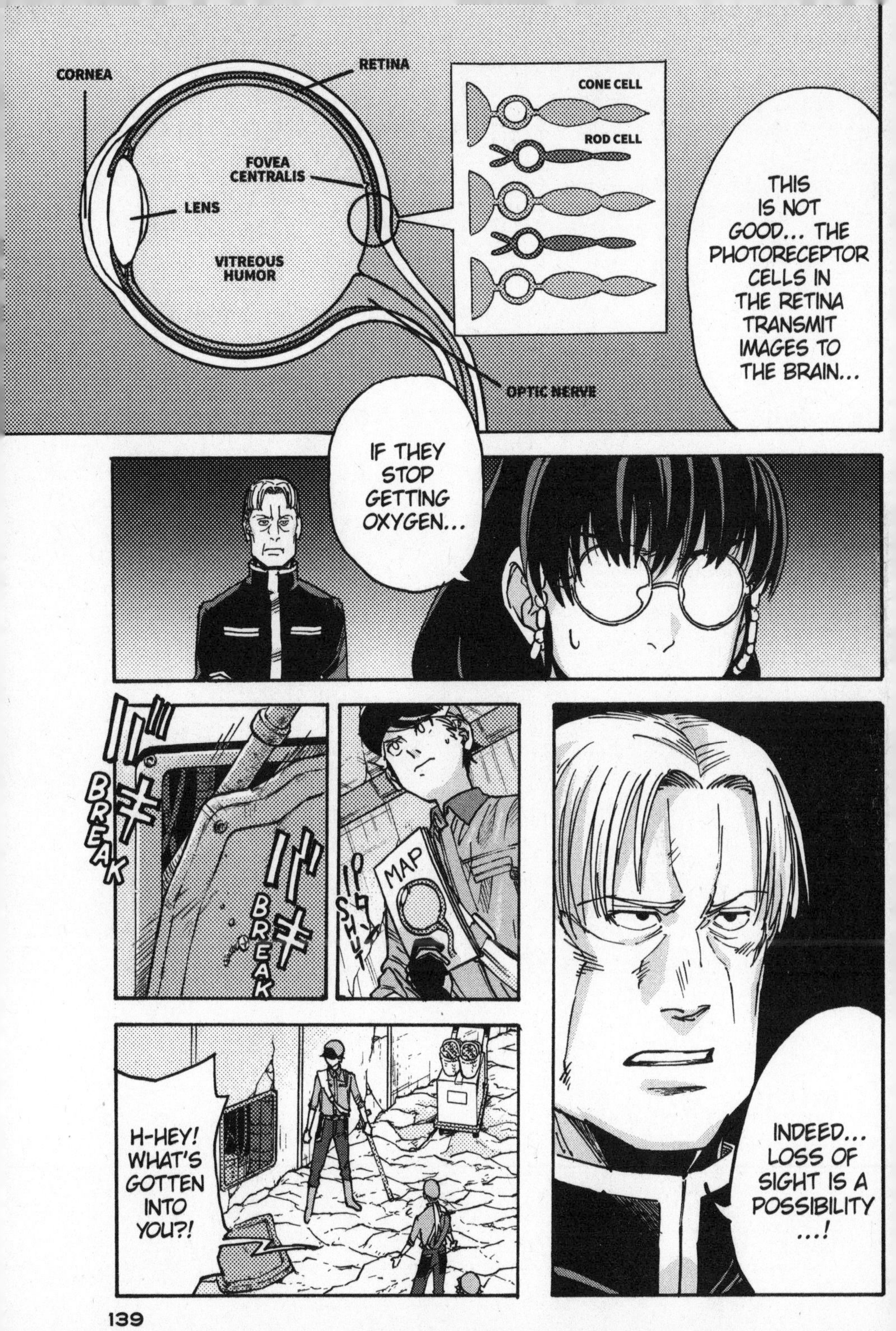
THIS IS NOT GOOD... THE PHOTORECEPTOR CELLS IN THE RETINA TRANSMIT IMAGES TO THE BRAIN...
CORNEA
RETINA
FOVEA CENTRALIS
LENS
VITREOUS HUMOR
OPTIC NERVE
CONE CELL
ROD CELL
IF THEY STOP GETTING OXYGEN...
INDEED... LOSS OF SIGHT IS A POSSIBILITY ...!
SHUT
MAP
BREAK
BREAK
BREAK
H-HEY! WHAT'S GOTTEN INTO YOU?!

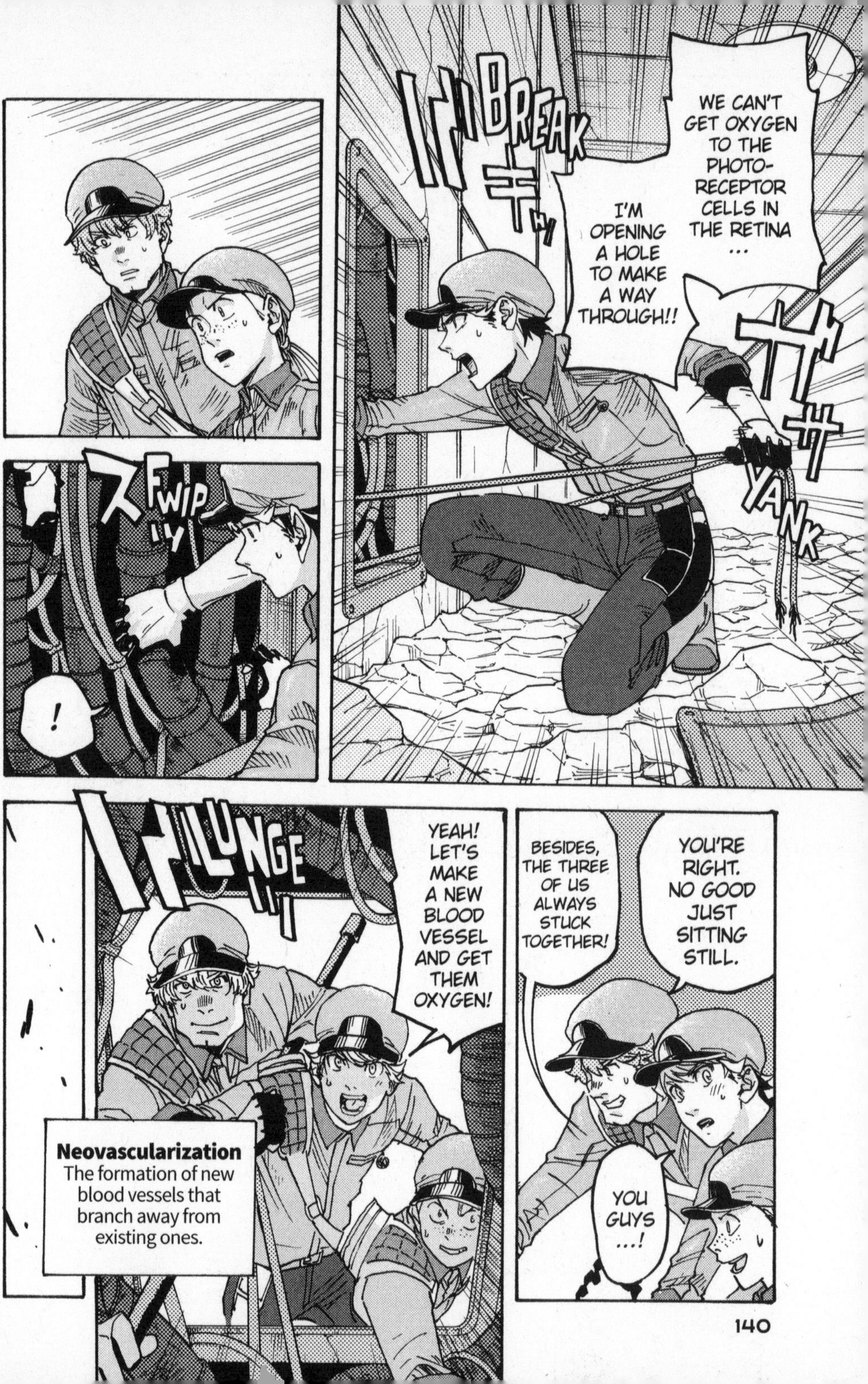
BREAK
WE CAN'T GET OXYGEN TO THE PHOTO-RECEPTOR CELLS IN THE RETINA ...
I'M OPENING A HOLE TO MAKE A WAY THROUGH!!
YANK
FWIP
!
YOU'RE RIGHT. NO GOOD JUST SITTING STILL.
BESIDES, THE THREE OF US ALWAYS STUCK TOGETHER!
YOU GUYS ...!
LUNGE
YEAH! LET'S MAKE A NEW BLOOD VESSEL AND GET THEM OXYGEN!
Neovascularization
The formation of new blood vessels that branch away from existing ones.

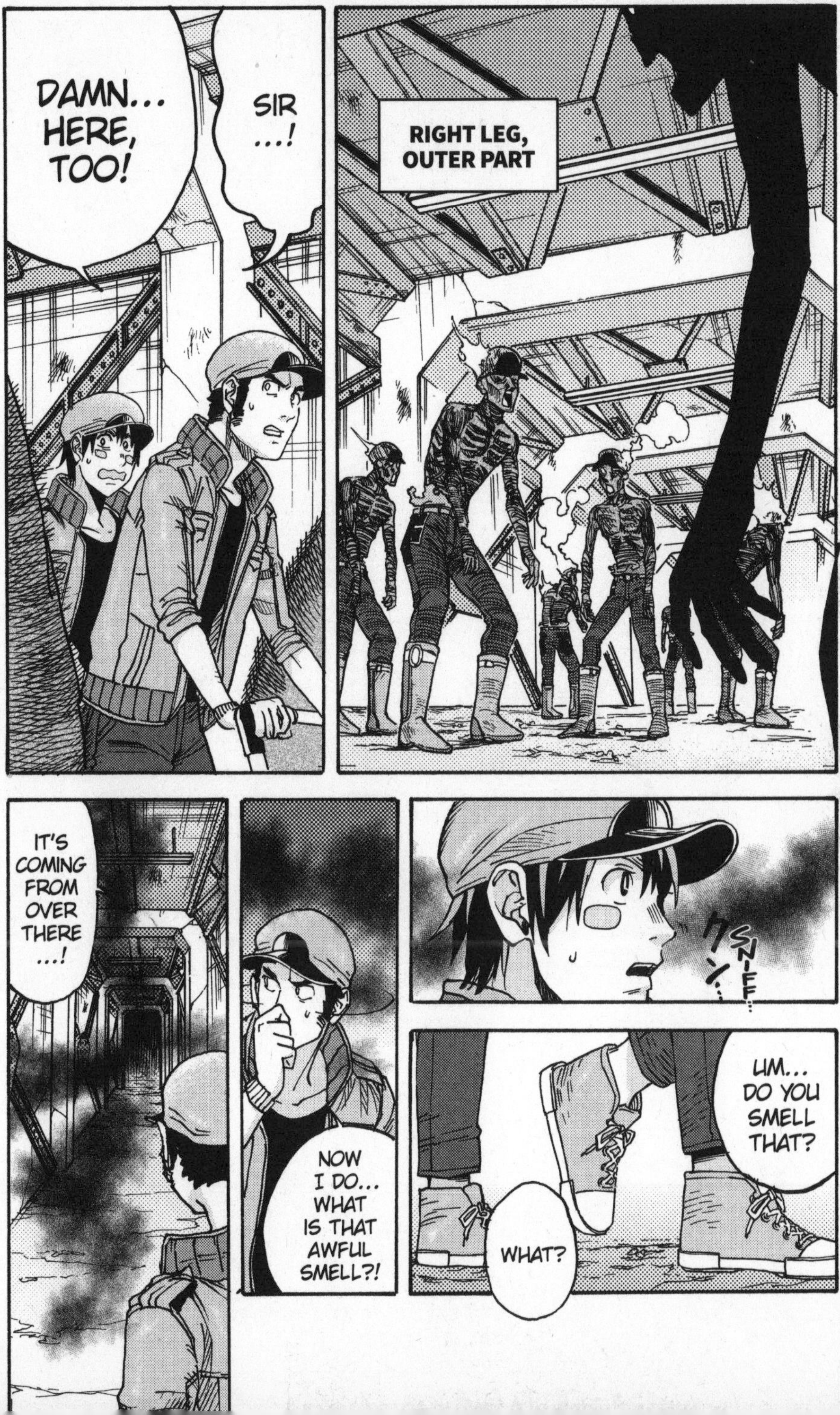
RIGHT LEG, OUTER PART
SIR …!
DAMN… HERE, TOO!
SNIFF…
UM… DO YOU SMELL THAT?
WHAT?
NOW I DO… WHAT IS THAT AWFUL SMELL?!
IT'S COMING FROM OVER THERE …!

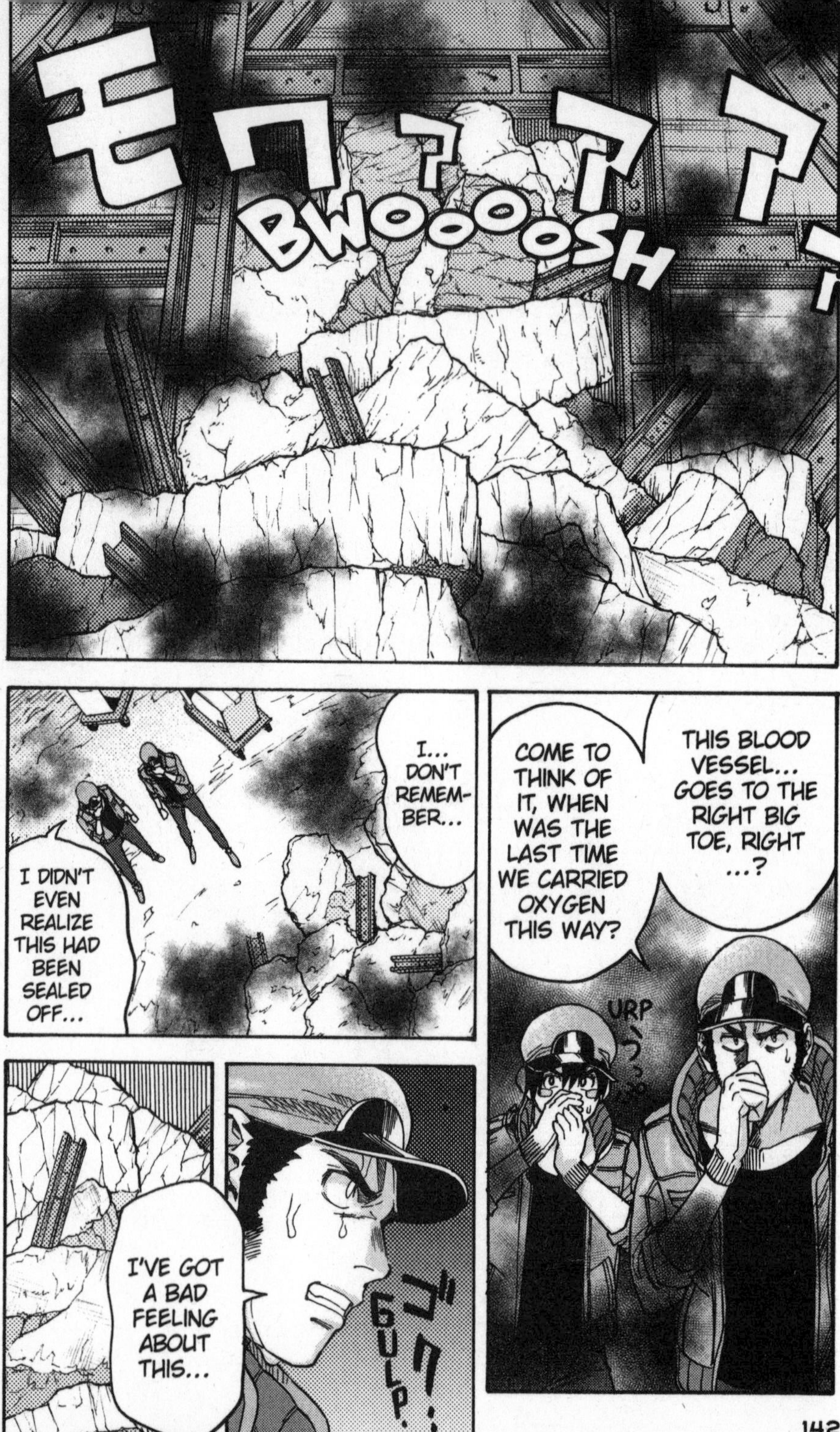
モワァァァ
BWOOOOSH
THIS BLOOD VESSEL... GOES TO THE RIGHT BIG TOE, RIGHT ...?
COME TO THINK OF IT, WHEN WAS THE LAST TIME WE CARRIED OXYGEN THIS WAY?
URP
I... DON'T REMEMBER...
I DIDN'T EVEN REALIZE THIS HAD BEEN SEALED OFF...
I'VE GOT A BAD FEELING ABOUT THIS...
ゴクッ
GULP...

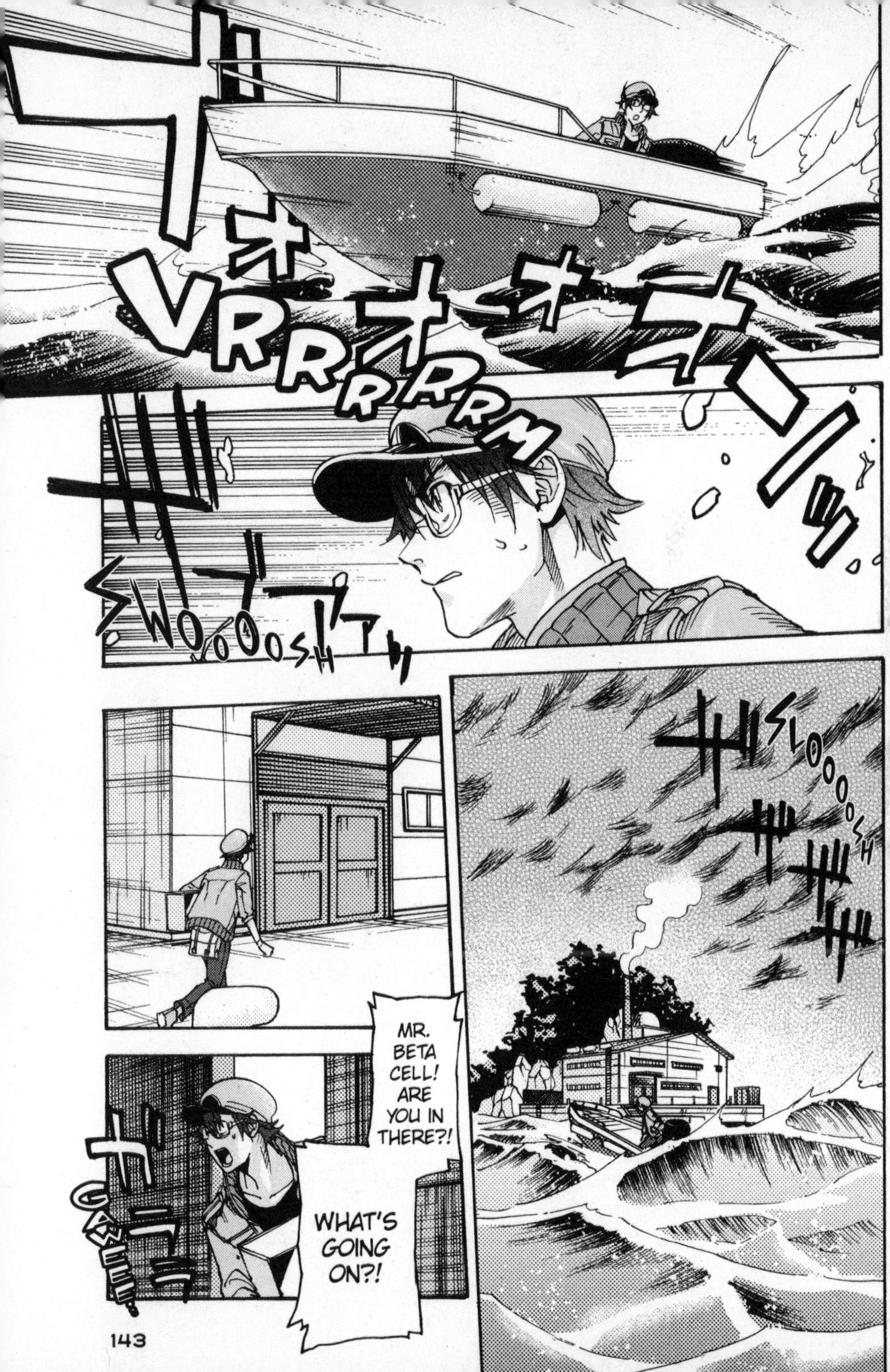
VRRRRRRM
SWOOOOSH
SLOOOOOSH
MR. BETA CELL! ARE YOU IN THERE?!
WHAT'S GOING ON?!
GWEEE

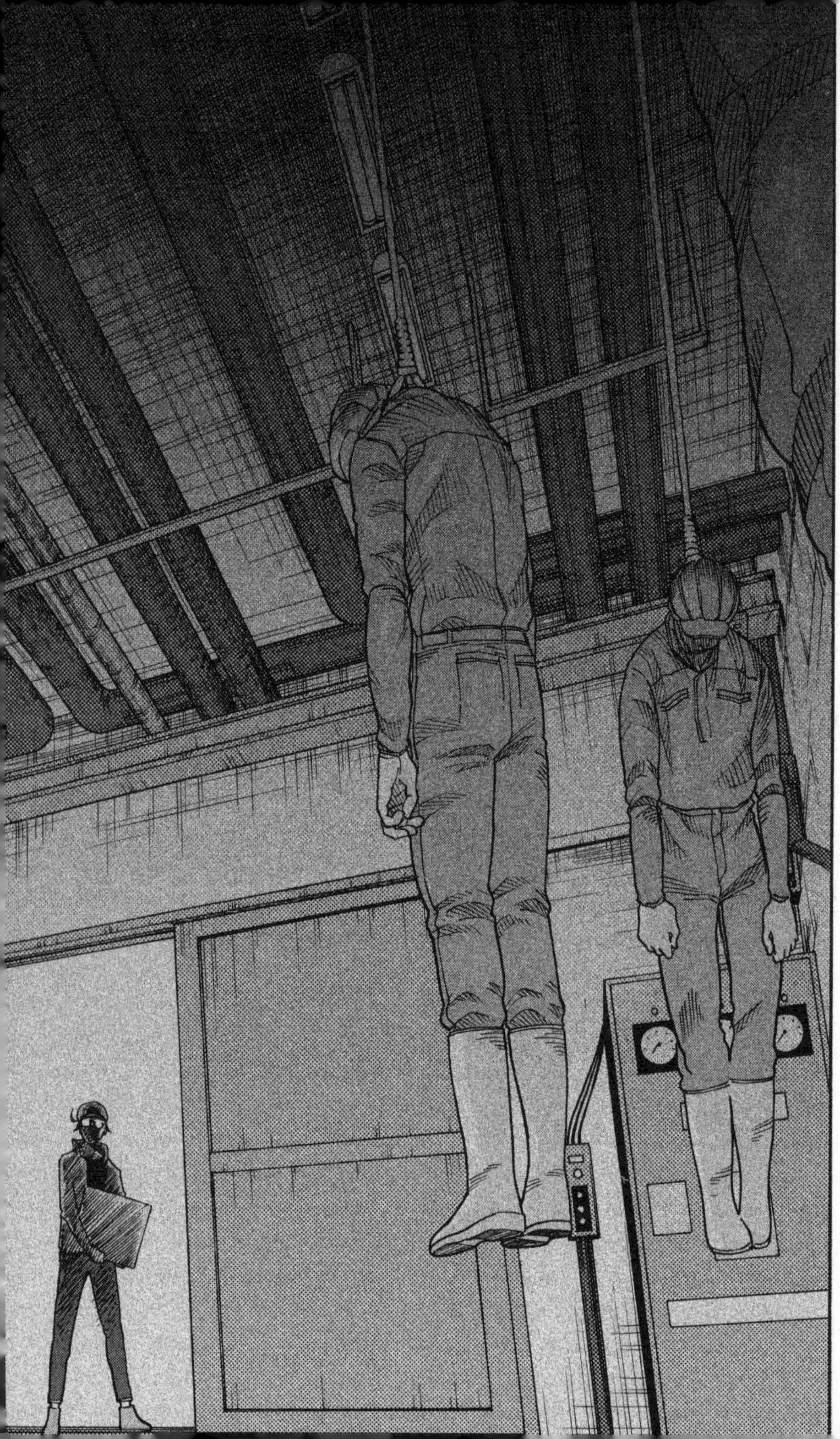

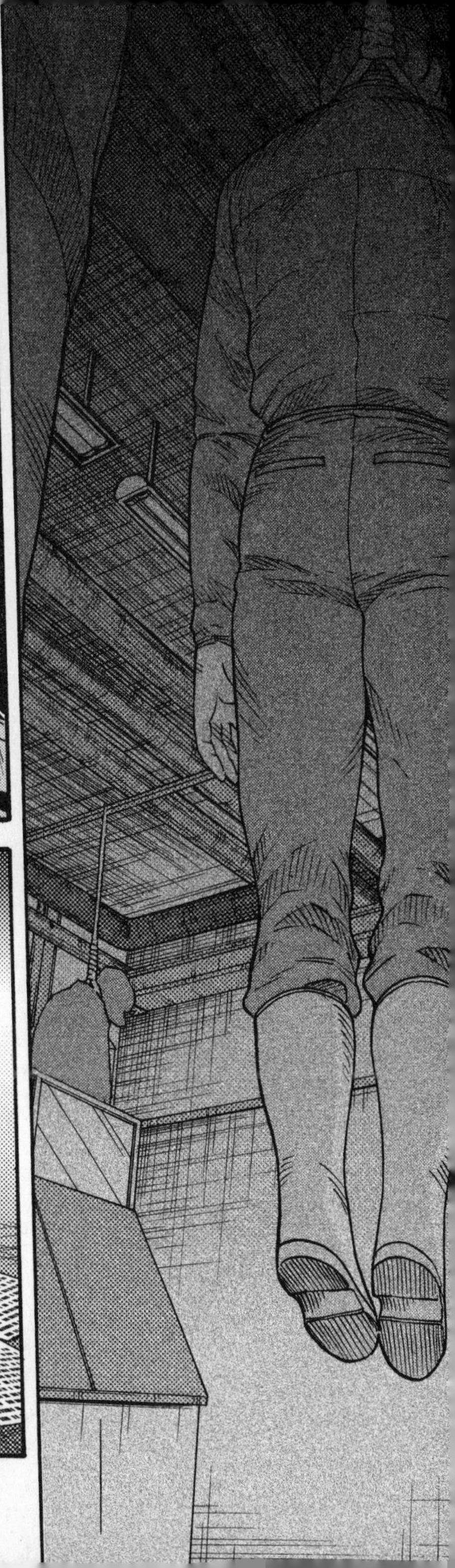

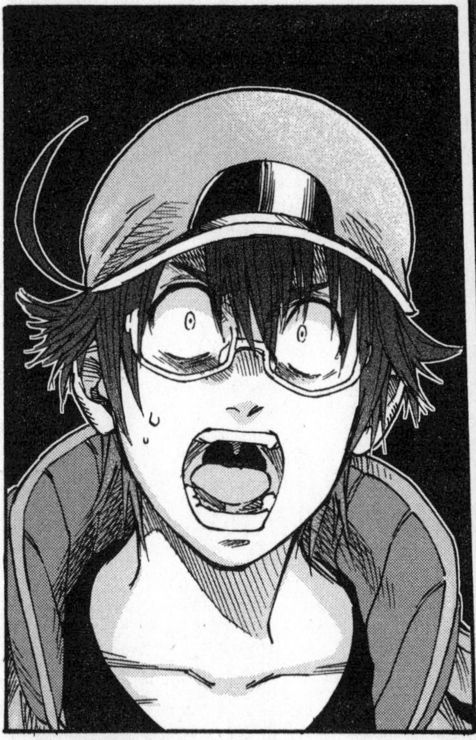

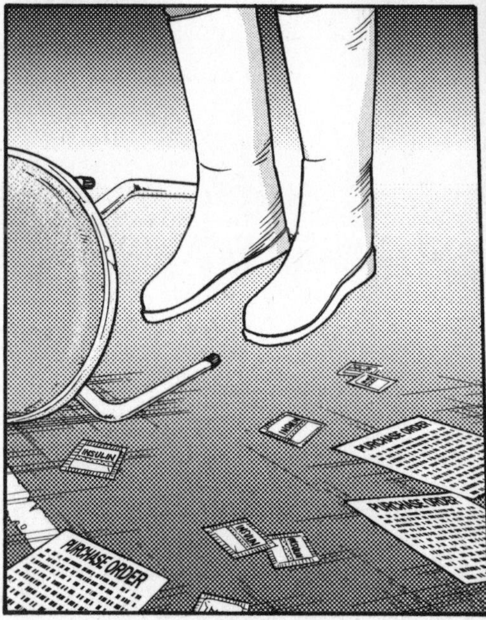
PURCHASE ORDER
INSULIN
PURCHASE ORDER
PURCHASE ORDER

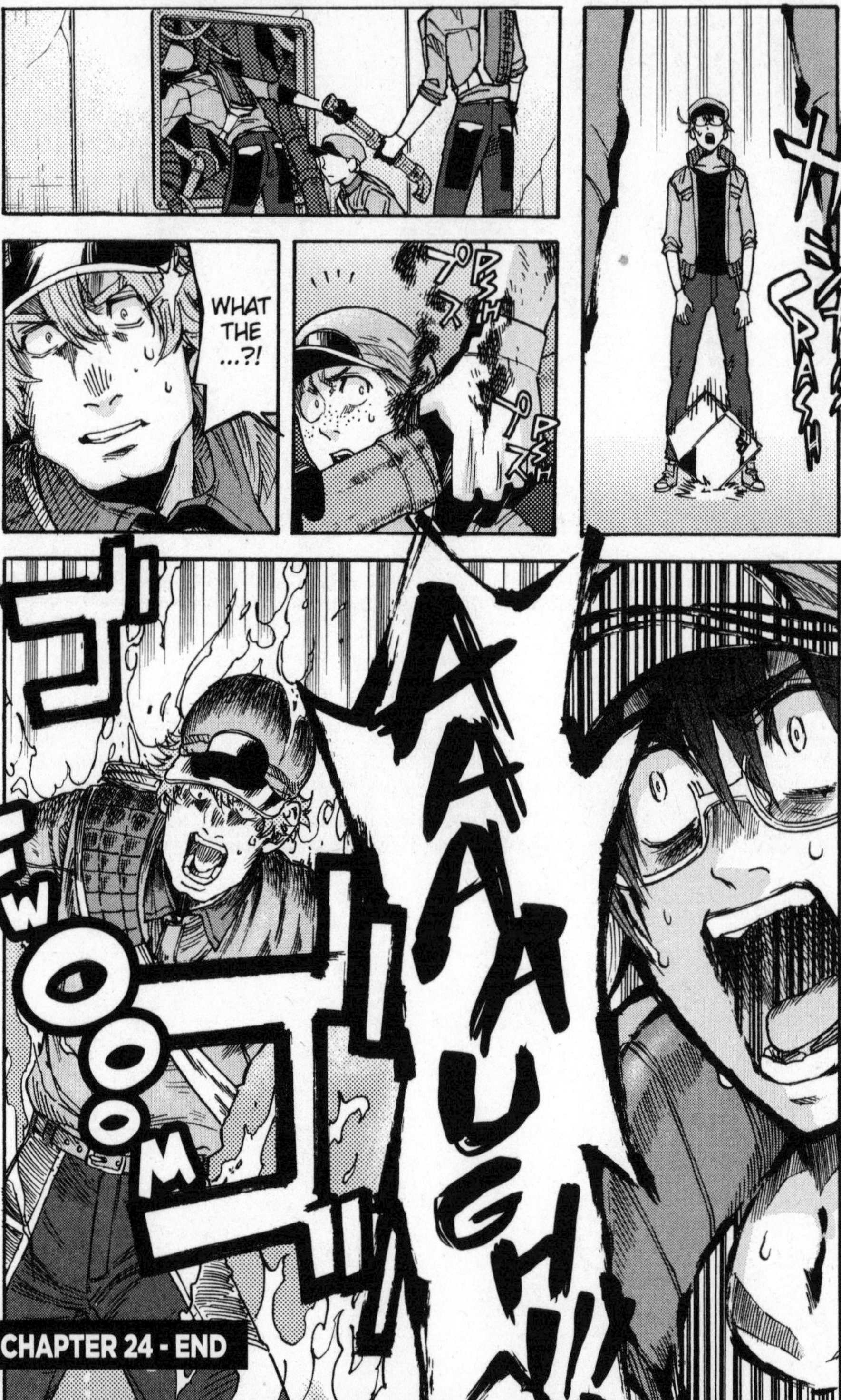
CRASH
P'SSH
P'SSH
WHAT THE ...?!
AAAAUGH!!
FWOOOOM

CHAPTER 24 - END

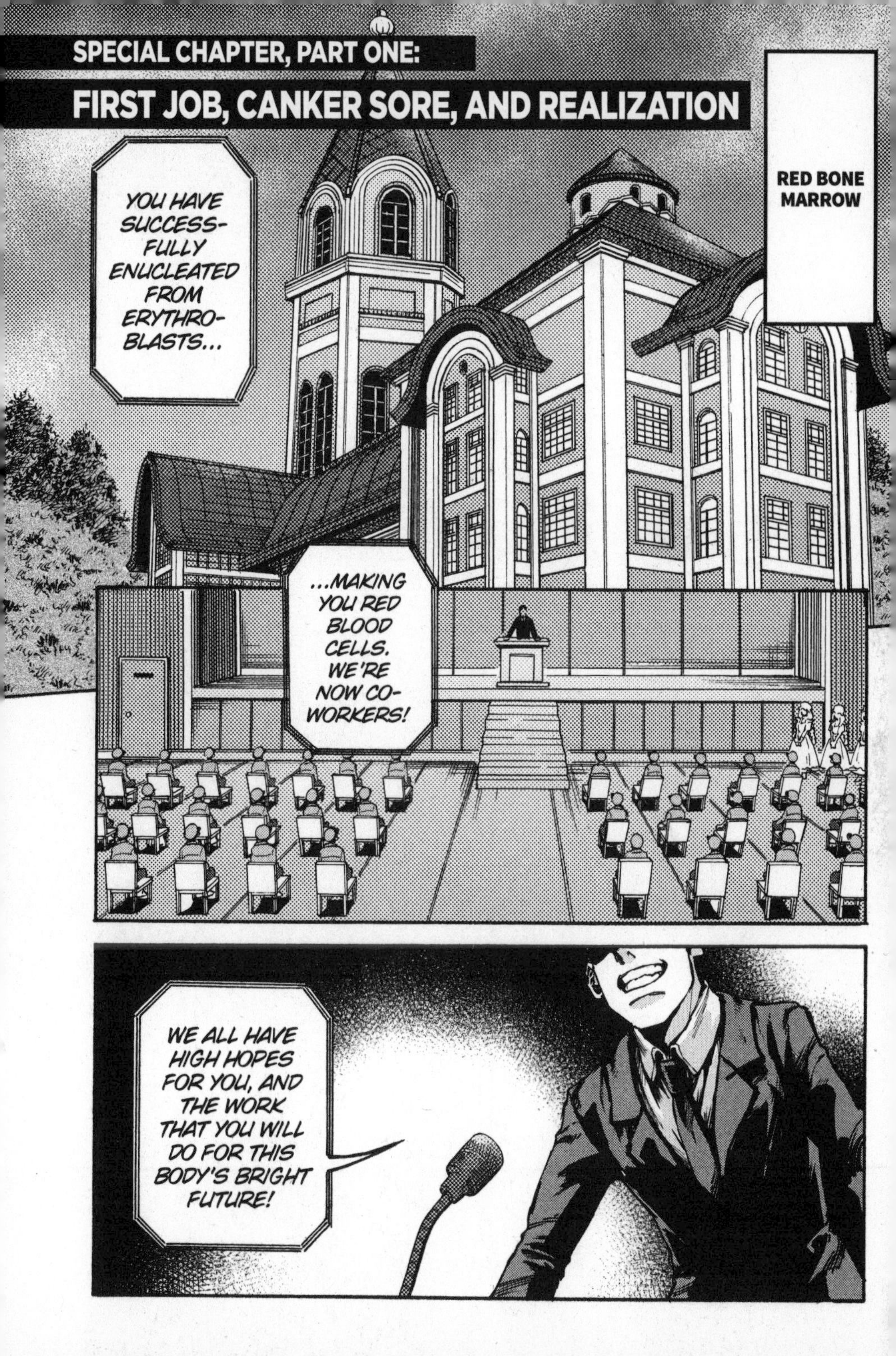
SPECIAL CHAPTER, PART ONE:
FIRST JOB, CANKER SORE, AND REALIZATION
RED BONE MARROW
YOU HAVE SUCCESS-FULLY ENUCLEATED FROM ERYTHRO-BLASTS...
...MAKING YOU RED BLOOD CELLS. WE'RE NOW CO-WORKERS!
WE ALL HAVE HIGH HOPES FOR YOU, AND THE WORK THAT YOU WILL DO FOR THIS BODY'S BRIGHT FUTURE!

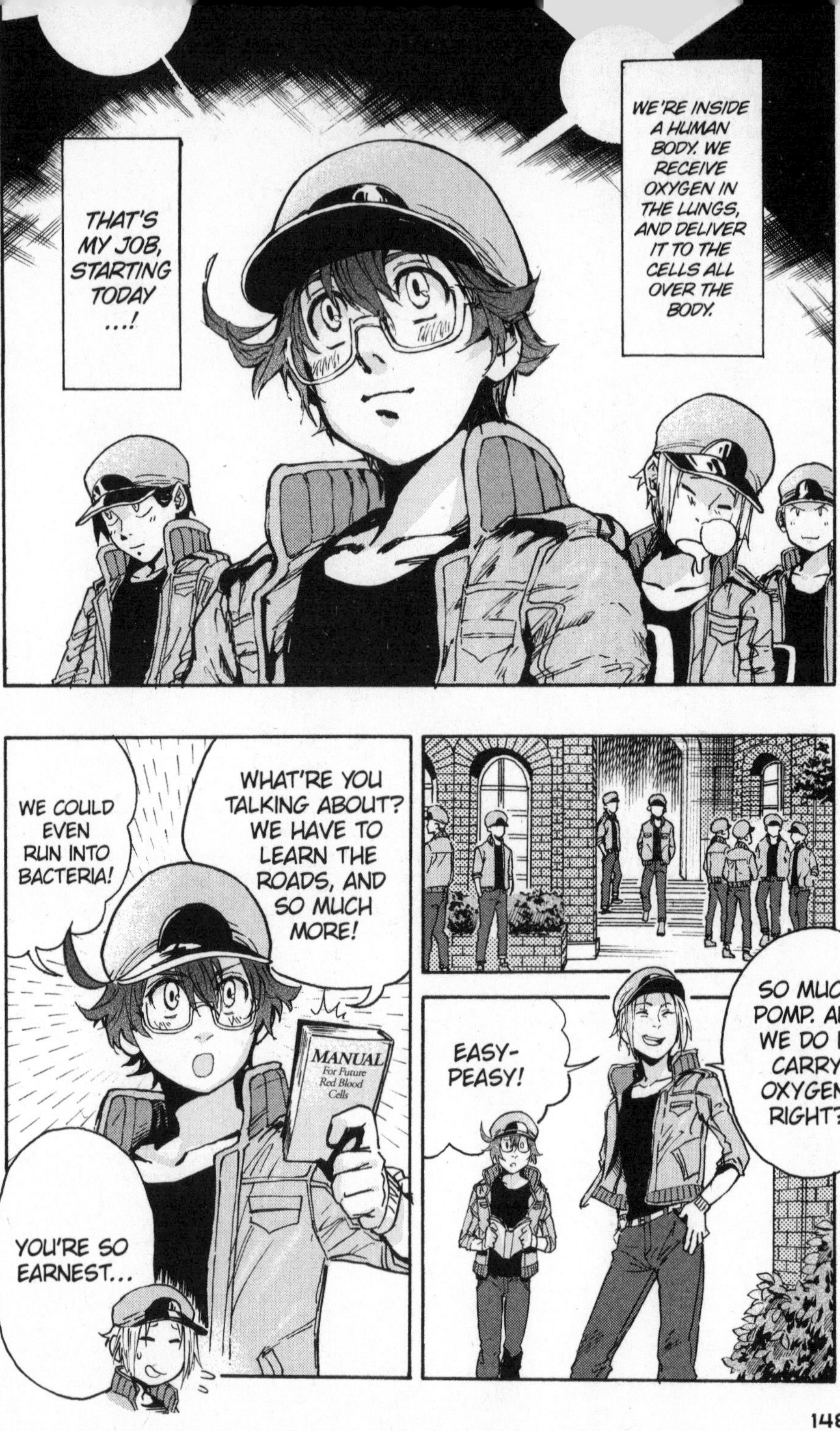
WE'RE INSIDE A HUMAN BODY. WE RECEIVE OXYGEN IN THE LUNGS, AND DELIVER IT TO THE CELLS ALL OVER THE BODY.
THAT'S MY JOB, STARTING TODAY ...!
SO MUCH POMP. ALL WE DO IS CARRY OXYGEN, RIGHT?
EASY-PEASY!
WHAT'RE YOU TALKING ABOUT? WE HAVE TO LEARN THE ROADS, AND SO MUCH MORE!
WE COULD EVEN RUN INTO BACTERIA!
MANUAL For Future Red Blood Cells
YOU'RE SO EARNEST...

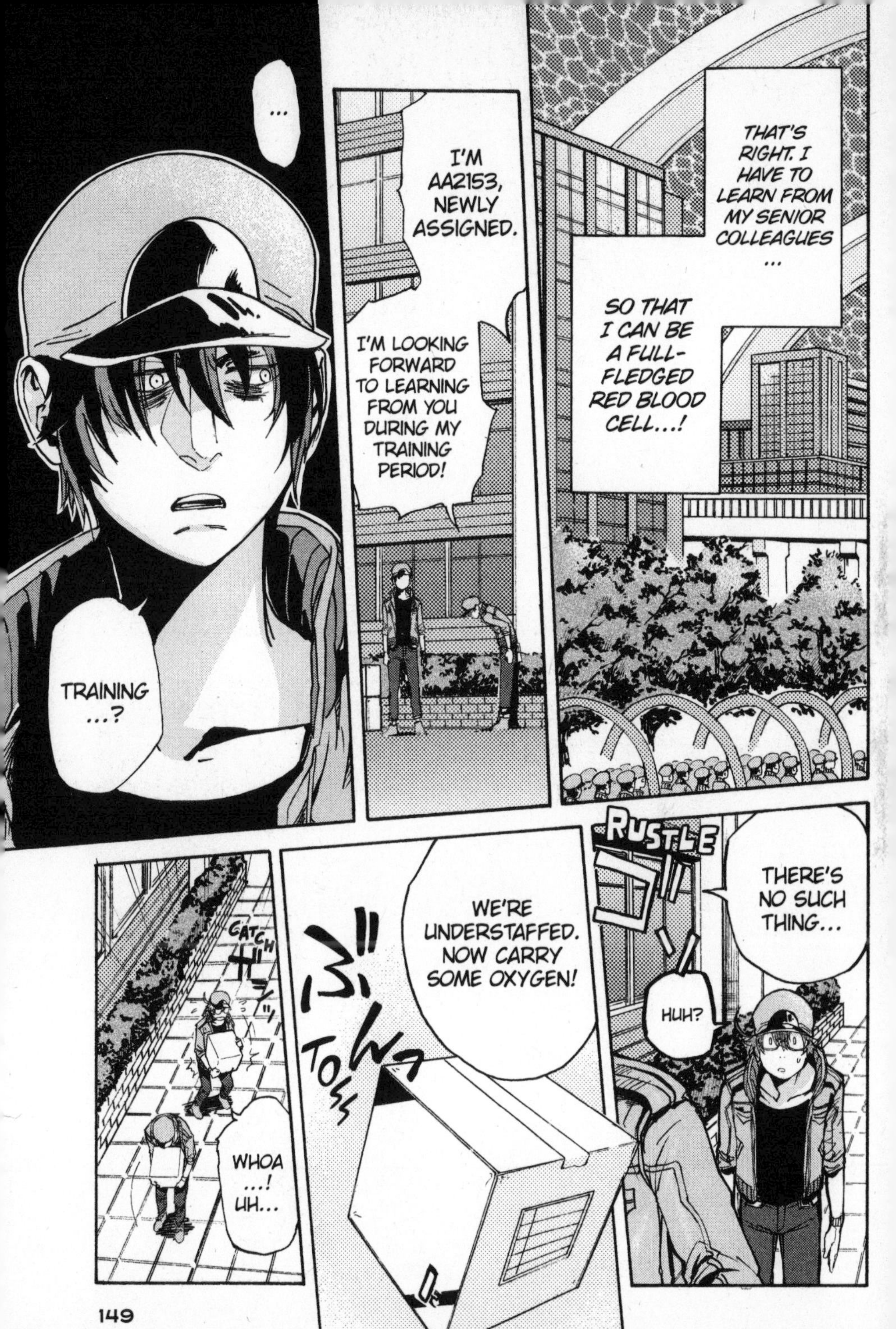
THAT'S RIGHT. I HAVE TO LEARN FROM MY SENIOR COLLEAGUES ...
SO THAT I CAN BE A FULL-FLEDGED RED BLOOD CELL...!
I'M AA2153, NEWLY ASSIGNED.
I'M LOOKING FORWARD TO LEARNING FROM YOU DURING MY TRAINING PERIOD!
...
TRAINING ...?
RUSTLE
THERE'S NO SUCH THING...
HUH?
WE'RE UNDERSTAFFED. NOW CARRY SOME OXYGEN!
TOSS
CATCH
WHOA ...! UH...

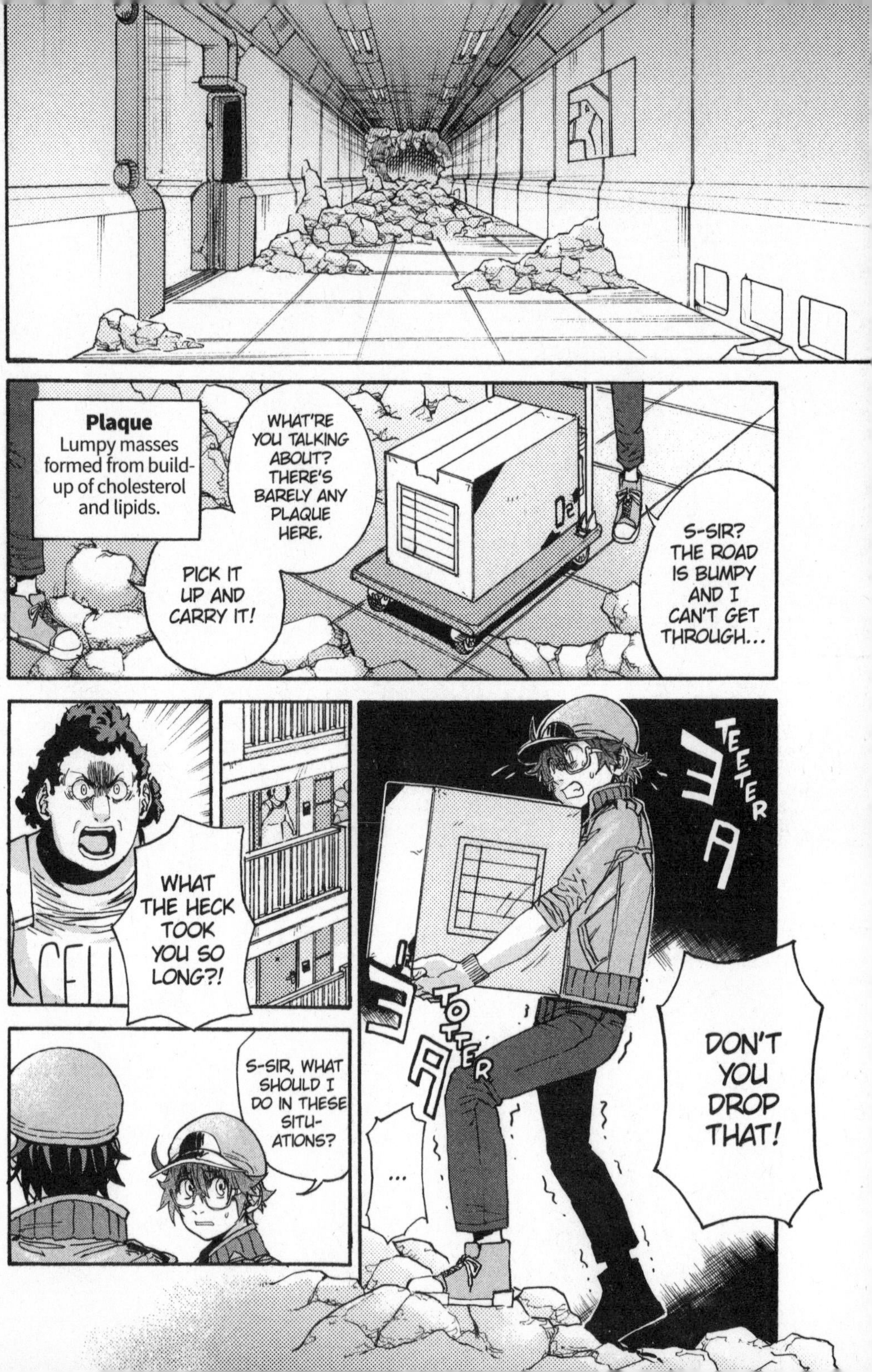
S-SIR? THE ROAD IS BUMPY AND I CAN'T GET THROUGH...
WHAT'RE YOU TALKING ABOUT? THERE'S BARELY ANY PLAQUE HERE.
PICK IT UP AND CARRY IT!
Plaque Lumpy masses formed from build-up of cholesterol and lipids.
TEETER
DON'T YOU DROP THAT!
TOTTER
...
WHAT THE HECK TOOK YOU SO LONG?!
S-SIR, WHAT SHOULD I DO IN THESE SITU-ATIONS?

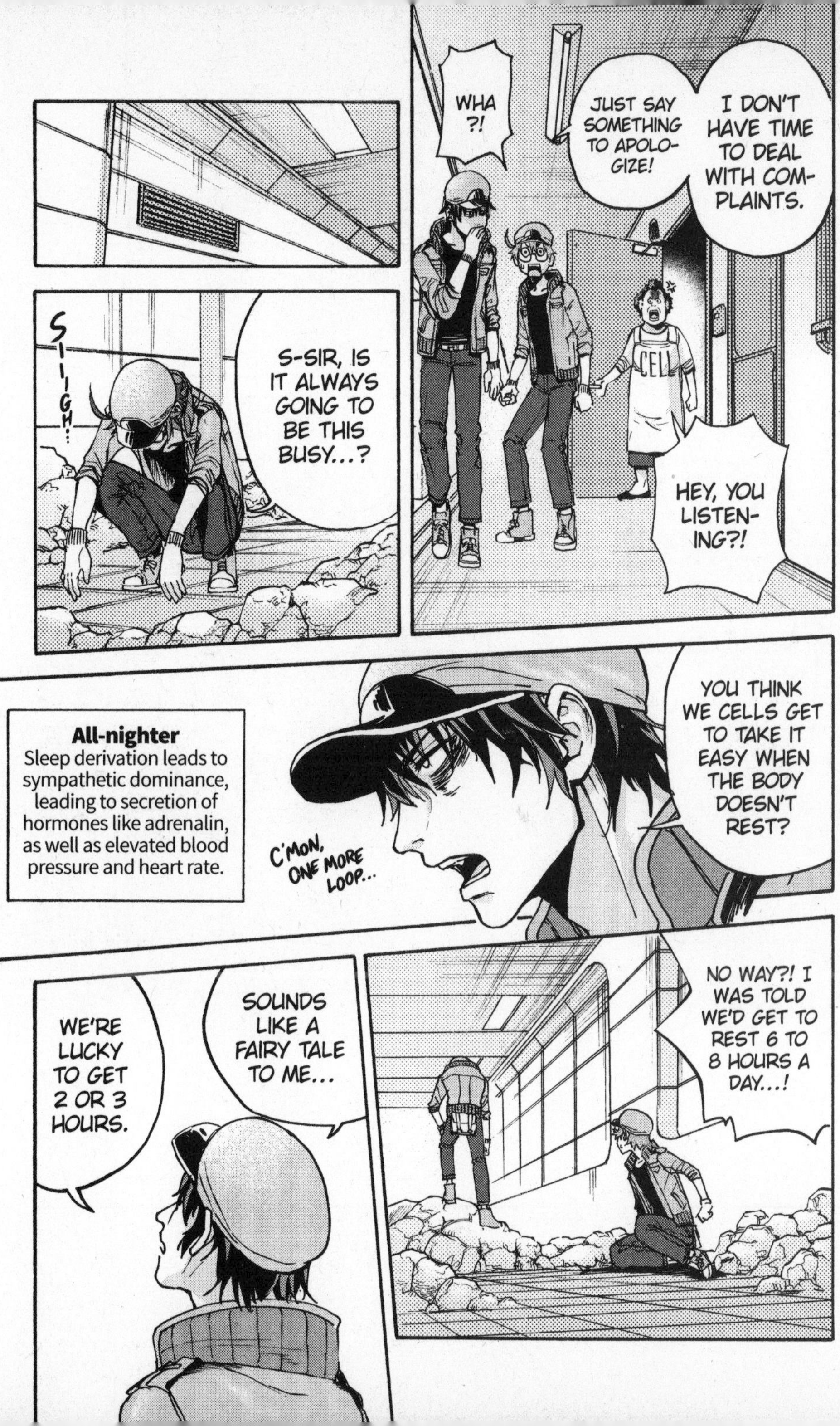
I DON'T HAVE TIME TO DEAL WITH COMPLAINTS.
JUST SAY SOMETHING TO APOLOGIZE!
WHA?!
HEY, YOU LISTENING?!
SIIIGH...
S-SIR, IS IT ALWAYS GOING TO BE THIS BUSY...?
YOU THINK WE CELLS GET TO TAKE IT EASY WHEN THE BODY DOESN'T REST?
C'MON, ONE MORE LOOP...
All-nighter
Sleep derivation leads to sympathetic dominance, leading to secretion of hormones like adrenalin, as well as elevated blood pressure and heart rate.
NO WAY?! I WAS TOLD WE'D GET TO REST 6 TO 8 HOURS A DAY...!
SOUNDS LIKE A FAIRY TALE TO ME...
WE'RE LUCKY TO GET 2 OR 3 HOURS.

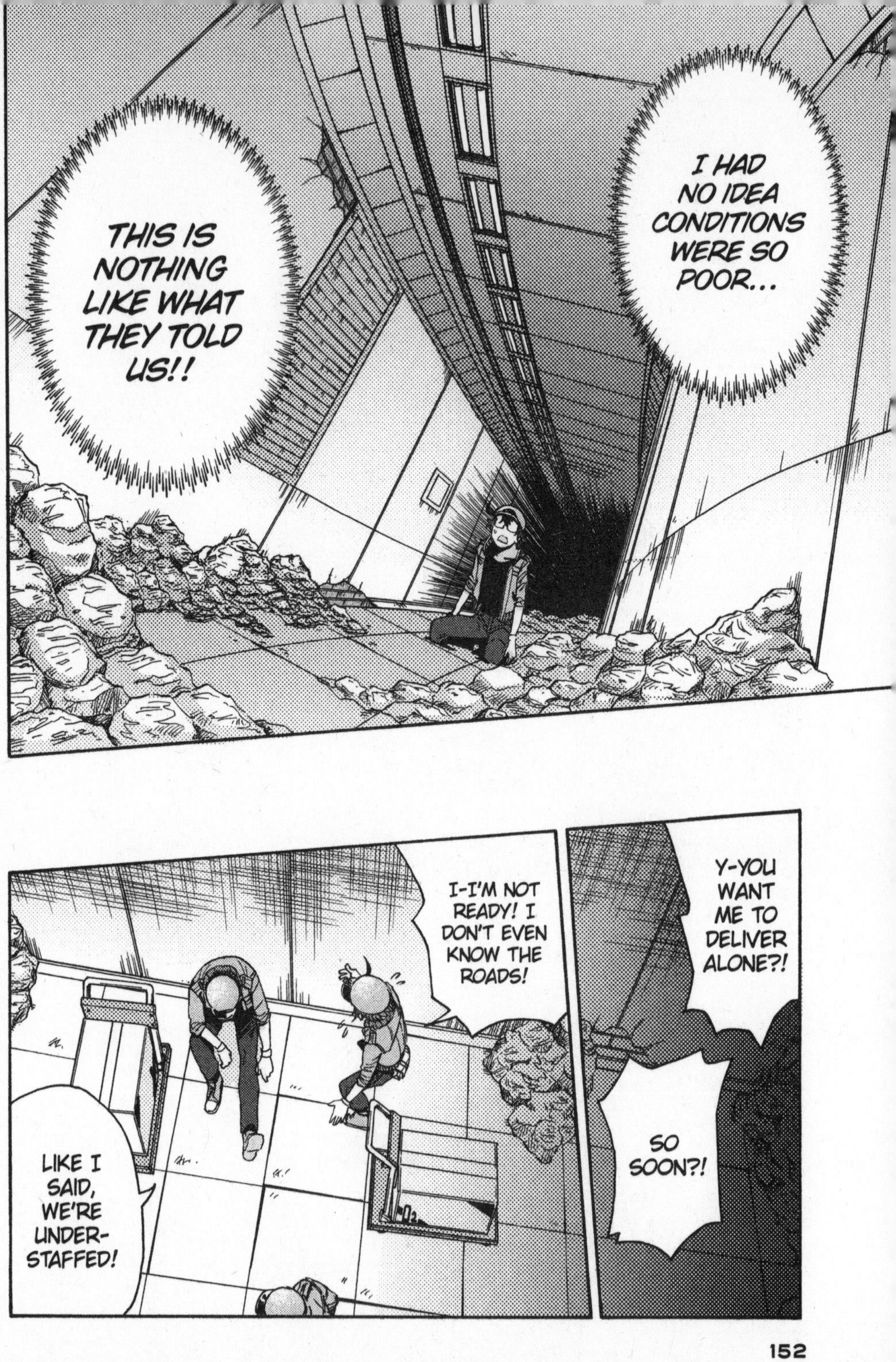
I HAD NO IDEA CONDITIONS WERE SO POOR...
THIS IS NOTHING LIKE WHAT THEY TOLD US!!
Y-YOU WANT ME TO DELIVER ALONE?!
SO SOON?!
I-I'M NOT READY! I DON'T EVEN KNOW THE ROADS!
LIKE I SAID, WE'RE UNDER-STAFFED!

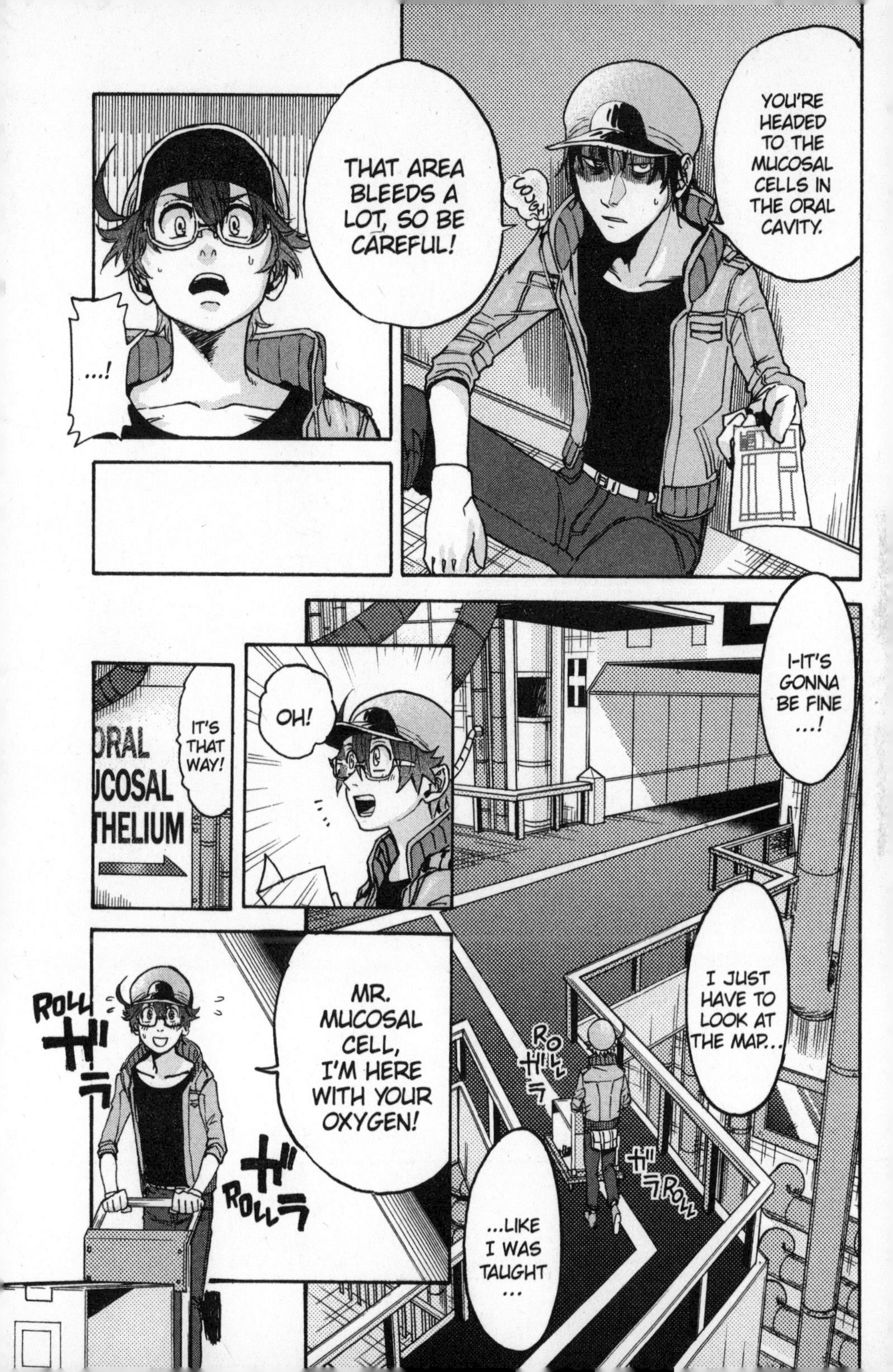
YOU'RE HEADED TO THE MUCOSAL CELLS IN THE ORAL CAVITY.
COUGH
THAT AREA BLEEDS A LOT, SO BE CAREFUL!
...!
I-IT'S GONNA BE FINE ...!
OH!
IT'S THAT WAY!
ORAL
UCOSAL
THELIUM
I JUST HAVE TO LOOK AT THE MAP...
ROLL
ROW
...LIKE I WAS TAUGHT ...
MR. MUCOSAL CELL, I'M HERE WITH YOUR OXYGEN!
ROLL
ROLL

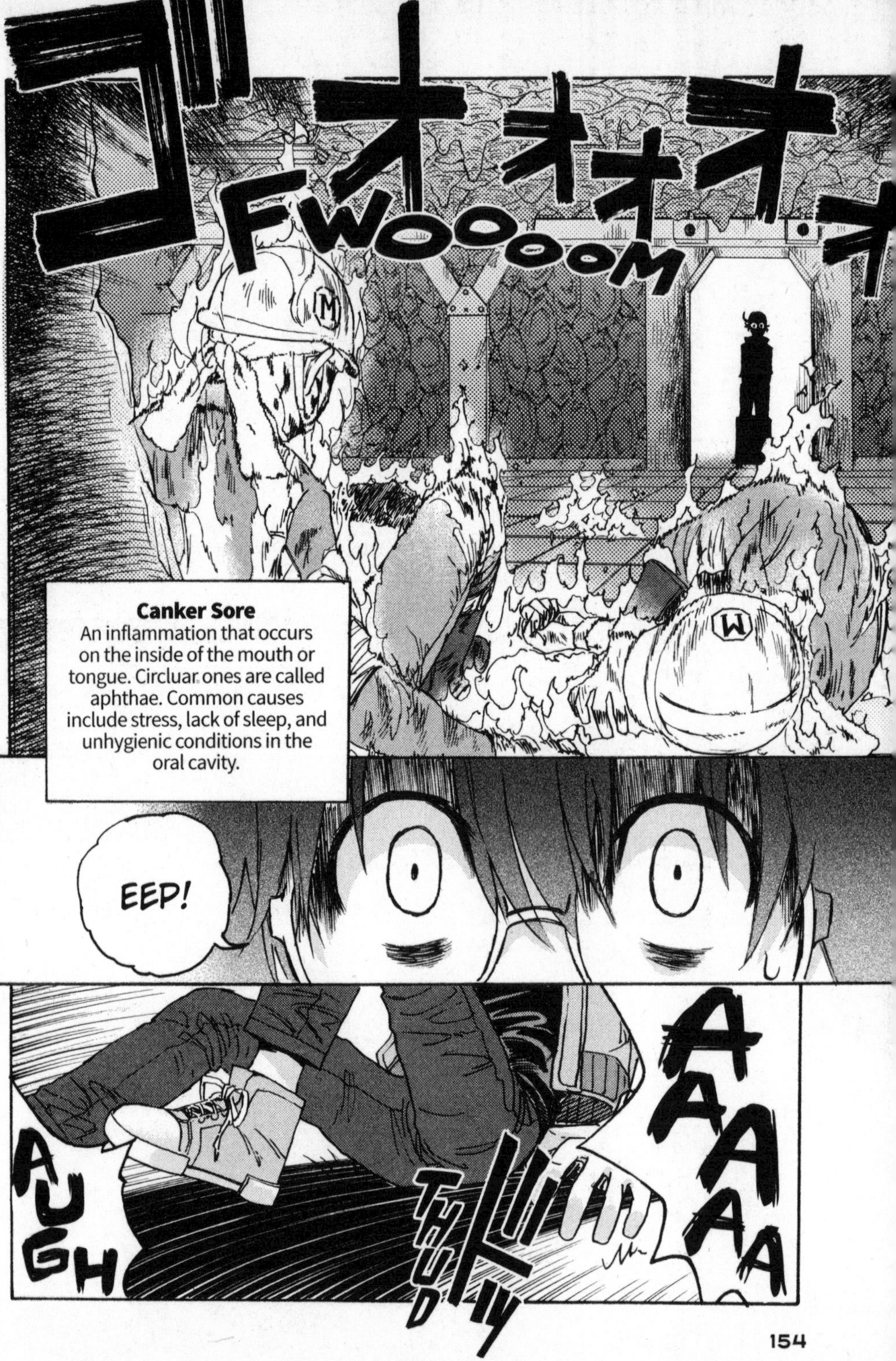
ゴオオオオ
FWOOOOOM
Canker Sore
An inflammation that occurs on the inside of the mouth or tongue. Circluar ones are called aphthae. Common causes include stress, lack of sleep, and unhygienic conditions in the oral cavity.
EEP!
AAAAAA
THUD
AUGH

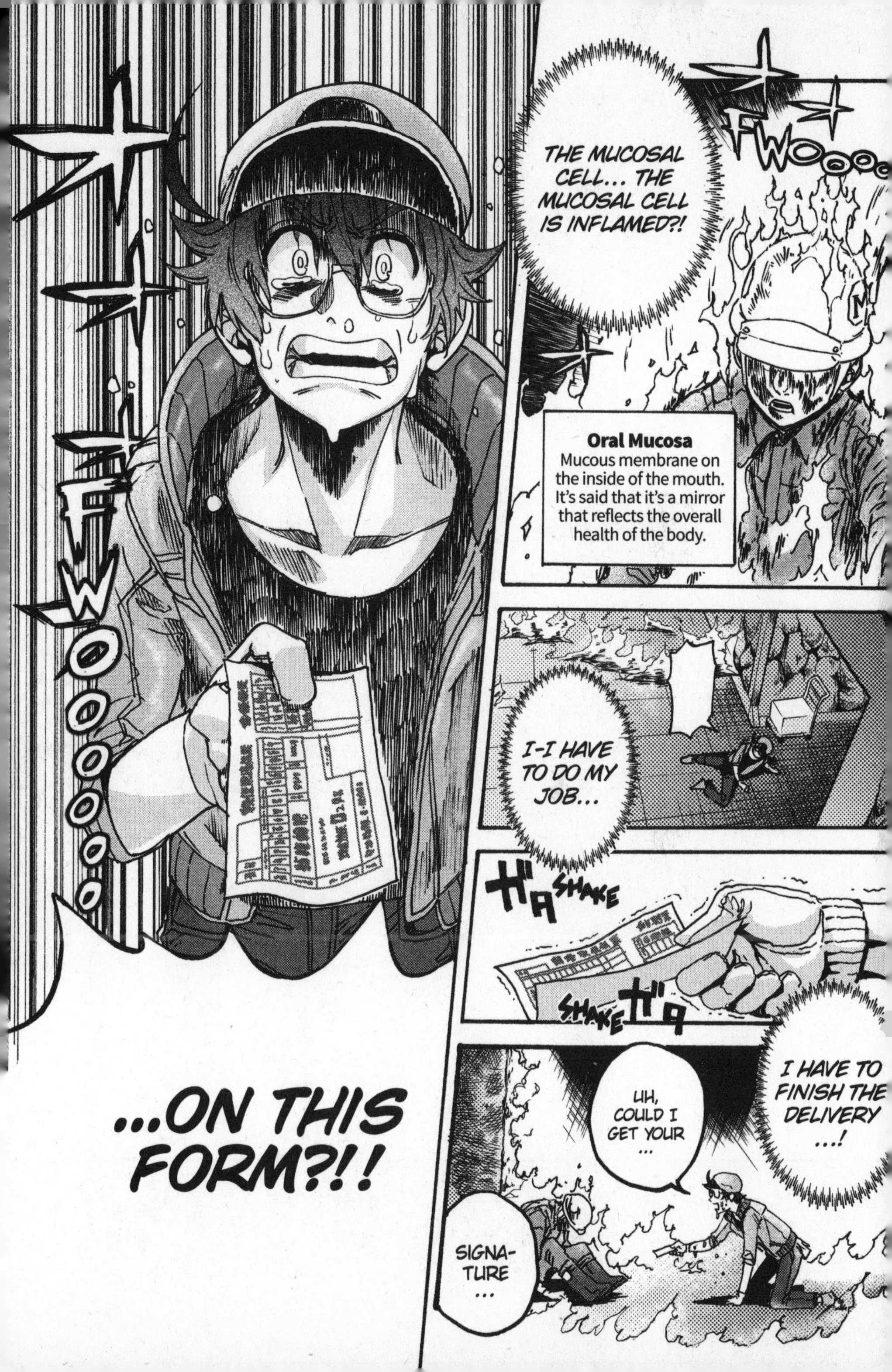
FWOOOOO
THE MUCOSAL CELL... THE MUCOSAL CELL IS INFLAMED?!
Oral Mucosa
Mucous membrane on the inside of the mouth. It's said that it's a mirror that reflects the overall health of the body.
I-I HAVE TO DO MY JOB...
SHAKE
SHAKE
I HAVE TO FINISH THE DELIVERY ...!
UH, COULD I GET YOUR ...
SIGNATURE ...
FWOOOOOOOOOOO
...ON THIS FORM?!!

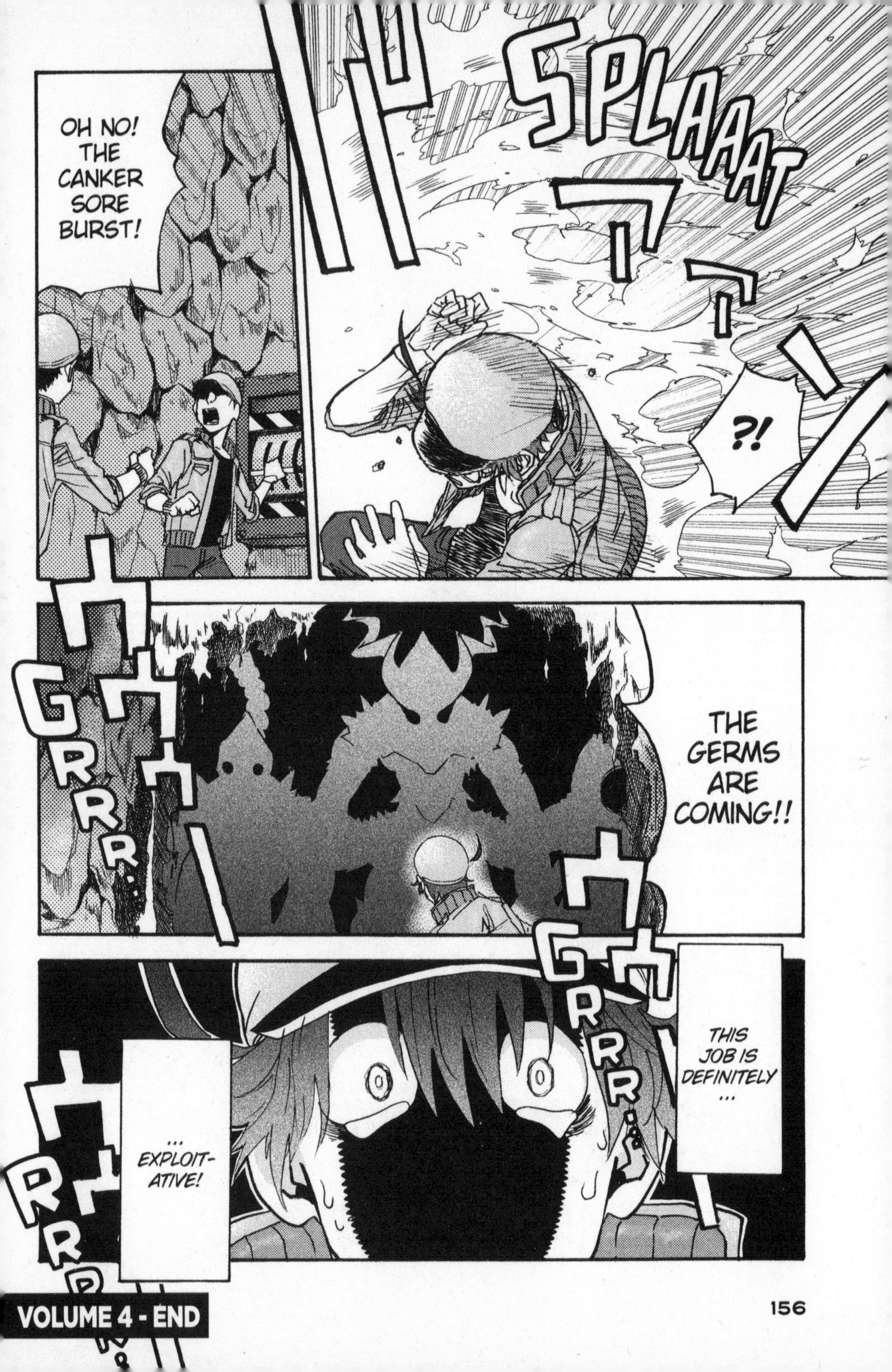
SPLAAAT
?!
OH NO! THE CANKER SORE BURST!
GRRR..
THE GERMS ARE COMING!!
GRRR...
THIS JOB IS DEFINITELY ...
... EXPLOIT-ATIVE!
RRR

VOLUME 4 - END

Cells at Work!
はたらく細胞
CODE BLACK

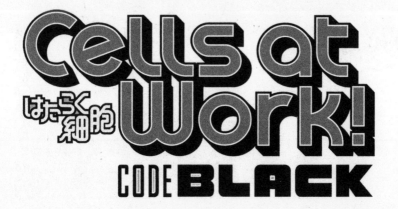

A dark and sexy body-horror action manga perfect for fans of *Prison School* and *High School of the Dead*!

Shuichi Kagaya is a smart kid, and most smart kids his age would be thinking about college. Shuichi is also a monster, and he's smart enough to know that monsters don't go to college. But after he uses his monstrous form to save his classmate Claire Aoki, it doesn't matter what his plans for the future were, because he's not the one making the decisions anymore. Now that the seductive, sadistic Claire knows Shuichi's secret, she's got her own ideas about what a monster is good for—because he's not the first monster she's met...

GLEIPNIR

"You and me together...we would be unstoppable."

Acclaimed screenwriter and director
Mari Okada (*Maquia*, *anohana*) teams up
with manga artist Nao Emoto (*Forget Me
Not*) in this moving, funny, so-true-it's-
embarrassing coming-of-age series!

When Kazusa enters high
school, she joins the Literature
Club, and leaps from reading
innocent fiction to diving into
the literary classics. But these
novels are a bit more...*adult* than
she was prepared for. Between
euphemisms like fresh dewy
grass and pork stew, crushing on
the boy next door, and knowing
you want to do that *one thing*
before you die—discovering
your budding sexuality is
no easy feat! As if puberty
wasn't awkward enough,
the club consists of a
brooding writer, the
prettiest girl in school,
an agreeable comrade,
and an outspoken prude.
Fumbling over their
own discomforts, these
five teens get thrown
into chaos over three
little letters: *S...E...X...!*

O Maidens in your Savage Season

Anime coming soon!

Mari Okada   Nao Emoto

KC
KODANSHA
COMICS

A Kodansha Comics Trade Paperback Original
Cells at Work! CODE BLACK 4 copyright © 2019 Shigemitsu Harada/Issei Hatsuyoshiya/ Akane Shimizu
English translation copyright © 2020 Shigemitsu Harada/Issei Hatsuyoshiya/Akane Shimizu

Published in the United States by Kodansha Comics, an imprint of Kodansha USA Publishing, LLC, New York.

Publication rights for this English edition arranged through Kodansha Ltd., Tokyo.

First published in Japan in 2019 by Kodansha Ltd., Tokyo as *Hataraku Saibou BLACK*, volume 4.

ISBN 978-1-63236-943-7

Printed in the United States of America.

www.kodanshacomics.com

9 8 7 6 5 4 3 2 1
Translation: Yamato Tanaka
Lettering: E. K. Weaver
Editing: Lauren Scanlan
Kodansha Comics edition cover design by Phil Balsman

Publisher: Kiichiro Sugawara
Vice president of marketing & publicity: Naho Yamada

Director of publishing services: Ben Applegate
Associate director of operations: Stephen Pakula
Publishing services managing editor: Noelle Webster
Assistant production manager: Emi Lotto, Angela Zurlo